D0386675

PRISONERS

PRISONERS

A MUSLIM AND A JEW ACROSS THE MIDDLE EAST DIVIDE

JEFFREY GOLDBERG

ALFRED A. KNOPF · NEW YORK · 2006

THIS IS A BORZOI BOOK
PUBLISHED BY ALFRED A. KNOPF

www.aaknopf.com

Library of Congress Cataloging-in-Publication Data
Goldberg, Jeffrey, [date]
Prisoners : a Muslim and a Jew across the Middle East divide / Jeffrey Goldberg.
p. cm.
ISBN 0-375-41234-4 (alk. paper)
1. Goldberg, Jeffrey. 2. Jewish journalists—United States—Biography.
3. Hijazi, Rafiq. 4. Palestinian Arabs—United Arab Emirates—Biography.
5. Arab-Israeli conflict. 6. Middle East—Ethnic relations. I. Title.
PN4874.G5335A3 2006
070.92—dc22 2006041026

Manufactured in the United States of America
First Edition

For Talia, Elisheva, and William Ze'ev

And for Pamela

The earth is a prison to man all his life.
Therefore I say this truth to the fool;
though you rush about, the sky
surrounds you on all sides. Try to get
out, if you can.

—Shmuel HaNagid, "The Prison"

CONTENTS

AUTHOR'S NOTE

Prisoners is a personal history. The events described in this book are real, but I have thought it appropriate, for reasons of security and privacy, to change the names of several individuals in this book. The following names are pseudonyms: Abu Iyad, Omar, Gadi, Yoram, Yehuda, Shlomo Efrati, and Evgeny.

My recollections of events have been reconstructed from contemporaneous notes as well as from interviews with many of the people who appear in this book.

PRISONERS

CHAPTER ONE

THE THIEF OF MERCY

On the morning of the fine spring day, full of sunshine, that ended with my arrest in Gaza, I woke early from an uneven sleep, dressed, and pushed back to its proper place the desk meant to barricade the door of my hotel room. I unknotted the bedsheets I had tied together into an emergency escape ladder. Then I hid the knife I kept under my pillow, cleaned the dust from my shoes, and carefully unbolted the door. I searched the dark hall. There were no signs of imminent peril. Most people wouldn't be so cautious, but I had my reasons, and not all of them were rooted in self-flattering paranoia.

I was staying at the Deira hotel, a fine hotel, one of Gaza's main charms. On hot nights, which are most nights, it brimmed over with members of *haute* Palestine, that small clique of Gazans who earned more than negligible incomes. The men smoked apple-flavored tobacco from water pipes; the women, their heads covered, drank strong coffee and kept quiet.

By day the hotel was mostly empty. The hotels of Gaza had been full in the 1990s, during the long moment of false grace manufactured by the Oslo peace process. In 1993, Yitzhak Rabin and Yasser Arafat shook hands on the White House lawn, and it seemed as if the hate would melt away like wax. At that moment, even a pessimist could envision an orderly close to the one-hundred-year-long war between Arab and Jew. But this was now the spring of 2001, and we were six months inside the Palestinian Uprising, the Intifada, the second Intifada, this one far more grim than the last. The land between the Mediterranean Sea and the River Jordan was once again steeped in blood: Arabs were killing Jews, and Jews were killing Arabs, and hope seemed to be in permanent eclipse. Optimists, and I included myself in this category, felt as if we had spent the previous decade as clueless Catherines, gazing dumbly from our carriages at the Potemkin village of Oslo.

So the Deira did negligible business, except after a noteworthy killing or a particularly sanguinary riot, which is the specialty of the heaving, thirsty demi-state of Gaza. Then, the press corps would colonize the Deira; reporters would come to catalogue the dead, and slot the deaths into whatever cleanly explicable narrative was in current favor.

The hallway was dim, and empty. I went downstairs to a veranda overlooking the Mediterranean, which shimmered in the early sunlight. Arab fishing boats spread their nets across the smooth water. An Israeli gunboat cast a more distant shadow. My breakfast companion was waiting for me. He rose, and we kissed on both cheeks. His nom de guerre was Abu Iyad, and he was an unhappy terrorist who I hoped would share with me illuminating gossip about Hamas—of which he was a member—and Palestine Islamic Jihad, two fundamentalist Muslim groups whose institutional focus is the murder of Jews. I bought him a plate of hummus and cucumbers.

Abu Iyad was a thin man, his face hollow and creased. His nails were yellow, and his hair was gray and thinning. I had known him for a dozen years. We weren't friends. We were more like companionable acquaintances; I could not be a true friend of anyone in Hamas. He had been a bomb-maker earlier in his career, but he no longer submitted himself to the group's hard line. His personality wasn't that of the typical Hamas ultra. The average Hamas man tends toward narcissism and humorlessness, and projects the sort of preternatural calm organic to people who believe that what follows death is exponentially better than what precedes it. But Abu Iyad seemed, on occasion, free of certitude, taking a jaundiced view of some of his more strident colleagues. He only tentatively endorsed the notion, common among Hamas theologians, that the Jews live under a cloud of divine displeasure. He was well-educated—Soviet-educated, but still—and he was cultured, for Hamas. He was familiar with Camus and he was partial to Russian literature, though not to Russians. We often talked about books. Once, we spent an afternoon on the beach, near Nusseirat, his refugee camp, eating watermelon and talking about, of all things, the nihilism in *Fathers and Sons*.

It was a year before the second Intifada, our day at the beach. The strip of gray sand was the property, in essence, of Hamas; each political faction ruled a stretch of Mediterranean seaside. The Hamas cabanas were rude concrete slabs, topped with green flags that read, "There Is No God but Allah," and "Muhammad Is the Messenger of God." A crust of garbage lay over the beach, which was frequently used as a bathroom by donkey and man alike, but a breeze pushed the smell of shit away from us. The few women on the beach sat separate from the men. They wore black scarves and cloaks of thick cloth, and they boiled inside them like eggs. Even when the women went to the water, they went in hijab. They waded in, up to their knees, splashed each other, and giggled. I could tell from the eyes, and the turn of their ankles, that they were pretty. I steered my own eyes away, though; even an innocent glance could have a terminal effect on me.

One of the men with us was a terrorist named Jihad Abu Swerah, a typically inflamed Hamas killer. He believed that the company of any women at all was an affront, even women who were serving us food. "Women by their presence pollute everything," he said. A real killjoy. He reminded me of something the Ayatollah Khomeini once said: "There is no fun in Islam."

Abu Swerah would eventually die at the hands of Israeli soldiers, who would find him in 2003 and cut him down in his Nusseirat hideout.

We tried to ignore him. Abu Iyad and I talked amiably on the beach that day with a few of his friends. The sky was soft blue and the water was gentle. It seemed to me an opportune time to throw an apple of discord into the circle. Just to make the day interesting, I accused Hamas—and the Muslim Brotherhood movement that gave birth to it—of succumbing to the temptations of nihilism.

ME: The Islamists believe in nothing except their own power. This frees them from the constraints of morality, allowing everything.

ABU IYAD: No, we believe in one surpassing truth, in *tawhid,* the cosmic Oneness of God. This is an overpowering belief. A nihilist, on the other hand, believes in nothing.

ME: This is true, in theory, the Islamist does believe in something. But that something is the supremacy of death, not the supremacy of God's love. No one, not even Turgenev's Bazarov, is perfect in his nihilism. But Hamas comes close.

ABU IYAD: Jews fear death, Muslims don't. Death isn't even death. It's a beginning. Love and death are both manifestations of God.

ME: You can't murder people and say you've done them a favor.

ABU IYAD: Hamas does not target the innocent.

After the chastising Abu Swerah and his janissaries left, Abu Iyad allowed that the actions of Hamas bombers could be seen as nihilistic, which is why he said he opposed some of the more bestial manifestations of his group's ideology. The men of Hamas, he said, sadly, were not his sort of Muslim.

Sometimes, I couldn't quite believe in his apostasy. His distaste for Hamas orthodoxy seemed real enough, but I sensed that it grew from some apolitical vendetta. Hamas, like any well-established terrorist group, is a bureaucracy, and, as in any bureaucracy, there are winners and losers, and I got the sense that he had lost—what, I didn't know.

There was something else, too: Every so often, when we talked, he would pare off the edge of his words, speak in euphemism, even deny what I knew he felt. The Shi'ites call this *taqiyya,* the dissimulation of faith, the concealment of belief in the interest of self-preservation, or temporal political advantage. Sacramental lying, in other words. I worried that the face of Abu Iyad I saw was only one in a repertoire of faces. He did, after all, kill a man once.

The man was a Palestinian, his own blood, but a "collaborator" with Israel; Abu Iyad killed the man with a knife, in an alley in Nusseirat. Abu Iyad only remembered the man's first name, which was Mustafa, and he remembered that he was taller than most Palestinians.

But then there were times when I stopped watching Abu Iyad through a veil of distrust, when I thought him to be a decent man, content to search for imperfect justice, not the world-ending justice sought by Hamas.

In the early 1990s, he favored, in principle, the murder of Israelis, in particular soldiers and settlers. But in November 2000, a group of Palestinians detonated a mortar shell near an armored bus traveling between two Jewish settlements, not far from Gaza City. Two settlers were killed, and three small children—all of the same family—lost limbs. This was unacceptable to Abu Iyad.

"It's not the children who are at fault," he said, an uncommon thing to say in Gaza, where children are both victim and perpetrator. Abu Iyad did not believe, for reasons both expedient and theological, that the slaughter of Israelis in Tel Aviv and Jerusalem would be helpful to his cause, and he questioned whether God smiled on the self-immolating assassins of Hamas. "A person can't be pure and admitted to Paradise if he kills himself, is my belief. There is a lot of debate about this among the scholars."

He sensed, even then, at breakfast, that the second Uprising, which was just beginning, would end badly for the Palestinians.

"The Israelis are too strong, and they're too ready to use violence against us," he said.

Nonsense, I said. Things will end badly for the Arabs because it is the Arabs who see violence as a panacea.

We went in circles on the question: Which side in this fight speaks more fluently the language of violence? I argued for the Arabs, and cited, as proof, a statement made to me not long before this breakfast by Abdel Aziz Rantisi, one of the founders of Hamas. Rantisi was a sour and self-admiring man, a pediatrician by trade, but one so perverse that he would work his rage on children. "The Israelis always say, when they kill our children, that they are sorry," he told me. "When we kill Jewish children we say we are happy. So I ask you, who is telling the truth?"

And I mentioned to Abu Iyad something said to me by Sheikh Ahmed Yassin, the so-called spiritual leader of Hamas, when I saw him at his home a few days earlier. I asked the sheikh about the three Israeli children on the bus, their limbs torn from them by a Palestinian bomb.

"They shouldn't have been on holy Muslim land," Sheikh Yassin said, his calm unperturbed by the thought of bleeding children. "This is what happens. The Jews have no right to life here. Their state was created in defiance of God's will. This is in the Quran."

I had no patience for Yassin. The thinking of scriptural fundamentalists seems, to the secular-minded, or even to the sort of person like me who feels the constant presence of God in his life but does not believe Him to be partisan in His love, as lunacy on stilts. It is also cruel beyond measure. Fundamentalism is the thief of mercy. These men, I told Abu Iyad, feel no human feelings at all.

Don't be so dramatic, he said, in so many words. "The sheikh is just saying this because this is what reporters want to hear." Dream murders, he suggested, do not constitute policy. They are to be understood as the last refuge of men stripped of all dignity.

"Well, it's pathetic," I said.

Abu Iyad asked, "It's the way you feel about the Germans, right?"

I didn't answer. I could have told him the truth: I was born, to my sorrow, too late to kill Germans. I could have said many other things, but I wasn't going to argue the point with a man who thinks the Shoah, the Holocaust, was a trifle compared to the dispossession of the Palestinians.

"Sometimes, I feel very satisfied when a Jew gets killed," he confessed. "I'm telling you what's in my heart. It gives me a feeling of confidence. It's very good for our people to know that they have the competence to kill Jews. So that is what Sheikh Yassin is saying."

So you build your self-esteem through murder?

You misunderstand me, Abu Iyad said. Sheikh Yassin, he explained, was not typical of the Palestinian people; he succumbed to the temptation of violence too easily. The sheikh represented one side of the divided Arab heart, the side hungry for blood. The other side craves peace, even with the Jews.

Abu Iyad was a fundamentalist, hard where the world is soft, but he was also soft where the world is hard.

I am not the only Jew who divides the gentile world into two camps: the gentiles who would hide me in their attics when the Germans come; and the gentiles who would betray me to the death squads. I thought, on occasion, that Abu Iyad might be the sort to hide me.

I was late for an appointment, and so I excused myself copiously. I did not want to offend Abu Iyad, who, like his brother-Palestinians, was as sensitive as a seismograph to rudeness.

It was not an appointment I was keen to keep. I was meant to visit a Palestinian police base that had been rocketed by the Israeli Air Force the night before. I was reporting a story, and the drudgery of reporting is the repetition, going back again and again to see things I had already seen, in the naïve hope that I would finally see something different, or, at the very least, understand it more deeply. But in the first months of the Intifada, I saw Palestinian cars rocketed by Israeli helicopters, as well as Palestinian police stations, government offices, and apartment buildings. I saw blue-skinned corpses on slabs in the morgue, and children whose jaws and hands and feet were ripped away by missiles. I was familiar with the work of Israeli rockets.

The base belonged to Force 17, the personal bodyguard unit of Yasser Arafat. My regular taxi driver, a man called Abu Ibrahim, delivered me there. Abu Ibrahim means "Father of Abraham." His given name was something else, which he seldom used since his wife gave birth to a son he called Ibrahim. He asked me once if I was father to a son. I said yes. He was relieved, on my behalf. I have two daughters as well, I said. But you have a son, he said, reassuring me. He could not pronounce my son's name, so he called me "Abu Walad," "Father of a Boy."

He wasn't much of a talker, in any case. He wouldn't tell me that he was a killer. Fifteen years before, he murdered an agent of the Shabak, the Israeli internal security service. He lured the agent to an orange grove, and there he killed him, with a grenade.

That's a great name you have, I told Abu Ibrahim once. There's peace in that name: Jews, Christians, Muslims, all of us are sons of Abraham. He just grunted.

He was a hard man. He never smiled, and his arms were roped with prison muscle. I don't think he cared about anything. Years before, I had learned from one of the chattier members of the Gambino organized crime family the expression *menefreghismo,* which means, roughly, "the art of not giving a fuck." Abu Ibrahim was an adept of *menefreghismo;* its practitioners were scattered about in the occupied territories. Once, in Hebron, I watched a Palestinian man, a cigarette dangling from his mouth, approach an Israeli soldier and stab him in the chest. The cigarette stayed between his lips through the attack. That's *menefreghismo.*

Gaza City is a compressed jumble of four- and five-story concrete apartment buildings, built at illogical angles on streets that are sometimes paved and sometimes not. Suddenly, out of the tangle, the Force 17 base appeared. It was a modest place—a few barracks, a parade ground, single-story offices. Its entrance was guarded by a life-size plaster statue of Arafat fixed on a battered plinth and gazing out over his ruined kingdom. The anonymous sculptor who created this homage to the Palestinian Ozymandias thickened the chairman's features, giving him the appearance of a fat-lipped Che Guevara. THIS CAMP WAS BUILT WITH FUNDS PROVIDED BY THE EUROPEAN UNION, a sign over the statue read.

Missiles had destroyed the base's communications room, a barracks, and a weapons warehouse. In the rubble were spent razors, shoes, cardboard containers of fruit juice, and the carcasses of rats.

I met a Palestinian reporter who showed me the damage, which was a testament to advances in the science of precision guidance. We were left with the impression that specific men were targeted. They were not hit, however.

"No one sleeps in the barracks anymore," a Force 17 commander told us. "We all sleep outside."

Force 17—the number refers, it is believed, to the first address of the group's headquarters in Beirut, at 17 Faqahani Street—is divided into two operating units, an intelligence division and a presidential security division. It has, in Gaza and the West Bank, roughly three thousand men under arms. What these men do with their arms on their off-hours had been a subject of study by the Israeli security services, which reached the conclusion, early in the Intifada, that they were using the arms for no good.

I knew someone in Force 17, a colonel named Capucci. We hadn't seen each other in some months, and I was hoping to say hello. Capucci's actual name was Muhammad Hassanen, but he took his nom de guerre to honor a former Greek Catholic bishop of Jerusalem, Hilarion Capucci, who was convicted in Israel in 1974 of smuggling arms in the trunk of his Mercedes from Lebanon to Israel on behalf of the PLO. Hassanen and the bishop shared a cell for a while in an Israeli jail.

One of the Force 17 men ran over to us, holding a bent piece of metal in his hand, a piece of the American-made rocket that took apart the communications room. He delivered a pro forma lecture that began, "America says it wants peace, but it sends missiles."

Then I saw Capucci, in the distance, getting into a jeep. I smiled, and waved. He looked at me curiously, and waved back, but tentatively. Then he sped away. How odd, I thought.

I didn't realize quite how odd it was until an hour later. I was sitting in the Café Delice on Izzedine al-Qassam Street in downtown Gaza City. The café was a regular spot for me. It was shabby and neglected; the yellow walls were water-stained, and a carpet of dust covered the shelves. But the café was well located, and there is not an extensive selection of cafés in Gaza City, in any case.

Izzedine al-Qassam Street is one of the main streets of Gaza City. It is named after an early leader of the Arab Revolt in Palestine, a proto-Arafat who murdered several Jews in the early 1930s before he was shot dead by the British. Hamas has named its terrorist wing after him. The street that honors his memory is potholed, without demarcated lanes, and is life-threatening. Braking is out of favor in Gaza, though honking is not. Officers of the Palestinian Naval Police were standing in the middle of the street, trying in vain to direct traffic. The Palestinian Authority has no actual navy, but it has a naval police. The whitewashed walls of the Shifa Hospital, across the street from the café, were covered in graffiti, drawn in violent strokes. "We Will Die Standing Up," one wall read. Near this was a sloppily painted picture, in red and black, of a bus, emblazoned with a Star of David. The bus was depicted in mid-explosion, and stick figures of green-uniformed and dead Israeli soldiers were scattered about the margins of the painting. Another line of graffiti, written against a backdrop of bleeding knives and exploding hand grenades, included a passage from the Quran: "The unbelievers will wish that they had surrendered. Let them eat, to take their joy, and to be bemused by hope; certainly, they will soon know!"

I was sitting at my usual corner table, underneath the café's dripping and gasping air conditioner, drinking coffee with an acquaintance. I chose the table, in Malcolm X fashion, because it gave me a wide view of the door and the street beyond. Not that it mattered. Three men, brooding in appearance, fantastically armed, and in a great hurry, burst through the open door and announced that I was under arrest.

The leader of the arrest party was a big man, his heavy shoulders straining against his brown suit coat. His brow was thick, and separated from the rest of his face by a single eyebrow. His cheeks were well padded, but he had a thin, elegant nose, not at all the nose one associates with Semites. He wore black shoes and white socks, and a gold bracelet on one wrist. He seemed to be about forty years old. The two other men, in their late twenties, were thinner at the waist. One of them carried an AK-47; the other a machine pistol. It was not at all clear which police apparatus these men represented, but this was not strange in Gaza, whose one and a half million people have been blessed with the protection of at least ten competing secret security organizations, not including the Naval Police.

The owner of the café, a small, soft-bodied man, maybe fifty, stood by the espresso machine. His expression suggested passivity in the face of superior firepower. I resented him just then, since he knew me, though I recognized that there was not much a seller of damp pastry could do to help.

One of the gunmen, the most ostentatiously menacing of the three—he kept his eyes purposefully narrowed, and he wore his black mustache thick, in the Ba'ath Party style—lifted me by my elbow, and pushed me to the door. He wore black pants and a black shirt. He said, in Hebrew, "Come with us." I feigned ignorance, and said, loudly, for public consumption, in Arabic, "I don't understand." He said, again in Hebrew, impatiently this time, "Just come with us." I waved my American passport in front of his face. "I'm an American!" I yelled. I had learned, in previous encounters with dyspeptic and well-armed Muslims, the tactical importance of behaving in the manner one associates with Steve McQueen, and so I resisted the urge to unleash, as I do in moments of tension, great gusts of words.

The man I was meeting followed us out of the café, onto Izzedine al-Qassam Street. A dark blue Jeep Cherokee idled by the curb. Its driver was smoking, and appeared unnaturally relaxed. My companion argued with the men, vouching for my good character. This had no discernible effect, which surprised me, since he was a leader of Fatah, Yasser Arafat's own political faction within the PLO.

I was maneuvered to the Jeep. Schoolboys in brown pants and white shirts were walking by, but only a few of them turned to watch; Gaza children see many unusual things—Gaza is notable for its complete absence of normalcy—and this drama, though large in my mind, could not hold their interest.

My own taxi was parked across the street, outside the gates of the hospital. I looked up and down the street for Abu Ibrahim, without seeing him. I think he was napping in the backseat.

I was pushed into the Cherokee. The three men got in; the chief in the front passenger seat, the two younger men on either side of me, in the back. They were so close I could feel their sweat on me. The driver pulled the Cherokee into the street and sped away. The four Palestinians looked out the windows, at the sky above. They feared, I guessed, the return of Israeli Air Force helicopters. It struck me, finally, that I was being arrested for spying. In the febrile imaginings of a Palestinian security agent, it would only make sense that an Israeli helicopter would be tracking my movements. I was not a spy, but that wasn't to say that I wasn't in trouble. I did have something to hide. Once, for a short time, I placed myself in the service of the people who hunted down men like these. This was something known only to a handful of people in Gaza. The men privy to my secret, I realized, included both Abu Iyad and Capucci.

The agent in the front passenger seat, the man in charge, turned around a few minutes into our trip. He said, in Hebrew, "Don't worry, this won't take long."

I again feigned ignorance. I said, in English, "Listen, I'm an American journalist and I demand that you release me. Do you understand me? Do you speak English?" He turned to his companions in the backseat, and said, in Arabic, something like, "The Jew is playing games."

The two men laughed.

"What were you doing this morning?" the thick-browed man asked, in Hebrew.

"I'm sorry," I said in Berlitz Arabic, "I don't speak Arabic."

"Come on already, give me a break," he said. His Hebrew was colloquial, and fluid, but low, from the street. There are several places Palestinian men of his age could learn alley-boy Hebrew: in the kitchens of Tel Aviv restaurants, on construction sites in Jerusalem, on the road gangs that pave the highways, or in prison. This man would have been in his twenties during the first Intifada. Tens of thousands of Palestinian men passed through Israeli prisons during the original Uprising, and it was ex-prisoners who filled the ranks of the Palestinian security apparatus.

"I don't speak Arabic," I said again.

"Okay, okay," he said, and turned back around.

"I want to call the American embassy," I said, loudly, in order to convince them of my Americanness.

"I'm going to take out my cell phone from my pocket," I said. The man in the front seat turned around. In English, he said, "Give me the telephone." I did, without protest.

We drove around Gaza some more. I had to go to the bathroom. I caught a glimpse of myself in a side mirror. My face shone like a well-polished boot.

"I have to go to the bathroom," I said. They ignored me.

I tried to keep track of our route, which was not easy. Gaza City is colored solely in differing shades of dun, and the streets are laid out at arbitrary angles.

I am not brave, in the fuller meaning of the word, but I do have the ability to stay hinged in moments of physical peril. Several years earlier, in the eastern Congo, at a roadblock of burning tires, a group of Mai-Mai rebels, who were notable for their consumption of formidable quantities of marijuana, as well as for their love of pillaging, pulled me out of a jeep and placed their spears at my throat. I talked my way through the Mai-Mai checkpoint. I could, I believed, talk my way through this.

We were, I realized, driving in circles. When we reached our destination, it was familiar to me: the headquarters of Palestinian Preventative Security, the largest of the secret services in Gaza. We drove through a gate into a nearly empty courtyard. I was encouraged, because I knew the chief of Preventative Security, a man named Muhammad Dahlan, and I was reasonably sure he would bring this sorry episode to a quick end. I was sure he would even make these men apologize (and I would graciously accept their apologies). Dahlan was, during the 1990s, a favorite of the Central Intelligence Agency, as well as the Shabak. He was charged, during the peace process, with suppressing Hamas and the Islamic Jihad in Gaza, which he did intermittently, but when he did it, he did it with iron. He was a greasy man, very Tammany Hall, but he was an effective security czar, and he was a pragmatist.

"Call Dahlan," I said in English, as I was helped from the Jeep. "He knows me." Never before had name-dropping seemed so urgently self-preservational.

The man in charge said in Hebrew, "This is not Dahlan's business." I said, again, "I don't know what you're saying."

I was led down a first-floor hallway and directed into an unadorned room, with two narrow windows set high on the wall. A thin-legged wooden table sat in the middle of the room, two chairs on each side. My captor, the most obviously malevolent of the three, instructed me, in Arabic, to stand against a wall, feet spread apart. I put my back against the wall. No, no, he yelled, and motioned me to turn. I did so slowly. He frisked me. His technique was well informed, though he performed his job with more enthusiasm than was necessary, giving my balls a savage squeeze.

Asshole, I said, in English.

He emptied my pockets: my wallet, a notebook, two pens, a miniature tape recorder, a packet of Pepto-Bismol, 25 shekels in coins, my passport, several random business cards, folded newspaper clippings, gum, gum wrappers, balled-up pieces of paper containing scribbled notes, and the keys to my car, which I had left to cook in the sun on the far side of the Erez crossing, the main border between Israel and Gaza. I think my captors were astonished by the mass of junk that fell from my pockets. My tape recorder was taken away, but everything else was thrown onto the table. I was told to sit. The men left, and I stewed. I reached for my pad, and took notes on the events of the day. This had a calming effect on me.

The air in the room was still, but I could smell thistles and the sea air, and sweat.

I was left alone for quite a while. I assumed the goal of my captors was to provoke in me a neurasthenic crisis, to give me time to manufacture dire thoughts about torture, or at the very least, habeas corpus, which is not a cherished value of Arab security services. It was clever of them to leave me alone. It was my misfortune to be familiar with the many creative methods of torture employed by interrogators of the Palestinian services. The previous June a Palestinian in the custody of Preventative Security was asphyxiated to death. Not long before that, a group of Palestinian students at Birzeit University, on the West Bank, were beaten and threatened with rape by other agents of Preventative Security. The crime of these students was to have thrown rocks at the visiting French prime minister. There were many stories of cruelty in Arafat's prisons. Two of the more common modes of torture were *shabeh* and *farruja*. In *shabeh,* a prisoner is bound in a kneeling position, his arms pulled back and tied to the ankles. The prisoner is then left hooded for several hours. This torture causes hellish pain in the joints, and it stimulates an overwhelming desire to die, according to people I know who have survived the treatment. In *farruja,* the prisoner is bound in similar fashion, but then lifted off the floor, suspended from a hook. (During the Inquisition, this was known as the "Queen of Torments.") Prisoners in Palestinian jails are often beaten—usually on the soles of the feet, with rubber truncheons. They are sometimes hooded for long periods of time; and burned as well, with molten plastic, or cigarettes.

On the other hand, this wasn't Syria.

I had one other thing going for me. Journalists were more or less inviolate, beneficiaries of a kind of unspoken policy of extraterritoriality. This is what I told myself. This incident occurred in a more innocent time—the definition of an innocent time being any time before the murder of the *Wall Street Journal* reporter Danny Pearl—and so the torture of an American journalist in an Arab jail seemed unlikely to me.

Finally the head man came back into the room, and sat down. He said in English, "My name is Abu Hamad."

I introduced myself, and extended my hand. He shook it, to my surprise.

Abu Hamad took my wallet, and emptied its contents on to the table.

He studied my Washington, D.C., driver's license, then my Costco Warehouse card, my credit cards, my expired New York Police Department press pass, and a card identifying me as a Friend of the National Zoo. In tradecraft, this mass of junk is known as "pocket litter," which

I would carry on me to convince counterespionage agents of my innocence. Of course, proper pocket litter wouldn't include a press pass issued by the Israeli Government Press Office. Abu Hamad picked it up.

"The New Yorker," he said.

Yes, I said with pride, *The New Yorker*. I told him *The New Yorker* is exceptionally popular among Palestinians in America. This may be true, or it may not. I had no idea.

In Hebrew, he said, "Why don't you speak Hebrew with me? I need the practice."

I have the sort of face that suggests guilt even in moments of virginal innocence, but I tried to contain myself.

I said, in English, "I'm sorry, I don't understand."

"Really," he said, his eyes slicing into me, "it's not a big deal. So you speak Hebrew. Everyone speaks Hebrew."

I said nothing.

"What do you think? We're going to hurt you because you speak Hebrew? *I* speak Hebrew," he said.

His logic was weak, but so was I. I gave in. "Look," I finally said in the language of my people, "you can't expect me to speak Hebrew on Izzedine al-Qassam Street, do you? That would get us both lynched."

This brought a smile to his face. I was happy to see him smile, and then my happiness curdled into self-loathing. Who knew I would be such an amateur? What a crashing demonstration of interrogational incompetence. This wasn't a spear at the throat. I wasn't being tied up like a chicken. He wasn't even yelling. He was the good cop, and there was no bad cop.

It was his stare, I think, combined with the fact that there are Arabs in Gaza with whom I speak Hebrew (and I'm sure he knows that already, I thought), that led me to believe that no harm would be done by an acknowledgment of the obvious. But wait. He had his victory. So why did the smile disappear?

"Lynched?" he asked, his face a black cloud. "You said lynched. What do you mean by lynched? You think we're really animals?"

I didn't get his meaning.

"The lynching," he said.

Several months earlier, two Israeli army reservists took a wrong turn on their way to their West Bank base, and wound up in the hands of the Palestinian police. The two were brought to a Ramallah police station, where they were swarmed by a mob, which tore them apart by hand, then rubbed their hands in the blood of their victims, and displayed them for the cameras. The lynching of these two reservists left many Israelis believing that their neighbors were not only unappeasable but barbaric.

"Well, that was Ramallah," I said. "What do you expect?"

Jokes at the expense of the West Bank usually go over well in Gaza. Not this one, however.

"You see what your people do to us," Abu Hamad said, a hard edge to his voice. "You were there this morning. How can you think we're the animals? The Israelis are the animals."

If I were quicker, I would have said: The difference between action and reaction is the difference between Palestinians and Israelis.

Instead, I asked, "Why are you following me?"

Abu Hamad answered my question with a question: "Why were you visiting the Force 17 headquarters this morning?"

"I'm a reporter," I said.

"Who do you work for?"

"The New Yorker."

"Who do you work for?"

"*The New Yorker*. If you don't believe me, check with anyone. Check with Dahlan."

"I don't work for Dahlan."

"Which police do you work for?"

"You're a spy, yes? For the Shabak."

"No."

"Mr. Jeffrey," he said, "what are you doing here?"

A very pertinent question. What I was doing here was trying to get out of here.

But there were many other answers to this question. I could have said: I'm here because I believe with perfect faith in the catechisms of solutionism, the American national religion, which holds that for every intractable problem there is a logical and available answer. I could have said: I am here in search of the secret afflictions of the Palestinian heart. I am here exploring the contradictions of Jewish power. I am here seeking the elimination of ambiguity. I'm looking for the bridge that will carry me across the black hole of cognition that separates Arab and Jew. I'm here to quiet the conflict in my heart. I'm here because I'm alive to hope. I'm here in search of the key to all mythologies. I'm here because I'm a fucking idiot.

"I'm working on a story," I said.

"What story?"

"Well, to see if it's still possible for Jews and Arabs to coexist."

"Why not?" he asked.

Why not what?

"Why not?" he asked again. "We can live together."

I asked him if he really thought it still possible.

"Of course," he said. "As you like. No problem."

"Well, it's not that easy."

"Why not?"

This seemed to be an auspicious moment to dilate on the subject of peace. I launched into the following speech, reproduced here with more coherence than it possessed in its initial delivery.

I told him I thought that there must be a way to create on this narrow ledge of land a place for Jews and Muslims to live in peace, side by side, without perfect justice, but without murder, either. Now, I know Jews better than I know Arabs. I think the Jews—not all, God knows, but many—are readying themselves for this day. But I don't know about the Arabs. There are people who tell me they know the answer, but I don't trust these people. In the Middle East, people who say they have the answers often don't know the questions. So what I'm doing (and if I keep talking without pause, maybe you'll forget about torturing me, or at least give me my cell phone back, yes?) is searching for the right questions.

He looked at me with a bored look on his face and asked: "What story are you writing?"

A factotum suddenly appeared in the doorway, holding a cell phone. Abu Hamad must be an important man, I decided; it is common for the top-ranking Palestinian security officials to be trailed by trained cell-phone-holders. My interrogator left the room.

While he was gone, I remembered another reason why peace is possible. The Book of Genesis tells us that, upon Abraham's death, his two estranged sons, Isaac, the father of my people, and Ishmael, the father of Abu Hamad's, came together to bury their father, the father of us all. This might be the single most hopeful image in all the Bible, a palliative against the despair that has seeped into all of us.

An old man, stooped and dark, came in with a tray of burning-hot tea. I took a cup and drank. The tea made me sweat. Were the Palestinians poisoning me? I'm so stupid! Twice in one day, acts of unendurable stupidity! Never drink the tea! Oh, what an ironic end! It's the Muslims who believe the Jews to be spreaders of poison. Even Arafat thinks so. It's not their idea, originally—they stole it from Christianity, but lately they've been improving upon it and marketing it with alacrity.

It wasn't poison. Perhaps it was the absence of air-conditioning that was making me sweat. My shirt, I realized, was soaked through. I tried to relax, and counted the minutes.

Abu Hamad returned.

"Why am I under arrest?" I asked.

"Why were you taking pictures of the Force 17 base?"

"I'm a reporter."

"As you like," he said.

"Really, I am."

"We know who you are," he said, smiling. "We know you work for the Shabak."

That was a highly implausible charge. For one thing, I was an enemy of both Hebrew and Arabic, fluency in which are prerequisites for Shabak service. For another, I am temperamentally unsuited for the secret life.

He paused for a moment. Then he said: "We know you were in Ketziot."

He let this last word hang in the air.

My face gave away the game. My double life in Gaza had just come to an end.

CHAPTER TWO

THE MYSTERIOUS CHILD OF LIES

The border between the Negev Desert and the Sinai Desert is not immediately apparent to the unschooled eye. The gravelly sand of the Negev gives way slowly to the graceful, khaki-colored dunes of the Sinai. But in the wastes of the Wilderness of Zin, the empty zone south of the city of Be'er Sheva—the Well of the Oath, where the Patriarch Abraham made a covenant with the Philistine King Abimelech—these two deserts meet, and their differences become more obvious.

The Book of Exodus records that the Children of Israel stopped twice in southernmost Zin, at an oasis called Kadesh-Barnea. The Jews had fled slavery in Egypt and were on their way to freedom in Canaan. On the first stop at Kadesh-Barnea, shortly after the crossing of the Red Sea, Moses dispatched twelve spies, one son of each tribe, to enter Canaan and bring back reports on its agricultural promise, and, of more urgent import, the war-fighting inclinations of its inhabitants. Two of the spies, Joshua and Caleb, went a great distance, to the mountains of Lebanon, and returned with good news: The Promised Land was sweet with honey, and the people did not seem unduly ferocious. The other ten spies, men of lesser faith, and greater cowardice, ceded one point to Joshua and Caleb—the land was fertile, shedding grapes and figs—but it was also a land of fearsome giants.

"And we were in our own sight as grasshoppers, and so we were in their sight," they told Moses. Joshua and Caleb argued that an irrational fear had seized the ten spies, but to no avail—the Israelites seemed ready to believe any news, so long as it was bad. God became angry at the Israelites, angry at their lack of faith in Him, but Moses asked God for mercy. As a punishment short of smiting, He decreed that the Israelites should wander the merciless desert for forty years, "until your carcasses be wasted in the wilderness." By doing this, he denied the faithless Jews of the slave generation the bounty of Israel.

The Israelites left Kadesh-Barnea and wandered for many years. When they returned, the generation of slaves was, in the main, dead. But still, Moses could not lead his people into the Promised Land. Even on their second visit to Kadesh-Barnea, the Israelites were sunk in self-pity. They spoke against Moses, cursing him for taking them out of Egypt and bringing them to "this evil place," which would be the death of them. Moses pleaded with God for water; God ordered him to speak to a rock, to demand that it give water, but Moses, in his frustration, struck the rock twice with his staff. The water flowed, but Moses had disobeyed God's word. It was at Kadesh-Barnea that God decided that Moses would die before being allowed to enter the Promised Land. The moral of the story, the rabbis say, is the importance of living one's life without anger.

There seemed to me another meaning to this story as well. It occurred to me, while trapped in this desert, not far from the desiccated wells of Kadesh-Barnea, that unhappiness clings to the Wilderness of Zin. This is the place, I realized, where the Jews became hardened to the demands of God.

It was in February 1991, in the Wilderness of Zin, at a place called Ketziot, not far from Kadesh-Barnea, that a friend of mine named Yoram tried, in my presence, to beat senseless an Arab by the name of Abu Firas. Abu Firas was a disagreeable and smug man, but his sourness was not a mortal sin. Yoram, whom I knew to be gentle but at that moment had blood in his face, was beating Abu Firas on the head with the handset of an army radio. The handset weighed five or six pounds, and it was sharp-edged. Abu Firas was hurt. Most men taking a beating like this would scream blue murder, but Abu Firas didn't. I was impressed. Yoram didn't stop when I came upon him. I took hold of his arm, knocking the radio to the ground.

Yoram was a religious Jew, and his kippah, knit and multicolored in the style of the modern Orthodox, stayed pinned to his head through his exertions. It was quite a sight—a yeshiva Jew, a God-fearer, delivering a bloody beating.

"You don't understand," Yoram said, gasping for breath. "You don't understand."

Abu Firas was on his knees, grabbing at his head. His hair shone with blood. He was barely coherent. He pleaded for water. Yoram tried to jack Abu Firas up onto his feet, but he couldn't move. Yoram, still panting, didn't tell me what it was I didn't understand.

We were standing near the solitary confinement cells, which were located in a corner of Sub-Block Two, which comprised one-fifth of Block Four of the Israeli army's Ketziot prison camp, which was situated in a closed military zone in the Wilderness of Zin, near the wastes of Halutza, two miles from Israel's border with Egypt. No one else knew we were there: It was twilight, the sun was burning down, the sky was dark red, and the sodium lights had not yet flickered on.

I had just returned from a run outside the prison wire. I enjoyed running in the desert. The desert matched my mood, as well as the mission of Ketziot. The prison belonged in these desaturated wastes. It would have been sordid to locate this vast prison in the green hills of the Galilee, or on the living soil of the Jezreel Valley.

I would run furiously down the road until the prison was just a gray smear behind me, all the way to the border, past the ruins of a Turkish railroad station and the crumbling graves of forgotten sheikhs. Sometimes I would stop at the station, and paw through the rubble in search of Ottoman relics, taking care to avoid the scorpions. But all that remained were piles of sand-colored stone. One hundred years from now, I imagined someone—a Jew? an Arab? an Arab and Jew together?—would pick through the rubble of our prison and find no evidence of civilization either.

The road was empty except for military traffic: tank transports, armored personnel carriers, the occasional self-propelled howitzer that would make the earth tremble underneath it. The signs warned in Hebrew and Arabic of firing zones on the right and left. The Wilderness of Zin, empty in the time of Moses, is, for the State of Israel, a wilderness of armor, crowded with artillery ranges, tank bases, and listening posts. Almost no one lives in this desert. A few small clans of Bedouins live in ragged camps, and a scattering of Jews live in a handful of lonely kibbutzim. The sun pours down on these farmers, turning them as brown as nuts. They struggle against the onslaught of sand, still committed to the vision of David Ben-Gurion, the first prime minister, who thought that a green desert would be physical proof of Jewish redemption.

But the biggest settlement in the desert was Ketziot, which did not feature in any dream of Theodor Herzl, the founder of Zionism, or in any program of Ben-Gurion, who made concrete Herzl's vision. Ketziot was a city of barbed wire, moldy tents, machine gun towers, armored personnel carriers, black oil smoke, sullen Arabs, and embittered Israeli soldiers. During my time as a military policeman at Ketziot, the prison held more than six thousand Palestinians. These men were the flower of the Palestinian Intifada. They were its foot soldiers, squad commanders, generals, and, from time to time, its propagandists, even its lawyers. The presence of so many notables in the prison had turned this far corner of the desert into a virtual Palestinian parliament.

The Palestinians did not generally call the prison "Ketziot," the biblical name of the place. They referred to it instead as "Ansar Three." Ansar One was a prison in South Lebanon, opened by Israel during its war against the PLO in the early 1980s. Ansar Two sat on the beach in Gaza City; it was a feeder prison to Ansar Three, the biggest prison ever built by Israel. The army officers who ran Ketziot did not care for the name "Ansar Three." In Arabic, *ansar* means "supporter," and the word holds a specific meaning in Islam: The *ansar* were the first loyalists of the Prophet Muhammad, brave and unforgiving fighters who carried the flag of Islam into Muhammad's first battles. For religiously minded prisoners, the Palestinian name of Ketziot gave them spiritual fortification.

The majority of the prisoners, however, weren't overly religious. The bulk of the prisoners, probably 80 percent of them, came from Fatah, and they had the run of the place. The prisoners who were members of Hamas, or of Palestine Islamic Jihad, or of the Popular Front for the Liberation of Palestine–General Command, or of the Democratic Front for the Liberation of Palestine, along with the handful of misled romantics who had pledged their allegiance to the Communist Party (true outliers in the Palestinian revolution, because they were committed to nonviolent protest), waged perpetual, Sisyphean battle to preserve their autonomy within the oppressive system of control instituted by the secret Fatah councils inside the prison.

Overseeing the prison was an Israeli Defense Forces military police colonel—three oak leaves on his shoulder. Four lieutenant colonels and majors, who commanded the main blocks within Ketziot, reported to the base commander. Each block commander had a deputy, a lieutenant, usually, as well as an intelligence officer. The intelligence officers often came from Israel's Druze minority. The Druze are members of an apostate Muslim sect whose rituals are obscure and whose resentment of Arab Muslims is potent.

The men in charge of Ketziot were not the finest commanders in the Israeli army. At Ketziot, two subtypes of Israeli military men flourished. The first was the *rosh katan,* literally, the "small head," the sort of soldier incapable of creative thought or the exercise of leadership. (The opposite of a *rosh katan* is a *rosh gadol,* a "big head," who is skilled at improvisation.) Then there were the *fuckyonaires,* soldiers who turned to shit everything they touched.

There were, at most, three hundred Israeli soldiers on duty at the prison. There was a small, permanent staff, supplemented by two hundred or so reservists serving short tours of duty in the watchtowers and guard stations; and eighty or ninety military policemen, who were charged with organizing the daily lives of the prisoners, feeding them, tending to issues of religion, health, and discipline, delivering them to interrogation, depriving them of the means of escape.

The majority of these military policemen were native-born Israelis, nineteen- and twenty-year-olds performing their compulsory service in the army's most detested division (the military police were in charge not only of prisons, but of enforcing orderliness among Israel's famously disorderly soldiers).

Alongside the nineteen- and twenty-year-olds, there was another contingent of military police, slightly older men who were new immigrants to Israel, chosen to serve in prisons precisely because they weren't native to the conflict. Their blood, it was thought, ran cooler than Middle Eastern blood. These soldiers were drawn from across the Jewish Diaspora: from Russia and its disintegrating empire; from Ethiopia, Argentina, Brazil, and Peru; from France, Britain, and South Africa. A handful came from America as well.

In the first months of 1991, during the Persian Gulf War, there were five American Jewish immigrants serving as Israeli military policemen at Ketziot. One of these men was marrying an Israeli woman, and so took on Israeli citizenship and the burden of compulsory military service. Two of these men left America to escape the stigma of material failure in a Jewish culture that sanctified success: The first was a former New York City police officer, a confused galumph with curvature of the spine; the second was a onetime part-owner of a defunct mattress and bedding store in a suburb of Los Angeles. The fourth was a minor financial criminal of some sort, under indictment in New Jersey for mail fraud; service as a jailer in the Israeli desert was, of course, preferable to service in the metal fabrication shop of the East Jersey State Prison at Rahway, and so he was pleased to be at Ketziot.

The fifth was also a misfit, but of a different sort: a true believer, whose cast-iron ideals carried him to Israel, to live as a free Jew in the Promised Land.

But not at Ketziot. Ketziot was not in my plan.

I never imagined that a place like Ketziot could exist. It was outside my frame of reference. Ketziot was a place bleached of color, and bereft of kindness. It was a monument to expediency, poor planning, and the ephemeral nature of cheap building materials. It was a place devoid of culture, an island of small-mindedness and cruelty in a brown sea of sand. And it was swelteringly hot, except at night, when the desert cold seemed capable of cracking bones.

Ketziot rose from the desert floor, tacked together at the outset of the first Palestinian Uprising in 1988, in a terrific hurry. Israeli soldiers were arresting Palestinians by the thousands, without discrimination—spray-painters, rock-throwers, knifemen, and bomb-makers were all bundled up together and shipped to the handful of army prisons already in existence. Confronted by a deluge, the army in early 1988 ordered the building of a central depot, an expandable, all-purpose dumping ground for these masses of Palestinians, and the flat land near the ancient Nabatean ruins of Ketziot, almost perfectly isolated from the rest of Israel (and from the burning cities of the occupied territories) became the place, a makeshift answer to a question Israelis hadn't, a few months before, even known to ask.

Ketziot contained few permanent structures. It consisted mainly of tents—rows and rows of gray army tents, and miles of steel fence and wire to separate the tents from the outside world, and from each other. Barbed wire snaked through the camp, so much barbed wire that we could have ringed half of Israel with it. There were four main prisoner blocks at Ketziot, each holding roughly 1,400 men. The blocks were separated from each other by high berms made of packed dirt that were wide enough on top to carry a jeep. The blocks were surrounded by metal watchtowers, permanently fixed with machine guns. The place stank of diesel, melted tar, body odor, and urine. The latrines—one latrine for every thirty prisoners—weren't dug deeply enough into the desert floor, on the faulty assumption that the army would be able to crush the Intifada before the Palestinians drowned the desert in shit.

The air smelled of boiling fava beans, which were a staple of lunch, dinner, and sometimes breakfast for the prisoners. And there were the rare smells: eye-watering aftershave, smuggled into Ketziot by new prisoners, who hid the bottles in their anuses; and the charcoal odor of burning sparrow—the prisoners would trap the birds and cook them in secret inside their tents.

And there was the noise: the coughing of truck engines, the screaming of F-16s flying low over the camp, and the dissonant Egyptian music that we played at top decibel over loudspeakers strung up on posts. The music was a reward to the prisoners in times of quiescence, but it was punishment for us—Umm Koulthoum, the Star of the East, singing "Alf Leyla wa Leyla," "A Thousand and One Nights," a thousand and one times.

"What the fuck are you doing?" I asked Yoram.

We stared at each other. Yoram looked as if he were ready to take a swing.

Abu Firas sat on the ground, watching now, his pain salved by the spectacle of two Jews at daggers drawn.

"Don't be a *manyak,*" Yoram said. A *manyak* is an asshole.

How am I a *manyak*?

"Get this dog out of here," he said, pointing to Abu Firas.

Abu Firas, who evidently understood Hebrew, spit out, *"Cus amak,"* at Yoram. Yoram lunged for him. *Cus amak* means "Your mother's cunt" in Arabic.

I held Yoram back. I told Abu Firas to move. Then I went in search of someone to take Abu Firas to the infirmary. I found another military policeman, and handed off the wobbling prisoner, who was by now bleeding on me. "He fell," I lied.

Yoram was not, in my experience, a sadist. He was an appealing person, usually. His parents were refugees from North Africa, a typical Sephardic family, as he described it. They kept kosher, and went to soccer matches on Shabbat. Yoram was kind, not coarse, and patient. Native-born Israelis are blessed with many qualities, but politesse and patience are not among them. That is why the beating surprised me; Yoram did not have a tripwire Middle Eastern temper.

The beating, I deduced, was prompted by something Abu Firas said. The prison had been especially tense in the first months of 1991. Yoram lived in Tel Aviv, which was, for a time, the target of Iraqi Scud missiles (Saddam Hussein was desperately trying to draw Israel into the Gulf War as a way of splitting the coalition arrayed against him). Abu Firas, in the course of a petty argument about some minor procedural matter, told Yoram that he would ask Allah to help Saddam burn Yoram's family to death. The Palestinian prisoners did not keep their opinions of Saddam's efforts to themselves. At night, when the air raid sirens warned of an incoming Scud, the prisoners, in their tents, would let out a roar of approval. *"Ya, ya, Saddam,"* they would sing, and sometimes, when their sap was high, *"Falastin baladna, wa Yahud kalabna,"* "Palestine is our land and the Jews are our dogs." They wouldn't stop until we threatened to fill their tents with tear gas.

Okay, so Abu Firas is an asshole, I told Yoram. What's the big deal?

Don't you understand? Yoram asked. "You can't let them talk to you that way."

So what if he curses you? It's the game. His role is to provoke you, yours is to ignore him. I kept going: Beating a man won't solve anything. It just drives the hatred deeper inside him.

I was embarrassed for Yoram. I thought we were the same, but I realized at that moment that we were different, crucially: Unlike Yoram, I never hit a Palestinian who wasn't already hitting me.

But if I was embarrassed for Yoram, for his brutality, for his darkness of mind, he was embarrassed for me, for my stupidity and my softness. I read his face: It said, *manyak* American, with your stupid American ideas. I had only been in the prison for a month but I had already made for myself a reputation as a *yafei nefesh,* literally, a "beautiful soul"—a bleeding heart.

They want to kill us all, Yoram said.

Beating them will make it worse, I said.

"You can't beat them enough," he said.

Goldberg doesn't understand the mentality of the Arabs. This was not the first time I had heard this; it was probably the fourth time in a month. You don't know the Arabs the way we know the Arabs, my commanders warned. Our guards told us: Give them your back and you'll get the knife. A lieutenant of the military police said, "The Arabs smile when they kill people." Never trust a smiling Arab, he said.

I rejected that particular observation as I rejected the premise on which it was based. Individuals have mentalities; whole peoples don't. Jews aren't cheap, blacks aren't shiftless, the Irish aren't drunks, and Arabs are not two-faced killers. It was Woggism to think this way.

I left Yoram to check on Abu Firas. A medic had cut away some of his hair and his skull was yellow with antiseptic. I stood there watching the stitches go in. Abu Firas said nothing. I was expecting him to say thank you. He didn't. Instead, he dead-eyed me, until I left.

A few days later, I fell into conversation with one of the leaders of the prisoners. I had become quite relaxed with a number of them. This one prisoner, Capucci—the same one who would one day go on to accomplish important things for Force 17—was a particular favorite. At the time, he was the *shaweesh,* the prisoner representative of his sub-block, but he was also said to be high in the ranks of Fatah. We talked through barbed wire. He already knew what had happened. "Are you a Communist?" Capucci asked. He wasn't smiling. He was seigneurial, and grave. He had a quiet in him that was most unusual. He was only thirty-five, but the other prisoners spoke to him as an imam speaks to God.

Capucci had heard that I had done something humane for a prisoner. Therefore, he suspected I was a Communist.

No, I'm not a Communist, I'm Jewish, I said, self-righteously. Capucci would not take the bait.

We spoke about Yoram. Capucci asked me if he was a settler. I said no. "He wears a kippah," he said, as if only settlers wore them.

"Yes, he does."

"Does he hate Muslims?"

"No, he hates *manyaks.*" On this last question I was unsure, but I thought it best, for Yoram's physical safety, to cover for him. I told Capucci that Abu Firas was ignoring me. I said I found this surprising. I thought he would be thankful.

Capucci looked at me. "That's what you thought?" he asked. Then he wished me a good day.

I had an unusual job at Ketziot. Most soldiers were forbidden to talk to the prisoners. But I was a "prisoner counselor," a job title that did not reflect accurately my duties in the related fields of discipline and punishment, but which did convey the notion that I was not meant to engage the prisoners solely with pepper spray and barked commands.

Unlike the guards, I moved through the prison camp without a weapon. My rifle was locked to the metal mesh of my bunk; I stored the ammunition in my kitbag. Once, early on, I gave myself a test: I wanted to see how long it would take me, in the dark, to unlock my rifle, open my kitbag, retrieve a clip, and be ready to fire. It took a very long time.

I did not go around entirely without defenses, of course; I was too skittish for that. I carried a small canister of tear gas in my pocket, and a knife of last resort in my left boot, and in the course of my duties—especially those that required me to open gates to the sub-blocks, and come into direct physical contact with prisoners—I was accompanied by two guards carrying M-16s, who sometimes paid sufficient attention to my back.

I didn't mind the company of reservists. I made a couple of friends among them. But they were in the prison for fifteen days, thirty days at most, compared to the four months my unit would stay, and they were useless in conversation for the first week, too unsettled by their surroundings, paranoia draining them of conversational energy. In any case, the Israelis were generally less interesting to me than the Palestinians. Israelis I knew. Palestinians I didn't. I was fascinated by them. Here they were, en masse, my enemy. Who wouldn't want to know about them? I asked them questions, ceaselessly, about their politics, their beliefs and desires, their families. I poured out questions about child-rearing and bomb-making and the menu for the Ramadan break fast.

Some of my colleagues thought my interest in the Palestinians odd—not odd in a quirky way, but subversively odd. The hatred between the Jews and the Arabs in Ketziot was a cold hatred—the camp was, more or less, a cease-fire zone in the Intifada—but the hate was still as wide as an ocean. To many of my Israeli comrades, reaching out to the Palestinians was a sign of something malevolent, rather than an indication of hopeless stupidity.

One day, my block commander called for me. Yehuda was a short, baggy-pantsed man of great poundage, a narrow-minded careerist, unlettered, all in all a man in over his head—a sergeant major gussied up in the uniform of a lieutenant colonel. He governed the block by ordering, in the most whimsical way, collective punishments for even minor prisoner offenses, and by fastidiously ignoring the block's most toxic, and morally complicated, problems. Yehuda was happiest when trouble visited the other blocks. He was also parochial—he lived in the dustbowl southern outpost of Yeruham (its American equivalent would be a one-gas-station town in the Nevada desert) and he was an Orthodox Jew of Moroccan descent. He was as sure of himself as only a God-botherer could be. He was the sort of God-botherer, though, who never absorbed Judaism's ethos of relentless questioning. As a Sephardic Jew, he felt he could say, as he often did, that he truly understood the mentality of the Arabs.

He also didn't care much for uppity American Jews.

I found Yehuda standing atop the ramparts overlooking the block, under a violent sun. His hands were on his belly. He gave the impression of a king surveying his realm.

There were two issues, he said. One, you were seen reading a book yesterday, while on duty. This is a violation. Is it true that you were reading a book?

Yes, it's true, I said. I was on a six-hour shift, in a guard shack, between Sub-Blocks Two and Four. There was nothing at all to do.

This is your last warning, he said.

He was right to threaten me; I was supposed to be organizing meal schedules, keeping an eye out for trouble, checking for holes in the fences, some damn thing. But instead I was reading.

My guilt having been ascertained, he proceeded with the questioning. What were you reading? he asked. "Amos Oz," I said, to bother him. (Amos Oz is Israel's greatest writer, but he is also one of the founders of the left-wing group Peace Now.) I was actually reading a book called *A Peace to End All Peace,* by the scholar David Fromkin. The book is an elegant indictment of the great European powers who, in the days after World War I, created the mess of the modern Middle East, but why would I want to get into that with Yehuda?

Number two: Why, he wanted to know, did I spend so much time talking to prisoners?

Because I'm not allowed to read, I thought. I told him I believed I could learn something from them. I suggested that my reckless sociability in fact served not only to enlighten me about the general nature of our enemy, but also served the intelligence goals of the Block Four command apparatus: By assessing the mood of the prisoners, I said, I could better help maintain the general peace.

He said that there was nothing I could learn from a Palestinian. You could learn, he said, that they lie, but he could tell me himself that they lie. They lie a thousand times a day. They'll lie about the time. They'll lie about the weather. They don't even know it's lying. There is no reason for you to waste your time finding out something I can tell you myself, Yehuda said. Then he dismissed me.

There was something I found in *A Peace to End All Peace* that spoke to Yehuda's ideas. Fromkin, early in the book, recounts the comment of the English writer George Steevens, who wrote the following about Francis Reginald Wingate, a premier British Arabist of World War I: "Whatever there was to know, Colonel Wingate surely knew it, for he makes it his business to know everything. . . . As for that mysterious child of lies, the Arab, Colonel Wingate can converse with him for hours, and at the end know not only how much truth he has told, but exactly what truth he has suppressed. . . . Nothing is hid from Colonel Wingate."

Despite Yehuda's order, I found it useful to talk to these mysterious children of lies, though not all of them; the rank and file would not, in general, talk to the military police—Fatah had its own rules about fraternization—but the senior men in the blocks, many of whom knew Jews, and knew Hebrew (most of them had worked for Israeli employers before the Uprising), were happy to talk, if for no other reason than to relieve their boredom and rehearse their arguments against Zionism. The clever ones would probe, as well, for information about the prison chieftains and the endless and contradictory *fatwas* streaming from the offices of the colonel in charge.

I would check in daily with Capucci, and with several others. In Sub-Block Three, there was a *shaweesh* named Jawdat Ahmed, from Bethlehem, who, before the Uprising, waited tables at a Sheraton hotel in Tel Aviv; there was Abu Bassam, of the northern West Bank town of Kalkilya, who told dirty jokes about the Arabs of Hebron, in the south of the West Bank; and there was Hamad Bikheet, a Goliath with gold teeth and yellow eyes, a Palestinian of Sudanese extraction who was the deputy chief of the block kitchen.

The kitchen—two connected tents in a separate barbed-wire cage—was, in part, my responsibility. I was charged, during my shifts, with knowing the whereabouts of the five just-sharp-enough knives allowed to Hamad and his cooks. Hamad would greet me every morning—before dawn, when I went through the block, collecting his staff from their tents—with a booming, *"Nu, vus macht a Yid?"* which is Yiddish for "How's it going?" Hamad spoke conversational Yiddish. He learned it when he worked as an assistant to a tailor, a survivor of Auschwitz, who kept a shop in an Orthodox suburb of Tel Aviv. I spoke only bacon Yiddish, and Hamad would mock me mercilessly for my ignorance of the *mamaloshen,* the mother tongue. He once told me he thought it a shame that the Holocaust caused the death of Yiddish.

He also told me the Jews were destined for hell. But he said it with a gold-toothed smile.

Then there was a Gazan named Rafiq Hijazi. There was something unusual about Rafiq. He was charming and placatory, which made him stand out in a prison of embittered mayhem-makers. He had a round face, padded cheeks, and alert, clear eyes. He appeared older than his twenty-one years. His hair seemed in danger of thinning and premature wrinkles radiated out from the corners of his eyes. And there was a stillness to him that was uncharacteristic of the younger inmates, who were kinetically twitchy, which I imagined was a symptom of extended confinement. Rafiq, though, didn't seem unmoored by incarceration. One day I asked him why.

"Sometimes I'm not really here," he said.

"Where are you, then?" I asked.

"In here," he said, tapping his temple. "Where are you?" he asked.

"I'm here in Ketziot," I said.

"Where else?" he asked.

"Far away," I said.

When we spoke we spoke between links of a fence, but sometimes I thought the fence was unneeded, because he did not present himself as someone capable of violence. He was instead bookish, which was an endearing quality, particularly in this place, and he was curious about everything, which was an outstanding virtue in my view. He also did not seem like the sort of person who saw empathy as an infirmity of character.

I spoke with Rafiq more than I did with any other prisoner. It was a delight to talk with him. Whatever personal grievances Rafiq nursed—and most of the prisoners had an unlimited capacity for complaint—he kept to himself. He was smart, observant, and analytical—this last quality, which demands both coolness and dispassion, was exceedingly rare in Ketziot, on both sides of the wire. It was Rafiq's sense of irony that secured my affection for him. We became co-conspirators, in a way, issuing commentary, only to each other, about the farce and absurdity of prison life. One day, Yehuda came barging through the block, spluttering and red-faced about an edict he issued that had gone unfulfilled, something of spectacular unimportance concerning the prompt collection of garbage from Sub-Block Three. I was standing with Rafiq just then, talking through the wire. We watched Yehuda storm past, two sergeants trailing behind. I gave Rafiq a look. "You should be more forgiving," he said. "The fate of Israel is in Yehuda's hands."

I laughed. Then he said, in a near-whisper, "We have those kinds of people, too."

Meaning what, I asked?

"Please don't tell me you think Palestinians are perfect," he said.

"No, don't worry about that," I said.

Rafiq was humble and devout. He would wake before dawn in the cold dark, emerge from his tent, wash his hands and feet—bare feet, in the desert night—at an open basin, and pray quietly in a corner of his enclosure. When I was assigned to the overnight patrol, I would watch him with admiration: Even the most religious prisoners had difficulty making morning prayers.

Unlike the other religiously observant prisoners, he would not try to convert me. I assumed he believed Islam to be superior to Judaism—to be its completion, in fact—but he had an academic's curiosity about my rival brand of monotheism, rather than a missionary's smug impatience. "The Jewish prophets are our prophets, too," he said once, in explaining his interest.

I wanted to make Rafiq my friend. I felt this keenly, almost from the moment we met. It was something I believed was actually possible. I sensed the presence between us of the enzymes of friendship. I believed that he liked me. He thought I was kind, for a Jew, and I thought he was smart, for an Arab. We had very little in common, of course, except that we were both in our early twenties, and we were both trapped in the same desert—he more than me, he seldom failed to note.

I never learned his crime. He wouldn't say what it was, exactly. He told me once that he was accused, by a military prosecutor in his case, of helping to lead the Uprising in the Jebalya Refugee Camp in Gaza. This was not an insignificant charge—the Intifada began three years earlier in Jebalya.

I asked him if the charge was true, but he wouldn't answer. It was usually this way with the prisoners: The Jews say I did this, the Jews say I did that. These men were proud, violent nationalists, the Intifada was a righteous fight, and yet nobody knew anything: six thousand Palestinians, and every one of them a virgin. The commander of the camp, a colonel named Ze'ev Shaltiel, told new arrivals to his staff not to bother asking the Palestinians what they did to earn a bunk in Ketziot. They would all answer the same way, Shaltiel said: *"Walla, Ani lo yodea"*—"By God, I don't know." The *"Walla"* was Arabic; the *"Ani lo yodea"* was Hebrew.

Rafiq and I would spend hours talking through the wire. We would ventilate our political stances. We would nitpick history. We didn't agree on much; he thought that Zionism was a form of kleptomania. But he did not mind hearing me rehearse for him the Jewish narrative. We would gossip about guards and prisoners, and we would, tentatively, with great gentility, talk about religion. We were both dedicated readers of our holy texts, though sometimes it seemed to me that he believed the Quran was written by the hand of God, and I could not say I believed the same thing about my Bible. Despite this difference, we shared a set of essential values, because his distaste for violence seemed as real as mine.

I wasn't sure, at first, which Palestinian faction received Rafiq's allegiance. I asked, but he wouldn't say. By the time Palestinian prisoners were ready for warehousing at Ketziot, they had already been run through the interrogation centers of the Shabak. But there was always more information to extract, which is why the Shabak men appeared at the prison, without warning, and with immediate demands. One day, overcome by curiosity, I went to a Shabak agent about Rafiq. He checked, and told me that Rafiq was Hamas. I asked, Are you sure? The information is *zahav tahor,* he said—pure gold, without a doubt true.

The next day, he came back to me, and told me he was wrong: Rafiq is Fatah, not Hamas. I was greatly relieved. But the man from the Shabak told me in so many words that they were all the same; the theological and political differences between Hamas and Fatah were Talmudic in subtlety and meaningless in practice, he said. The important thing to remember is that Fatah and Hamas both seek Jewish blood; they are different fangs in the same mouth.

Paranoia was communicable, and I was soon infected. The Israeli prison staff slept in a command sub-block located less than a hundred feet from the prisoners. We were separated by a scalable wall and a loose coil of barbed wire. We were so close we heard their snoring. And we would hear other noises in the middle of the night—murmuring, grumbling, moaning from the tents. One of the men in my tent said once, "God knows what goes on inside those tents."

I let my imagination go. I would lie in my bunk and allow marauding Palestinians to pillage my mind. There were so many prisoners, and so few of us. This is the way it would happen: They would plot their rising in secret (our intelligence officer couldn't have found a plate of hummus in Cairo), and then one night, on a silent signal, they would build siege-works of mattresses and then hurl each other across the fences and swarm like the Black Hundreds into our compound. We would kill whomever we could, but there would still be more, an unstoppable wave, filling our tents. I would be feeling in the dark for a clip, and then I would hear a scream, and then I would feel a length of barbed wire cutting into my neck. Maybe it would be Rafiq himself killing me, a smile plastered on his chubby face.

One day, a prisoner in the next block was killed by Fatah. He had been accused of collaborating with Israel; he was tortured, tried by a secret Fatah tribunal, found guilty, and executed. All this happened inside a closed tent, not twenty-five feet from a guard. We, the military policemen, were shocked and terrified: Who are these people, who would inflict such cruelties on their own kind?

"Animals," Yehuda explained. Palestinians are people who pierce the anuses of suspected collaborators with sharpened broomsticks. Imagine what they would do to a Jew.

A few days after the killing, I proposed a scenario to Rafiq: Imagine that it is five years from now and you are a free man, working in Jerusalem, on a building site. You see me walking down the street. I'm in civilian clothing, but you remember me as a soldier of the Israeli army, the army that occupies your land and oppresses your people. Would you kill me if you had the chance?

To which Rafiq replied, in Hebrew, "Come on."

No I'm serious, I said.

Jeff, this is stupid, he said.

Listen, I told him, I'm not going to drag you to solitary confinement if you give me the wrong answer.

He hesitated.

I was desperate for an answer. I was desperate, though, for the right answer—it was surpassingly important to me. He could, with the wrong answer, tear down the scaffolding of my beliefs, the belief in the power of friendship to bridge the abyss between our two tribes, the belief that I could make him my friend. I believed, with morbid sincerity, that if I could make him my friend, we would together, in some small but consequential way, defy the wicked logic of hate and war, that we, together, would stand as a rebuke to the grotesque idea that our problem was without a solution.

Finally, he said, "Look, it wouldn't be personal."

I thanked him politely for his answer and walked to my tent.

What was I thinking? What, I asked myself, could I expect of a man living in a hem of barbed wire? It was then that an idea began to gather in my mind: One day, I would find Rafiq when he was a free man, and I would ask him this question once more, and then he would give me the answer that I so zealously desired.

That night, though, alone in my bunk, the thought struck me: Maybe they were right. Maybe the Israelis were right. Maybe I didn't understand the mentality of the Arabs. Maybe I didn't understand anything at all.

CHAPTER THREE

OUR LADY OF LOURDES

On the other hand, why *should* I have understood the mentality of the Arabs? I was, after all, from Long Island. If you're searching for the secret meanings of Billy Joel songs, I'm your man. But Arabs?

There was only one Arab in my school, in Malverne, on the South Shore of Long Island, not far from Queens. Malverne is a tribally Catholic, deeply American town that borders, to the misery of at least some of its residents, an enclave of blacks, who share Malverne's public schools. This fact explained why some of Malverne's whites sent their children to the Catholic school down the street from my house.

The Arab's name was Omar. His parents brought him to New York from Egypt, and his father worked in a gas station. My outstanding memory of Omar was of his dangerous incompetence in dodgeball, a game for which—in the days before the rise of liability awareness and sensitivity training for gym teachers—a boy of twelve or thirteen, to avoid humiliation and to protect the bones of his face, would want to build certain skills. There was no mercy for Omar; he was creamed, daily. It wasn't his fault, though. He was thin and mild in personality, and soccer, which I think was his game, had not penetrated the consciousness of Malverne by 1977.

I knew one other Arab in childhood. When I was fifteen, I met a girl named Joy, a Catholic, a daughter of Palestinian immigrants, who was a student at the Sacred Heart Academy of the Sisters of St. Joseph. She was the most enraged teenager ever to cross my path, quicker to fury than all the children of divorce in my high school, all the proto-Goths, all the Johnny Rotten–lovers in dog collars, even the black girls who smeared their faces with Vaseline for protection before nail-slashing their enemies in the parking lot behind the school.

I met Joy at Beth Ann Seccia's Sweet Sixteen. Music from *The Rocky Horror Picture Show* was on the record player. Mrs. Seccia served baked ziti and rice balls, Mr. Seccia hovered, but not too oppressively, and it was a slap-up good time until Joy and I ruined everything by turning Beth's streamer-filled basement into a steel-cage Middle Eastern blood-and-thunder death match, J.V. division. At first, when the subject of Israel came up, and her eyes narrowed, I thought she wasn't mad at me, but *for* me, which was a delusional but seductive idea, if only for the double transgression she represented. Not only was she a Catholic girl, which held its own taboo allure (see Billy Joel, "Only the Good Die Young"), but she was an Arab, which was hopelessly exotic, in a Montague and Capulet sort of way. But our conversation took an irreversibly dark turn when I suggested that the Palestinians were primarily responsible for their own misery. I no longer remember the contours of the fight, but in ten minutes we careered from an argument about the transmutation of idealism into evil to the spectacle of Joy howling with both lungs, "Deir Yassin! What about Deir Yassin!"

Deir Yassin was an Arab village near Jerusalem. One hundred and ten or so of its inhabitants were massacred by the Irgun Tsvai Leumi, the National Military Organization, a Jewish terror group in pre-Israel Palestine under the command of Menachem Begin. The massacre came shortly before the expiration of the British Mandate in Palestine, and the declaration of Jewish independence. For the Palestinians, Deir Yassin is the apotheosis of misfortune and injustice. Later in life, I would understand the inescapability of the *argumentum ad Yassinum,* the Katyusha rocket in the arsenal of Palestinian rhetoric. I'm never surprised, in debates, to hear a Palestinian immediately invoke Deir Yassin as the truth that trumps all Jewish truths (the Munich Olympics? Deir Yassin! Entebbe? Deir Yassin! the Hebron massacre, which took place eighteen years before Deir Yassin? Deir Yassin!).

I told Joy (and our slack-jawed friends, who were mesmerized by this car wreck of an argument, despite their complete lack of interest in the affairs of the Middle East) that I was a socialist Zionist, that the actions and beliefs of the right-wing Zionists were anathema to me. In fact—and I hid this from Joy, quite obviously—I had once considered myself a supporter of Vladimir Jabotinsky, the founder of the militaristic nationalist Zionist movement called Revisionism, but that was back when I was fourteen.

The mainstream of Jews in Palestine was horrified by what happened in Deir Yassin, I said, and they felt grief for those who died there, and, oh, by the way, none of this would have happened had the Arabs possessed the foresight and compassion to accept the United Nations partition plan, which split Palestine into two halves, one Jewish, one Arab.

Well, around the bend she went. Who gave the United Nations the right to steal my people's land? Zionism, she said, is the worst thing to ever happen in the history of the world.

I fought back, but I was on the ropes: No one, in my limited universe, thought these thoughts, and I was unequipped to parry them. I knew well that Jews were disliked—I knew this in an uncomfortably personal way—and, more to the point, I knew that Israel was, in many quarters, reviled, but this I learned from the newspapers.

When I was fifteen, Zionism, the liberation movement of the Jewish people, was so self-evidently the righteous response of a lamblike people to demonic threats that I was crushed by the idea that the world didn't share my view. Israel was the polestar of my existence. This sounds outlandish, I know, and I don't mean to suggest that the fruitless pursuit of girls, and the early scramble for the right college, and an obsession with rap music, and the dissolution of my parents' marriage, didn't all combine to fill up my days. But I was convinced, by fifteen, that I was an American only because of some terrible, cosmic accident of birth. I'd been born too late, and in the wrong place. I was a victim of existential dislocation: Israel was home, Long Island was exile.

I'm still not entirely sure how I reached this conclusion. I discovered, long after my conversion to the cause of Jewish nationalism, an important clue in the thinking of Jean-Paul Sartre, who, in his writings on anti-Semitism, did not have the South Shore of Long Island in mind, but might as well have.

Sartre, in *Anti-Semite and Jew,* which he wrote shortly after one-third of the Jews on earth fell victim to the German hangman, argued that Jews are merely the constructs of anti-Semites, that the Jew exists only because the anti-Semite invented him. There is no Jew inside the Jew, in other words; the Jew exists only in the cold stare and clenched fist of the anti-Jew. Sartre ignored the existence of positive Jewishness; he could not seem to imagine that Judaism, its texts, traditions, and beliefs, could draw the voluntary allegiance of a person freed from the compulsion of the ghetto.

Sartre's understanding of Jews is insulting, dehumanizing, and historically perverse: The anti-Semite did not of course create the Jew. The anti-Semite, in his most enduring form—his Christian form—was created in reaction to the Jew.

But part of the reason I despise Sartre's analysis is because it is truer—about me, at least—than I care to admit.

I was not raised in an observant home. In many ways, my parents, who did not observe the Sabbath, who did not pray or speak a Jewish language, and who packed my lunch with ham-and-cheese sandwiches, were only nominally Jewish, in the usual understanding of Jewishness. My family was, in practice, the Mosaic equivalent of lapsed Unitarians. We paid dues to the nearby Reform temple, a sterile place of yellow hallways, organ music, women in fur, and garmentos talking through Shabbat services. But we were thoroughly disconnected from the spiritual life of the place, such as it was. The occasional relative strayed into religiosity. My Uncle Julie, a kind and unusually short upholsterer from the Bensonhurst section of Brooklyn, was the most religious in our family, which meant that he went to synagogue on Rosh Hashanah *and* Yom Kippur and that he wasn't a Communist. But we weren't much for ritual. A hard anticlerical streak, it seemed, ran in our genes. My grandfather, who was born in the *shtetl* of Liova, Bessarabia, spoke happily of the time he glued his rabbi's beard to a desk. When the rabbi awoke from his nap and sliced himself free, he beat my grandfather, causing *his* grandfather to storm the *cheder,* a battered shack of a Hebrew school by the River Prut, and beat the rabbi with his fists. My grandfather, even late in life, felt no regrets. Not long before he died, he said, "The only thing I don't know is where I got the glue."

My family's Judaism was a free-to-be-you-and-me Judaism of "social action," of liberal Democratic politics, of civil rights, abortion rights, and boycotts, always boycotts; my parents, who were both teachers, and union members, boycotted whatever it was that the United Farm Workers told us to boycott. We protected our refrigerator from green grapes and iceberg lettuce with a commitment that would impress a Wahhabi. (Even today, the sight of a bunch of grapes conjures in my mind a vision of César Chávez's sorrowful face; such grapes, for me, are the madeleines of collective bargaining.)

My parents were unswervingly agnostic and we lived without the consolations of religion. We were taught that religion was not the basis of morality, but that it was often the source of immorality.

We did have saints, though, men who sacrificed their lives for the cause of justice and whose beatification by my parents and their liberal friends taught me about the intoxicating romance of martyrdom: There was Martin Luther King, Jr., above all. (I was partial to Malcolm X; I would memorize his speeches, diligent little Jewish radical that I was.)

I remember my father's rhetorical question, "Did you know that Martin Luther King's closest aides were Jewish?" and answering yes, my chest inflating with pride. And there were Schwerner, Chaney, and Goodman, the young Freedom Summer volunteers—two Jews and a black—who were murdered outside Philadelphia, Mississippi, in 1964. And then there was Allard Lowenstein, who served, briefly, as our congressman, and who counted my parents among his most earnest supporters (my earliest, inchoate memories include a raucous Lowenstein rally, viewed from atop my father's shoulders).

Lowenstein, who was murdered in 1980 by a mentally deranged man, was among the first people, in his book *Brutal Mandate*—which I read at a young age, even before I read Malcolm X—to expose America to the horror and absurdity of apartheid in South Africa. He also led the Dump Johnson movement in 1968. Lowenstein was, before becoming an actual martyr, a living martyr: The Republicans gerrymandered his congressional seat out of existence, and he spent only two years in Congress. A poster from his losing race hung in our house. It was purple and featured a peace sign and a quote attributed to Lincoln: "To sin by silence when they should protest makes cowards out of men." This was, epigrammatically, our Jewish faith, and Lowenstein was the embodiment of that faith.

The Long Island district Lowenstein represented was split between liberal Jews and conservative Catholics, though it contained pockets of blacks, and the occasional understated WASP, adrift in a sea of dispossessed and high-decibel Brooklyn exiles.

In 1968, when my parents made the *hejira* from roiling Brooklyn to the green stretches of Long Island, they chose to buy a house not in the plushy Bagel Belt towns of Cedarhurst or Great Neck, but in a place in which white children could go to school with black children. When they moved to Malverne, they were under the mistaken impression that it was part black (my mother said she saw blacks shopping on Malverne's main street, and extrapolated, incorrectly). Our street came to an end at a racial DMZ, the aptly named Ocean Avenue, across which sat the all-black neighborhood of Lakeview. The sons and daughters of Lakeview attended Malverne's schools with those white children whose parents didn't mind a little bit of race-mixing. A father of one of my friends once told me that "the colored" sicced their dogs on white children: "Son," he said, "be careful."

It wasn't only our politics that were Jewish. We were New York Jews, which meant that we were Jewish gastronomically and culturally, as well as neurotically. And in this neurosis could be found an unspoken contradiction in our faith. Despite our belief in the brotherhood of man, despite our adherence to the utopian vision of universal justice that was in the weave of our progressive faith, we possessed a melancholic and mostly unmentioned understanding of the gentile world: Though I was not a Zionist by inheritance, it was made obvious to me that the world would always see us as Jews, no matter what we did. Oppression was a birthright. There is a link, of course, between the Jewish vision of the world as it should be, and the understanding of the world as it is: The Jews of America, when they go to the polls, are voting against memories, memories of Cossacks, Nazis, and blood libels.

Anti-Semitism is a constant. So, too, is the urge, among Jews of cosmopolitan, universalist bent, to separate themselves from their tribe. Being in rebellion against Judaism is in itself a form of Judaism. These Jews separate themselves by conversion, by public disassociation, or by excoriation of the tribe for its moral and spiritual failings. Marx, whose worldview had the tacit sympathy of one branch of my family, was such a Jew.

But we were not among the anti-parochialists; there were few attempts by my Russian Jewish family to engage in the self-deceit of all-out assimilation. Very few people around us behaved in the manner of the posh German Jews of Manhattan, for whom Cohen became Kane, Weinstein became Winston, and Schwartz became Stewart. No one in my family ever considered the benefits of deracination through name-change, even though no name signals quite so clearly the Semitic nature of its owner as does Goldberg; Cohen, perhaps, Einstein, we hope, but Goldberg, no doubt.

We felt something, I think, that many Jews in this country still feel: a kind of involuntary apartness, an unease, rooted in an incontrovertible truth about America—that, no matter what the Constitution says, it is a Christian country. It could be argued that no country in the Diaspora has so successfully inoculated itself against Jew-hatred as has America. But the fear of anti-Semitism is the forge on which many American Jews build their identities. This is how I built mine.

I learned about the inevitability of anti-Semitism early on, below the level of consciousness, from my grandfather, that rabbi-abusing miscreant from the Pale of Settlement. His birth name was Gedalia, but it was changed to George at Ellis Island. He was a tough, quiet man with a tattoo on his arm who came up through the sweatshops and who scraped his way to success as a manufacturer of Venetian blinds and who, late in life, would melt at the sight of his grandchildren.

When I was a small boy, he would tell me stories of his childhood that were so strange and thrilling that they could well have taken place on Mars. The Jewish ghetto in Liova was destitute; the family horse was blind, the house had one room with a single window, and my grandfather told me how the cold would enter his bones when he hid under his bed, pressing himself against the dirt floor to escape the attention of Cossacks—Cossacks as cruel as Pushkin's—who came hunting for Christ-killers to crucify. By day, of course, the Jewish children in his czarist school were made to pray to Jesus.

My grandfather was born into the whirlwind of Russian anti-Semitism. Liova was situated not far from Kishinev, in Moldova, the scene of one of the most dastardly pogroms in the martyrology of Judaism. The pogrom took place in 1903, a few years before his birth. The Jews of Bessarabia (and all across the Pale) spent their lives cowering before berserk mobs, and before the priests who blessed the spilling of Jewish blood in the name of Christ.

On March 30, 1903, a letter addressed to "Brethren Christians" was posted in the taverns of Kishinev. "The base *Zhids* are not satisfied with the blood of Our Savior crucified by them," the letter read. "Every year they shed the innocent blood of Christians and use it for their rituals. Have you not heard that they crucified a Christian boy in Kishinev and bled him? This is the way they jeer at us, Russians. Brothers, in the name of our Savior, who shed his blood for us; in the name of our Father the Czar . . . let us exclaim in the forthcoming great day: Down with *Zhids*! Beat these mean degenerates, blood-suckers drunk with Russian blood!"

In the pogrom that followed, forty-nine Jews were murdered; another five hundred were injured. More than seven hundred houses were destroyed and six hundred shops were looted. The poet Hayyim Nahman Bialik, dispatched to Kishinev by the Zionist leaders of Odessa to investigate the pogrom, wrote of its obscenities in the poem "In the City of Slaughter":

Descend then, to the cellars of the town,
There where the virginal daughters of thy folk were fouled,
Where seven heathens flung a woman down,
The daughter in the presence of her mother,
The mother in the presence of her daughter,
Before slaughter, during slaughter and after slaughter!

Bialik aimed his rage at the Jewish men of Kishinev as well. He was a Zionist and, at the time he wrote "In the City of Slaughter," he was a Zionist in the thrall of Vladimir Jabotinsky, the unremitting militarist who carried the banner of Jewish iron. And so Bialik, sickened by the unmanning of Kishinev Jewry, wrote:

In that dark corner, and behind that cask
Crouched husbands, bridegroom, brothers, peering from the cracks,
Watching the sacred bodies struggling underneath
The bestial breath,
Stifled in filth, and swallowing their blood!
The lecherous rabble portioning for booty
Their kindred and their flesh!
Crushed in their shame, they saw it all.

The Kishinev massacre provoked a seismic, global reaction: Theodor Herzl asked the Russian government to move its Jews to Palestine; Theodore Roosevelt wrote a letter of protest to the czar (it went unanswered), and even Tolstoy, no lover of Jews, organized protests against the slaughter. The peasant Jews of the Pale had little time, however, for Tolstoy, or for the czar, or for the amelioration of Bialik's burning embarrassment. They were in search of a path of escape. The Zionist argument gained little traction; most poor Jews sought salvation in the steel-and-concrete promise of Roosevelt's America, and not in the Palestine dreams of the *luftmensch* Herzl. My grandfather's father was one of those who went west. In 1913, he left his wife and children in Liova and made his way to Bucharest and then to Berlin, then Paris, Cherbourg, and a boat to New York. It would be eight years before he could send for his family. He left them knowing they might fall under the Cossack sword.

"They would come through town on the way to Kiev," my grandfather told me when I interviewed him about his exotic youth. "One day they came knocking on the window—it had iron bars. They were looking for a house of ill-repute. They started breaking through the window, the door. We started screaming. They were drunk, they were always drunk."

He went on, "They decided to skip our house. It looked too poor. They went to the house across the street, and they took that man out, bedding and all, and they took him off, and we found him dead the next day." The Jews, he said, did nothing in response.

He remembered only one Jew who fought back. It was his Uncle Mendel, a blacksmith, a huge man with arms the size of briskets. He was also one of the *shtetl*'s only competent drinkers. "We were having Simchas Torah"—the holiday that celebrates the giving of the Torah by God to the Jews at Sinai—"and it was a joyous holiday, big noise, and my uncle, he used to get drunk on Simchas Torah and he insisted that the musicians walk him home from *shul*," the synagogue. "And he used to fight with everyone in the *shul*, with everyone. It was a rumpus. He was home when a Cossack came onto the street, drunk, swinging his sword around. My uncle walked out of his house and he went up to the Cossack, but then he went to the left, and got around the Cossack, and he picked him up and he broke his back and took his sword."

Mendel ran from town; my grandfather never learned what happened to him.

I would demand that my grandfather tell stories of Mendel the blacksmith again and again, and I would often wonder what became of him. My imagination took him to Palestine, of course, where he fought for his people; Mendel, *my* uncle, was not one to cringe in the face of violence. He did not behave in the manner one associates with the soft-shelled Jews of the Diaspora.

In my grandfather's stories, one question never arose: Why? Why did they hate us? My grandfather never asked. He accepted the existence of Jew-hatred in the same way he accepted the existence of weather.

For a time, so did I.

When I was eleven or so, in the yard of my middle school, I was taught, against my will, a game known variously as "Jew Penny," or

"Bend the Jew." My tormentors were representatives of the more physical races: red-faced Irish kids, a cackling bucktoothed German boy, and the occasional Italian, the sort who took up smoking even before they grew underarm hair, and who blew up cats with M-80s. Lenny Bruce once said that all Italians are Jewish, but he never met these *cugenes*. They were, generally speaking, dumb as rocks, but just as hard. They taught me how to play "Bend the Jew" on the fields of our school, and in the parking lot of Our Lady of Lourdes Roman Catholic Church and School. The school was a three-story orange-brick fort topped by a wrought iron crown of thorns. Our Lady of Lourdes is the church where they took Communion, and where they were taught, I imagined, to feel superior to Jews.

"Bend the Jew" is a simple game, with ad hoc rules. A group of miniature Torquemadas surround a "cheap fucking Jew," and then they throw pennies at his feet. If the sheenie doesn't bend, his tormentors throw nickels, and then dimes. If the Jew still won't bend to pick up the coins, out of pride or fear, he is jumped and beaten. Of course, if he bends down to pick up the coins, he is jumped and beaten. I never bent, but I can't say I fought back, either. I was no Mendel.

I would be embarrassed today even to suggest an analogy between inconsequential playground beatings and cutting words, on the one hand, and the desecrations and blood-letting of the pogroms, on the other. And I would prefer to think of myself as someone who does not justify the decisions and mistakes of his adulthood through the prism of minor childhood traumas—and my traumas, by any reasonable standard, were minor. They were, however, mine, and they have not, alas, left me alone.

Perhaps this is because they were not sporadic. They were for a period of time my existence, and I did nothing to alleviate my plight, except call myself a faggot and silently blame my parents. I kept them ignorant of my starring role in this schoolyard passion play, though of course I blamed them for settling in a wasteland of Irish pogromists.

It was blackest night when I woke up to the smell of fire. Our Lady of Lourdes was burning. No one else was awake. I was eleven, or twelve. There were no fire trucks. I ran out of the house, in my pajamas, and pried open the great oak church doors. Fire was whipping through the sanctuary. Jesus Christ was burning on the cross. I ran to the altar, in my bare feet. There, on the altar, were the sacramental wafers. I grabbed up the wafers, and the chalice, and then I dove through a stained-glass window.

The firemen came; they were all Irish Catholic (Jews didn't join the fire department). "Here," I said, handing the fire chief the chalice and the wafers, the body of Christ. The chief looked like a boy named Harrington who pitched pennies at me.

There was a parade the next day: It even went past the synagogue. I was seated on top of the fire truck. The Catholics cheered me as I went by. The next morning, the police came to school and arrested me. They accused me of setting the fire. No one would listen to my denials. I screamed my innocence to the sky. A priest made the sign of the cross as I was taken away.

I always woke up just then. I never did figure out where I was being taken.

Soon after I had this dream, I would take my bicycle by Our Lady of Lourdes, to make sure it was still standing.

I didn't like the dog's life of the Diaspora. We were a whipped and boneless people. What good were these brains—doctor brains, lawyer brains, accountant brains—without the muscle to protect them? I don't remember much about Hebrew school, except the feeling of suffocation it induced in me each Tuesday and Thursday, but I do remember that one day one of my teachers—a gray man in a brown sweater who was reputedly related to a supporting actor on the sitcom *F Troop*, but about whom nothing else was even passingly interesting—told us that we should be proud to be Jewish because Sandy Koufax is Jewish. That raised the question: Sandy Koufax? That's it? That's all you got? Okay, there's Hank Greenberg and Sid Luckman, but really? A quarterback from the forties? Only a single member of the Mets was Jewish, Art Shamsky, who batted .300 in the 1969 championship season but soon retired with nagging back problems.

What was the source of this curse? "It is expected that we and our fellows will strive and succeed in the traditional pursuits of a landless people," David Mamet, the Uncle Mendel of American Jewish letters, once said. "But a Jewish *football player* . . . that person would stand as a magnificent and welcome freak. That person is an image which gets the heart beating a bit faster with pride."

This is not to suggest that immediately upon gaining understanding of the apocalyptic consequences of my disembodied passivity, my attenuated not-yet-manhood, I took up tae kwon do, or stock-car driving, or the chewing of smokeless tobacco. My early response to the petty physical trauma of my life—and how stereotypical is this?—was to find refuge in the public library, behind walls of books. It is the place where I drowned myself in the literature of the Shoah. I found in the Holocaust a perverse form of consolation. The slaughter of the Jews by the Germans meant that the world was always thus, that my inconsequential problem was a minor link in an eternal chain of terror. But my discovery of the Shoah was also emphatically destabilizing. Twelve-year-old Jewish children should not be exposed to the unfiltered evil of the Shoah, in which the worst that could happen did happen. My mind, stuffed with facts about firing squads, Zyklon B, and Mengele, would wander back four decades to images of mothers and fathers, shoveled into boxcars, with no air, no food, no water, ragged bodies cascading onto train platforms, children ripped from crying fathers, the fathers disappearing from sight, carried away in a crush of bodies, the mothers and children stripped naked, screaming for help, herded to oblivion. It is all true, of course, and the eyes should not be averted, but it is too much truth at a young age. Such knowledge turned the ground under my feet, already giving way, to quicksand.

Then, in our modest library, I discovered the Black Panthers. The words of Huey Newton, Eldridge Cleaver, and Stokely Carmichael read true to me, their call to violent resistance somehow reasonable to my Holocaust-haunted self. And soon enough I came across the writings of Meir Kahane, on a high shelf, and it was Kahane who provided a not un-Panther-like but specifically Semitic model of self-defense. Kahane was the Brooklyn rabbi who founded the Jewish Defense League in 1968 to shake Jews out of their fatalistic and feminized passivity. He argued, infamously, in favor of the bat, the bomb, and the gun. ("Every Jew a .22," he said, to the shame and horror of the Manhattan Jewish elite and to the secret joy of every beaten-down Jewboy in the tristate area.) Later in life, I would come to know Kahane personally, and I would see him for what he was: an ayatollah, a hater obsessed with the purity of Jewish blood and the chasteness of Jewish women. But for a time he held all the answers for me. In the locker room, I was a kike, but in the sanctuary of the library, I was a revolutionary kike, one of Kahane's *chayas,* a beast, a street-fighting Jew.

There was one thing I could not understand about Kahane: The man hated black people, just hated them. The JDL was founded for the ostensible purpose of protecting the remaining Jews of Brooklyn from the black deluge. In my case, though, the whites were the enemy, and the blacks were my comfort. Never—not once—did a black call me a name (I did not know, until reaching college, that blacks and Jews were supposed to despise each other). I thought, naïvely, that the Black Panthers and the JDL were of a piece.

It was a black boy, in fact, who turned into my schoolyard savior. His name was Chuckie Greer. He was muscled and cool, a splendid athlete on the ball fields and intimidating in the hallways. One day, in the locker room, he saw the splotchy, red-haired bully named Harrington push me against the wall. Chuckie suggested a course of action I had contemplated only in my dreams.

"Hit him," Chuckie said.

I couldn't. I wasn't weak—I've always had thick arms—but I could not use them. There was something wrong with the genetic wiring.

"Hit him," Chuckie said, and finally I did.

It worked. The Jew-haters slunk away.

It wasn't just Chuckie Greer, Malcolm X, and Meir Kahane who turned me into the Moshe Dayan of the Howard T. Herber Middle School. My parents played a role, inadvertently. When I was thirteen, against convention, they scheduled my bar mitzvah for the Western Wall in Jerusalem. They were not motivated by reasons of spirit. For them, it was an exercise in avoidance. Long Island bar mitzvah parties in the 1970s stank of ostentation, gluttony, and almost otherworldly tackiness (I do not think that much has changed). At one such party, in the ball room of our temple, I recall standing, dumbstruck, with the aggrieved bar mitzvah boy—he was wearing a powder blue tuxedo, with ruffles and tails—as he watched his grandmothers dance to an extended version of "Push Push (In the Bush)."

God forbid this should happen to me.

So we went to Israel. We boarded an El Al 747 at Kennedy Airport. Two hours into the flight, I became violently ill. But I remember the beautiful, if truculent, stewardesses, and I remember the seamless way the Mediterranean met the white beaches of Tel Aviv.

The bar mitzvah came, and then, thank God, it went. It took place on a sunny day. I carried the Torah across the plaza of stone before the Western Wall, and I offered God, in whom I don't recall believing, my most sincere prayers, asking Him to steady my hand, because these fanatics—hundreds and hundreds of frantically religious black-hat Orthodox, rocking violently in supplication, wearing fur hats in the desert heat—would surely murder me if I let the Torah fall to the ground. I also remember the cabbage smell of the hired-gun rabbi, whose name was Yitzhok Weisfish. I had never met a Jew who looked like Weisfish; he wore a beard of brillo, a black velvet kippah, a black coat, and a white shirt stained through with sweat. I was not completely unfamiliar with the black-hat Orthodox. My grandparents, who stayed behind in Brooklyn when we left for Long Island, lived across the street from a Lubavitcher yeshiva, and the streets of their neighborhood were crowded with the dented, muffler-dragging station wagons favored by the God-tremblers, who drove without much skill but with great faith. "They have very bad teeth," my grandmother explained.

Weisfish was no more than thirty, but looked fifty, and we exchanged no words at all because he spoke no English and my Hebrew education at the Reform temple centered on rote memorization.

I was greatly relieved, by the end, to escape the Western Wall plaza. I understood that this was the holiest site in Judaism, God's earthly home, and so I expressed, when called upon, pieties about sanctity and wonder, but in truth I was left cold by this enormous pile of stone. I wasn't quite old enough to grasp the revolutionary idea at the core of monotheism, but I would soon: God, I would realize, did not live in a retaining wall of the Temple Mount, or on top of the Mount, or in any other rock, or in the wind, or on the moon, or in the oceans blue.

But fetish-making is a human weakness, and Jews don't possess immunities against this weakness, and so the descendants of the discoverers of the incorporeal God come from the four corners of Exile to lay hands on the Wall and kiss it and leave sycophantic and pleading notes to God in its weed-filled cracks, and, while I was glad the Old City of Jerusalem fell to my people in the Six-Day War, the holiness of the place did not saturate me.

For me, the wonder was modern Israel, the greatest wonders being Jews with guns, and not just .22s, but Uzis and M-16s and bigger guns than these, grenade-spitting guns, great barking machine guns. On a bus tour across the Galilee, we drove in the wake of a tank transport, a mammoth truck carrying a deadly Jewish tank. A Jewish tank! And

Jewish armored personnel carriers! It was a miracle. Enough of thinking and suffering! Let's do some shooting!

Ordinary sights were euphoriants: the cops, all Jewish; soldiers, everywhere—Jewish, swaggering, cool, impervious to abashment. Mean Jews, tough Jews, big Jews, and no gelded, Diaspora Jews in sight, except on my tour bus.

A Jewish fire truck! A fire truck with a Star of David, stenciled right on the side. Would wonders never cease? We visited Yad Mordechai, a kibbutz just north of the Erez checkpoint, the entrance to Gaza. At Yad Mordechai, in 1948, the Jews held off Egyptian tanks for six days, armed only with Bren guns and Molotov cocktails. The men of Yad Mordechai did not cringe; they fought like lions, they fought like the man for whom their kibbutz was named, Mordechai Anielewicz, who led the Jewish Combat Organization in the Warsaw Ghetto. Outside Rachel's Tomb, in Bethlehem, I took a photo of a soldier; I kept that photo in my desk drawer and looked at it every night, telling myself that one day I would be this soldier.

By the time we came home, I burned with love for Israel. I began this mystic pilgrimage a speck of a Jew, but I emerged utterly different, invested with a mission much larger than myself, larger, certainly, than the quotidian and occasionally terrifying life of a Long Island Jewish boy. Israel was my main chance: For nineteen hundred years, since the final Roman obliteration of Israel (they even changed its name to Palestine, in order to erase from the world's memory its existence), the Jews were chased across the earth. But in 1948, just seventeen years before I was born, the Jews reentered history, building a country out of the cinders of the Holocaust. How could I miss out on this drama?

My parents didn't discourage my zeal. I was given a paperback copy of *Exodus,* the Leon Uris novel that served as the script notes for my dream life. I identified, body and soul, with the hero of *Exodus,* Ari Ben Canaan, a Hebrew (not, somehow, Jewish) warrior, brave and cold-eyed, who defended Jewish honor and whose existence seemed vengeance enough for the Holocaust. He was smarter than his British foes (not merely cleverer, which would be the trait of a Diaspora Jew). He was smarter, surely, than the Arabs who threatened to suffocate his new country, and he was handsome in a quite obviously non-Jewish way. The freeborn Jew Ben Canaan was very nearly an *Übermensch.* Uris meant him to serve as an antidote to the prevailing self-image of the post-Holocaust Diaspora Jew, the chin-stroking, self-doubting, smothered-in-mother-love Jewish male. Uris captured in writing my ruthless feelings about American Jews. The principal American character in *Exodus,* Kitty Fremont, a nurse giving aid to Holocaust survivors, voices anti-Jewish feelings that Uris suggests hides in the hearts of America's Christian majority. Fremont, this "girl next door," in Uris's words—he wrote that she "was one of those great American traditions like Mom's apple pie, hot dogs, and the Brooklyn Dodgers"—notes that there is "something different about Jews. They aren't like us." But in Ari Ben Canaan, whom she beds (and whose performance, it barely needs to be said, is satisfactorily virile), Kitty finds her "kind of people," that is to say, Jews who, if you didn't know better, might very well be Christian.

By my early teenage years, I was what you could reasonably call an obsessive reader, and Ben Canaan was one of many Jews I came across. I didn't, in general, like what I read: I fell acutely in love with *The Great Gatsby,* but the presence of the "small, flat-nosed Jew," the great corrupter of the American dream, Meyer Wolfsheim, discomfited me. I could almost feel the grease come off the page when Wolfsheim appeared. It didn't strike me that Fitzgerald could be a Jew-hater; it struck me that maybe the portrait was true. And then there was Robert Cohn, in *The Sun Also Rises,* the archetypal unmanned Hemingway man, a boxer (he took up boxing to defend himself against anti-Semites) who is nevertheless a cowering, quivering mess, pathetically in need of inclusion, his desperation for acceptance alienating the (Christian) men he hoped to befriend—plus, he cries, and can't hold his liquor. Thank God I hadn't yet reached for T. S. Eliot, because my spirit would have been crushed by Eliot's portrait of Bleistein, the "Chicago Semite Viennese," and Sir Ferdinand Klein.

No, Ari Ben Canaan was the Jew for me.

My vision of Israel also conformed to Uris's. In his Israel, sloth, corruption, lust, and ennui, all the imperfections of man, are held in abeyance by the superior power of will, belief, and total commitment. No one even littered in Leon Uris's Israel. Nor did they litter in mine. All they did was the selfless, righteous thing.

I blazed through every book on Zionism I could find: I charged through Herzl, who was stripped of his cosmopolitan illusions at the trial of Dreyfus, and who came to the idea of a Jewish national home as the cure for anti-Semitism. Then I found writings by Max Nordau, in whom I found an early echo of Uris's yearning for tough Jews—

Nordau called for a rebirth of "muscle Judaism." He demanded of young Jews to become "deep-chested, sturdy, sharp-eyed men." And I read Jabotinsky, the revisionist. In his novel *Samson,* Jabotinsky has the great destroyer of the Philistines send a message to the people of Israel: "They must get iron. They must give iron. They must give everything they have for iron—their silver and wheat, oil and wine and flocks, even their wives and daughters." I understood this intuitively—Mordechai Anielewicz died for a lack of iron—but the passage struck me, especially the business concerning daughters and wives, as a bit much, perhaps because of my early indoctrination in the philosophy of Marlo Thomas. But what did I know, anyway?

But then I read Ben-Gurion, whose enveloping contempt for Jabotinsky (he called him "Vlad Hitler") was sparked by Jabotinsky's devotion to capitalism and opposition to the program of self-restraint endorsed by the Jewish leadership in Palestine: self-defense, and only self-defense, and certainly no preemptive aggression against innocent Arabs. Jabotinsky thought the Jews in Palestine would survive only if they surrounded their Sparta with an "iron wall" that would stand—had to stand—until the last remaining "gleam of hope" in the Arab eye could be extinguished by the grinding application of superior Jewish force. The majority of early Zionists believed, however, that the Arabs would come to understand the logic and promise of the Jewish project in Palestine. The Arabs, after all, lived in squalor, and the Zionists who came to Palestine in the senile years of the Ottoman Empire brought with them innovation, energy, and modernity. My Hebrew school textbook, published by the Reform movement after the Israeli victory in 1967, put it this way: "Side by side with the Jews lived the Arabs. . . . Most of them were farmers, working on backward farms and living in primitive villages. Modern life had hardly touched them. . . . The Arab farmers saw the fertile Jewish farms and the rapidly growing settlements. . . . 'See!' said the Jewish farmers. 'There is a better way to live!' "

Another commentator wrote: "One of the most extraordinary features of the Jewish rebuilding of Palestine is that the influx of Jewish pioneers has resulted not in the displacement and impoverishment of the local Arab population, but in its phenomenal increase and greater prosperity." It was Einstein who wrote this.

Ben-Gurion also opposed the revisionists for the economic injustices embedded in their ideology. Jabotinsky took the side of the grubby mercantile class of Tel Aviv over the New Jews of the kibbutzim, those uncharacteristically tanned, Trotsky-reading, Diaspora-denigrating pioneers mucking out the swamps and greening the deserts of Palestine. I couldn't help but agree with Ben-Gurion's indictment, because, by the age of fourteen, a short time after my Zionist awakening, I came to see the egalitarian beauty of democratic socialism as well. This was an inevitable ideological evolution, of course, for the son of a Lowenstein family.

But I could make this leap only because I saw no conflict between Zionism and socialism, or between socialism and Judaism. The books of the Prophets Amos and Isaiah were the wellspring of socialism. I had come upon the perfect synthesis of the parochial and the universal. There was no contradiction here, just two impulses, both organically Jewish: the first, a belief in the defense of my tribe against a cruel world; the second, a belief in Judaism's message of universal liberation, a liberation that might one day obviate the need for tribe at all.

My reading in progressive Zionism brought me to the Tolstoyan mystic Aharon David Gordon, father of the philosophy called *avodah ivrit,* or Hebrew labor. Gordon argued for the salvational power of open air, soil, and muscle; the Jews must build their nation with their own hands, and, in so doing, be built by it. Jews were divorced from nature, he said, and in a Semitic echo of Jefferson, this estrangement from the land fostered decadence and dependency. The Jews will be reborn as a nation only when they come into intimate contact with the soil of their once free land. I soaked myself in Gordon's ideas, which seemed to me noble and true and antithetical to the unphysicality of Diaspora Jewish existence, especially in the purgatory of suburbia, graced neither with the creative ferment of the city nor with the authenticity and liberating self-reliance of rural life. Jews, the rabbis always taught, should seek clean and easy trades, in order to free themselves for the study of Torah and Talmud. But Gordon thought differently: Only donkey-work could straighten the crooked backs of the Jews in exile.

"A people that has become accustomed to every mode of life save the natural one—the life of self-conscious and self-supporting labor," Gordon wrote, "such a people will never become a living, natural laboring people unless it strains every fiber of its will to attain that goal. . . . We need fanatics of labor in the most exalted sense of the word."

Must I mention that I was the only follower of A. D. Gordon in Malverne High School?

I was, for a while, wrapped up in loneliness, having no one to dream these dreams with me. Then one Sunday, while leafing through the summer camp advertisements in *The New York Times Magazine,* I found the answer: a camp called Shomria, an ad for which was hidden amid those for canoe camps, fat camps, and camps for rich Jewish children from the North Shore of Long Island, which were easy to identify because they had elaborate Indian names and promised no Jewish content whatsoever. What they did promise was access to Jewish girls with reengineered noses, as well as an outstanding summer equestrian experience. Camp Shomria offered something different: six weeks of progressive Zionism. Shomria had no horses, but it had a cow, and a half-dozen chickens, and soon these creatures were the unfortunate objects of my Hebrew laboring.

Shomria was a most unusual place, a redoubt of socialist ideology in a post-socialist and post-ideological age. It was, for a time, my salvation, a Catskills Valhalla of universalism, progressive Zionism, Jewish self-defense, Hebrew labor, and coed showers.

The camp was an outpost of the international socialist Zionist movement called Hashomer Hatzair, the Young Guard, and its cadres were known among the rest of Zionist Jewry as *shmutzniks,* Yiddish for "the dirty ones." It was not clear if this epithet, which was worn like a badge of honor, was originally meant to derogate the movement's politics (radical), its sexual mores (loose), or its approach to matters of hygiene (laissez-faire). Hashomer Hatzair was positioned on the far left of the Israeli political spectrum; even in the 1980s, in the twilight of socialism, many of its seventy kibbutzim observed May Day with red flags and parades of tractors.

Hashomer was founded during World War I in Galicia by a group of young Jews who were in open rebellion against the shopkeeper Diaspora values of their parents. It was, at first, an experiment in romanticism, in the style of the Wandervogel German youth movement. Later, it dedicated itself to the Jewish colonization of Palestine, though, like other Communist-leaning Jewish parties, it did not support the idea of an exclusively Jewish state, even into the 1940s, even when the Arabs resolutely rejected the idea of a binational workers' state in Palestine.

Camp Shomria was located off a hilly country road outside Liberty, New York, a small and ragged town that was most famous for the hotels situated on its outskirts, the great mambo-in-the-sunshine chopped-liver palaces like Grossinger's and the Concord, which were considered by the adolescent socialists up in the hills to be symbols of lumpen middle-class degeneracy. Shomria was a ramshackle place, by the standards of Jewish camps, or even by the standards of Brooklyn slumlords. The movement in Israel was the source of few funds—the kibbutzim, by the late 1970s, were socialist ships sinking in the sea of capitalism. And so we had that cow, but no tennis courts. Tennis was not missed, however. Most of the campers came from first-generation families from Brooklyn, Queens, and the Bronx, places I had been led to believe were empty of Jewish children.

Though the kibbutzim sent little money, they did send us emissaries, Sabras, native-born Israelis, who supervised the running of the camp, drove its old vans, and tried, in a limited way, to steer us into the ideological currents of the movement.

We did some of the things other camps did: There was a pool, and a barn for arts and crafts, and there was hiking and music, and, as at other camps, the whiff of sexual possibility was in the air (though the coed showers were deemed by the counselors to be an experiment in egalitarian collectivization and not in copulative adventurism). And we played basketball without pause, though on our court was drawn a map of Israel—without the occupied territories. One night, in the early 1970s, I was told, the brown shirts from the Betar camp nearby—Betar is the youth movement of Jabotinskyites—swept down from the woods onto our basketball court and painted in the West Bank and Gaza.

We also did things other camps didn't do. We played, for instance, a game called "Warsaw Ghetto Uprising." Our counselors would wake us in the middle of the night and send us into the woods to accomplish secret tasks, including the smuggling of messages in and out of our pine-tree-filled ghetto. We would, as well, reenact the various struggles of the Haganah, the pre-state Jewish defense organization, and play "Siege of Jerusalem," in order to commemorate the destruction of the Second Temple and the beginning of Jewish exile. And we lived collectively one summer, camping out in the woods, in the style of an early kibbutz. For a time, I was tasked with waking up at four in the morning and milking our cow, a job I shared with a boy from Brooklyn named Emile (after Zola, naturally).

On Fridays, at sunset, we dressed in white and met on the main green for *mifkad,* or formation. We stood by age group, our counselors before us, in the manner of drill sergeants. The head of the camp would command in Hebrew, "Attention!," and we would snap, more or less, to attention, feet together, clenched fists held to our sides. Then he would announce, "At ease!," and we would relax our posture. We did this five or ten more times. Then we counted off in Hebrew. At the end, we would scream, *"Shomrim chazak!"* which means "Strength to the Guardsmen!," and we would shout *"Chazak Ve'ematz!"* "Strength and courage!" The Israeli flag would be raised, and we sang "Hatikvah," the Israeli national anthem, with strong purpose and great happiness, even though, as Saul Bellow once noted, it is not the cheeriest national anthem in the world: "Our hope is not yet lost / The hope of two thousand years / To be a free people in our land."

Then there was a godless and not infrequently vegetarian Shabbat dinner, and more songs of progressive Zionism—"Shir LaShalom," the Song of Peace, the anthem of the Israeli left—along with songs of proletariat uplift, including, inevitably, "The Internationale":

Arise, you prisoners of starvation
Arise, you wretched of the earth!
For justice thunders condemnation
A better world's at birth!

On occasion we would sing, this clutch of children from striving Jewish homes in Queens, New Jersey, and Long Island, the Woody Guthrie song "Plane Wreck at Los Gatos (Deportee)," a paean to oppressed migrant workers:

Goodbye to my Juan, goodbye, Rosalita
Adios mis amigos, Jesús y María

Though we could not relate directly to the plight of these particular Mexican workers, since none of us was in danger of deportation, and none of us was even distantly related to anyone named Jesús, we sang without cynicism, in the spirit of utopian solidarity.

And we would have our entertainment—skits, music, scenes from the plays of Clifford Odets, all invested with useful left-Zionist political meaning. These evenings were built around themes: coexistence between Arab and Jew, the cruelty of feudalism, worker solidarity. Then there would come hours of folk dancing, and then the counselors would go off and have proletarian sex with each other, and their campers would attempt same, sometimes successfully, and even safely, because condoms were made available, though without the knowledge of most parents, many of whom wouldn't have objected, because they were from the 1960s.

Though there was sex, there was no smoking, and, remarkably, this being the late 1970s, no drinking or drugs, because these ugly bourgeois vices were expressions of individual selfishness that would only serve to undermine the ethical austerity of the collective.

Really.

We would often meet in formation during the week as well; this time, not in white, but in our *chultzot shomriot,* our Young Guard shirts, which were blue, Russian-style peasant shirts, tied in the front with white lace. At the end of each summer, we would gather in the dark by the lake to award deserving new *Shomrim* their *chultzah.* Names would be called out, and these initiates would march to the front of the formation, and there they swore allegiance to the principles of Hashomer, and they would receive their shirts, and then barges holding huge signs made of gasoline-soaked burlap would be lit on fire, and the flames would spell "Strength and Courage" in Hebrew, and our cheers would fill the night. And thus we would be fortified for the coming year's battles against materialism, egotism, and racial injustice in the high schools of the New York area.

Hashomer Hatzair in the Diaspora meant to inculcate in its campers the values of the anti-capitalist kibbutzim, including manual labor and the rights of the oppressed worker. But ultimately, the goal of Hashomer was to promote the *aliyah,* or immigration, of its young members to Israel. *Aliyah,* which means "ascent," was the highest value of the movement. It was assumed, with a kind of Bolshevik inevitability, that *Shomrim,* by late high school age, would be on track to make *aliyah.* At the age of eighteen or so, we would be slotted into a *garin,* or seed group, which would travel collectively to a movement kibbutz.

We were encouraged to consider ourselves incipient Israelis, even to the point of changing our names. When I announced early one summer that, henceforth, I would be known as "Eitan" and not as Jeffrey, there was general praise. (*Eitan,* which means "strength," is not even my Hebrew name, the name used when I am called to the Torah; that is "Ya'acov," Jacob, after my maternal grandfather. But "Ya'acov" didn't sound sufficiently Israeli to me.) By renaming myself, I was following in the footsteps of one of the counselors I greatly respected, a preternaturally serious twenty-year-old from Manhattan named Raviv Schwartz, whose exile name was Roger. Raviv spoke movingly of his coming ascent to Israel, and I was intoxicated by the grandeur and mystery of it all.

The paramount value of *aliyah* was sometimes transmitted subtly to us, even slyly, because *aliyah* was not a cherished value of our American parents, who, as a rule, loved Israel, but not that much. And since it was our parents who paid our camp fees, which allowed us to live as socialists in the first place, we danced around the subject of leaving America. The Israeli emissaries did not themselves make the strenuous case for *aliyah,* in large part because we shared no common language with them. They spoke some English, of course, and our counselors knew some Hebrew, but this was not a problem of vocabulary, but of culture. These emissaries were generally hard-fibered, unsentimental, short-haired kibbutznikim, ten or fifteen years older than our counselors. They were also—most of them, at least—combat officers. The left-wing, give-peace-a-chance kibbutzim were in fact factories of war, providing Israel with many of its greatest generals, Arab-killing commandos, and fighter pilots. These men were as tough as we were soft, and they were stoic and self-effacing, even by the standards of pre-confessional early 1980s America.

One of these emissaries, a scion of a leading Hashomer family named Bini Talmi, was, in some ways, the closest thing to Ari Ben Canaan I had ever seen. He was self-possessed, lean, sunburned, and competent in all the endeavors of the Hebrew laborer, at a time when I still couldn't correctly hammer a nail. He was also, I was sure of it, a killer of Jew-haters.

He once told me, after some prodding on my part, that a person who has seen war cannot explain it to someone who hasn't. He did not say this to put me in my place, though he did. He said it because he meant it; he did not have the words, certainly in English, or in Hebrew, to talk about what he did. Bini fought in the Six-Day War and in the Yom Kippur War; that much I knew, though not from him. He would talk about his kibbutz, but never about the army.

We spoke a few times about peripheral matters. He told me that in the field, on maneuvers, no matter how primitive the conditions, he shaved with hot water, without fail; he always found a way to boil water, and shave with a clean razor. He was vain about nothing else except this. I was impressed, of course; I did not yet shave, and I did not know how to make a fire. But about war, he said nothing. I was aching to ask: Did you kill anyone, Bini?

But this would have been a most outré question at Camp Shomria. Modern war was absent from our Hashomer education. It was not the subject of our midnight forest games. The ghetto uprisings, the Maccabees—those were the texts, but not the Sinai campaign, the Six-Day War, the Yom Kippur War, and certainly not the Lebanon War, which was Israel's first true war of choice.

My comrades did not seem interested in Israel's wars. There were those my age who were considering *aliyah,* but they were not eager to serve in the Israeli army, as young immigrants are required to do. I did not fear army service. Quite the opposite: There was no contradiction between my politics and the idea of military service. But by the time Ariel Sharon set out in 1982 to remake Lebanon by force, the Israeli army had become, for many of my friends, an object of derision. For me, it remained an object of aspiration, and joining seemed like a good idea.

I recall these thoughts first forming after one of our evening programs, in my last summer in the movement. We were singing a song by Phil Ochs, a once-famous folkie who was a Yippee fellow-traveler, a writer of hard-left political music (there was nothing oblique or commercial about him), and a lyrical genius, who hanged himself in 1976. We were particularly fond of one of his songs, called "Love Me, I'm a Liberal," which was an evisceration of the dilettante left, a denunciation, in essence, of political moderation. Ochs' stereotypical liberal sings of crying when he hears of the death of Medgar Evers, an NAACP leader in Mississippi who was assassinated in 1963, but about the more radical proponents of black liberation, he had this to say:

But Malcolm X got what was coming
He got what he asked for this time.

Ochs' songs tended to reinforce the vanity we felt about our cost-free radicalism. At this particular evening program, we were singing an Ochs song called "I Ain't Marching Anymore." The program was built around our collective opposition to Selective Service registration, and "I Ain't Marching Anymore" seemed to be the appropriate musical accompaniment. It is a catalogue of the grotesqueries of American militarism, and it condemns the United States for, among other things, dropping atomic bombs on Hiroshima and Nagasaki:

When I saw the cities burning,
I knew that I was learning;
That I ain't a-marching anymore.

It's a vivid and urgent song, but there's something missing. Ochs mentions nothing of the Shoah, which ended not because the Germans awakened to the horror of genocide, but because the Allies physically prevented the Germans from killing even more Jews. In Ochs' universe, only American imperialism, and not German genocide, was fit for excoriation.

It was strange for Jews to count themselves out of the marching, when the marching saved Jews. Even a seventeen-year-old could see that.

Much later, I imagined that the Israelis, standing in the back of the dining hall, observing us silently, were trying to understand our innocent pacifism. Bini, the only emissary I knew well, never betrayed feelings of contempt or pity for us; he was a man of unexpressed thoughts, in any case. But it occurred to me that our make-believe lives—lives free of violence, exploitation, and meanness—must have seemed, to actual Israelis, the stuff of farce.

This is not to say I was reconciling myself to Jabotinsky. I felt all the proper feelings about Sharon, and I paraded about New York in a PEACE NOW T-shirt. But I did not blame Zionism, or the Israeli army, or the Jewish people, for Sharon's immorality.

We were, however, in the midst of a revolution in the spirit of left-liberal Judaism. Israel, already a bogeyman of the International Left (though it was once a project of utopian socialism), was becoming a target even of Jews. And this feeling, which manifested itself as acrid criticism of even the smallest of Israel's sins, was beginning to infiltrate the Zionist movement in America.

Many of my friends were drifting away not only from the idea of *aliyah,* but from the idea of Israel itself. They were finding new ideological homes among people feverishly hostile to the idea of Zionism. My friends were for the *campesinos* in El Salvador and against the contras in Nicaragua, they supported Leonard Peltier and the American Indian Movement, condemned South African Jewry for its complicity in apartheid, they fought for baby seals and whales and for oppressed laboratory animals everywhere. One friend marched to protest the use of rabbits in cosmetics testing carrying a sign that read PROGRESSIVE ZIONISTS FOR ANIMAL RIGHTS. Though I was unswervingly anti-contra and ardently pro-rabbit, these causes seemed beside the point. But universalism uncomplicated by history or nuance was drawing my friends away from Zionism—so tribal, so jejune. I remember a conversation with one of my campmates, a sophisticate who attended the

United Nations International School, who was raised in Greenwich Village, a person knowledgeable about the properties and use of marijuana (the first time I even smelled pot I was with him, watching *Network* in the Bleecker Street Cinema). He told me once that he thought Israel was becoming a Jewish South Africa, a corrupt state built on repression and exploitation. He didn't care if it was filled with Jews. He could not bind himself to the Jews, if the Jews were wrong.

We were diverging. I had taken to reading the letters of Yoni Netanyahu, the martyred hero of the raid on Entebbe, whose writings were collected by his brothers Iddo and Binyamin, the future prime minister, and had just been published in America. Yoni seemed part of an uninterrupted chain that stretched back to the Maccabees and Gideon and Joshua; his life, and his death, were a source of pride to me, and a reproach: He gave his life for his people in a mission that was, rather directly, an answer to the Holocaust. The challenge for young Jews was to match, even in some small measure, Netanyahu's example. One Passover, in a letter to his family, he wrote, "When I go back over our history, I pass through long years of suffering, of oppression, of massacres, of ghettos, of banishments, of humiliation; many years that . . . seem devoid of light—yet it isn't so. For the fact that the idea of freedom remained, that the flame of liberty continued to burn through the observance of this ancient festival, is to me testimony of the eternity of the striving for freedom and the idea of freedom in Israel."

I could not understand my friends who weren't feeling what I felt. I joined Hashomer more for its Zionism than for its socialism. For some of my friends, it was the opposite. They didn't see the poetry of Entebbe, they didn't see justice in the sword of Israel, they didn't feel kinship with their people. Didn't brotherhood trump everything? It is the impenetrable mystery of blood: For some it is glue, for others water. The world was going topsy on me. The victim was now the perpetrator?

My feelings about Arabs were too inchoate to express, too confused and contradictory, but it will suffice to say that, though I wished them well, I did not count them among the noble oppressed.

I could not abide the idea that the Jew was Goliath. This notion was formulated in defiance of morality, and in defiance of observable fact. The Jews were surrounded by implacable enemies. The Jews came into possession of the Gaza Strip and the West Bank only because they refused to acquiesce to their own murder. They seized the land from which the murderers meant to come.

And the fight for Jewish liberation, for Jewish freedom, was incomplete, beyond the borders of Israel. The Jews of the Soviet Union—three million of them, the third largest community of Jews in the world—were under the boot of Soviet communism. Jews were exiled to Siberia, to the gulag, simply for standing in opposition to their own extinction.

The left held its cultural and aesthetic attractions for me, and some political ones, too. I feared Ronald Reagan as my parents feared Richard Nixon, and I would still read *The Village Voice, The Nation,* Jonathan Schell on nuclear peril, and Peter Singer on animal liberation, and like every New York Jewboy of a certain age I could rap backwards and forwards (I still can) Grandmaster Flash's "The Message." But it was another record that made me realize just exactly what I was meant to do—the soundtrack to the Jimmy Cliff movie, *The Harder They Come,* which featured the Melodians singing Psalm 137: "By the rivers of Babylon, where we sat down, and there we wept, when we remembered Zion." I listened to this song as if in a trance. It moved me in ways that Phil Ochs never could.

I was trapped, I felt, in the strange land described by this most transporting of psalms. All power to the Sandinistas, but I was a Zionist.

CHAPTER FOUR

THE HILL OF JEWISH BONES

My undergraduate Zionism did not take me to Israel right away. I first went on a detour, to the Rumbula Forest, outside Riga, in Latvia. It was a visit that only fortified my sense of Jewish nationalism.

In the Rumbula Forest is a mound of earth, smooth, gently sloping, white with snow in winter, that covers the burned remains of 25,000 Jews, murdered by the Germans over the course of three days in the late fall of 1941. The killings began on November 30; there was a pause, then the guns opened again, on December 8. The men of the Einsatzgruppen, the mobile killing units of the SS, and their Latvian Christian collaborators, did the killing. Before the war, Riga's 35,000 Jews represented about one-tenth of the city's population; Jews had even served on the city council.

After the forest massacre, the Germans roped Riga's remaining Jews, five thousand or so, into the city's Jewish ghetto; they would soon be slaughtered as well, though Riga's ghetto-fighters, in concert with the partisans in the forests of Latvia, gave the Germans an umbrella poke or two before the inevitable defeat.

Three years later, the worm having turned irrevocably against them, the Germans set out to rid themselves of the evidence. The SS forced prisoners to dig up the decomposing Jewish bodies in the pits in Rumbula, and then set them on fire. They turned the quiet forest into a great open-air crematorium. The SS then murdered the prisoners, and burned their bodies as well.

The murder of Latvia's Jews ended on October 13, 1944, when the Soviet army entered Riga. By then a Jewish community had been nearly extinguished. There was a remnant of Jews, a few in hiding in

Riga, others scattered in the forests and the camps. Some of these Jews went home. The Soviets, unlike the Nazis, did not set out to murder Latvia's Jews, but they launched another type of exterminating war: For the next fifty years, they brought down the smothering weight of totalitarianism on those Jews who still felt the command of tribe. The Soviets tried to obliterate not the Jewish body, but Jewish memory.

By March 1986, when an Aeroflot plane, its engines spitting smoke, its cabin smelling of fish, carried me from Moscow to Riga, there were only a few thousand Jews left in Latvia, living in conditions of economic degradation and spiritual debasement.

I was traveling with a friend named Kevin Aaronson, a student, like me, at the University of Pennsylvania. We were driven to Rumbula by a man named Alexander Maryasin, an engineer by training, and a wide-faced, gray-haired man who seemed bemused by the absurdities of the Soviet Union. In 1972, fourteen years earlier, he asked the authorities for permission to immigrate to Israel. He was one of thousands. It was a great awakening, all across the Soviet Union. Jews, inspired by the miracle of Israel's victory in 1967, insatiably curious about their history—a history stringently denied to them by the Soviets—made a simple request: *Let us go home*. The Soviets saw these requests as an explosion of bourgeois, imperialist chauvinism. Israel was an enemy of the Soviet Union, the offspring of hateful colonialism, built on the malicious fiction that the Jews constituted a nation (and never mind their official Soviet documents, which read, in the space reserved for nationality, "Jewish"). The rascality of these Soviet traitors was unforgivable.

Nevertheless, a good number got out, in the early days. The West put on pressure, and the door opened, for a time. But Maryasin was not among the lucky. He worked for the state, he managed an industrial plant, and his head was thought to be too full of secrets to be set free. He was fired from his job, and whatever secrets he might have possessed became stale with age. Still, the Soviets would not let him go. So he became the protector of Rumbula, of its Hill of Jewish Bones, as he called it. The Jews of Riga had placed a small marker at the site to commemorate the murdered Jews (the Soviets declined the opportunity to erect such a monument), and Maryasin's job was to preserve the sanctity of the place, a difficult task, given the Cossack-like predispositions of some of Latvia's youth. Maryasin was also a leader of the refuseniks in Latvia, and he was their representative to visitors from the outside world, mainly American Jews bearing cigarettes and matzoh.

Kevin and I were visiting the Soviet Union over spring break. Most of my friends had gone to Florida, equipped with beer money and an optimistically large supply of condoms. But Kevin and I were on a mission from God.

Well, at least Kevin was. We were, despite our friendship, different in rather crucial ways. I was, in my mind, still a democratic socialist. Kevin, on the other hand, was a student at the Wharton School of Business. I was nearly without religion. Kevin was Orthodox. I knew more Arabs than I did Orthodox Jews, which is to say, I knew no Orthodox Jews before meeting Kevin. I liked him, but I did not understand him, especially after I got to know him well. I could not fathom how a sharp young man from Chicago—Lake Shore Drive, no less—the son of a doctor, the brother of a lawyer, a young man tracked for worldly success since childhood, someone acquainted with the awesome power of rational thought, believed the things he believed, namely that God Himself wrote the Torah, and personally handed it over to Moses on Mount Sinai. I could not believe that Kevin took seriously the idea that the world was created in six days, some 5,700 years ago. I could not understand his devotion to the laws governing the use of electric lights and can openers on Shabbat, or his rigid adherence to the kosher laws. Kevin believed that to stray from such regulations would violate his responsibilities to God.

I most certainly did not believe that God carved the Ten Commandments with a chisel, and though I no longer ate pork (it was a way to separate myself from the broader culture), I liked cheeseburgers very much, and every so often I would eat a McDonald's cheeseburger in front of Kevin, not to goad him, but because I underestimated the amount of pain such a sight could cause in someone so devout.

I did, however, confess to him that I was no longer positive about the nonexistence of God. I would, from time to time, attend Friday night services, but quietly, so as not to provoke the scorn of my friends. My friends were concentrated on the staff of the college newspaper, *The Daily Pennsylvanian,* of which I was the editor. They were as irreligious as I purported to be; the entanglements of religion, just like the entanglements of politics, seemed distasteful in the skeptical culture of college journalism, which is similar to the culture of professional journalism, only more so.

I am not suggesting that it was hard to be Jewish at Penn. Penn was, in the 1980s at least, the most Jewish of the Ivy League universities. It was so thoroughly Jewish that the center and power forward of our basketball team were named Bernstein and Lefkowitz, respectively. The "Tel Aviv Towers," we called them. I was surrounded by Jews; they were part of the ecology. But I kept myself remote from their organizations and certainly from their prayer services.

I had found my calling. I was, by my junior year, establishing a notable record of academic malfeasance, in part because my commitment to the newspaper was absolute. There seemed no greater mission than that of a muckraking reporter, and it was, I told myself, a calling in harmony with organically Jewish values, of a certain kind; not the values found in the tribe-and-law books such as Leviticus, but the universal values found in the justice-seeking books of the Prophets. The Jews in journalism tend to be among the more deracinated members of the tribe, because the mission of journalism is most attractive to people free of the burden of sectarian loyalty. (It is one of the unnoticed ironies of anti-Semitism that many of the Jews accused of controlling the media are notable mainly for their disloyalty to the dictates of tribe.) There were plenty of Jews on the newspaper, but the Jews who dominated its staff were suspicious of the agendas of their more devout brethren.

So when I volunteered for the mission to the Soviet Union, I kept it quiet. I was in permanent conflict with myself. I was, I knew, committing a sin of journalism by making myself part of a story, believing too much in a cause. But I couldn't help myself: I was still fired by the ideology of Jewish nationalism. And besides, who could resist a free trip to the land of the Cossacks?

Later on, as a professional reporter spending inordinate amounts of time with anti-Semites, I realized that I had all the hallmarks of a counterphobe, a person who seeks out close encounters with the thing he fears most. And I realized that this visit to the Soviet Union was my first exercise in counterphobia.

The Jews of the Soviet Union were trapped in appalling circumstances. Upright men and women were being imprisoned, exiled to Siberia, ostracized, evicted from their homes, simply because they acted on an outlaw desire. They were living the story of Passover, they were the children of Israel, held captive by stone-hearted pharaohs. Though I had grown distant from my youth movement, it still seemed inevitable that I would go on *aliyah* after college. To think that a Russian Jew, by accident of birth, would not be allowed the same privilege made me overflow with anger. Despite our rather obvious differences, Kevin and I built a friendship based on a shared feeling of Jewish rage. And like me, Kevin hoped to channel that rage into something constructive, meaning a brilliant, post-Penn career in the Jewish army.

Our mission was sponsored by a group called the Student Struggle for Soviet Jewry. We were trained, in the winter of 1986, by a group of Jews—Penn graduates, some of them—who once every couple of years left behind their mundane lives as Philadelphia lawyers and dentists and went gallivanting about the Soviet Union, dodging the KGB, agitating the American embassy in Moscow, and bringing a small dose of solace to Jews abandoned by the civilized world.

We were taught rudimentary tradecraft. We were shown how to encrypt the telephone numbers of refuseniks, and to conceal, to whatever extent practicable, our mission. We were to masquerade as college students on an art tour of the Soviet Union. Our briefers recognized that our cover story would become tattered soon enough, because we would be carrying into Moscow, our first destination, Jewish books and the implements of Jewish worship, meant for delivery to the most spied-upon citizens of the Soviet Union. Also, we didn't know anything about art.

We were diligent, though. On the first leg of our flight to Moscow we were still memorizing our briefing books. In the airport in Zurich we spent forty-five minutes shredding our notes and surreptitiously depositing the remains in wastebaskets down the length of the terminal. Such behavior today, in an international airport, would almost certainly lead to our arrest, but in 1986 the obsessive antics of two would-be Mossad agents caused no alarm.

Of course, we fooled no one. When we landed at Sheremetyevo Airport in Moscow customs agents emptied our suitcases and took our shoes for dismantling. The agents found the prayer books and Shabbat candlesticks and the books about Judaism we had cached away, not too well. Several of the books were taken from us, in exchange for a receipt.

But they did not take all the books. We had replaced the covers on every one of them (I switched the dust jacket of a book about the raid on Entebbe with the cover of a book about Fabergé eggs). Nor did they seize our cassette tapes, which contained speeches delivered in the West by the former refusenik Natan Sharansky, who had, not long before, been released by the Soviets. We taped music onto the first five minutes and the last five minutes of each cassette, just in case the customs men thought to listen.

For some reason, they let us out of the airport, and into Moscow, where we found our hotel, then proceeded out into the snowy night to pay phones to call the refuseniks whose telephone numbers we had memorized. We met them, in the days that followed, on train platforms or on crowded streets. They would identify us by prearranged signal—a folded-up newspaper, for instance—and then we would follow them to their apartments. Many of these refuseniks had previously received visitors from the West, but we had our uses. The wife of the imprisoned refusenik Yuli Edelstein cried when we gave her long underwear for her husband, who had been sent to a prison camp in Siberia. Edelstein's crime—the crime of all these Jews—was to ask for permission to leave the Soviet Union.

On our first Friday night in Moscow, Kevin arranged for us to see one of the few Orthodox Jews in the city, a man named Pinchas Polonsky. He lived in an apartment on a dirty and narrow street in an anonymous district of Moscow. The apartment was damp, dark, and cold. Polonsky was self-taught in Jewish ritual, which he observed with Levitical rigor, and he made his living by teaching underground classes on Judaism. The sun went down, and Kevin and Polonsky prayed the Sabbath service. I was a double-stranger here—I spoke no Hebrew, and knew nothing of Jewish ritual. And Polonsky, who looked as if he had stepped out of a woodcut depiction of the *shtetl* in deepest winter—the yeshiva *bocher* with a bent-over spine, wool coat, black cap, untrimmed beard, skin as white as the moon, a man born to suffer without end, now absorbing the abuse of mean and low atheists—did not seem, I thought, ripe for a lecture on muscle Judaism or socialist Zionism.

What harm did these people cause the Soviet Union? They were not terrorists. They destroyed nothing. They accepted their suffering. They sat, and waited.

Polonsky served us herring and spoke of his unquenchable desire to place his feet on the holy soil of Israel. His desire was palpable, as was his purity. He and Kevin prayed and prayed, and I could not imagine that God would intercede on their behalf. This man should be fighting instead of praying. I wandered the few square meters of his cagelike apartment. He had no art on his walls, but he had books—on plum-colored shelves warping under the weight, in stacks against the furniture, yellow, cracking commentaries on the Torah, and commentaries on commentaries on the Torah. A man could hide behind these books.

It was late. Kevin and Polonsky had worked their way through two or three prayer books, and we headed out into the frigid night. We could not take the subway, because it was Shabbat. So we walked the three or four miles to Red Square, our heads down against a driving snow, across high drifts and over roads slick with ice.

Two days later, we left for Riga. Within hours of our arrival, Kevin and I both reached the conclusion that we were being followed, but followed in a flamboyant way, not in order to track our movements, but to let us know that we were being followed.

We met Maryasin on the morning after our arrival, in his apartment. He told us his story. We asked him if he thought we were being watched. Of course you're being watched, he said. On his advice, we decided to ease back for a while. That night, we went to a concert of Sibelius, played screechingly by a local orchestra, in an underheated hall, surrounded by dour Letts.

The next morning we drove to Rumbula. It was windy, the sky was the color of dishwater, and I felt as if we were attending a funeral forty-five years late. Kevin said Kaddish, the prayer for the dead. Then we drove to a shack, by the river, to meet an aged stevedore named Janis Lipke, and his wife, Johanna.

Lipke was permanently bedridden. His skin was yellowed, his white hair brittle, and his sleeping clothes looked moth-eaten. His wife was in better health, but still half-blinded by glaucoma. The shack was squalid, in need of airing. The Lipkes, who were Christian, survived on the charity of Riga's last Jews; the Soviets took away the Lipkes' pension a few years earlier, after Janis accepted a medal from Israel, for the things he had done during the Shoah.

In December 1941, having witnessed the dire hour of Latvia's Jews, Lipke, despite having no blood connection to those still alive in Riga's Jewish ghetto, decided that he must try to save them nonetheless. He first made contact with the underground. Then he offered his services to the Nazi occupiers of Latvia as a contractor, which allowed him to recruit labor from the ghetto. He would drive up to the gates of the ghetto and requisition Jewish slaves. He loaded them onto his truck and distributed them to safe houses in the countryside. He would not overreach; only a handful of Jews would disappear each month. By war's end, there were only two hundred Jews still alive in Latvia; at least forty of those Jews were saved personally by Lipke.

I asked him why he did it. I was ready to capture the profound and moving testament of a living saint. But as he spoke (Maryasin translated) there was no eloquence, just a simple declaration: It was wrong to kill innocent people. He didn't, in any case, know why people didn't like the Jews.

Kevin asked the Lipkes if we could get them anything—food, clothing, medicine. Their possessions consisted of a battered tea kettle, several sticks of Communist furniture, and a quarter-cord of firewood. Maryasin mentioned that the Lipkes were in constant need of basic medicine—flu medicine, painkillers, aspirin. We said we had these things back at our hotel. We told the Lipkes we would be back soon. We left for the hotel, telling Maryasin we would meet him again in a couple of hours.

We fetched our supplies and walked purposefully into the street. There, at the end of the block, were two men staring directly at us, meeting our looks without averting their eyes. We walked toward them. Another pair of men, on the opposite sidewalk, were staring as well. They moved when we moved, parallel to us. Another pair of men, in caps and heavy overcoats, stepped in behind us. Were we imagining this? At the end of the block, the first pair—one of them was squat, the other lanky, with a pockmarked face and a mustache didn't seem as if they were preparing to move for us. We crossed the street. The two men trailing behind us crossed over as well. A car went by, slowing as it passed by, its occupants coolly eyeing us.

They were telling us something: *Zhids,* we've got your number. We decided to abort. If we continued, we would draw these men right to Maryasin and the Lipkes, who needed no more trouble.

Then one of the men on the street, one of the thugs keeping us from our mission, smirked.

In the hotel, we paused for a bit of lacerating self-recrimination. Maybe they weren't following us. Maybe we watched too many movies. Maybe we were a pair of cringing little ghetto Jews.

So we cowboyed-up and armed ourselves with blister-packs of Sudafed and Tylenol. But the street again pulsated with malice, and we could not bring danger to the Lipkes. That night, we left for Leningrad by train, having failed a Christian who had not failed the Jews.

The KGB was alert to our appearance from the moment we arrived in Leningrad. We saw the first refusenik on our list. When we came back to our hotel, we were met by a group of men in leather coats who took us to the basement of the hotel and lectured us on the anti-Soviet nature of our activities. They let us go with a warning, and we filled our backpacks with the remainder of our supplies, and stole out of the hotel to the home of the refusenik Evgeny Lien, who was among the most unafraid of all the Jews in Russia—he had passed through a half-dozen Soviet prisons in the early 1980s—and would not be fazed by a visit, after ours, from the KGB.

We spent a couple of peaceable hours with Lien. We warned him we were being followed, but he said not to worry. Shortly after we left the apartment, we were picked up, brought by car back to the hotel, to the basement, where a courtroom of sorts had been established for disagreeable Jewish tourists.

Overseeing the proceedings was a high official of the OVIR, the Soviet border authority, an aging female colonel in a green dress uniform. Her lipstick was poorly and liberally applied. I studied the epaulets on her square shoulders. She was surrounded by sallow men in leather coats. Presumably they were KGB specialists in Jewish affairs. Near us sat a translator, a prim woman of about thirty who smelled of hairspray and whose nerves interfered with her ability to speak English, and Russian, as well.

Perhaps it was because we were only twenty and dumb to the world, or perhaps it was because we were poisoned on fantasies of Jewish toughness, but we were not at all frightened. The colonel said something interrogatory, and mean. She had a voice that could scare the bark off a tree. We looked to the translator. She stammered. Kevin, who is a translucently kind person, told her to take a deep breath. She managed to repeat the question, which had to do with our activities—whom we had seen, why we veered from our official itinerary. We played it as we were trained, and denied everything. Then we remembered to behave as inconvenienced American tourists would behave, and said something about paying good money to see the Hermitage. We demanded to speak to someone at the American consulate. The colonel stared at us, without expression. She asked more questions, and then she issued her ruling, which I must paraphrase, because the translator was still only half-coherent: We had, in defiance of the condition of our visas, engaged in neo-imperialist, anti-Soviet activity but we would, because of the warm relations between our two nations, be punished not with imprisonment but with expulsion from the Soviet Union, never to be allowed to return.

Kevin and I suppressed the urge to laugh. If only the Jews of Leningrad could have our luck.

That night was the eve of Shabbat. Kevin lit candles in our room. Guards were posted outside the door. The next morning, we were told to get ready, we were leaving. It was Saturday, the Sabbath. Kevin had never before driven on the Sabbath. He seemed dismayed. I reminded him that this decision was beyond our control. He considered registering a protest, but I argued against this.

We were driven to the train station, two men in the front, Kevin and I in back. Kevin prayed in silence. For the first time, I understood that he meant it, he really meant it. We were escorted into the station, first to the ticket booth—the Union of Soviet Socialist Republics would not be paying the bill for our expulsion—and then onto a train. We were given a bare cabin, and the door was shut behind us. The train jerked. For a moment I thought we were moving east, not west. But we were Finland-bound. At the border, customs agents came to our cabin and upended our suitcases. We were frisked with vigor. Their petty torments went on for half an hour. Then we were let off the train. The Russians were through with us. We dragged our bags to the border and passed through Finnish customs with a minimum of drama. And there we were, on a silver day in frozen March with no easy way home, but we were giddy with relief.

Before we went in search of a train to Helsinki, Kevin made a suggestion that surprised me, coming from someone so religious. We walked as close as we could to the border, drew the attention of a pair of Soviet guards, and gave them the finger. They didn't seem to understand the significance of the gesture. I suggested mooning them, but Kevin took note of the temperature. We enjoyed the moment, but the feeling of relief was fleeting; it was the feeling of impotence that stayed with us.

CHAPTER FIVE

GOD'S GOLDEN SHORE

Exile was the disease, and Israel was the cure. I felt this in my cells. So I dropped out of Penn and bought a one-way ticket to the Promised Land. No looking back, baby. Even my hardest-edged, Zionistically inclined friends suggested I buy a round-trip ticket, which would at least allow me to come back to America to get my stuff. But I didn't have stuff, and I didn't have money, either. My one-way ticket was meant to be seen as an act of devotion, but in truth it was a concession to a cruel-hearted economic system that refused to discount El Al tickets even for committed socialists.

I left from Kennedy Airport in New York. My parents, divorced by then, came to see me off in separate cars. My father, making a slow fade from my life, suggested to my mother that she cry. Maybe the guilt would stop this madness, he said, this lunatic desire—which was her fault, he added, for taking me to Israel for my bar mitzvah—*My fault? You were there, too, you schmuck*—to become a farmer and a soldier and God knows what other Leon Uris bullshit he has planned. But my mother wouldn't order up the tears. She was a Jewish mother, and the six thousand miles that separated Long Island from my soon-to-be-home on a Jezreel Valley kibbutz was an insuperably long distance, but she had read, without my knowledge, the letters of Yoni Netanyahu, because she wanted to understand, so I flew away without the abjection of a sobbing mother.

On board, I sat next to an Israeli, forty years old or so, who lived in New York—an émigré from Jerusalem. I disapproved of him immediately, but silently.

He asked me what I was going to do in Israel. I tried to answer with detachment, with sophistication. I said I was hoping to live there. I was just going to try it out, to see what kibbutz life is like, maybe join the army.

He smiled. That's nice, he said. Are you really sure?

I said I'm sure I'm sure. I know what I'm doing.

He asked me how I could be so sure. How many times have you been to Israel? he asked.

Once, I said, when I was thirteen. But it's not like I haven't been around the block once or twice.

Israel isn't so easy, he said. The army, especially, can be a rough go.

I'm ready for it, I said. I'm a big believer in Israel.

Then he asked: How big is your asshole?

I said, what?

How big is your asshole?

I was panicked. I hadn't, of course, been around the block once or twice. I'd barely been out of the house.

I don't know what you're saying, I said, my face purpling.

Look, he said, you want to go into the army, right? Well, they're going to fuck you. They're going to fuck you!

Fuck me?

You don't understand, do you? Every day, you get fucked another way. You think it's a party? You think it's a picnic? It's the army!

It's tough, I said, I know, I have friends in the army. But it'll be okay. I mean, it's Israel.

He didn't answer, he just smiled, and went back to his newspaper. I tried to sleep, but couldn't. I would not let this bitter man upset my plans.

He was not the first to try. My mind was sent drifting back to a doctor's appointment I had a month before, in Philadelphia, a checkup. I had never met the doctor before. He asked me about my plans. He was Jewish, so I told him.

He looked at me incredulously. Why would a young American with his wits and his health move to Israel?

I said: Because I believe it is the responsibility of every Jew in the world to serve the nation of Israel. I said it just like that, as if I were reading from an index card. But I have never in my life been more sincere.

He smiled the most condescending smile one could imagine, so condescending that even a twenty-year-old could read it.

Do you think it's so safe here for Jews? I asked, bristling.

I did not quite believe that a second Holocaust could happen in

America. But I believed that there were limits to America's acceptance of the Jews. Certainly, I believed that Jews in distress could not rely on the United States government for help. The sordid history of the Shoah bears this out. When Jewish doubters suggested to me that America might in fact be the Promised Land, I replied with the name Breckinridge Long. If America were paradise, it never could have appointed to government service such a wicked man. His name has been buried by history, but he was once a man of power, appointed by his friend Franklin Roosevelt—that great friend of the Jews—to take charge of the State Department's visa section in the days before America entered World War II. Long was a Jew-hater of the most unambiguous and unrelenting kind. He considered *Mein Kampf* to be "eloquent in opposition to Jewry and to Jews as exponents of Communism and chaos." Long instructed his consular officers to deny visas to any alien "who has close relatives or who is acquainted with other persons" living in areas under Nazi control. This edict was meant to shut down Jewish emigration from Europe to America during the last possible moments of escape. Thousands perished because the spirit of pharaoh lived in Breckinridge Long.

Long is dead, but who knew for certain whether his beliefs died with him? A lecture on Long was my answer to this fool of a doctor.

He wasn't sold.

"Of course it's safe for Jews here," he said.

I had no patience for doubt, or disbelief. It was as if I were fourteen again, filled with zeal, unbending in my convictions, living inside my Ari Ben Canaan dreams. Perhaps my stiff-neckedness was the residue of humiliation. Humiliation, I was learning, had a long half-life. A year later I was still having homicidal fantasies about the Soviet border guards who manhandled me on the train to Finland. But maybe my revivified Zionism was the result of something slightly more elevated: a mature, but still deeply felt, understanding of the essential abnormality of Jewish existence in the Diaspora, an understanding driven home by the uncompromising Jews of the Soviet Union, who risked everything for the chance to take part in history, to live authentic and full Jewish lives.

Kevin and I had vowed to each other, in a fit of undergraduate earnestness, that we would redouble our efforts in the cause of Jewish freedom, and I wanted to keep my vow. I still suffered, of course, from a conflicted heart. I wanted to be a reporter—it was my main chance to change the world. But I also wanted to join the Peace Corps—which was also my main chance to change the world. I wanted as well to bring justice to the benighted residents of the inner city. And I wanted to work on a fishing boat in Alaska—not to change the world, but to see the world, which I had not yet done.

But what I wanted most was to undergo the metamorphosis that would make me Israeli.

I tried to sleep on the plane, but couldn't. My imagination was fired by the possibilities before me, the idea that I was meeting my destiny. My misbegotten years as an American were over, now my life was beginning, as a New Jew, in Israel. In any case, sleep is not easily available on El Al planes, because New Jews are as obstreperously loud as Old Jews: Cramming four hundred of them into a flying aluminum tube is not a formula for tranquillity, particularly when a substantial minority of the Jews is Orthodox. There were flying squads of Orthodox Jews in a frenetic search for minyans—quorums of ten men necessary for prayer—and they were knocking into me, tripping on my legs, smashing into the seat-back, without apology, or even knowledge of their disruptiveness. I tried to think sympathetic thoughts; these were, after all, my people.

Then morning broke, and the plane began its descent over the Mediterranean, and we crossed God's golden shore. The beaches of Tel Aviv, visible through a screen of mist, were dotted with swimmers, and then the biggest Jewish city in the world spread out before us, clean-lined, cross-hatched by wide boulevards. Boxy, whitewashed apartment buildings stretched north and south, separated from each other by palm trees.

We landed, and the cabin erupted in raucous clapping and whistling. The cheering grew in large part from the recognition of a simple miracle: Jewish pilots, flying a Jewish plane, have brought Jews to the sheltering harbor of a Jewish land. I clapped as well. And so did my neighbor. "Welcome home," he said, without cynicism, when we touched down.

Kevin, who was by then a student at a Jerusalem yeshiva, met me at the airport and soon we were on a bus to Jerusalem. We rode up the highway, into the mountains, and I could not believe my great fortune—I was here, a grown man, a free Jew in his own land.

Three days later, I was on another bus, heading for the kibbutz where I would try to become a New Jew, or at least learn Hebrew and grow the calluses of a Hebrew laborer. The kibbutz was called Mishmar Ha'Emek, the Guardian of the Valley, and it was located on the southern edge of the Jezreel Valley, across a wide plain from Nazareth. The closest junction was at Megiddo, four miles to the east of the kibbutz. Megiddo is Hebrew for Armageddon. The valley is watered and green. It was the promise of water that drew small bands of Jewish revolutionaries from the cities of Eastern Europe, men and women who discarded their books, the rituals of their parents, and then their parents themselves, and built many of the earliest and most illustrious kibbutzim, including Mishmar Ha'Emek, which is known throughout the Hashomer Hatzair movement for the socialist steadfastness of its members.

The bus dropped me at Megiddo junction, which sits at the northern tip of the Wadi Ara, a narrow gap of a valley that is solidly Arab; Umm al-Fahm, one of the largest, and most radical, Arab towns in Israel, sits above the wadi, as do several other Arab villages. The more adventurous, and more resolutely naïve, among the valley's kibbutznikim, would, in the days before the Palestinian Uprising, visit the villages of the Wadi Ara to participate in European-sponsored coexistence workshops, and eat falafel.

Megiddo junction is austere. A handful of squat concrete shelters protect bus riders from the hard weather of the Jezreel winter. To the west of the junction is the tel, the manmade hill of Megiddo, covered in white stone and palm trees, and, in summertime, by spirit-infused Christian pilgrims, who gaze out at the valley below as their Jewish guides read them the battle scenes from the Book of Revelation.

Opposite the tel is the Megiddo Prison, built by the British, now under Israeli management. Guard towers and high gray walls keep the Arabs in and everyone else out. Five miles to the north is the cow town of Afula, home to the valley's hospital, and to its movie theater, which in the late 1980s featured American movies from the early 1980s. Twenty-five miles up the road is Haifa, Israel's main port. Down this same road, the opposite direction from Megiddo, is the city of Jenin, on the West Bank. The Megiddo junction marks the beginning of the frontier zone between Israel and the occupied territories.

In a letter from the organizers of the kibbutz ulpan, its Hebrew-language course, I had been told that a van from Mishmar Ha'Emek meets the buses coming from the south. There was no van, so I waited, alone, at the edge of a broad field. I stared up at the sky and all around me, at the emerald beauty of the valley. This was the last time Israel ever seemed big to me.

The van came. The driver was a large-biceped man in his fifties, open-shirted and wearing sandals, despite the cool weather. He grunted when I said hello. My friendliness seemed to put him off. I decided to keep my happiness in check around these leather-necked kibbutznikim. I needed to remind myself that these were not shtick-friendly American Jews. Israelis, in my limited experience, did not understand American humor. Sometimes it seemed as if they didn't understand any humor. This wasn't a negative, in my mind: Jews didn't need a sense of humor when they had an air force.

I was the only passenger, but the driver—his name was Tsvi, I later learned—didn't mutter a word. He was probably a war hero; he was preoccupied. Why should he care about an American Jew like me, anyway?

We drove past the fields of Kibbutz Megiddo, and then a Yemenite farming village, dilapidated in appearance, the hulks of battered farm equipment piled up near the road. Two miles further, we turned left down a lane lined with palm trees and poles flying red flags—the kibbutz. It was lush, green, and funereally quiet. My silent friend Tsvi dropped me in front of the main dining hall, a low-slung building that is the communal center of the kibbutz. I asked for walking directions to the ulpan. Tsvi pointed me down a path, and left me. I heaved my pack up, and walked the half mile to the ulpan. There was no one in the office, but I did discover a few signs of life, a small number of incoming students sitting on the porch of one of the motel-like buildings that would house us. The most exuberantly friendly of them was a young Dutchman named Eff, who had the skin coloring and posture of a heroin addict. He took me to find the woman who registered new students. Her name was Galia. She was in her one-room house in a colony of bungalows called, I was to learn later—when I took an apartment there myself—"Little Poland." It was called this either because its residents originally came from Warsaw, or because they were muddleheaded.

Eff knocked, and Galia called out for us to come in. She was watching television, a soap opera, it seemed. It had never struck me that there would be television on a kibbutz. There was no television at Camp Shomria.

Galia walked me down to the office, which was located in the lowest spot of a wadi. It was a shabby one-room hut located equidistant from the dairy and a pair of two-hundred-yard-long chicken houses. I commented on the collision of odors—the sweet smell of cow flop and hay clashing with the nostril-burning ammonia stink of chicken shit. Galia took my observation as a complaint. "It's the ulpan, what do you want?" she said. The implication, I think, was that the Hebrew education of Diaspora Jews was not the raison d'être of the kibbutz.

I told her how glad I was to be there, and I could not help but mention the fact that I was a veteran of Hashomer Hatzair. "I bet you were in Hashomer Hatzair, too," I said, this being a Hashomer Hatzair kibbutz, and, by the way, I was, you should know, a recipient of a *chultzah*.

"A *chultzah*?" she asked disbelievingly. In the argot of Camp Shomria, of course, the word *"chultzah"* served as shorthand for *chultzah shomrit,* the bright blue, Russian-style, open-necked, lace-up-the-front shirt that was awarded to Young Guardsmen of exceptional pioneering promise. In actual Hebrew, however, *chultzah* means just "shirt." So what I told Galia was that I received, for my service in Hashomer, a shirt. I did not understand that at the time, so I could not intuit exactly why Galia was looking at me with open-faced disdain. I was also to later learn that membership in the youth movement of Hashomer Hatzair in the late 1980s signified to the young generation of the kibbutz what membership in the Audio-Visual Squad signified to most of the students of Malverne High School.

Mishmar Ha'Emek, I would learn over time, was not Camp Shomria, because Camp Shomria was Brigadoon. Mishmar Ha'Emek was a village of more than a thousand modern and confused people who were struggling to find a place in post-socialist Israel, in an economy that could no longer afford to subsidize the kibbutz experiment in radical egalitarianism, and in a country that was divided against itself on matters of faith and meaning and justice for the Arabs it had supplanted. In the years ahead, some kibbutzim would fail; one sold off fields to a developer of shopping centers. Mishmar Ha'Emek, however, made the collective decision to grapple with the new economic and political realities—to adapt, rather than die. It was an important decision for the movement, because Mishmar Ha'Emek was one of its flagships. It produced several of the leaders of Israel's left-wing political parties, and it was known for the competence of its fighters. In April 1948, a month before the Jews of Palestine declared independence, the kibbutz came under attack by the irregulars of the Arab Liberation

Army, a mostly Syrian force that mistreated the Palestinian Arabs with just as much enthusiasm as it mistreated the Palestinian Jews. The ALA, under the command of a brigand named Fawzi al-Qawuqji, shelled the kibbutz, destroying most of its buildings. The kibbutznikim, along with reinforcements from the Haganah, held off the attack, but the Arab army then laid siege to the kibbutz. Three days after the original attack, a cease-fire was declared, and the kibbutz evacuated its women and children. By that time, though, Jewish reinforcements arrived in the region, and the Arab forces, demoralized by the energetic resistance, fled in the direction of Jenin, as did many of the Arab villagers from the hills above Mishmar Ha'Emek.

The kibbutz, part of a movement that still argued for the creation of a binational state and still hoped, in the teeth of hate, for reconciliation between Arab and Jew, had covered itself in martial glory. The members of the kibbutz generally supported Mapam, the party of the far left, substantially to the left of Ben-Gurion. But the men of Mishmar Ha'Emek were first into battle. The pattern did not change. It seemed to me that every man on the kibbutz over twenty-four fought on the front lines in Lebanon; every man over thirty-two fought in the Yom Kippur War; and everyone over thirty-eight fought in 1967. And not just fought, but led. The cemetery of Mishmar Ha'Emek, in a grove at the end of a long graveled path, was filled with the young dead.

By the late 1980s, it was the onslaught of capitalism that was threatening the kibbutz: Mishmar Ha'Emek was still centered on agriculture: giant combines roamed the valley floor, reaping and threshing wheat; groves of avocado and almond trees covered the hills between the kibbutz and Megiddo; a hatchery produced thousands of chicks each week, and the dairy collected the milk of four hundred cows. The kibbutz even maintained a modest herd of beef cattle, which were tended to by actual Jewish cowboys. But Mishmar Ha'Emek could not continue to subsidize its old and its sick, send its members on vacation abroad, and pay for the higher education of that minority of its children who expressed an interest in college, if it didn't extend itself into the industrial economy. So it did. And it found its fortune in . . . plastics.

"Plastics are the future of the kibbutz," Bini Talmi told me when he took me on a tour of the Tama plastics factory, which made enormous egg collection systems, plastic plates and cups, and twine. Mishmar Ha'Emek was one of the leading manufacturers of twine in Israel, Bini said, though plastics gave the kibbutz its good name.

I hadn't seen Bini, a hero of my adolescence, the Ari Ben Canaan–like emissary to Camp Shomria, for five years. I was quite glad to have him around, since most of the rest of the kibbutz seemed indifferent to the students of the Hebrew course.

Bini and his family adopted me, taking me in on Friday nights, and providing me with occasional but cutting insights into the life of the kibbutz, not the least of which concerned its core contradiction: a socialist collective entering, full-throttle, the world of capitalist competition in order to preserve the utopian vision of its founders. Mishmar Ha'Emek was especially orthodox in its adherence to the principles laid down by its creators, two generations before. The children of the kibbutz still slept together in dormitories, not with their parents—an act of radical collectivism. Originally, the innovation of collective child-raising was meant to liberate kibbutz women from the hour-to-hour drudgery of motherhood and free them for productive work, in the A. D. Gordon understanding of work; instead, the productive work they were assigned to perform by the kibbutz most often concerned the changing of diapers in the children's houses. The kibbutz members were officially barred from keeping private bank accounts. The manager of the plastics factory earned the same salary as the lowliest cow-milker, which is to say, nothing: Members of the kibbutz were all placed on allowances, which were supposed to cover their basic needs. No one starved, and no one got rich. But what about the man who invented the Tama Automatic Egg Collection System? Doesn't he want to own the patent to his miraculous device? Did he ever feel resentment? "We're all good socialists here," Bini said, with an ambiguous smile.

Every decision on the kibbutz was made by the collective. This is a beautiful thing, but also a corrosive thing. I noticed, over time, the existence of a good deal of hostility in this very small village. There is friction in all relationships, of course, but I met people on the kibbutz who had not spoken to their neighbors in thirty years.

Few people spoke to the ulpan students. This seemed mean, though understandable. The kibbutz did not, to my unhappiness, attract the Diaspora's best Jews. I thought I might find like-minded people, struggling to become absorbed into Israeli society. But the ulpan's draw, for many of its students, was its isolation from the pressures of the larger world; here, a person could do unthinking labor for a modest number of hours each day, and then spend the rest of the time subsidized and unpressured, drinking beer and organizing sleeping arrangements according to the demands of the unmediated libido. Among my fellow students were a considerable number of stoners: Eff, the Dutchman, was in fact a former heroin addict, sober now, except for the hashish he would buy during his hitchhiking trips to Jenin. Then there was Zuckman, who had a tattoo of a red devil on his leg and drove the garbage tractor through the small residential neighborhoods of the kibbutz. An ex–truck driver named Feinstein, who had come to the ulpan with twenty cartons of cigarettes and a dexamphetamine habit, introduced me to Johnny Cash. My roommate was a South African named Cohen, who was an army veteran—he had spent time in the bush, he said, fighting the kaffirs.

The kaffirs? Jesus Christ, where was I?

I didn't see much of Cohen; he moved in with Galia during the first week of class. (I had ruined my chance with Galia, of course, on account of the shirt.)

Where did God find these lost boys, these leftover Jews? Where were the committed Jews, high-minded Jews, nonaddicted Jews?

Bini explained it one day: Many of the native kibbutznikim, the Israelis, were mistrustful of these outsiders, who came to Israel in flight from failure. They were—each crop, time after time—not very bright, not very industrious. The sad fact, he said, is that the only American Jews, the only English-speaking Jews, who were coming to Israel were the God-poisoned Orthodox and the secular Jews who couldn't hack life at home.

And then there's you, he said, quickly.

I decided to spend my time with the Israelis, rather than my slacker Diaspora compatriots. I threw myself into Hebrew, and into work. I was spared an assignment in the plastics factory, and instead I found work in the chicken houses, the *lool*. Each of the ten houses was home to about six thousand hens and six hundred roosters. The fertilized eggs were collected by the Automatic Egg Collection System—a balky, brittle device that extended the length of the shed, and that brought the eggs to a central sorting bin, from which they were transferred by truck up the hill to the hatchery, a steaming, sulfurous building without windows that produced, on a good week, ten thousand or more new chicks for sale. Once a week, my alarm clock woke me at four. I hiked up to the hatchery where, under the supervision of its manager, a man charmingly named Herzl, I donned a raincoat and hosed down two hundred or so plastic hatching flats, learning, in the process, that endless repetition, even more than joint pain, is the defining feature of manual labor.

My job in the *lool* was no better; it was filthy and low. I cleaned the belts of bloody eggs and hardened shit, unclogged the automatic feeders of congealed grain, and collected the carcasses of hens, murdered by sex-crazed roosters. The roosters were aggressive, territorial, and though they had been de-beaked they had not been de-clawed, and humans were at the low end of the pecking order: The roosters launched brazen attacks on our calves as we walked through the house; we carried truncheons to fend them off. It was all quite horrible. My lungs filled with feathers and my fingernails were stained black with muck.

But I loved the work. This was the fulfillment of my dream: I was a Hebrew laborer, a Tolstoyan ascetic—or as close as one could come on a kibbutz with a plastics factory and color television—and, lo and behold, calluses were forming on my hands.

The Israelis in the houses were mostly young, and more accepting of outsiders than others on the kibbutz. However, they were unacquainted, as most Israelis seemed to be, with etiquette, and they were unskilled in the art of pleasant conversation. They possessed the quality known as *dugre,* which is the Arabic word for "straight." The *dugre*-type can be exasperating. Conversation with them is bone scraping bone; the cartilage of indirection and euphemism is missing. Oren, one of the workers, asked me my first week, "Are you crazy to leave America for a chicken house?" He followed this with a series of questions meant to calculate how much money I could be earning in America. *Dugre* Israelis are incapable of harboring hidden agendas.

Most of the chicken house workers had only recently finished their mandatory army service, but they were already subject to frequent call-ups to the reserves. They all served in combat units; one was a patrol boat captain, two were paratroopers, and another one was an operator in a commando outfit called Unit 5101, a long-range reconnaissance team that penetrates Arab territory and tags targets for air force bombers. Several of them had served in Lebanon, and to a man they opposed Sharon's invasion. They were all members of Peace Now. They were too good to be true: They did not shirk their duties as soldiers, nor did they shirk their duties as citizens.

They were commanders, some of them, in charge of squads, platoons, tanks, and boats. But now they were collecting eggs, and the glorious thing about egg collection on the kibbutz was that these commandos saw nothing demeaning in the work. Nor did they consider it a source of spiritual uplift. They just didn't think much about it. They became farmers and soldiers because their fathers were farmers and soldiers. It was natural. It was the triumph of Zionism.

I applied myself to the cause of personal reinvention. I put myself on a training schedule: work all morning, learn Hebrew in the afternoon, then run for an hour in the fields, or in the forests behind the kibbutz, in the Menashe Hills, through clearings that long ago were Arab villages. Then I would lift weights in the exercise room, a converted bomb shelter. I worked out with a kibbutznik named Gadi, a former commando who was rejected from the paratroops because of his large size (he would fall too fast). Gadi could bench-press extraordinary amounts of weight. It was my goal to match his achievements.

One evening, the kibbutz work manager, a man who went by the nickname Schubic, saw me outside the dining hall. Schubic possessed a kind of rough gemütlichkeit, unlike most of the citizens of the kibbutz. He knew I wanted to be a soldier. "Goldberg, which way is east?" he barked. He was wearing a sleeveless T-shirt, the sort of shirt known in America as a "wife-beater." He was a piece of meat with eyes. He was not the type to complicate his life with Diasporish self-doubt. He was also a paratrooper—a reservist, still, though he must have been approaching fifty. "*Nu?* Which way is east?" he barked again.

I took a guess.

"That's south!"

He gave me a violent clap on the back.

"What are you going to do in the army when they tell you to move west, or east? Wait for someone to drag you along?"

It was easier to take the Jew out of Exile than the Exile out of the Jew. But I was trying.

Sometimes, my runs would take me across the Hills of Menashe, along footpaths that brought me to the shoulder of Megiddo. Once, a friend showed me a way to sneak atop the tel. I went often, in the late afternoon, after the Christian pilgrims had departed for Nazareth. Megiddo's stone paths made for a hard run. But Armageddon was also an excellent place to bring girls.

I was drawn to Megiddo for reasons I didn't understand. It stood at the center of things, which is where I wanted to stand. And though Armageddon is a Christian myth, not a Jewish one (it is, however, rooted, like all Christian stories, in Jewish writings, in this case in the psychedelic visions of Ezekiel), I found the story intoxicating: It appealed to my Manichaean sense of the world, a world cleanly divided between good and evil. And I found the idea of living my life in the land of the Bible hopelessly romantic.

There was a man on the kibbutz I knew only as Ijo. He was a mountain Jew (there are only three kinds of Jews, a friend of mine once suggested: mountain Jews, book Jews, and money Jews. I was a book Jew trying to become a mountain Jew). Ijo looked like Moses, not a Charlton Heston Moses, but a low-to-the-ground, olive-skinned, Jewish-beaked Moses. He wore shorts through the cold winter, and sandals, and walked with a staff, and had an undisciplined gray beard. His job was to lead kibbutz members on nature hikes. These were not nature hikes in the pack-a-lunch American sense of the term, but relentless scrambles down the canyons and up the mountains of Jewish history. One day, I asked Ijo if I might borrow an English guide to the valley. He gave me a Bible, with instructions: Read from the Book of Judges; you'll understand where we live. It never struck me to see the Bible as a *Fodor's* of Jewish geography. But I went out walking.

"The spirit of the Lord came upon Gideon, and he blew a trumpet." The Jezreel was the scene of great drama during the time of the Judges. I read about the reign of Deborah, who smashed the Canaanites at Mount Tabor, which I could see from the top of Megiddo. The Midianites, too, threatened the Israelites in the time of the Judges. But the Jewish farmer Gideon, heeding God's word, gathered the people on the southern edge of the Jezreel Valley and led them to battle at Mount Gilboa, to the north.

I read and read. This was my history. A new feeling came over me. I became conscious of ancient greatness, and of my connection to this greatness. Though my family had made innumerable car trips to Williamsburg, Mount Vernon, and Fort Ticonderoga in the interest of intellectual betterment, those places produced in me feelings of dislocation. There were no Jewish names to be found among the country's main founders, and on the lists of Revolutionary War dead. The blood of Washington and Jefferson did not run in my veins.

When I was small, my family was friendly with a family named Martin. The Martins lived a couple of blocks away. They were undiluted WASPs, splendidly exotic by the standards of the South Shore of Long Island. They even drank milk with dinner. They were lovely people. Mrs. Martin's family came from Kennebunkport. Her parents ran a hotel there, the Colony, that was once a "restricted" hotel. We visited one winter. My mother whispered to me, "I think we're the first Jews ever to step into this place." Mrs. Martin took out a book one night, a book of yellow, crackling paper—a family tree. She could trace her line back to the *Mayflower*. I wanted to be rooted the way these people were rooted.

Well, I was rooted in Israel. I wasn't part of the *Mayflower* generation, but I wasn't late-drifting flotsam, either. In Israel, I felt something that no Diaspora Hebrew school could ever impart: that my ancestors were not merely peddlers and tradesmen but kings and prophets. It was to this land that I was tied. It was on this land, by the way, that I decided that maybe God did, after all, exist—not the God of Orthodoxy, who controlled every muscle twitch of humanity and who worried without end, on His high throne, about my use of electricity on Shabbat, but a God who inspired a revolution in morality among the people who first discovered His existence, His burdened people, the Jews, and a God who bound up His Jews together, as one family.

Here, I felt at home. It was here that a Jew could become something noble.

CHAPTER SIX

THE BLANKET PARTY

On the day I received my first M-16—actually the first gun I had ever held in my enlightened hands, guns, naturally, being anathema to us violence-loathing Diaspora Jews, even to the summer guerrillas of the Catskill Mountain Liberation Front at Camp Shomria (in our forest games, we defended the Warsaw Ghetto with whittled sticks and moxie)—my drill sergeant, a maple-faced Russian immigrant, 230 pounds of muscle, told us to fall in love with our weapons.

The sergeant was darkly moody, a terrible bastard, and I worshipped him. He said: "Your rifle is your best friend. You must take care of it. You must keep it clean. It must always be with you. It goes with you when you take a shit. It stays with you when you sleep. In barracks, you will sleep with it under your mattress. In the field, you will sleep with it in your sleeping bag, between your legs. You are never to let go of your weapon. Is this clear?"

"Ken, hamifaked!" we screamed. "Yes, commander!"

I was on an army base called Tsalmon, located atop a mountain in the Upper Galilee, within rocket distance of Israel's border with Lebanon. It was late afternoon on a cool fall day, and we stood under a wet sky in our uniforms and blister-making boots. A few days earlier, the sullen supply sergeants gave us these boots, along with uniforms, web gear for holding rifle cartridges and canteens, sleeping bags, moldy kitbags in which to stuff all this equipment, but only now did we feel like real soldiers. I was exceedingly happy—the rifle was electric with the promise of Jewish power—and so, too, were my new comrades, all of us from the Diaspora, most of us having lived our lives in the company of quisling Jews who, for reasons inexplicable and bizarre, believed that the main lesson of the Shoah was that those who forget the past are doomed to repeat it, instead of the actual lesson of the Shoah, which is that it is easy to kill a unilaterally disarmed Jew but much harder to kill one who is pointing a gun at your face.

We did not have much time to appreciate the weight of the metal in our hands, to inspect before a mirror our potently armed and dashingly uniformed selves, to imagine the damage we could do to our enemies with the weapons now entrusted to us—that came later, after final inspection, when one of the boys in my barracks, an Australian, the son of survivors, said, "Could you imagine what it would have been like . . ." and he stopped before completing his thought, but he didn't have to, because we knew what he meant, we *felt* what he meant. But now we were ordered to run in our boots down a plunging hill to a long potholed road, and then to the front gate of the base, where we were to reassemble, in perfect formation, in sixty seconds.

"Move!" the drill instructor yelled, and we moved, M-16s slapping against our legs. We made it in seventy-five seconds. We were told this was not good enough. So we did it again, and again, and again, into the darkness.

We wanted to shoot our rifles, but the inculcation of discipline came first, then instruction, and only then, firing. The next morning, the lessons began. We were taught field-stripping and cleaning. Field-stripping is surprisingly easy; the M-16 cracks open in half, with a push of a button. The bolt slides out, and the firing pin mechanism comes apart in seconds. We were taught the best methods of cleaning, and it was impressed upon us that a dirt-filled barrel was as gross a sacrilege as a dropped Torah. And we were taught how to unload the rifle—to press the loading catch, remove the magazine, pull the cocking handle until the bolt holds steady, inspect the chamber through the ejection port, point the rifle at a forty-five-degree angle, take hold of the cocking handle, pull the trigger, and let the bolt slide back into place.

I am not mechanically inclined, or greatly interested in the secrets of machines. But I was fascinated by my rifle—its construction, its lines, the mystery of its physics, but most of all by the fantastic, ahistorical juxtaposition of my rifle and me.

We were, by the end of the day, sufficiently educated in the disassembling of the M-16. Learning to fire, however, would come only after we mastered the art of blind field-stripping. We were marched, after dark, to a stone-covered field. It was a moonless night, and we could see neither the rocks under our feet nor the rifles in our hands.

We were ordered to drop to our knees and take apart our rifles, lay the parts on the ground, then reassemble our rifles on command. Misplacing a component would be punished without remorse; the firing pin itself, the smallest of the M-16's removable parts, is known in the Israeli army as the "pin Shabbat," because losing it means losing the privilege of a pass home on Friday afternoon.

It was chaos. It took us many minutes of frantic groping to stumble through the exercise. Four or five tries later, it still took several minutes. The drill sergeants made sure we understood that the contempt they felt for us was real and quite possibly immutable.

But they kept to their schedule. Two days later, after receiving instruction on basic sighting, and on the breathing techniques necessary to maximize accuracy, we marched to the firing range. Boxes of 5.56mm ammunition were laid out like a buffet, and we loaded our clips for the first time. We were instructed on the three basic firing positions—standing, kneeling, and prone. We were told to place the butt of the rifle in the soft spot between the shoulder and the collarbone; the kick is strong, it could break a bone if you're not careful. And then we fired, at paper targets, twenty meters away.

In the moments before I reached the firing line, I was consumed with fear that I would betray myself, in my incompetence, as a soft Exile Jew. I wished, in those moments, that I had been a hunter. In America—not my America, but the *real* America, Christian America—the children came downstairs on Christmas morning to discover BB guns under the tree, and then, when they were older, .22s, then shotguns, and their fathers dressed them in cammies and woke them before dawn and drove out to the woods and bagged dinner. The thought of murdering herbivores and strapping their carcasses to the roof of a station wagon was not appealing to me, but if only I had been given the chance to practice on deer, or woodchucks, or even Coke bottles lined up on a country fence, I would have been ready for this moment, ready to confound the stereotype of the Jew who could not defend even his own life.

I aimed, I fired, and somehow the bullets flew from my weapon and pierced the paper target. If I had been firing from forty meters, I would have posed no danger to a side of a barn, but at twenty I performed well enough to keep humiliation at bay.

I grew to love everything about shooting—the precision, the deadly seriousness of it (the Israeli army is a sloppy army, but not on the range; on the range, Israelis become very nearly Swiss in their fastidiousness), the smell, the noise, the sound of the casings falling to the ground. What I loved most, though, was that, if I concentrated, really concentrated, my imagination turned those paper targets into the faces of Hitler, the Cossacks and the KGB agents who kept Kevin and me from Jan Lipke, and the Irish louts whose petty humiliations I should, by rights, have laughed off years ago, but still hadn't.

There were fifty of us, Jews from twelve countries, brought together by the Israeli army for this training course, which was called Marva, after the base on which it was founded, several mountaintops over from Tsalmon. We were not yet Israelis—the course was meant to coax us toward Israeli citizenship, but in a sadomasochistic sort of way: by hardening us to military life, rendering out the fat, converting us from Jewish to Israeli. In the three months of the course, we suffered as all young Israelis suffer, at the hands of nineteen- and twenty-year-old drill sergeants, who subjected us to the physical and emotional terrors of basic training, with the crucial difference that we were allowed, at any point, to give up and walk away, because we weren't bound by Israeli law or the Israeli draft. But our commanders knew something about us that we also knew—that most of us came from soft homes and wanted to prove our hardness. We would not subject ourselves to the shame of quitting.

There were fifteen or so Americans on the course, a dozen Australians, eight or ten South Africans, a handful of Londoners, a couple of Parisians, six Mexicans, four Argentines, a Belgian, and one lost Rasta-Jew named Mordecai from the island of St. Maarten, whose father owned a liquor wholesaler that supplied visiting cruise ships. We were all in our early twenties. We had different motives. Some of us were planning to stay in Israel forever, first serving a full tour in the army (Marva for us was a kind of prep school), and then finding Israeli girls who looked, with luck, like the female drill instructors at the Marva base: tan, raven-haired, heavily armed, self-confident, beyond reach. For others in the course, veterans of Zionist youth groups—most of the Australians were members of Betar, Jabotinsky's movement—Marva provided a chance to play soldier, to develop actual combat skills without risking exposure to Arab bullets. Some landed in Marva by mistake (one person, an eventual dropout, thought it was a kind of nature school). Still others, steroidal weight lifters, patrons of Samson's gym in Jerusalem, the home of Jewish muscle-boys of Kahanist sympathies, just wanted to shoot things. I was lifting weights myself at the time (it seemed to me that a specific lesson of the Shoah was for Jews to get to the gym). But these boys were here not merely for the physical challenge, but for the promise of killing.

We were divided into squads haphazardly. In my squad were some very agreeable Americans, among the ablest soldiers in the course. The Australians, Betaris who strutted about manfully but reacted to army discipline with petulance, were concentrated in another squad, led, to their misfortune, by a martinet immigrant from Uruguay who was reputed to have only one testicle, which accounted, according to his squad, for his persistent bad mood.

My drill sergeant, the towering Russian, was named Evgeny. He was a blessing and a curse. Evgeny was born in Odessa, but he came to Israel as a boy. His family was among the lucky Jews who escaped during that first burst of nationalist Jewish feeling in Russia, before the gates clanged shut. It was interesting to think what Evgeny would have been, had he stayed in Russia—a humiliated Jew, downtrodden, oppressed, unarmed. The journey from the Soviet Union to Israel for him was a journey from slavery to manhood.

Evgeny's family settled in Karmiel, the development town that anchors Jewish Galilee. He was a mystery to us—he was the pillar of fire in our camp, we lived and died by his whims, but we knew virtually nothing about him, other than his origins. Certain things, beyond his provenance, could be deduced, however. He wore the brown beret of the Golani Brigade, the meanest of the army's four infantry brigades. Golani men were mainly Sephardic, drawn from Israel's Moroccan Jewish underclass, and from its communities of Tunisians, Turks, Yemenites, and Iraqis, the Jews who populate the development towns and the low neighborhoods of south Tel Aviv. There are not many blond heads in the ranks of Golani. (It is the Paratroop Brigade that receives, in general, the Ashkenazi sons of kibbutzim, and the children of privilege of north Tel Aviv.) Evgeny was a "gingi," a redhead (with a red beard, as well), and we speculated that he must have been a poor match for the Golani Brigade, but that he survived because he was tougher than the rest. Evgeny expected us to measure up to his standards of manliness. He took special satisfaction, I think, in making American Jews vomit, from the pain and exhaustion of full-pack runs and hill-climbing and, in particular, stretcher marches.

Stretcher marches are a form of torture perfected by the Israel Defense Forces: seven men, one collapsible stretcher, the heaviest of the men atop the stretcher (the lightest only when the drill sergeant is sweetly disposed, which is never), the other six carrying the stretcher (four at a time, two in relief) at shoulder level, over rock, through sinking sand, up pathless mountains, and into deep wadis. Even during water breaks, the stretcher remains hoisted high in the air. Should the stretcher fall, if shoulders should dislocate, if a man falls out in exhaustion, this would cause their friend, helpless atop the stretcher, to tumble to the ground, and the entire team would be punished, the punishment taking the form of more stretcher drills.

Evgeny worked us from five in the morning to near midnight, without pause: a morning run, with full kit, in boots, through the dark valley, then push-ups and crunches, then a rushed breakfast, followed by navigation class, or Zionist history class, then barracks inspection (we could spend hours folding and refolding our ratty blankets, and hunting down renegade balls of dust), then running drills, rifle inspections, firing range, lunch, a fifteen-kilometer stretcher march (often right after we ate, when our stomachs were filled with bully beef and rye bread), boot-polishing, push-ups, close-quarter combat drills, dropping and rolling and crawling and firing. Then there were punishment drills, punishment for showing up ten seconds late to a formation, or five seconds, or one. The punishment was collective; if one man in fifteen stood late for formation, the other fourteen suffered. The effect of this, at first, was to encourage the entire squad to help the slow, the feeble-minded, and the scatterbrained. But after sixteen or eighteen hours of constant movement, when every muscle in the body was making itself felt, the effect was different; exhaustion breeds selfishness and swamps the ideals of the *gibbush*—the "melting together" of many men into one cohesive unit—and a squad, under this sort of pressure, can quickly turn against the man who can't keep up. We had one such weak link in our squad, a kid named Scott, from Brooklyn, a rabbity, chinless, tough-guy manqué who drove us to distraction, from the very first day, with stories of his manly exploits on the streets of Flatbush. He was a braggart and a fool. One day, he displayed a photograph of a naked woman, spread-eagled on a bed. "My girlfriend," he said, with pride.

All of us were hurt, all the time—pain in the knees, in the ankles, the head, every sort of cut, abrasion, and blister—which was all part of the transformation. But Scott was a shirker. He excused himself from work by reciting his manifold, and mostly imaginary, injuries. He ducked his turn under the stretcher, he meandered to inspection, and we ate punishment for him every single day.

Most of the rest of us had become inured to the physical hardships, me included. We complained, of course, but we did our duty. This lesson was brought home to me, caustically, by Evgeny. On the first week of the course, a virus had flattened me out and the platoon medic had ordered me to bed. When Evgeny saw me in the latrine, puking, he said: "You can't get sick if you want to be a fighter in the army." I must, he said, "overcome." The word for "overcome" in Hebrew, *"L'hitgaber,"* means, literally, to be a man. And so I found my canteen, gargled with mossy water, laced up my boots, and reported for weapons inspection. I was expecting praise for this act of steel-gutted courage. Ten minutes later, Evgeny was mocking me for the elephant-sized dirt balls clogging the barrel of my rifle. I spent half the night throwing up, but I didn't let Evgeny know. I was determined to be an Israeli man, not an American Jew.

Midway through Marva, we were bused to a place called Givat Olga, on the Mediterranean, near the gray industrial town of Hadera. We pitched our tents and endured a week of brutish physical training with virtually no sleep. "Beasting" is the English term for it, one of the London boys said.

All day long we practiced stretcher runs in two and three feet of Mediterranean water. Our boots were drenched, and the salt burned the raw skin on our heels. We stormed up and down sand dunes and trenched hills. We attacked sham bunkers in the noonday heat. We ran for miles to a firing range, where, chests heaving, we tried to put bullets through a bull's-eye. And we were punished for infractions, real and imagined. We stood in formation on the first night as Evgeny announced a series of exercises that would bring us to dawn. He asked us if we had any questions: One of my friends, dizzy with fatigue, asked him if we needed to bring the squad's jerry-cans with us on the long march to the exercise. "Yes," Evgeny said, smiling wickedly. "Bring the jerry-cans."

At that moment we could have committed murder. My friend had asked a classic Israeli army "kitbag" question—the entirely unnecessary question that only serves to make things worse. Only a schlemiel asks a kitbag question. At least my friend didn't ask whether to bring our actual kitbags; they weighed even more than the jerry-cans.

By the third night, we had been moving, more or less constantly, for sixty hours (we would sleep for two or three hours at night, except that, at any given moment, four or five of us were on guard duty). The day had begun with a rifle run—a long jog in the water, rifle held over the head, until the muscles of the arm go into rebellion. We had spent hours on the firing range, missing with greater and greater frequency, which brought abuse from Evgeny and the other drill instructors. "You shoot like girls," Evgeny said.

The goal of the exercise was to draw us closer together; our success or failure was not individual, but collective. We were working as well as could be expected, all except for Scott, for whom the demands of this exercise outmatched his capacity to meet them. By the third day, we were carrying Scott—quite literally—through many of the drills. He had been, in the previous weeks, dissolving before our eyes. We were punished, on his behalf, five or six times a day, and he was making himself a burden and a danger to others. On the firing range one day, a friend of mine, a self-effacing American whose Diaspora name, Norman Winer, belied his un-Diaspora-like toughness and physical competence, noticed Scott pointing his rifle, unknowingly, we thought, well to the left of the target, at the jeep of the course commander. Norman, loose-limbed and strong, rushed up to him, and turned him around. One night, on guard duty, Scott told Norman that it would be better if Norman would step aside in case of an attack: Scott said he was better equipped to repulse the Arab onslaught. We feared for our lives around Scott.

On the third night at Givat Olga, we were running in the sea. It was about nine p.m. We were fully loaded, and exhausted. The sweat was stinging our eyes. Evgeny showed no signs of boredom. He put four men under each stretcher, rather than six, so there would be no rotation, just continuous muscle-ripping pain. Scott, however, would fall out, every ten minutes or so, letting go of the stretcher. Each time he did so, the stretcher would tip until the three men under it could balance themselves. The man on top was strapped down, but almost broke free once. Evgeny, watching from the beach, laughed. Then he added more drills to the exercise, more thirty-second stretcher dashes.

We tried to help Scott. When we went back to six-man rotations under the stretcher, we pushed Scott aside, and told him to run beside us. I took his rifle from him; now I had two M-16s draped over me, stabbing me in the ribs.

After a while, Scott stopped running altogether, and we were punished again. It was our fault, Evgeny said, that our squad mate fell behind.

The atmosphere had turned scabrous and grim. The trajectory of Scott's downfall was compressed: A few hours before, we were making sincere efforts to help him; now we hated him. His failure was not our fault, we agreed. Scott was a poor physical specimen, but he was not the weakest among us. His problem was not physical; it was moral. We began to curse him. On the next round of stretcher races, Scott was put on top and strapped down. The men under him made sure the ride was unpleasant. At one point, when he felt as if he might tumble into the water, he let out a girlish scream.

Just after midnight, Evgeny decided that Scott needed to be taught a sustained lesson. He announced a water break. Everyone collapsed on the beach. Evgeny called a few of us over and told us to teach Scott a lesson. Give him the blanket, he said. We nodded solemnly.

But how? In a barracks, or in a tent, the blanket was a fairly straightforward exercise in intimidation: The soldier in need of discipline—for being a screwup, a small head, a sloth, a thief, whatever his failing—would be attacked, while asleep, by his comrades. A blanket would be thrown over the soldier's head, then he would be held down and pummeled, most often with fists, but sometimes with socks stuffed with hard soap. The soap hurt more than the fists, I was told. On the beach, there would be no anonymous beating. Scott would know exactly who was hitting him. We didn't care. We were swollen with rage.

A plan was hatched. I gave Scott's rifle to a friend to remove the firing pin, just in case Scott's thoughts turned to revenge. We told Scott to get back on the stretcher. He was relieved—he knew we would make it bumpy for him, but it meant he would not have to run. We strapped him on, and lifted him up. There were ten of us now, under this one stretcher. We began running through the waves. Suddenly, blows flew. My friends reached up and punched Scott on the legs, in the kidneys. I hit him, too. I wanted to kill him. We were slogging through the water in the dark, Scott screaming and writhing. Someone tripped. The stretcher came down into the sea. Two of my friends turned it over. Scott was facedown in the water. We were foggy with exhaustion, but Norman understood immediately the jeopardy of the moment. He called out to me. We reached into the water and pulled the stretcher out. Scott was choking and gasping. We dragged the stretcher up to the beach and loosened his straps. He rolled into the sand. Someone yelled "Asshole!" as Scott ran off behind a dune. Someone else chased him and knocked him down.

Then I noticed Evgeny. He was sitting atop a rock, smiling. He seemed unconcerned, relaxed, as if this were a picnic, not a near-murder committed at his instigation. He lifted himself up, slowly, and went after Scott. He calmed him, and walked with him.

We laid ourselves out on the beach. We didn't feel much, we were so overtaxed by tiredness and resentment. A couple of guys fell asleep in the sand.

Evgeny came to us. "Scott wants to stay in the course," he said. This was an astonishment. Why would he want to stay?

Evgeny told us it was our decision to make, whether or not he stays.

It was four in the morning. Someone said, Okay, Scott, let's hear it.

We sat in a circle, Scott in the middle. He apologized for letting us down. We told him it was too late for that. Scott was desperate for our approval. He needed us to tell him we admired him, respected him, that we acknowledged his toughness, that we were all friends. We said, no, Scott, you can't stay.

He began to cry hard. Then he got on his knees, and begged, as if he were begging for his life. "I promise," he said. "I promise I'll do better. Just don't kick me out."

An Australian named Paul Hakim stood up, red-faced in anger.

"Get off your knees!" he said. "Jews don't beg!"

Scott was unspeakable, a half-man, a disgrace to himself, and to our people. He was finished.

Evgeny took Scott's rifle and ammunition and we hiked back to camp, where we slept for a couple of hours. Early the next morning, we watched Scott turn in his kitbag. A jeep was waiting to take him to the bus station in Hadera. No one would speak to him.

He came up to me. He tried to give me a four-finger-lock soul brother handshake. "It's not a problem," he said. "I'm still going into the army."

I said I hoped not. And then the first and only Jew I ever hit was driven off to meet a bus.

In the joy produced by the end of hell week, we forgot, almost instantly, about our scapegoat, about what we did to him under orders, and what we would have liked to have done to him even without orders. No one talked about him again, except for Norman, who said once, at the end of the course, that he wished he hadn't seen what he had seen.

We graduated in December 1987, after our final, all-night stretcher march, across the north of Israel, to the Sea of Galilee. We arrived after dawn. The water was calm and blue, and we went swimming.

On December 8, unknown to us, an event occurred that would change everything. An Israeli truck driver struck a car at a junction in Gaza. Four Palestinians were killed. A rumor spread through Gaza that the crash was premeditated, an act of vengeance by the driver for the death of a friend, killed in Gaza the week before. It was not true, but a fire was lit. Rioting broke out first in Jebalya Refugee Camp, north of Gaza City. The rioting did not end, as it usually did. The main high school in Jebalya emptied of students; they took to the streets, and threw rocks at soldiers. The soldiers were severely outnumbered—the Israelis in charge had no plan, and no conception that Gaza was volcanic. In a panic, the soldiers fired on the Palestinian teenagers with live ammunition, and they killed one, a boy named Hatem al-Sisi, who was the first casualty of the first Intifada.

In the dining hall of the kibbutz, a couple of weeks after I returned from Marva, I saw a friend of mine, just back from reserve duty. He seemed depressed. He had been in Gaza. A few days earlier, a gang of Palestinians had thrown Molotov cocktails at his jeep. The soldiers in the jeep fired on the Palestinians. They killed one.

"What were you supposed to do?" I asked.

"Not be there in the first place," he said.

His attitude was not universally shared. One night, I met up with an acquaintance, a boy of nineteen whose father helped run an institute devoted to the furthering of Arab-Jewish cooperation. The institute was funded by our bleeding-heart kibbutz movement. We had worked together in the hatchery; now the boy was a rifleman with the Givati Brigade, a frontline infantry unit, and home for Shabbat leave. We were sitting in the clubhouse of the kibbutz, with a few friends, drinking instant coffee and playing backgammon. One of the others in this group of friends was heading off to Gaza after the weekend. "Give them some good smacks for me," the boy said.

On the last day of Marva, the course commander, a captain named Natty, had called me to the empty dining hall and asked me if I was planning to go on to the regular army. He put the question in such a way that made it impossible to say no.

"Do you want to serve the Jewish people?" he asked. "Intelligence could use a man like you." Flattery works: I agreed to visit with some "friends" of Natty's, who could talk about my options.

One day in late December, I left the kibbutz to visit these friends, who, in short order, introduced me to some of their friends, who sent me on to some of their friends, who invited me to visit them on their base. One morning, an army jeep picked me up in Netanya, on the coast, and we drove a short distance to a checkpoint that separated pre-1967 Israel from post-1967 Israel. A month before, the checkpoint had not existed.

We were traveling in an unarmored jeep, without shatterproof glass. The intelligence lieutenant seated beside me in the back of the jeep explained the Uprising as a failure of the Shabak, the internal security service, rather than the army. I nodded. I would agree with almost anything said by an Israeli in uniform.

In truth, though, the Uprising was the fault of neither the Shabak nor the army. It was everyone's fault. Only later, in Ketziot, would I understand the inescapable poisoning effects of occupation. The Israelis had convinced themselves, in the sweetly satisfying days after the Six-Day War, that theirs would be an enlightened occupation. We will be different, the Israelis argued. Implicit in this assertion was a kind of Jewish exceptionalism. And for a while, it was true. It was a gentleman's occupation. In the first years after the war, many of the Palestinians of the West Bank and Gaza grew prosperous, at least compared to the debased standards of Jordan and Egypt, which had occupied the West Bank and Gaza until 1967. Israelis built the first universities in Gaza and the West Bank, and brought electricity to small villages. Still, there was a limit to enlightenment: A succession of Israeli governments refused to concede the obvious, that Palestinian nationalism was no less resilient than Jewish nationalism, that it was part of the fiber of Palestinian society, that the Palestinians did not want to be ruled by anyone but themselves.

We wore helmets on the drive to the base, but the road was quiet, until we reached a junction, not far from Nablus. The infantry was out in numbers. There were jeeps parked pell-mell all across the junction. Apparently there had been an incident of rock-throwing. We were held up there for a few minutes, while arrests were made. The lieutenant got out of the jeep, and I followed.

On the ground, seated cross-legged, were ten or twelve young Palestinians, their hands bound behind them, blindfolds pulled down over their faces. Most of them were hunched over, as if they were trying to make themselves small. Up on a hill, we saw three soldiers bring down an Arab teenager. The boy slipped down the hill. A soldier caught him roughly, and pulled him back to a standing position. The soldiers were red in the face. The boy was wide-eyed and panting.

They reached level ground, and that's when one of the soldiers swung his truncheon at the back of the boy's legs, behind the knees, dropping him in an instant. Then the soldier brought the truncheon down on the boy's knees. The truncheon was wrapped in plastic, but it still made a crack. He screamed. The soldier gave him two more thwacks. Then the soldiers yanked him up and dumped him with the others. He was flat on the ground, but the soldiers forced him into a sitting position. Then they tied his hands behind his back, and draped a blindfold over his face.

The soldiers said it would be safe now for us to travel on, but the lieutenant wanted to stay and watch. Perhaps there were more Arabs up in the hills awaiting capture.

A sergeant went down the row of prisoners, canteen in hand. He took hold of the jaws of the prisoners, and squeezed, forcing open the jaws of the prisoners. "Drink!" he barked, in Hebrew, and then poured water into the open mouths.

When we left, our route took us directly through an Arab village. On the inside door of the jeep, on the driver's side, was taped a copy of the Traveler's Prayer, and the driver—a kippah under his helmet—chanted it softly in Hebrew. It is written as an urgent plea to God: "May you rescue us from the hand of every foe and ambush along the way, and from all manners of punishments that assemble to come to earth."

The two-lane road entered a narrow valley. The town was built up the sides of the hills. We peered upward, waiting. The streets were empty, and the driver raced us through. A sign soon appeared, announcing the turnoff to the base.

"Those guys they arrested," the lieutenant told me, as we

approached the gate, "they were throwing Molotov cocktails at our soldiers, from a hill. One landed on top of a jeep and set the roof on fire."

It was an odd day with the men from this intelligence unit. They couldn't tell me what they did, because I had no security clearance. So the conversation was filled with hints and intimations, an unusual sort of conversation to have with Israelis, who ordinarily rush right to the point. I took a series of tests, and passed, evidently, because I was invited back. Everything would depend on my security clearance: You're going to have to account, they said, for your whereabouts these past twenty-two years.

A soldier gave me a lift to a nearby settlement, where I waited for a bus. Across the wadi was a small Arab village, a wisp of a village, really. But it was very close, maybe five hundred meters away. I asked a woman waiting at the shelter if she knew the name of the village. She was a settler; she wore a kerchief over her hair, and a long black skirt. "I don't know," she said, in a tone that suggested she couldn't be bothered to store such information. "It's Arabs."

The bus to Tel Aviv arrived. I sat in a window seat. We were stoned along the way. Once, the soldiers on the bus ordered the driver to stop. They rushed out and fired live rounds into the air to disperse a group of rock-throwers who looked, from my imperfect vantage point, to have been about twelve years old.

One day on the kibbutz, I happened to tell my friend Gadi how lucky he was to have been born in the Jezreel Valley. The joy never diminished for me: To walk on earth conquered by Solomon, Gideon, and Deborah was a gift; as it was true for Antaeus, it seemed as if the ground itself was a source of strength.

"So what?" he said.

"You're just spoiled," I said.

"I don't care about that stuff."

I asked him, jokingly, "Are you sure you're Jewish?"

"No," he said savagely. "I'm not Jewish."

I was confused. He did, after all, look like a Teuton. Maybe there was something I didn't know. "You're Israeli," I said, "what are you talking about?"

He paused, and assessed me coolly.

"I don't feel Jewish," he said. "What's Jewish? I don't go to synagogue. I'm Israeli." He said "synagogue" with contempt.

What did Gadi want out of life? He wanted to lift weights, find a job, maybe move to Tel Aviv, or perhaps find a wife—maybe an Israeli, maybe one of those big-boned, lubricious Swedish kibbutz volunteers. He would become a high school teacher, perhaps, or maybe he would take a job with El Al security; that was one way to see the world, without charge. His desires were normal desires: for money, a car, a girl.

Gadi, in his normalcy, symbolized a paradox of the kibbutz experiment, and of the entire Zionist experiment. His grandparents came to Palestine with an idea, to make whole the Jewish people, to build "New Jews," strong and competent and close to the land, like all the other peoples of the world. For them there would be no more hand-wringing and cringing self-doubt. Well, they made Gadi and his generation normal, so normal that they wanted nothing to do with Jews. They were indifferent to the idea that Israel was meant to serve some sort of cosmic purpose, either a universal purpose, as a light unto the nations, or a tribal purpose, as an ark of refuge for lost and suffering Jews. They did not, as a rule, want to absorb Russian Jews into the kibbutz (not that the Russians, then arriving in Israel in numbers, were in general hoping to lead new lives of agrarian socialism).

As for Western Jews, those few still clinging to the fantasy of physical and spiritual redemption, they were pitied.

The parents, and grandparents, of these young Israelis weren't much interested in Judaism, either, but with one difference: The grandparents were in revolt against the texts, parched rituals, and superstitious beliefs of their parents, against the *shtetl,* against the Diaspora itself. But they at least knew the texts, and knew the rituals. They understood the thing they were rejecting. The grandchildren believed themselves to be in revolt, but they were revolting against nothing. They were rebels in a vacuum created by their own ignorance.

There was no synagogue on the kibbutz, no fasting on Yom Kippur. Passover was celebrated not as the story of a just God's war against slavery, but as the history of a successful proletarian revolt: Spartacus, with matzoh.

I asked Gadi, "Why live in the Jewish state if you don't feel Jewish? Why don't you leave?"

He said, "Maybe I will."

Was that the chill of disillusion I felt coming over me?

Even the secular religion of Hashomer Hatzair held no allure for the third generation. It was not just the blue shirt that was out of favor, but the ideology of Jewish labor itself. These Jews labored, of course, and dirt got under their nails and their necks were as red as any tractor driver's, but they were laboring without consciousness of labor's meaning.

I kept these thoughts to myself: I knew better than to lecture these farmers on the Gordonian holiness of chicken shit. Instead we spoke of the things my friends wanted to speak about: nightclubs in Haifa, trips to Thailand, and jobs in New York with Israeli-owned moving companies.

The kibbutz was becoming a hollow place for me. Its members, with some exceptions—the kind family that made me their adopted son, most notably—were narrow, clannish, and cold. Farmwork, I feared, dulled their senses. As for the work—well, over time, I came to hate chickens. I didn't hate cows quite so much, and I had found a temporary place in the dairy, where I learned bovine obstetrics, which is to say, my hands went inside the birth canal of more than one cow. This was actually an affecting experience (so long as you remembered to take off your watch), but my mind could not adjust to the repetition of farmwork. I wanted something new every day, which kibbutz life could not give me.

One day, I packed my bags and left for the city.

I found a job on *The Jerusalem Post*. A family in a suburb of the city, friends of a friend, the best sort of Israelis, giving in ways Americans don't usually give, opened their home to me, this double-refugee fleeing his native land and the fallen utopia of a collective farm.

I was still keen on an army career. I checked in with the men in the intelligence branch. There were opportunities there, to be sure, but because I was born and raised in the Diaspora, I would never attain the topmost security clearances, the sort that would allow me access to the secrets that mattered. Jews in America were sometimes suspected by their countrymen of dual loyalty. In the age of Jonathan Pollard, the traitor who stole American secrets on behalf of Israel, this was to be expected. But now the Israelis were telling me that, as an American, I could not be trusted.

So that was that. As an alternative, the infantry held little allure for me. It did, once, before the Intifada, but now my friends in the paratroopers were telling me their days consisted of chasing rock-throwing children through the alleys and casbahs of the occupied territories. I wasn't interested in being a cop.

But Israel, like God, has a strange sense of humor, and so on a cold fall day in 1990, I was bused, with a hundred other men, from the draft board headquarters in Jerusalem to the army's main personnel base. And there I was assigned to the military police.

CHAPTER SEVEN

DESERT EAGLE

I was dreaming about the desert when the air-raid siren sounded. I woke with a start. I heard boots pounding the ground outside my tent. Iraqi Scud missiles were falling again somewhere in Israel. The Scuds were terrifying, but I was happy to be wakened from my dream. I had been dreaming that I was running breathless through the desert. There were no people anywhere, no prisons, no army bases, no border posts, nothing. Everything was still. But then I realized that someone was chasing me. I didn't know who it was, and I could not turn my head to look because my neck wouldn't swivel.

My friend Yoram came into the tent. "You coming?" he asked. The siren wailed in the background. I shook my head. It's not as if we had a proper shelter, anyway, just a trailer, its windows covered in plastic, poor defense against gas, no defense against high explosives. I rubbed my neck, testing its flexibility. (Early in my service at Ketziot my commander told me to keep my head on a pivot.) I had forty-five minutes until the start of my shift. Yoram asked: "You sure? Do you know where your mask is, at least?"

The Arabs, the prisoners, had no masks. This was why I wouldn't wear a mask. It wasn't fair. We were level with the Arabs in so many things—our food came off the same trucks, our tents were all antediluvian, we all coughed up the same desert dust. But we were not equal on the question of gas masks.

The prisoners complained, of course. They complained about all sorts of trivia, but this was important. The prison commanders told the Arabs that the army didn't have any masks to spare. This was the politic answer. But in fact the army could always find more masks. The honest response should have been: Saddam is your friend. Go ask him for masks.

I hated the Arabs when they cheered Saddam. But I stopped hating them when I realized that I would cheer, too, if I were an Arab in Ketziot, and someone were bombing Tel Aviv. I would yell *Allahu Akbar!* My spleen would dance a *debka*. As an Arab in Ketziot, how could I not be angry, after all this humiliation and shame?

Ah, yes, humiliation: the Arabs, and their insufferable egos, as fragile as old bones.

Of course I wouldn't cheer. Violence, violence, violence, that's all the Palestinians seemed to know. Peaceful resistance isn't even a minority interest among the Palestinians. If only they would try a little Gandhi, I thought, maybe they would get somewhere.

I fell back asleep. The dream didn't have time to reassert itself. I woke up with five minutes to spare. My tent was trembling in the wind. In the back, someone was snoring. I pulled on my uniform and went out into the dark.

The night was better than the day. The cold was numbing, but it killed the flies, and it worked against the ripeness that hung in the air until dusk, that rank smell of burning oil, urine, rotting vegetables, and sweat. At night, the wild wind of the desert swept the prison clean. And the Arabs were scared of the night. That's what we thought, anyway.

Most everything was shut down at night except for the harsh sodium lights, which were kept at half-brightness along Dizengoff, the wide, paved path that cut through the center of the block. It was named after Dizengoff Boulevard, the Fifth Avenue of Tel Aviv, which is lined with shops and cafés and is bursting with life. Our Dizengoff was without such merits, though it was wide enough to allow passage of a platoon of Merkava main battle tanks. At night, the public address system was quiet, and so, too, were the water boilers, but the silence was not absolute: The rats, creeping from their hiding places to sniff out garbage and drink from the shallow pools of filmy water, squeaked without pause. And the quiet was broken by the snoring of fourteen hundred prisoners.

In basic training, a person learns his tolerances—for sleeplessness, for insult, for blisters, but most of all for male snoring. I suffered through the military police training course in a barracks that housed soldiers from fifteen different countries, all of whom snored. We sang a song sometimes, before inspections, as we made our shantytown barracks at least superficially acceptable in appearance: *"Baruch HaShem, sh'yesh li chaverim, m'kol ha'edot, v'kulam manyakim,"* which translates as, "Praised be the Lord, that I have friends from all the tribes, and every one of them an asshole."

I slept in that barracks inches from an Ethiopian, a diffident young man named Shlomo whose septum deviated tragically. Had he been white, I would have said something mean about his snoring, but this fellow had walked four hundred miles to Addis Ababa in order to find a plane to Israel, and I wasn't going to burden him. I didn't sleep, however.

In Ketziot I didn't mind the sound of snoring because I knew that nothing could go wrong while the prisoners slept. But then the day would come and the promise of harmony would dissipate under the white light of the sun.

There was nothing much to do on the overnight shift. Only a small crew of Israelis was awake. One man was in each of the guard towers, watching the tents and trying to hold in his piss until the end of the shift. There were two military policemen on duty, each one posted to the guard shacks on Dizengoff, one situated at the far end of the block, half a kilometer from the entrance gate, the other at the block's center. Two guards, reservists on thirty-day tours, were assigned to each military policeman. I was lucky that night; the two men with me were Jews, not merely Israelis, which meant that they knew how to tell a joke.

Here's a joke I learned in the Israeli army: Two soldiers, infantrymen in the Golani Brigade, were on patrol in Hebron, getting ready to enforce the six p.m. curfew. The streets were mostly empty already, but one of the soldiers saw an old Arab man hobbling down the lane in the distance. The soldier dropped to one knee, took aim, and fired, taking off the old man's head. The other soldier watched this in shock. "What are you doing?" he cried. "It's not six yet!"

"I know," said the first soldier. "But I knew where that guy lived. He never would have made it home in time."

That night, my two guards and I talked about the sharp cold, the strange ways of Arabs, and sex. But mostly we talked about our commanders, in particular the deputy chief of our block, the run-amok Lieutenant Shimon Efrati.

Efrati was twenty-two years old. He had short black hair, and two buckteeth. His lips were perpetually, lasciviously, wet. His face was narrow, and he was as thin as grass. He was, by common consent, a rogue. His expression was consistently one of displeasure, except after he dispensed punishment, or engaged in an act of manipulation; then his face went shiny with satisfaction. He moved about the block disproportionately armed, a Desert Eagle semiautomatic pistol strapped to his waist, and he carried an M-16 with a sniper scope as well. I would not have been surprised to find a buck knife and a .22 in his boot. Sometimes, when he was off-duty, he would walk out into the desert and shoot his guns in the air. He was frightened of Arabs, I thought, but he hid his fright behind a wall of bluster. He was also stupid. Jack Ross, an American and my closest friend on the block, decided that Efrati might be the stupidest Jew on the planet. We had never met anyone like him.

Jack, like me, had difficulty accommodating himself to the realities of Ketziot. We were so limited by the insulation of our American upbringing. Jack made no pretense of understanding his surroundings—he was unfledged and he knew it. I didn't understand a thing, either, but I would never admit it.

One day, early in my tour, I made an attempt to befriend Efrati. He seemed to dislike me very much. There was something presumptuous about me, something privileged, something very white, that seemed to tick him off. Though I sought no career in the military police, it seemed a wise idea to do a bit of toad-eating, to somehow counter his antipathy. I searched for a topic of mutual interest. Finally, one came to me.

"Can I see your pistol?" I asked him.

Why?

"I'm curious. I just want to see it," I said.

He was not a trusting person, but he unholstered his 9mm and handed it lightly to me. "It's smaller than I thought," I said.

"Did you ever want to shoot someone?" he asked.

"No, not really," I said.

"If you become an officer you get a pistol," he said.

"Is that why you became an officer?" I asked. I regretted the question immediately.

"What's your problem?" he asked darkly. He took back the pistol, and turned his back.

I could not make him like me. He was after my blood, no matter what I said. Then I gave him reason to hate me. I refused to carry out one of his orders, and refused it, unforgivably, in open view of the Arabs. It happened on a hot, parched morning. I was stationed on Dizengoff, supervising the kitchen crew, which was collecting the huge empty breakfast pots from around the block. Suddenly, I heard yelling, just down Dizengoff. I turned. A guard, a reservist, was holding his head in pain. A rock, someone yelled. An Arab had thrown a rock.

I knew immediately what had happened. The prisoners did not generally throw rocks at the guards. To throw rocks would be to invite tear-gassing, and a spray of rubber bullets. In their tight pens, there would be no escape, just certain pain—and the worst kind of pain, anonymously felt pain, fifty miles from the nearest television cameras. Our prisoners were predisposed to martyrdom, but martyrdom in the cause of public relations.

Nevertheless, a rock had indeed been thrown, but it was, in the lexicon of Ketziot, a "fax," not a weapon. In the first days of Ketziot, the prisoners devised a simple system of communication. Notes would be tied to rocks, or sometimes written on the rocks themselves. These rocks were called faxes. In the morning, the air over the prison whistled with flying faxes. Fax-throwing was prohibited, of course, not because of the danger, but because cross-block communication was forbidden—the faxes contained messages from the secret leadership councils of the prisoners to the rank and file. Hunger strikes and protests, among other excitements, were coordinated by fax. Messages from the outside, messages from as far away as Tunis, the headquarters of the PLO, were brought into Ketziot by new prisoners, and then disseminated by fax. Sometimes these faxes would fall short of their destination. Part of our job was to collect these faxes and turn them over to our intelligence officer, who spent much of his day in a tin shed reading captured rocks.

The punishment for a prisoner caught throwing a fax was twenty-four, forty-eight, or even seventy-two hours in solitary confinement, *zinzana,* in Arabic. The *zinzana* was the size of a refrigerator box, into which three, four, five, or six prisoners were shoveled. The prisoners slept seated on a cold and hard plastic floor, limbs draped over limbs, and they shat in a bucket that was emptied once a day. After a few days in the box, prisoners could no longer stand unaided. I despised the isolation tanks for their cruelty. I felt there was very little a prisoner could do to me to deserve time in the box.

The errant fax had skinned the guard's scalp. There was a spot of blood, no great damage. This is not to understate the pain caused by a rock to the head. Palestinians called rock-throwing an act of "symbolic violence," and I had tended to agree with this view, until the day on the West Bank when I was hit by a rock on the back of my skull. There was nothing symbolic about the pain, or the blood that ran down the back of my neck.

The guard was fine and quieted his comrades, who had gone a bit banshee on his behalf. It was decided, however, that the misdirected fax was an acute challenge to our authority.

The *shaweesh,* the prisoner representative, of the nearest block called me over frantically. *"Shoter, shoter,"* he said, using the Hebrew word for police officer. "Come here." He was anxious. The *shaweesh* was from Kalkilya, on the West Bank. His name was Mahmoud, and he was about twenty-five years old, and like all the *shaweeshim,* he was from Fatah. The *shaweesh* was the titular leader of the block, titular because the identities of the real leaders remained a carefully kept secret.

I was surprised he called out to me. We happened, Mahmoud and I, to be *broges* at the time. "I'm *broges* with you," Mahmoud said, the week before.

"What's *broges*?" I asked.

Broges is a Yiddish word that means something akin to "angry to the point of not speaking." It was, like much of the Yiddish I know today, a word I learned from the Arab prisoners.

Mahmoud, from the moment of my arrival at Ketziot, had set himself to be my adversary. New military policemen were invariably tested by the prisoners. The prisoners sought to know the limitations of the *shoter*'s patience, his endurance for complaints, and they were desperate to know if he was a *freier,* a sucker, because having a *freier* around is a very good thing for an Arab prisoner. Mahmoud was apparently assigned the task of testing me. On my first day out on the block, Mahmoud's prisoners were engaged in a Ping-Pong tournament. The Ping-Pong ball would fly over the fence with regularity. *"Shoter! Shoter!"* they would yell. I came to the fence. "The ball, please," Mahmoud said, pointing. I would hunt down the ball. This happened five or six times on my shift. I would fetch the ball, then fifteen or twenty minutes later, there it went, over the fence. Eventually, my replacement arrived. "They hit the ball over the fence a lot," I told him. "It's really annoying."

"You don't have to give the ball back," he said.

The next day, the ball came flying again. I fetched it once, twice. The third time, I called Mahmoud over.

"They're very strong," he said. "They hit the ball hard." He turned to the players. *"Shebab,"* he said, making a big show of it. "Don't hit the ball over the fence again." The *shebab* were the young men of the block, the foot soldiers of the rebellion. They said nothing.

I told Mahmoud I would return the ball at my leisure. He started to yell. He threatened to report me to Efrati. He said I hated Arabs.

I gave him the ball back.

Twenty minutes later, the ball came over the fence again. One of the two guards assigned to my post turned to me, red with frustration. *"Dai, kvar!"* he said. "Enough already." He went to the ball, resting in a puddle of stagnant water, and crushed it under his boot. Game over.

Mahmoud was apoplectic: "That ball was from the Red Cross!" he yelled.

The guard said, "Go fuck yourself."

Later in the shift, this same guard asked me: "You're a *yafei nefesh,* right?" Was I a "beautiful soul"? a bleeding heart?

The first rule, when answering this question, is to lie: A beautiful soul in such a ruthless place is a *freier,* and a *freier,* to Israelis, is the absolute worst thing.

I suppose I should have expressed to him my Nietzschean disdain for the weak. But instead, I said, idiotically, "I don't know. Maybe."

I was trimming, of course I was very clearly a wet. He said: "I bet you never thought when you made *aliyah* you'd be eating shit from Arabs." I stared at him, dumbly, so he went on, sharing with me his philosophy, in an epigram: "Either you eat his shit, or he eats your shit. But you can't both eat each other's shit."

This was not a lesson I learned at Camp Shomria.

Mahmoud wanted me to eat more shit. One day, I was searching the fence of Mahmoud's sub-block for holes. In the rear of his block, behind the tents, I came upon a prisoner, maybe seventeen years old, kneeling and scraping a rock ferociously on the concrete. I asked him what he was doing. He looked up, goggle-eyed, and ran for Mahmoud. A crowd of prisoners trailed Mahmoud as he came over.

We greeted each other solicitously. He put two fingers through a gap in the fence, and I extended my hand to shake them. "Good morning," I said.

"Good morning," he said.

"How's your health?" I asked.

"Fine, thanks God," he said. "How are you feeling?"

"Blessed is the Lord," I said.

"Every day," he said.

We could have gone on for an hour.

I finally came to the substance of our impromptu meeting. "I saw your friend scraping a rock on the ground. Is he making a weapon?"

Mahmoud laughed with all his teeth. "A weapon?" he asked.

By now, twenty-five or thirty of his block's residents had gathered in a circle around Mahmoud, and I knew he would have to stand his ground with me.

"What is he doing with the rock?" I asked. Mahmoud said he didn't know.

"So ask him," I said, annoyed.

Mahmoud called the boy over, and spoke to him quietly in Arabic.

"He said he doesn't have a rock," Mahmoud said.

I laughed. "He has a rock. He put it in his pocket. I'll pull him out and search him if you want."

They spoke again. Mahmoud decided to tack a bit. "He has a little stone. He was making jewelry."

I asked to see it. Mahmoud signaled to the boy to empty his pocket. He did, and out came a piece of stone, maybe an inch and a half long, carved into the shape of Israel—the Greater Land of Israel, a reflection not merely of pre-1967 Israel, but of the West Bank and Gaza as well.

"It's Israel," I said, surprised.

"It's Palestine," he said.

Right. Of course. Palestine.

"You guys are Fatah, right?" I asked. Mahmoud said yes, of course.

Didn't the PLO say it recognized the State of Israel? Didn't it say its goal was to create a Palestinian state on the Gaza Strip and in the West Bank?

Yes, Mahmoud said.

So, in fact, this piece of stone jewelry, its very shape, has been created in defiance of PLO resolutions, against the will of Chairman Arafat himself?

Mahmoud found this only marginally amusing.

I turned to the young prisoner and asked him, in Hebrew, if he believed in the existence of the State of Israel. Mahmoud translated, and the boy mumbled his answer. "He believes it exists," he said. Nicely put, I responded.

But you support the PLO in all its endeavors?

Yes, of course.

So you know that your state will be built on the West Bank and Gaza alone?

The boy stammered. But Mahmoud answered for him: "Have you ever tried to carve a rock into the shape of the West Bank and Gaza and put them on a string? You can't do it. It's impossible. They're too small."

Now it was time for me to play Johnny Law. It was illegal for the prisoners to possess any sort of nationalist symbol: no T-shirts, flags, drawings, carvings, banners, necklaces. We couldn't very well turn the prison into a Fatah summer camp, could we?

Of course, the prisoners spent many waking hours defying this order: Sometimes, it seemed as if we weren't running a prison, but a vast arts-and-crafts workshop, staffed by genius alchemists of kitsch. Out of the debris of prison life, our captives could create the material symbols of Palestinian nationhood: the Dome of the Rock, born of tin foil and fossilized pita; the red, green, and black Palestinian flag, formed from torn T-shirts, tomato paste, and melted tar. These ad hoc workshops produced harmless trinkets as well, like gold-colored tissue boxes and tiny sailing ships. They offered these creations to us, as bribes. Some of my colleagues took them, in exchange for cigarettes and candy bars.

"I'm going to need that rock," I said. "You know the rules."

"No, I can't make him give it up."

We went on, in circles, for a couple of minutes.

I said, quietly in Hebrew: "How long do we have to do this?"

It was at this point that Mahmoud was supposed to say something like, Three minutes. But instead, he set his jaw and said, "He's not giving you the rock."

"Then we'll have to come in there and get it," I said. Doing so would mean mounting up an invasion: a platoon of gas-mask-outfitted soldiers, the threat of tear gas and rubber bullets, and the creation of intense bad feeling across the block. Mahmoud knew that I would not pull the trigger. More to the point, he knew I couldn't—Yehuda, the colonel, would never authorize such an operation.

"Fine, come in," Mahmoud said.

"Better yet," I offered, "let's just take your friend to solitary confinement."

Had I just said that?

"Okay, take him," Mahmoud said.

He was not going to back down. Neither was I. Mahmoud sent the rock-carver to his tent for a coat and a change of clothes.

"Mahmoud," I said. "We don't have to do this."

"What do you want from me?" he whispered. "I'm not a *mashtap*," he said, using the Hebrew acronym for collaborator.

A collaborator? No one thinks you're a collaborator.

The boy returned with his coat.

I told Mahmoud to clear the gate, to move his men back four meters. *"Yalla, shebab,"* he said in Arabic. "Let's go, guys."

I opened the gate, the boy came out, and my two guards aimed their M-16s at him. "Let's go," I said. I locked the gate. Mahmoud had won. He won by losing.

I walked the boy—his name was Hatem, he said—down the narrow, fenced-in run to Dizengoff, and then on to the isolation tanks behind the kitchen compound, near the command block. As we walked, I said, in broken Arabic, "Give me the thing." He looked around furtively, then reached into his pocket and handed me the carved rock of Palestine. I stopped him. "Let's go back," I said. My two guards looked at me quizzically. "I got what I wanted," I explained.

I took Hatem by the elbow and tried to turn him, but he resisted. "No!" he said in Hebrew. *"Zinzana,"* he said, pleadingly.

"What?"

"I don't know Hebrew," he said in Arabic.

What a mess. One of my guards, a Moroccan Jew, interjected. "What's the problem?" he said in Arabic to Hatem.

"I have to go to solitary," he said. He went on in Arabic, frenetic, nearing a breakdown.

The guard, who was older, a father, I think, said, "Let's just take him. He can't return. It will look like he's a collaborator."

So we went. The *shoter* with the keys to the three isolation tanks was there. One of them was open; the prisoners inside—four of them, in a space fit, at most, for two small dogs—were sweeping it out. "Put this one in there," my comrade said. Hatem went inside, the other prisoners finished sweeping, and the door was locked. I was nauseated.

I went back to see Mahmoud in his sub-block a few minutes later.

He was in a tent. I told one of the men outside the tent to get him for me. A minute passed, then two. No Mahmoud.

"Mahmoud!" I yelled. "Get out here now!" Still no Mahmoud. "Tell Mahmoud," I said to one of the *shebab,* by the fence, "that if he doesn't get out here right now, I will—"

What, exactly, was I prepared to do? Extract Mahmoud, and put him in *zinzana* with the wretched Hatem? Beat him? Fire him as *shaweesh*? Cut his ration of baklava?

I realized quite quickly that I would lose this rally of wills.

"—Tell Mahmoud," I said, to one of the boys, "that I'd like to speak to him, if he wouldn't mind."

He appeared a minute later. He looked as unhappy as I felt.

"What is *wrong* with you?" I asked quietly.

"Why did you do that?" he asked back.

"You gave me no choice," I said.

"I gave you no choice? How is that rock going to hurt Israel?"

"Rules are rules," I said.

"You're just like all the rest of the Jews," he said.

So on the day the fax hit the guard, I was surprised when Mahmoud called out to me. He was standing in the corner of his pen, close to the barbed wire. A *shaweesh* in a neighboring pen named Yasser told me the day before that he wanted to arrange a *sulha,* a forgiveness ceremony, between Mahmoud and me, so that we could move beyond our dispute over the Palestine-shaped rock. I agreed to participate, so long as we wouldn't have to prick fingers or kiss each other on the lips. Not to worry, Yasser said. But the *sulha* had not yet taken place.

"Jeff," Mahmoud said, "it was a mistake. The fax was a mistake." I looked at him crosswise. But he was pleading and sincere. "We'll take care of this," he promised. What he meant was that the internal security committee of Fatah, which policed its members—and the other factions as well, despite their grumbling—would identify the fax-thrower, and administer punishment for his wild pitch. The punishment might be something as simple as a tour cleaning the latrines. At worst, it might end up as a beating, what in my tribe was known as a blanket party.

"Fine, fine—" I said, and then I was interrupted by more shouting. Efrati had arrived, and he was calling for me.

Efrati often violated the cardinal rule of prison etiquette, which was never to let the prisoners see you upset. We were, for instance, forbidden to run in front of the prisoners. No problem was so grave that the Arabs should see us hurrying anywhere. This would suggest we were not in control.

But Efrati could not check himself. We stood in the middle of Dizengoff, watched silently by hundreds of prisoners, as Efrati waved his arms and yelled, "Who threw the fax?"

"Ein li musag," I said. "I don't have a clue."

The fax, I said, might not have even been thrown from my sub-blocks. It might have come from another sub-block, further down Dizengoff, or possibly from another block altogether, Block Five, for instance, which was hidden from view by a massive berm, but was no more than fifty yards away. These Palestinians were the Nolan Ryans of the territories, and they could painlessly launch inter-block faxes.

"Think about this," he said. "Who threw the fax?"

I said I didn't know.

Jack Ross, my American friend, came up to me and said in English, "Efrati's really mad."

"I don't know who threw it," I said.

Efrati was silent for a moment, furrowing his brow, evidently searching the dark corridors of his mind for a solution to this dilemma. Soon enough, he found it.

"Take a prisoner to solitary confinement," he said.

I did not grasp his meaning. It was a language problem, I thought. I was still, after all this time, an incompetent speaker of Hebrew, and at least a quarter of the commands I received flew right by me.

"I don't understand."

Efrati, agitated, said: "Take a prisoner to isolation."

"Which prisoner?" I asked.

"Any prisoner," he said, indifferently.

This made no sense. I blurted out, "What are you talking about?"

Efrati said, "Take—someone—to—solitary."

"No," I said.

"You can't say no."

But I did. I did not believe in collective punishment. I found it repugnant.

I studied the ground for a moment, and then I motioned Efrati to move with me out of earshot of the prisoners. He came, reluctantly. I told him that this was a terrible idea, to punish a man for something we knew he did not do. This violated common sense. This violated the Fourth Geneva Convention governing the treatment of war prisoners, I said. Efrati, through clenched teeth, issued his order once again: Pick someone, and take him to isolation. The Geneva Convention, he said, did not apply here.

Maybe it didn't. I was bluffing. I had never read the Geneva Convention. It was not provided to us in the prison.

Again I refused. Jack had joined us now. He was in a state of boundless worry.

"What is Efrati thinking?" I asked Jack, in English.

"I have no idea. Are you going to do it?" he asked.

No, I answered. I couldn't do it. It was un-American.

It was not my intention to resist the order. I was not known for my disobedience. But something came over me, and I could not move. If I carried out this order, I thought, I would destroy myself.

Efrati threatened me with imprisonment. Still, I wouldn't do it. "I'll deal with you later," he said. He ordered me away, and I went to my post, to collect my canteen, and the book I was trying to read.

Efrati went to the fence of the nearest sub-block.

"I need someone to go to solitary," he barked. Twenty Arabs immediately volunteered.

I turned in surprise. Efrati gave me a withering look.

I was so sure I understood things. But my knowledge was thin armor against Efrati and the prisoners.

Why didn't I learn? Didn't Mahmoud teach me that the Arabs want to be our victims?

I watched as my colleagues opened the gate to the sub-block and marched out a young prisoner. The prisoner, a smile plastered to his face, threw up his hands in victory. His comrades in the sub-blocks across Dizengoff called out encouragement. A moment earlier, he was an anonymous soldier of the Intifada. Now, thanks to Efrati, he was a hero.

I waited for Efrati to take his revenge. Finally he summoned me to the command trailer. "Should I pack my kitbag?" I asked the MP who came for me. He said nothing. Efrati's feet were up on the desk. It was Yehuda's desk, but he was off-duty.

"Why are you scared of the Arabs?" he asked.

"I'm not scared," I answered reflexively. I hastened to add that not only was I not scared of the prisoners, I was not scared of anything.

"You think it's smart to take their side instead of mine?" he asked.

Not at all, I said.

"How many prisoners have you taken to isolation?" he asked.

Two or three, I answered.

"Exactly. You're scared of the prisoners."

"You don't understand," I said.

"Shut your mouth!" he said. He sat up, and leaned over his desk. "Don't be a failure."

"If you want to punish me, then punish me," I said, suddenly feeling brave.

"Get out of here," he said. I left unpunished, but not unbruised.

A friend of mine named Dror once told me about a confrontation he had at a base near Nablus. He was a paratrooper and the blond son of a German Jew. He was walking one day to the dining hall of his base when he came across a group of Palestinians sitting in the open sun. They were blindfolded, their hands were tied, and they were shoeless. A group of *jobnikim,* rear-unit guys, clerks and the like, were on their knees in front of the Arabs, burning the soles of the prisoners' feet with lighters. "It was the middle of the day," Dror said. "They were torturing them for fun." He kicked their hands away and forced them to stop. Later that day, three of the soldiers came up to Dror. "You shouldn't ever do that," one of them told him. "Forget that you shouted at us—but in front of an Arab?"

They were Sephardim, the *jobnikim*. The best way they knew to fight their inferior feelings was to make the Arabs feel worse.

I went to Jerusalem on leave, and I stopped by the American library, near the King David Hotel. I would go there to read magazines. But on this day, I was looking for a copy of the Fourth Geneva Convention. I found it in a compendium of human rights law. This is what Article 87 stated: "Collective punishment for individual acts, corporal punishments, imprisonment in premises without daylight and, in general, any form of torture, or cruelty, are forbidden."

The Geneva Convention, however, said nothing about prisoners who asked to be punished.

CHAPTER EIGHT

RAFIQ

I was working the graveyard shift on the morning of the day everything went sideways.

I was sitting in the guard booth, in the artificial twilight created by the sodium lights that were burning at half strength. The moon was large in the sky, but still there wasn't enough light to read. In any case, the desert night had so thoroughly digested the heat of the day that keeping still brought on feelings of frostbite. I went outside and did jumping jacks in the dark.

I despised the prison, but I loved the exoticness all around me. On those overnight shifts I waited eagerly for the onset of morning prayers, which began usually about the time my feet lost sensation. The muezzin's cry would float over the camp, and it would remind me how far I was from America.

The first Palestinians awoke a little before five. These were the most religiously observant of the prisoners. That morning, as usual, the first of the prisoners to exit the tents of Sub-Block Three, nearest my station, was my favorite, Rafiq Hijazi, late of the Jebalya Refugee Camp. My encounters with so many of the other prisoners were often limited in subject to the banalities of prison life, but Rafiq and I would range far from Ketziot in our encounters. I liked that he had the dispassion of an analytical academic in a place notable for its absence of thought. He also had an open-mindedness that to me was a clear sign of inner benevolence.

I still recall the feeling I had after our first conversation, a feeling of connection. It was a strange and traitorous feeling, but it was also a true feeling, and it was accompanied by a satisfying frisson of danger and dissent. Nothing much happened in that first conversation; just a bit of intelligent talk, along with the mutual recognition of some small, now forgotten irony, and the shared acknowledgment that Ketziot was a kind of appalling joke. "Believe me, I have better things to do than be here," he said, smiling.

"Me, too," I said.

"What do you want to do?"

"You go first," I said.

"I want to fight for the liberation of my people," he said.

"No, not like that," I said. He smiled; he knew what I meant.

"I like school," he said. "I'd prefer to be in school. What about you?"

"I'd rather be fighting for Israel," I said.

"Isn't that what you're doing?" he asked.

I noted the pacific sky above us, and the absence of shooting. "This place is kind of ridiculous," I said.

"Really, what do you want to do right now instead of talking to me?"

"Well, I like talking to you."

"Okay, but you don't want to be here. Where do you want to be?"

"In Jerusalem, reading," I said. "Maybe walking through the desert."

"Why do you want to do that?" he said, in the manner of someone who had grown up in sand.

"It's quiet."

"This prison is very noisy," he said.

"It's pretty unpleasant," I said.

"So will you help me escape?" he asked.

I was raised to search out the familiar in the stranger, on the theory that we are all alike. I looked for the familiar in Rafiq, and found it. Of course, Rafiq and I shared no common experience. Rafiq's life—from what I could glean of it—was quite unlike mine in its impoverishment.

The materialization of a relationship came suddenly. Within a few days of our introduction, I would stop by his block every few hours, to see how he was getting on, to share a harmless confidence, to interrogate his beliefs. It was a compressed, pinched relationship, of course. We could not go anywhere or do anything. No double-dating, no football games. We could not, for that matter, shake hands in an even approximately normal way. The openings in the fence were too small. A streamlined hand—four fingers pointing straight out, the thumb held to the side—could work its way through, up to the knuckle. So when we shook, we shook fingers.

The feeling of connection I felt with him was not political. We were officially, as well as factually, each other's enemy. We were on opposing teams. I wore army green, he wore prisoner blue. He believed in the basic goodness of his tribe, as I did in mine, despite the perversities of Ketziot.

But I soon discovered that he was the only Palestinian I could find in Ketziot who understood the moral justification for Zionism. For his part, I might have been the only soldier he met who didn't deny the existence of misfortune in Palestinian history. He did not accept the morality or justice of Zionism (just as I didn't believe that Palestinian suffering represented the determining moral truth of the conflict), but he understood it in a way that was free of the cant, illogic, and resentment that was typical of the Palestinians. His comrades, even those who were formally educated, embraced a set of theories that were foolish in their simplicity, those that attributed Israel's existence to the hidden hand of a worldwide Jewish conspiracy, or to the plottings of late-stage European imperialism, or outlandishly, both. Rafiq's heart was closed to the temptations of Masonic conspiracies and open to Jewish pain. "I don't like to see anyone get hurt," he told me once, and he said this without qualification.

Ours was a bond of the mind. The desert's desolation was not merely physical. There was no one to talk to in the desert. Rafiq had his friends, of course, and I had mine—well, I had one, in Jack. But I could learn things from Rafiq I couldn't learn anywhere else. I did not know if these encounters meant to Rafiq what they meant to me, but he seemed to welcome me into his life. He, like me, was fond of argument. I would try to talk him out of his positions, and he would try the same on me. But his arguments were never ludicrous, or tinged with anger.

We would talk most frequently about what we all called "the situation." Rafiq was a clever commentator on Middle Eastern politics. He was convinced—and he convinced me—that Saddam's falling Scuds would turn out to be good for the camp of moderation. The Palestinians were made friendless by their decision to side with Saddam in his war against the world, he explained, and this friendlessness would eventually convince their leaders to seek out the approval of America, as well as those Israelis inclined toward compromise. The Scuds would have an even more profound effect on Israel. No Arab state had attacked Israel since the Yom Kippur War, eighteen years earlier, he said. Israel was impervious. Then the missiles came, and they reminded Israelis that they were vulnerable not merely to the stones of the Palestinians, but to the armies of the Arabs. This renewed fear might serve to provoke Israelis to seek peace. Rafiq's analysis made a great deal of sense. He and I felt the same thing: We were close to something new.

I had consoling thoughts about Rafiq—thoughts about the thickening possibilities of peace, a peace that could be made first by two inconsequential soldiers. If Rafiq Hijazi could somehow extend the border of his compassion to take in Jeffrey Goldberg, then why should peace be impossible? Hope, the saying goes, is the last prop of the desperate, but I located a larger meaning in this modest relationship.

I told Jack one day I had found a true moderate behind the barbed wire, and I told Jack that I thought Rafiq was my friend. Jack was dubious. He was not an excessive right-winger—I could not precisely figure out Jack's politics, but they were generally centrist—though he believed fiercely in tribalism. "I look at these guys and I don't see individuals," Jack said. "I see members of a group."

I thought this was harsh, and said so.

"It doesn't matter if he's a good guy," Jack said. "He's not here as an individual." Rafiq was in prison, Jack believed, because he was a member of a group, a group that felt morally superior to our group, a group that wanted to kill our group. "They smile at us all the time," he said, "but there's something else going on behind their eyes."

This one was different, I said. For one thing, Rafiq has never told me to go home. The other Arabs said this persistently. Why don't you go home? This is not your place. At first I thought they meant me, specifically—my accent, my limited Hebrew, and my demeanor gave me away as a foreigner in the army. But the prisoners said this to natives of Israel, too: Go home, meaning, go home to Morocco, France, Iraq, Tunisia, even to Poland, Russia, and Germany, the countries of your ancestors. This isn't your home. You have a country. To the prisoners, the Israelis were equivalent to the French, and the Palestinians were the Algerians. But Rafiq knew the difference, he understood that Zionism wasn't quite the same thing as colonialism.

So what? Jack would say. What do you really know about him?

Well, I said, I thought he was Hamas, at first, but then the Shabak told me otherwise.

So what? Jack would repeat. Are you sure he likes you?

Yes, I said. He smiles when he sees me. He enjoys talking with me as much as I enjoy talking with him.

Jack did not think what I had was a friendship. "When does his mask come off?" he asked of Rafiq.

There was a *shaweesh* named Abdel near Rafiq's cage. He would smile each time I came near. One day he called me over. "I have a gift for you," he said. He summoned another prisoner, who came to the fence with a model ship, eight inches long, made of aluminum foil, empty toothpaste tubes, and cloth. It was quite handsome. "This is for you," he said. I couldn't take it. It seemed corrupt. He wasn't offended.

A few weeks later, Fatah, for some reason, fired him as *shaweesh*. Soon after, I went over to talk to him. He was sitting on the concrete, with some of his *shebab*. "Hey, Abdel," I said.

He looked at me, squinting. *"Lech lihisdayen,"* he said in Hebrew. "Go fuck yourself." And that was that: He cut me dead.

His mask came off, Jack said, because he had no reason to keep it on. Abdel was no longer *shaweesh*. There was no reason for him to manufacture friendliness for someone whose death his heart desired.

I went to Rafiq soon after my confrontation with Efrati. I told him about my troubles. He listened for a while.

"I think Efrati is a drunk," he said.

There was something teetering and beery about Efrati, but he wasn't a drunk. Rafiq, however, was sure. "He always looks like he's going to fall down," he said.

I started to laugh. What do you know about drunks? I asked. Have you ever even tasted alcohol?

"Of course not," he said. He had reared back at the mention of such a despicable idea. "It's *haram,*" forbidden.

Then he gave me some advice. Let Efrati have his rage. People like him need to storm around a bit, so let him storm. Be nice to him, but don't do what he wants you to do if you don't like his orders.

I told Jack about my conversation with Rafiq. He was incredulous. It was naïve to share my problems with a prisoner. He thought I was suffering from some kind of reverse Stockholm syndrome, in which the captor identifies with the captive.

I didn't admit to Jack that the same thought had already crossed my mind.

The muezzin's call went up. It was time for the *fajr,* the morning prayer. *"Allahu Akbar, Allahu Akbar,"* he cried, from inside a tent somewhere, "God is Greater." *Allahu Akbar* is often translated in the West as "God is Great," but as Rafiq explained to me: "God *is* great, it is true. But there are many things that are great."

I interrupted: "The Israeli Air Force is great."

"Maybe to you," Rafiq said. "But to say that 'God is Greater' means that of all the great things, God is greater than them all."

The muezzin went on, *"Ashadu Allah ilaaha illa-Lah,"* I bear witness that there is no god but God. *"Ashadu anna Muhammadar Rasulallah,"* I bear witness that Muhammad is the messenger of God. *"Hayya 'Ala-s-salah,"* Come quickly to prayer, which is followed by: *"Assalatu khayrun, min an-nawm,"* Prayer is better than sleep.

This last bit was honored in the breach by most of the prisoners. There was a protest song, written in the original Ansar prison, in Lebanon, called "Ansar Sings to the Dawn," that went, in part: "Break my ribs under the butt of your gun, crucify a child in the burning sun, but Ansar will always sing to the dawn!" Most of the prisoners did not—the number of early morning worshippers was small on most days, even from the ranks of Hamas and Islamic Jihad. Rafiq said, by way of excusing the shirkers, "It's very hard to get up in the cold," and it was true; it took a man of uncommon religious feeling to rise before dawn and make his ablutions at an outdoor sink in the frigid dark, under the gaze of Israeli soldiers.

Still, the laissez-faire approach of the Hamas men to Allah brought them some ridicule. Once, a Fatah man, a defiant secularist, noted sardonically to me that one of the block's most illustrious prisoners, Abdel Aziz Rantisi, the Hamas leader, regularly slept through morning prayers, particularly after nights of inconvenient cold.

That morning, like all mornings, Rafiq emerged, sleep still written on his face, and turned to his ablutions.

There was nothing halfway about Rafiq's faith. "You have to believe everything the Quran says," he said. "You can't be a Muslim if you don't believe in the truth of the Quran." I explained to him the hallmarks of liberal Judaism—the shedding of ritual and the transmogrification of literal truth into metaphor. "It's not a religion," Rafiq said matter-of-factly. "Do they believe in God?"

Sort of, I answered.

Do you? he asked. Yes, I answered, without amplification. He was greatly relieved. Had I said no, our relationship would not have recovered.

The camp stirred as the sun rose. I moved from sub-block to sub-block collecting members of the kitchen crew—the fifteen or so prisoners designated by the block's Palestinian leadership to cook for the remaining fifteen hundred. With me were two guards, but their M-16s were unneeded. The kitchen workers were, at six in the morning, groggy and stiff from the cold, and, in any case, they had little incentive to make trouble. They were the block's elect, blessed with daylong access to unlimited food and constantly flowing hot water. The prisoners weren't underfed, but they ate as if wolves lived in their stomachs. The kitchen workers took their time eating. There would always be enough for them.

I lined them up by a fence, took the roll, took the roll again and marched them to the kitchen, which consisted of two tents in a barbed-wire pen that abutted the rectangle-shaped command block.

I opened the gate to the kitchen, counted the prisoners as they walked through, and then asked the crew chiefs—a Bedouin from Khan Younis, in Gaza, named Hassan, and his deputy, the Sudanese-Palestinian named Hamad (he of the gold teeth and semi-fluent Yiddish), to produce the five knives in the kitchen for inspection, which they did sluggishly. *"Walla, shoter, ata adain mifached memeni?"*—"By God, officer, you're still scared of me?" Hassan asked this each morning, without fail. This was a game of the prisoners, to needle us, and it did wind up some of my more irritable colleagues, but I found it easy to parry: "Of course I'm scared of you," I said to Hassan. "You're a terrorist."

Then we continued on with the day.

The camp was waking up unhappily for the first roll call. The prisoners stumbled out of their tents wearing what they wore to sleep: blue prison clothes, gray sweaters, faded keffiyehs. Some of them, especially the Gazans—a rougher bunch than the delegates from the West Bank—came out barefoot, even in the cold morning. Their feet were horny and thickly padded. "Beasts," Yehuda once called these shoeless men. But most of the prisoners were bundled against the morning cold. The graybeards wore torn and stained *dubonim,* Israeli army winter coats, our discards. The younger prisoners wore heavy shirts or thin, ratty jackets, and they rubbed their hands together for warmth, and did jumping jacks, to get the blood moving.

The kitchen crew was just getting to work, clanging huge pots and emptying sacks of beans, when an administrative sergeant came over from the command block. A new shipment of inmates was arriving shortly at the front gate. He was shorthanded, could I help him off-load the new arrivals?

The prisoners were coming by bus directly from the prison at Dahariya, in the Hebron Hills of the West Bank. This was unusual; most of the time, prisoners came to our block from Ketziot's central intake facility. There was a great deal of turnover in Ketziot—at the time of my service, we held 6,200 prisoners, and many of these men were serving six-month or one-year terms.

Many of the prisoners serving short sentences were so-called administrative detainees. They had been put in jail without charge and without trial, by military order, for a six-month term, renewable at the discretion of a military judge, who did what the Shabak told him to do. The law was a holdover from the British Mandate period, which ran from the end of World War I to Israel's War of Independence in 1948. The British used the law against Jews.

The administrative detainees included many of the intellectuals and lawyers of the Palestinian national movement. These men were concentrated in Block Three. Our block tended to receive the harder cases: the "military" leaders, as they called themselves, of the Uprising, as well as hundreds of their teenage foot soldiers. The hardest cases in my block were housed in a special sub-block, just across Dizengoff from the command block, called the *lool*. This "chicken house," unlike the other sub-blocks, was a walled-in enclosure of concrete and barbed wire and, unlike the other blocks, it had a roof, of sorts, a screen of black netting that caught flying faxes and cast the *lool* into constant shadow. The Arabs didn't call it the *lool,* Rafiq told me once. They called it *al Areen,* the lion's den.

The prisoners on the bus were destined for the *lool,* which meant they were more dangerous than the average rock-thrower; knifemen, perhaps. The sergeant suggested I armor-up. The only thing I brought with me to the front gate, though, was a pocket-sized tear gas canister.

A snub-nosed green bus pulled up to the chain-link gate, now closed behind us. The bus jerked to a stop, and down the steps came Ron, a friend from the military police training course I attended two months before. We became friends the day we were assigned to scrub white the porcelain foot grips of the base's squat toilets. The base originally served the Jordanian army, and the Israelis had left crucial parts of it unrenovated. Ron, who was preternaturally sunny, took the opportunity to explain to me the gastrointestinal benefits of squatting, as opposed to sitting. The American way, I told him, was just fine for me.

Ron and I caught up quickly. I looked inside the bus. There were five handcuffed and blindfolded prisoners seated on uncushioned benches, separated from the driver by a mesh gate.

I noticed that Ron was carrying a truncheon. It was about two feet long, black and smooth, except for the grip, which was ridged. The army truncheons were made by an Israeli company that employed Palestinian labor.

"That's a big stick," I said.

Ron slapped it against the palm of his hand. "Yep," he said languidly. "A big stick." He asked me if we carried truncheons as well.

We didn't, I said. We had them, but they were stored in locked containers. "We motivate the Arabs with love," I told him.

"Well, we motivate the Arabs by shoving a stick up their ass," he said.

"Do you beat people up?" I asked. Dahariya, by reputation, was the meanest prison in the army penal system. At the outset of the Intifada, especially, conditions inside the prison were said to be crude and cruel: Prisoners slept on the concrete floor, often on nothing more than a mat or a piece of cardboard. It was more a fortress than a prison camp, and its cells, I was told, were dark and airless. Prisoners were seldom allowed out of these cells for exercise. They were, however, let out once a day to empty their slop buckets; toilets came late to Dahariya.

Unlike Ketziot, Dahariya served the Shabak as an interrogation center, which meant that some of the prisoners there were, in some sort of limited way, subject to "moderate physical pressure," which is a term—very un-Israeli-like in its euphemistic quality—invented by the Shabak and adopted by the Supreme Court justice Moshe Landau in 1987. Landau recommended that the Shabak, while in pursuit of certain types of intelligence—ticking-bomb intelligence—could hood prisoners, deprive them of sleep, expose them to extremes of heat and cold, and bind them to small chairs. The Shabak was also allowed to engage in the vigorous shaking of prisoners, in order to extract information. A small handful of prisoners died during these sessions of vigorous shaking, according to human rights groups in Israel.

No, no, Ron said, Dahariya isn't so bad. Yes, it's true, the prisoners are brought to Dahariya fresh from the street, and they are therefore temperamental, so on occasion it is necessary to break them down through the use of physical force. "It's not like we're the Border Police, though," he said. The Border Police, a paramilitary group whose recruits were almost uniformly of low stamp, was, by consensus, the roughest Israeli unit in the territories.

We boarded the bus. The driver had already wandered off for coffee. Ron told the other military policemen, in American-accented Hebrew, to remove the blindfolds, which they did. The prisoners, I saw, were young—eighteen or nineteen years old. They blinked against the early morning sunlight, and looked around nervously. One said something in Arabic to another, across the aisle. "Shut your mouths!" Ron yelled in Hebrew. They stopped talking. *"Yalla, yalla, yalla!"* Ron said. *"Yalla"* is an Arabic word for "let's go." Benignly inflected, it is similar in meaning to "Come on, guys." But said with impatience, or condescension, *"Yalla"* is a term of disrespect. It is used, for instance, by Arabs who are trying to move stubborn donkeys. Ron's *"Yalla"* was said with a curl of his upper lip.

The prisoners stepped gingerly off the bus. They were cramped-up from the ride. We lined them up against the outside wall of the block—the retaining wall of the *lool,* in fact. I told them in Arabic to face the wall. My Arabic was improving every day: Now I could say, "Give me your identity papers," and "You're in violation of prison regulations," and "You don't want me to use the tear gas."

The search was pro forma—they had been searched in Dahariya—but it was a rule. I kicked out the feet of the first prisoner and patted him down, starting at the shoulders, and moving all the way to the ankles. I went nowhere near his genitals. I searched fifteen or twenty men a day, and an alert prisoner would have soon deduced that I was too delicate in my searches, particularly in the nether regions. I refused to touch the prisoners on the crotch, even after another guard discovered in a block-wide search a shank, sheathed in masking tape, in a prisoner's underwear. I did, however, learn to stop apologizing to the prisoners as I felt them up.

The search successfully completed, the administrative sergeant took over, and delivered a lecture in Hebrew outlining the rules and regulations of Ketziot Military Prison Camp, Block Four. It seemed as if two or three of the prisoners did not understand Hebrew, but he forged ahead anyway. There were many commonsense rules: no fires in the tents, which was often ignored; no throwing of objects (almost always ignored); and no standing by the fence, which most veteran prisoners didn't even seem to know was a rule. Then there were regulations meant to suppress expressions of nationalism, or religious fervor: no dancing the *debka,* an Arab line dance, or any other form of group dance in which men cling together; no praying in groups larger than three, except for morning prayers, when groups of five could form; no wearing of the Palestinian national colors; no wearing of the *jalabiya,* a loose-fitting Arab robe; no playing of the flute or drums. It was also a violation to sing nationalist songs (we, the Arabic-illiterate prisoner counselors, were supposed to judge whether or not a song contained "national content").

When the sergeant finished, Ron turned to them and said, in Hebrew, "Now be good boys, okay?"

The sergeant ordered the prisoners to form a line, which they did only after I pantomimed the action for them. I opened the gate and we walked through together, to the top of Dizengoff.

The prisoners seemed startled, almost dumbstruck, by the sight. It was, to a first-time visitor, a dizzying picture. I looked at Ron, who had not been here before. His eyes seemed unable to take in the size of the place. What one sees, from the top of Dizengoff, is a picture to provoke dread. Everything seemed to be moving at once, and all the images commingled menacingly: black rivers of barbed wire; sooty smoke from tall chimneys against a faint blue sky; machine guns aimed at swarms of prisoners, bearded, white-eyed men, hundreds and hundreds of them, who were pacing back and forth in teeming pens, grabbing at the fences, yelling out to each other along the half-kilometer length of the block. The heat blurred the edges off things; everything melded together. But from the air—from the cockpits of the F-16s that flew over us each day, rattling us with sonic booms—Ketziot must have looked like a vast, smoke-filled honeycomb.

"Jesus," Ron said. I reminded myself that Ron's entire prison was one-third the size of this block alone. I was, for a moment, proud.

I told the first prisoner to move. He did so, with some hesitation. In the near distance we could see dozens and dozens of prisoners pressing up against the fences, straining to see the new arrivals. I noticed something, then: My prisoners seemed scared, actually physically scared. The Uprising brought about such a spectacular shift in my understanding of Palestinians that it no longer occurred to me that they ever felt fear.

A few months before, I happened to be in Nablus, at a riot. I was off-duty, visiting a friend in an infantry unit. We were called out to confront a group of Palestinians. I wasn't called, actually, not being a member of the unit in question, but the promise of trouble lured me into a jeep that soon enough became the target of a small group of Palestinians—not the group we were meant to confront, but a metastasis of this mob, apparently. Several of these young men, their veins rivers of adrenaline, their faces discolored by rage, tore open their shirts, and thrust their bare chests out in our direction. One of them screamed, "Shoot me, Jews!"

Another Palestinian rushed to the center. "I'll fuck your sisters!" he screamed at us, and then he yelled, "What are you scared of?" He threw a rock at us; it landed on the concrete.

One of the soldiers from a jeep that had come up behind us took aim at the cursing Arab, and fired rubber-coated steel bullets at his chest. The Arab fell back, onto the pavement. His friends ran forward and dragged him out of sight. A Red Crescent ambulance I had not noticed before was parked twenty meters behind the rock-throwers (these riots weren't quite as spontaneous as they appeared on television) and its crew ran up to grab the wounded man. I don't know if he lived or died.

I had assumed until the Uprising that the Palestinians were cowards. The terrorism they committed—the school killings and market bombings—was not, as the partisans of Arafat maintained, a last-resort weapon of the weak, but a weapon used *against* the weak. But here, on a potholed street in the shade of the Nablus casbah, this new generation of Palestinian men showed only untempered courage.

So why was my prisoner, this young lion of the Uprising, shaking? At one point, he grabbed his right hand with his left, to stop the tremors.

We divided up the prisoners. I took mine to the sub-block in the left-rear of the cage. The *shaweesh* came to the gate. It was the lugubrious Capucci, he of the commanding eyes and pillarlike dignity.

I said good morning. He said good morning. I asked after his health; he asked after mine. "Cold, last night," I said. "Yes, very cold," he said. Then I asked him to step back, and I opened the gate. I signaled for the new prisoner to enter. The prisoner stood inside the gate, and I stayed and watched. Capucci and the prisoner kissed on both cheeks, though I don't think they knew each other. It was a triple-kiss—right cheek, left cheek, right cheek again. Three kisses signified a certain level of comfort and affection; four or more signaled trust and intimacy; two was pro forma; one, I guessed, was death.

Capucci walked the prisoner to a tent. The flap was open, so I could see inside. Usually, the new arrivals received beds—wooden slats under thin mattresses, each one touching the next—by the tent flaps, the draftiest, least desirable place to sleep. But Capucci gave this prisoner a bed further down the row.

A day later, I was in the *lool,* and I asked about the quivering prisoner.

"Why do you ask?" Capucci said flatly. I told him I thought the new arrival was scared. I hadn't noticed that before in the prisoners.

"He wasn't scared," Capucci said. "He's very brave."

I said that he didn't seem all that brave to me.

So Capucci told me a story. This prisoner—his name was Muhammad—spent two months in the prison at Dahariya. The army suspected Muhammad of being a leader of a Fatah cell in Hebron that stabbed a Jewish settler.

"Was he?" I asked.

"Walla, ani lo yodeah," Capucci said. "By God, I don't know."

He continued: "He was there in Dahariya for so long, and every day the Shabak would torture him. They poured water over his head, and they made him stand outside in the courtyard under the sun for four hours, and if he fell over they would hit him. They kept him for six weeks and every day they did these things. But he didn't say anything. Then for a reason he doesn't know he was let out of jail. He wasn't charged. He went home. But then the Shabak man came to his home and said we will take you again, unless you work for us. Muhammad had a brother who worked in Tel Aviv and the Shabak man said they would put Muhammad's brother in a difficult position. Muhammad refused to do what the Shabak said, but he knew that they would come to arrest him again. So each day after that he would practice torture in his house."

"Practice torture?" I asked.

"He would put a hood over his face for a minute or two minutes, to make himself not panic. He was practicing holding his breath. He would stand naked in a bucket of cold water at night, to freeze. He would stand up in his room all day long. This way he made his knees stronger."

He continued, "The Shabak man came for Muhammad. They took him to Dahariya and they did the same things to him that they did before. He didn't become a spy. Then they charged him and convicted him, and sent him here. But his Shabak man told him that at Ansar Three they use electricity to torture prisoners. He made up a whole story about how Muhammad was going to get electric torture on his parts"—his genitals—"starting the day he got here. Muhammad believed him."

So he was scared?

"Not scared," Capucci said adamantly. "He is not scared. When he saw you come onto the bus with the other men, he became upset that the electric torture would start. That's all."

Not scared?

"Not scared."

I asked Rafiq one day if he felt fear. He said he did not. I had no reason to disbelieve him. He did not generally posture for my benefit. He readily admitted that he felt fear when he was first arrested. He was only seventeen, he said, when the Shabak first came for him.

"I didn't know what was happening when I was arrested, so of course I was scared," he said.

He was fearful only once at Ketziot. It came the year before, shortly after five prisoners escaped into the desert. "We were all taken out of our tents at once," he said. "I didn't know what the commanders were going to do. They were really upset." He was reminded then, he said, of an Arab proverb: "It is a comfort to die with others."

The Israelis weren't going to do anything, I told him. What do you think, that you were all going to be gunned down?

Rafiq smiled. "Why not?"

Jews don't commit massacres, I said.

"Sure," he said.

And nothing happened, after the escape?

No, he admitted.

And that was the only time you were scared?

"Once you get here, everything has already happened to you."

Like what? I asked.

But he decided to keep his secret.

"There's one thing that's good about this prison," he said, lowering his voice. I looked at him with some surprise.

"What is that?" I asked.

"I have a lot of time to read. When people leave me alone, I have a lot of time to read."

CHAPTER NINE

THE ARMY OF MUHAMMAD

After I finished helping to deliver the prisoners, I went to bed, but it was difficult to sleep in the dank tent. We slept on the same kind of beds as the prisoners. As Inspector Clouseau once said, prison is hard enough without uncomfortable furniture.

I went to the showers, where I bumped into a lieutenant named Chaim, a reservist who was pleasantly bookish and not at all a *manyak* but who developed a phobia in Ketziot that made him wash his hands fifteen or twenty times a day, and, in moments of special stress, three or four times an hour. He would spend five minutes at the sink, manically lathering, as if he were punishing his hands. He carried his own soap, in a plastic bag, and his own towel, likewise sealed in plastic against outside contamination. Chaim and I were coming on duty together, in time for the second roll call of the day.

The schedule at Ketziot was built around the count. Each prisoner was counted three times a day, a time-eating enterprise in a block of fourteen hundred men. But it was necessary. On my platoon's first day at Ketziot, we were told about the great escape the year before. Five prisoners had disappeared through a fence one night; by the time the breakout was discovered, two of them had made it across the border to Egypt. It seemed to me like the Passover story in reverse, men fleeing captivity in Israel for freedom in Egypt. There was no opportunity for me to share this piquant observation at our first briefing, because this was serious business, and I was learning to avoid the temptations of humor in the army, because the army, with some exceptions among the reservists, did not value humor. An escape was a sin, and it would not, we were told coldly, happen again.

The count had one other purpose: It was the only moment in the day when a collaborator, real or imagined (but either way in mortal peril), could raise his hand and be safely removed from his block by the military police. Exposed collaborators, or men suspected wrongly of collaboration, were housed in a separate facility, away from the mass of prisoners. The Shabak had remarkable success turning Palestinians against their brothers. Their methods were low, but effective. Shabak men called it "the three Ks"—*kesef, kavod,* and *kussit,* money, respect, and pussy. The penalty for a Palestinian who collaborated with the Israeli authorities was death. In the six years of the first Intifada, more than nine hundred suspected collaborators would be killed by their brother-Palestinians. Many of the murdered men were not collaborators, but many were. Most of the killings would take place on the streets of Gaza and the West Bank, but a substantial number took place in the prisons. One morning soldiers in another block discovered a dead Palestinian draped across the razor wire. A young prisoner immediately stepped forward to take responsibility. Blame is assigned by the ruling councils inside the tents even before the deaths occur.

The prison would awake to singing after the midnight murders of suspected collaborators. A demolished corpse was carried out one morning from a sub-block near Rafiq's. The body was beaten blue. A young prisoner offered himself up as the killer and he was marched away, to the care of the Shabak. The head count continued.

The roll call was fastidiously choreographed. In the minutes before the count, a reserve lieutenant received a printout containing the names and serial numbers of every prisoner in the block. Outside the block's war room (an extravagant title for a prefabricated shed that contained both a radio room and a weapons closet), the lieutenant organized his security team: two gunners manning a jeep-mounted machine gun, six guards carrying M-16s rigged to fire canisters of rubber-coated steel pellets, and a military policeman entrusted with a malevolent-looking gray metal device, a container filled with tear gas that could, with the opening of its nozzle, knock down dozens of men in seconds. Use of the tear gas container was dangerous for the men using it, because the gas did not exit in a jet. Instead, it came out as a cloud, and, if the wind was wrong, the gas would quickly turn on its users.

The jeep led the way, the guard team following on foot, down Dizengoff. The jeep parked outside the double-fence of the first sub-block on the list. The machine gun was trained on the prisoners, more than one hundred in each sub-block. The revving of the jeep's engine was the signal, up and down the block, that the roll call was to commence, and the prisoners gathered in rows, sitting (or squatting, on cold days) in anticipation of the count. It was vitally important that they not stand: A prisoner standing during the count could be shot, all except the *shaweesh*. The *shaweesh* organized the count, and stood before the lieutenant.

The lieutenant approached the inside gate of the double-ringed sub-block. The *shaweesh* stood back, ten or fifteen feet, one eye on his assembled charges, making sure they were in line and quiescent. The six guards, armed with the M-16s, lined up on two sides of the block, and aimed their rifles directly at the prisoners. The gate was opened, and the lieutenant, accompanied by an administrative sergeant and the man with the gas, walked through. This was the only time of day Israelis entered the pens. Inside the typical pen were three tents, each capable of sleeping up to twenty-five men uncomfortably. The tents were army-issue, and dated back to the period of the Six-Day War. Before them was an open space—a "plaza" we called it—which held a Ping-Pong table, and to the side, a lean-to with toilets and showers. Actually, the toilet and the shower were the same thing: The shower head was an open pipe that was placed directly over the squat toilet. Outside the toilets was an open army sink, shaped like a half-barrel, and just outside the fence loomed the water heaters, which burned kerosene for one or two hours a day, and sent up balloons of black smoke.

For the count, the prisoners were organized in rows in the plaza, waiting silently for their number to be called. The lieutenant, if he were clever, would begin not with the brusque accounting, but with an elaborate set of greetings to the *shaweesh*. The Israeli economy of manners can be grating and debilitating, when it is not comical. But in prison it was dangerous. The smart officers understood the importance of providing their prisoners, who came to humiliation so easily, with the simulacrum of dignity. Many years later, the scholar of Islam, Bernard Lewis, told me the fight between Palestinians and Israelis represented a collision between the world's most polite society and its least. This was true, in microcosm, in Ketziot.

"Asalaam aleikum," the lieutenant said in Arabic. "Peace be upon you." It was Chaim the handwasher who was in charge, and he was smart, and not coarse. The *shaweesh* responded, *"Wa-aleikum salaam,"* "And upon you, peace." Once, I heard a *shaweesh* begin the exchange by saying in Hebrew, *"Shalom aleichem,"* the Hebrew equivalent of

"Asalaam aleikum." The next day, the Fatah ruling council in the block called him a sycophant and threatened to take away his job. He didn't start the day with a *"Shalom aleichem"* again.

"Is everybody fine today?" Chaim asked. "Yes, thank you," answered the *shaweesh*.

I stood to Chaim's left, carrying the gas. On Chaim's right stood a military policeman, with the master list of inmates.

"Let's begin," Chaim said. My colleague to Chaim's right read off serial numbers. On hearing their numbers, the prisoners shouted their names with their whole throats and then spun in place, giving their backs to us.

In the first sub-block, two men were sick and in bed, the *shaweesh* said. Chaim ordered him to have the sick carried outside, so we could see for ourselves that they were in fact in bed and not in Egypt. The *shaweesh* dispatched eight prisoners from the count to the tents, and they carried out the beds, the prisoners buried underneath mounds of brown blankets.

We moved through the sub-blocks as quickly as the asthmatic jeep would allow. We arrived on the Gaza side of Dizengoff, and entered the first sub-block. We were in the middle of the count when suddenly the sound of gunshots split the air. The prisoners, seated on the ground, came to their knees. I looked at the guards, lined up just outside the fence, ready to fire into the mass before them. I put my hand on the trigger of the tear gas. Chaim looked around, and said, "Let's go." We backed out, and locked the gate.

We didn't know what had happened. Jeeps raced in the distance. The shot, we surmised, came from Block Three, invisible behind the berm. Our prisoners were agitated, milling about; they assumed the worst—that one of their own was dead. But the *shaweeshim* kept things calm. We decided, jointly, the prisoners and the guards, to continue the count. We hurried through it, and then rushed back to the command block.

A prisoner was shot, that's all we knew. No one was telling us anything. Absent news, rumors would flash through the block, setting the prisoners on edge. Efrati stepped out of his trailer and chambered a round in his M-16, which seemed senseless and provocative. He told us a prisoner was shot in the next block, during roll call; he stood up during the count, Efrati said. The *shaweesh* ordered him to sit down, but he ignored the command. The prisoner told the officer that he needed protection—his fellow inmates were trying to kill him—and then suddenly he screamed *"Allahu Akbar"* and attacked a military policeman with a knife. He was not given a chance to draw blood. The lieutenant opened fire at close range with live ammunition.

We heard the thwapping of a helicopter overhead. Word was passed that the prisoner was still alive, that he would be flown to a hospital in Be'er Sheva. But our block was churning now. Sleeping reservists were woken, and placed on duty. The weapons closet was opened; extra clips were handed out.

I went to Dizengoff. The prisoners were pacing their cages. I asked one of the *shaweeshim,* a thirty-year-old Fatah man named Abu Bassam, what he knew. Abu Bassam scratched his head when he was nervous, and he was scratching now. He had good information, which had just arrived by fax. The prisoners of Block Three reported that the night before a Fatah security committee had accused the gunned-down prisoner of collaboration. The information had come to Fatah from the outside. The prisoner had been interrogated already, Abu Bassam said, though he wouldn't say how. A secret trial, behind the closed flaps of the tent, was meant to be held tonight, he said, but the prisoner, in anticipatory dread, tried to preempt the trial by proving his fidelity to the Palestinian cause. It seemed, Abu Bassam suggested, that the *shtinker*—the Yiddish word for "rat"—believed that Israeli blood would wash away his sins.

It was not an operation sanctioned by Fatah, or the other factions; quite the opposite. Still, Abu Bassam said, the Palestinians were fired with rage: You didn't have to shoot him, he said. Why didn't you just tear-gas him, or hit him over the head? In Abu Bassam's logic, it was permissible for the Palestinians to torture a confession out of this man—the accused collaborators were always tortured—but Israelis weren't allowed to defend themselves. I said, hoping Abu Bassam would carry this idea to the others, that this crisis had nothing to do with Block Four and that we should all remember that.

Abu Bassam shook his head. That would not be possible.

I was called back for a meeting. Yehuda was on leave, so the panjandrum Efrati was in charge. "If they do something, we'll be ready for them," he said.

I went back to my post on Dizengoff. My guards were nervous. One kept his rifle, which is usually slung low across the belly, at shoulder-level, his finger resting near the trigger. I told him to lower his weapon. His actions were not helping the general morale. A chant arose from one corner of a sub-block. I went to check the commotion. There were men—Hamas, by the cloud of beards I saw—standing up against the fence, screaming. I could not understand what they were saying. I signaled to their *shaweesh*. He refused to come to the fence, which was a bad sign. I moved down the fence, to the next cage. It was daytime, but half the prisoners were in their tents, and the flaps were down—flaps, the rules stated, must be rolled up during the day. The chant continued: *"Khaybar, Khaybar, ya Yahud, Jaysh Muhammad sawfu ya-ud."* It was a Hamas chant, apparently. One of the *shaweeshim* told me later that day that it meant, "Oh, Jews of Khaybar, the Army of Muhammad shall yet return."

Khaybar is the name of an oasis not far from Medina that, in the time of Muhammad, was populated mainly by Jews. In the year 628, Muhammad led his army against these Jews, defeating them in battle and subjugating the survivors. Later, Muhammad expelled the Jews from all of Arabia.

The intent of the slogan was obvious—the reconstituted army of Muhammad in Palestine would do to the Jews today what the first army of the Prophet Muhammad did to the Jews in Arabia fourteen hundred years ago. It seemed a bit much. Sometimes, the prisoners would chant the slogan *"Falastin baladna wa Yahud kalabna,"* "Palestine is our homeland and the Jews are our dogs," which makes the point and is certainly not oriented toward the possibility of reconciliation, but does not invoke an ancient Arabian curse. We shoot a *shtinker,* and Hamas waves Muhammad's sword? These Hamas men behaved as if the defeat of the Jews at Khaybar took place the previous Tuesday.

I saw Rafiq. He said by way of explanation: "They believe that everything that happened once will happen again."

A soldier came up to me. A riot had broken out in Block Five. The prisoners were throwing chunks of wood, rocks, and balls of hardened pita at the guards. Our prisoners would surely learn of it, if they hadn't already. We stepped out onto Dizengoff. He went right, I went left, to the guard post situated between the cages furthest from the command block.

The guards—reservists who had been mobilized only a few days before and were disoriented and overwhelmed—stayed close by the booth. One day, you're a computer programmer in Tel Aviv, the next, you're putting down riots in the Middle East's biggest prison. Such were the joys of army reserve duty.

In the distance, we heard the muffled thud made by the firing of tear gas. We stored our own supply of tear gas in a locked bench in the booth, and now we broke it open quietly.

The block seemed still, but in the half-light of dusk, I could see movement inside the tents. Then the prisoners, seemingly all at once, came out and walked silently to the fences. I stepped out of the booth. A thousand eyes bored into me. I looked up and down. The prisoners, anger etched on their faces, stared at me. I realized I was the only Israeli out in the open.

I left my guards in place and walked slowly down Dizengoff, to find Efrati, to suggest an immediate, prophylactic, 100 percent deployment, in the hope that fifty or sixty soldiers, armed, plus the tower machine guns and the jeep-mounted machine gun, might persuade the Palestinians to get off the fences.

They continued staring me down as I walked. I went slowly—I strolled, I ambled, I did not run.

Who was I fooling? The block was as quiet as a grave. There were Abu Bassam, Hamad, Hassan, and Rafiq, people I chatted with regularly, standing there, a blue wall of hostility. Why was Rafiq looking at me that way? There was no recognition in his eyes.

Efrati came out onto Dizengoff, looked around, and ran back—running, again, the idiot—to the weapons closet. He broke out a case of truncheons. I turned the corner and entered the command block. There was great excitement. We collected gas masks and tear gas canisters, rifles, and clips. An armored personnel carrier lumbered in through the gate. Out of the back came the prison's rapid reaction team, a floating squad of riot-enders.

We lined up in formation. Efrati gave us his orders. We were to put on our gas masks and march purposefully onto Dizengoff, truncheons visible. Every gas-blaster would be sent out as well. We would take up positions at the corners of each block. If the prisoners began rioting, we would choke them with gas. If they persisted, we would fire on them with rubber bullets. If they didn't move from the fence, but didn't riot, we would still fire tear gas, because hanging on the fence like this was not permitted.

I was carrying one of the gas-blasters. My thoughts were crashing into each another. Did Efrati just say that we're to spray them with tear gas, even if they do nothing but stand by the fence?

We marched out, gas masks covering our faces. The jeep led the way. There were forty of us now, not including the men in the towers, and extra pairs of guards patrolling the perimeter. As fate would have it, I took the corner of Rafiq's pen. I hoped—it was an urgent hope—that Rafiq would not recognize me in my gas mask. Then it occurred to me that in a few minutes I would have to gas him. If they got violent, well, I could be violent back. But what if he just stood there?

This was new to me. It seemed as if these prisoners were engaging in nonviolent resistance. I had not yet seen this among the Palestinians. The idea did not seem to exist in their moral vocabulary. It was a shame and a waste that the Palestinians had blinded themselves to the ideas of Gandhi and King. If they hadn't, they might have broken the occupation in a week. In my desire to convince Rafiq that violence was no solution, I asked him once to think about what would happen if ten thousand Palestinian men marched on an Israeli checkpoint, as Gandhi once marched on the salt sea. Imagine, I said, that these Palestinians resisted the temptation to throw rocks and Molotov cocktails, but instead simply sat in the road and blocked traffic, keeping settlers from their settlements and soldiers from their bases. It is quite possible that the Israelis would meet them with violence, just as the British often met Gandhi's followers with violence. But the Israelis would stop soon enough. I was sure of that. The Israelis, like the British soldiers of India, could not sustain such one-sided violence. Germans could slaughter the defenseless at close quarters, but not Jews—not most people, especially in front of the television cameras. The Israelis would be forced to negotiate with you, I told Rafiq, and, after all, isn't that what you want? Recognition, a seat at the table?

Rafiq said this scenario was beautiful, but hopelessly unrealistic, for two reasons. Israel, he said, was too committed to the occupation—for reasons of religion, nationalism, and also greed—to be driven off the West Bank by passive resistance. The Palestinians were too dependent on Israel's economy to boycott it, in any case. "We would starve in the meantime," he said.

Another, more convincing, answer to this question came from the *shaweesh* Jawdat Ahmed. "We're men," he said. "We're not going to let someone hit us on the head and not hit back. We're not women."

There is strength to be found, I said, in absorbing the blows. He laughed at the absurdity of this. "No Arab man is going to let a Jew beat him, believe me."

"Jeff, is that you?"

Rafiq had worked his way down the fence.

"Yes, it's me," I said, my voice muffled by the mask.

"Shalom," he said, and walked away.

My transformation was complete. All my life I wanted to be a Freedom Rider. Now I felt like Bull Connor.

Suddenly a message rippled down the line of prisoners. Almost as one, they moved back off the fence. The leaders—the secret leaders, whoever they were—had made a decision. There would be no confrontation in Block Four, not tonight, at least.

The prisoners hustled to the tents, and dropped the flaps. We waited. In the dark, I felt tremors. So did the others. The ground was vibrating. I looked down to the main gate and saw five Merkava tanks in a line come smashing through the block. These are the main battle tanks of the Israeli army, each one weighing sixty-nine tons. The noise was shattering. Those of us standing in the funnel of Dizengoff pushed ourselves flat against the fence. Dizengoff was barely wide enough for the tanks. I looked into the blocks—prisoners were crammed together in the corners of the tent, staring. As the tanks moved past, their crews threw stun grenades into the sub-blocks, but they only served to deafen the soldiers, not the prisoners. The tanks exited the far side of the block, and went right, to Block Five.

You're a little late, I thought.

Efrati came up to me and two other military policemen, all of us carrying gas. "If I give the order, you put the gas right at the corners of the tents, where the flaps meet," he said.

"Why would we hit them with gas?" Yoram asked me. "They went in the tents."

The prisoners gave Efrati no excuse. In other parts of the prison city, though, it was chaos. The three of us were soon pulled from Block Four and shifted to Block Three, where the shooting took place. We put on our gas masks again, and an officer I did not recognize led us to a far sub-block, where the prisoners were cursing, screaming, and throwing trash.

The tanks had been through once already. Their treads carved tracks in the tar. "Put the gas over there," the officer said, pointing in the direction of a band of Palestinians, dismembering a slat-bed, hoping to turn the pieces into projectiles. So I opened up the tear gas, and so did the others. One of them did so behind cover, dropping to one knee behind a crate, and spraying gas as if someone were shooting back, as if this were some kind of fair fight. The gas streamed forth and I could see through the visor of my mask the prisoners scrambling into the tents, grabbing at their blinded eyes. I shut down my gas tank a second later. The prisoners were behind barbed wire, for God's sake. What was I doing? I had once experienced the dire effects of tear gas—the vomit that tasted of acid, the cascade of tears. How could I deliver that same misery to men who posed no threat to me?

I felt pity for them, and for myself, but mainly I felt relief, relief that the tear gas sent the prisoners back into their tents, relief that we would have no world-ending revolt, no mass murder, we wouldn't have to kill anyone, and our own throats would go unslit. And I felt relief for something else: At least I wasn't in my own block. At least I wasn't gassing Rafiq.

The next morning, we came out at seven for roll call. The jeep's engine had died, so, in an opéra bouffe coda to the previous night's excitement, we employed an armored personnel carrier instead. Several of the prisoners could not choke back their laughter at the sight of the APC banging its way down Dizengoff. Later on, when I was speaking with Rafiq—I approached him with some trepidation, but he told me he found the sight of me in a gas mask amusing—he said the use of the APC convinced the *shebab* that they were truly lionhearted. "Everyone thinks the soldiers are scared of us," he said. "We're just prisoners without weapons, and you use armor to threaten us."

I explained that the jeep wouldn't start. He didn't believe me. Of course, *I* wouldn't have believed me.

The prisoners were truculent, the guards unhappy. Some in the military police believed that we did not confront the prisoners with sufficient hardness. Efrati seemed noncommittal on that point, though he scheduled a series of exercises on the block that involved a great deal of gunfire and yelling. I happened to think that a day in which no one died (even the prisoner who was shot survived) was a successful day. This was the official view of the army as well. A few days later, the general who led Israel's Southern Command, Matan Vilna'i, toured the prison from berm-level. Word filtered down that he was pleased with the handling of the unpleasantness, and especially by the fact that the events at Ketziot barely made the news, covered only in brief items in the big dailies. KETZIOT PRISONER SHOT WHILE ATTACKING GUARD read a small headline in *The Jerusalem Post*.

A few mornings later the prisoners were punished for their disobedience, when we launched a search of the entire block. The prisoners were adept at hiding contraband—radios, knives, notebooks, even cameras—and we would find it. Reinforcements from other blocks poured in, and we swept through the compound in a rush, removing the prisoners of entire sub-blocks. We marched them to the outside wire, and kept them there for two or three hours, while we tore through their meager belongings. We wrecked everything. Notebooks were ripped, clothes were dumped on the ground, pictures of small children were destroyed by our boots. We discovered a great deal of banal contraband: a photograph of Yasser Arafat; a three-inch-long knife, decidedly dull; notebooks covered in violent, juvenile drawings. The prisoners hamstered away the better class of contraband in slicks, deep holes mined through the tar and concrete. The slicks gave up the secrets of clandestine prison life: long knives carved from slabs of asbestos, lengths of barbed wire, makeshift clubs, a radio. The best hiding places, however, we did not usually explore. Some of the prisoners were bangling, wrapping illegal contraband in plastic and stuffing the packages up their anuses. Lighters, even knives, were rumored objects of bangling. Messages were smuggled from the Unified Uprising Command in the territories by means of bangling. Once, the leaders of the prisoners decided to invite Jimmy Carter, who was then traveling the Middle East, to inspect Ketziot, as a way to embarrass Israel. They knew the army would never allow them to make this invitation, so the message to President Carter was carried out of Ketziot in a prisoner's ass. And some poor Palestinian anus was the location, we assumed, of the List, a document of near mythic importance, which contained the names of suspected informers. It was kept by the Fatah internal security committee. Our intelligence division wanted very much to know what the Palestinians knew. But so far as I could tell, the Israeli intelligence officers in Ketziot did not even know the identities of the security committee leaders, much less the location of the List.

A foul mood continued to blanket the camp. I would escape whenever I could. It was when I returned from my one of runs in the desert that I found my friend Yoram beating the life out of one of the prisoners. Though I ended our friendship, I never turned him in. I was not a *shtinker,* I told myself. But I *was* a moral coward. That piece of self-knowledge, however, only came to me later.

A few days after the big search, I was waiting for a bus in Be'er Sheva when I saw Scott, the Course Marva dropout, waiting for the Tel Aviv bus, eating falafel. His face was covered in acne. He was beefier than before; it looked as if he had been lifting weights.

He was in uniform. He said he was in a unit stationed in Gaza. He said he was "seeing action." He asked me, "You seeing action?" I told him where I was serving. "We're sending you a lot of customers, huh?" he asked. He said his unit was "kicking ass and taking names."

Whose names? I asked, in annoyance. "A-rabs," he said, in the manner of a redneck. His boys were cracking heads, he said, taking it hard to the A-rabs.

I was quite ready to accept the fact that both head-cracking and ass-kicking were taking place, but I refused to believe that Scott was doing any of it; even in his new, bulked-up state, I couldn't imagine him capable of cracking an egg. But he needed me to know that he could deliver a beating.

CHAPTER TEN

THE GIVING FAMISHES THE CRAVING

Block Four was not staffed by large-hearted men, but most soldiers weren't malevolent, either. Guards and MPs generally maintained simple goals: avoid entanglements with the Arabs, and return home without stab wounds. Our ranks contained men of noticeable compassion, like the medic from Haifa—an Iraqi-born Israeli—who made sure, even on his day off, that a certain prisoner with high blood pressure was supplied with a sufficient quantity of medicine. There was, on the other hand, Yoram, and a few other miscreants, like the reserve medic whom I saw spray pepper into the eyes of a complaining prisoner, and the reserve officer who slammed the head of a prisoner into the concrete during the block-wide search.

But the real cruelty of Ketziot was systemic. The army banned family visits. Some of these men, many with children, did not see their families for two and three years, though the prison was situated only twenty miles from Gaza. And the very location of the prison was a violation of the Fourth Geneva Convention—the harsh climate was in itself a form of cruelty.

The guilt was rising in me. For a while I had been making a show of toughness—scolding prisoners, yelling at the recidivists, ignoring their occasionally reasonable demands—but now I decided to place on open display my obviously clement heart. I felt that a little bit of thoughtfulness, a gentle word here or there, might make the Palestinians see the humanity of the Jews. It was anathema to me to let anyone think that Jews were cruel by nature.

I told Rafiq one day that I thought I could change the world with small acts of kindness. He laughed. "Are you joining our side?" he asked.

"I didn't say I was becoming a terrorist," I said.

In one sub-block, Hamas had picked a fight with Fatah over the distribution of Ping-Pong balls and baklava. Ordinarily, this would not be a matter requiring Israeli intervention, unless it resulted in a stabbing. But I decided to help, and so I settled this controversy in the style of an American liberal: I gave everyone more Ping-Pong balls.

The baklava controversy was not fully in my control. I mentioned to Hamad, the deputy chief of the kitchen, the accusation made by some Hamas men that baklava was distributed unevenly in the block. Baklava was the lunchtime dessert on Friday, the Muslim Sabbath. It played an inordinately important role in the psychological balance of the block. (On the other days, the prisoners ate fruit.) Hamad moaned about his supply chain; the army, he said, did not give him enough nuts. I told him I would investigate. He asked me, standing at the fence, if I would like to try the baklava; he had a tray already made.

"Do you want a *schtikl* baklava?" he asked.

"A what?" I said.

"A *schtikl,*" he said, annoyed. "A little piece."

"Schtikl?"

"It's Yiddish," he said.

It was against the rules for soldiers to take food from the prisoners, for the obvious reasons. I said no, thank you. He became offended. "You don't trust me?" he said.

"Maybe you've poisoned it," I said.

He went into the tent, and came out with a slice of browned and honeyed baklava, which to the eye was indeed deficient in nuts. He broke it in two. "Take half," he said.

I looked around; there were no commanders in sight. "I really shouldn't," I said.

"You insult me," he said.

"God forbid," I said.

So I took half. He ate his first. Then I ate mine. It was a fine piece of baklava. "Not too sweet," I said approvingly.

"That's because the army doesn't give us enough sugar," he said.

I thought the problem was nuts, I said. We talked for a moment about the lethargic flow of baking goods into the kitchen. I promised to talk to the supply sergeant.

Then I went to my tent and waited to die.

One afternoon, I was called over to a sub-block by a *shaweesh*. One of his men was hurt. He produced the prisoner, who was bleeding from a cut on his head. The origin of the wound was a mystery: The *shaweesh* told me that the man tripped on a tent pole and smashed his head on the concrete. I didn't believe him. I suspected his injury was the product of an "investigation," as the Palestinians called it, their spiteful, never-ending hunt for moles. Of course I couldn't prove it. Everything was a mystery inside the tents, and people died when the tent flaps were down. The military police command knew this, and yet did nothing. The colonel in charge of all army jails came to the prison now and again, and one day he spoke to a group of military policemen. He acknowledged that we had no way to see inside the tents at night, and that therefore we were unable to prevent murder. He also acknowledged that electronic surveillance would be of great use—listening devices and the like—but he said the cost would be too great.

I arranged for the bleeding man to be taken to the infirmary, where the wound was stitched. In the medic's tent, I asked him if he thought it wise to return to his sub-block. He looked at me blankly. I was too ambiguous. If you want to leave, I said, this could be arranged. His eyes narrowed. "I'm not a *shtinker*," he said peevishly. Very well. I returned him to his block. A week later, I happened to be speaking to his *shaweesh*, and I asked after the injured man's health. The *shaweesh*, a worldly man, a university graduate, went gape-mouthed. "You must have a white heart," he said. The *shaweesh* could not contain his surprise that I had asked after the health of an Arab. He had never experienced an act of kindness from a Jew, he said.

That's ridiculous, I said.

No, he said, Jews are without hearts. The Jews, he said, are "enemies of the sun."

We are not enemies of the sun, I countered, absurdly. (How, exactly, do you defend yourself against such a charge?) I said: Jews are filled with mercy. Our ancestors invented mercy. Read the Bible. Do you think we want to be here? Do you think we like being here in this place?

You like it too much, he said.

I tried to prove him wrong.

A few days later, I was placed in charge of the garbage detail (an honor bestowed upon me by Efrati). The detail comprised a crew of

Palestinians who moved from sub-block to sub-block, pulling a cart, and hauling trash. These prisoners, selected by their leaders, were lower in station than the kitchen crew; they were younger, and noticeably darker—three of the seven were of Sudanese origin. They did not despise the work, though, and they enjoyed the chance to leave the confines of their cages.

To supervise the garbage crew, as I did, did not require stamina of the mind or body. (Rafiq once asked me, "Did you think that when you came to Israel you would be in charge of collecting cooking pots and garbage for Palestinians?" I answered, "It has always been my dream.") I was to make sure the garbagemen didn't exploit the gift of cross-block mobility to pass messages; to make sure, of course, they didn't escape (how cinematic would that be, to hide in a reeking mountain of garbage until it was trucked out of Ketziot?), and to see to it that they executed their jobs. "The health of this camp depends on you," I told them, to buck up their spirits, and mine.

Their supervisor was an eighteen-year-old from the Balata Refugee Camp, near Nablus, named Sufiyan, who had a good nature and complied readily with my modest set of requirements. The boys worked hard, in the heat of the day, amid flies and rats, collecting steaming piles of food for our foul dumpster. One day, I asked Sufiyan if his crew was allowed to shower after work. He said no, there was only enough hot water for about ten or fifteen showers a day, and Sufiyan suggested mischievously that rank had its privileges: The dark-skinned refugee boys of the garbage cart would be ill-advised to cut in line in front of senior Fatah men.

This was not fair. That was my ruling: It was not fair, and unhygienic as well. I devised a solution. The kitchen compound, which had unlimited hot water, was equipped with a shower. I decided to take the garbage crew to the kitchen at the end of each shift, and let them shower there. I checked with Hamad; I had found him a couple of extra bags of nuts, for his baklava, so he was in my debt. He had no objections.

And so the garbagemen showered each day after finishing their route. They were inordinately grateful, and I was pleased with myself.

This went on for a week. Then Efrati found out. He wandered over to the kitchen one day, just in time to see Sufiyan, his hair wet, a towel around his neck, emerge from the shower tent. Efrati called him to the fence and asked him what he was doing. Sufiyan told him.

Efrati looked around, and called me over.

"Why are the cart boys in the kitchen?" he asked. I explained: I thought it would be best, for camp hygiene, if they showered each day.

"You decided that by yourself?" he asked. He was already vibrating with anger.

"Yes, I decided this by myself."

Efrati turned to Sufiyan. "Get the *shebab* out here now!"

And so Sufiyan dragged his crew out, including one sixteen-year-old boy who was in mid-shower. They lined up against the fence.

"It is forbidden to go into the kitchen except if you work there," Efrati said quietly to Sufiyan, who nodded to me and said, "But the *shoter* told us—"

Efrati exploded. "I'm in charge here! Not the *shoter*!" Sufiyan looked frightened. He was not one of the hard-barked men of the underground, I realized. He was probably a kid who threw a rock and got caught.

I tried to explain my thinking to Efrati, but he turned to me contemptuously and said: "I'm in charge."

He ordered a guard to fetch the administrative sergeant, the one who carried the keys to *zinzana*, the solitary confinement tanks.

He told me to march Sufiyan's men to their sub-blocks. Sufiyan, however, would be spending a couple of days in solitary.

I struggled to control myself. "It was my decision," I said. "I decided to do this." But Efrati smiled at me and led Sufiyan away.

"God save us always from the innocent and the good," Graham Greene wrote in *The Quiet American*.

Later that day, I visited Sufiyan. I arrived as he was slopping out the cell. He held himself erect and kept his eyes on me the entire time. He didn't say a word. I did not hold his gaze.

He still didn't speak to me when he was returned to his sub-block, two days later. I couldn't blame him. He believed, his *shaweesh* told me, that I had drawn him into a trap, that my heart was cruel.

I didn't bother answering these charges. He believed it, and that settled the matter.

It was true, of course, that I did not understand the mentality of the Arabs. I did come to recognize this. But the realization was dawning on me that it was also the Israelis, the flesh of my flesh, that I did not understand.

One afternoon, in the mess tent, I found a seat at a long table crowded with guards from another block. I sat down across from a man who seemed familiar to me. He was about twenty-eight or thirty, thin, with black hair, and he slouched. He seemed tired; I guessed that he was new to the prison.

He looked up. "Eitan?" he asked. No one had called me Eitan in seven years.

"Raviv?" It was my onetime camp counselor in the Catskills. Several years earlier Raviv had made *aliyah* to a kibbutz called Harel. He was now living in Jerusalem. He was in Ketziot for a thirty-day tour of Block Five.

We said the sort of things over lunch one says in such circumstances—"What's a girl like you doing in a place like this?"—and we gossiped about friends. But I was feeling squirrelly. Actually, I was embarrassed, meeting in this place a person who taught me the values of democratic socialism and universal liberation. But my embarrassment was mitigated by *his* embarrassment. Raviv was outstanding in the movement for his strong character, his selflessness, and his mature, sincere radicalism. Meeting here, after many years, in this mess tent, was so very fin de siècle. This is how the story of Camp Shomria ends? Here?

We didn't speak much about the prison. We talked instead about the difficulties of kibbutz life. It was not easy to engineer the transformation of subway-riders into farmers in the fields. Most of Raviv's friends, even those who argued unabashedly for the superiority of rural life over the degradations of the city, had abandoned their kibbutzim as well. You could not, apparently, keep us down on the farm.

In any case, my disillusionment with the kibbutz movement was complete. I told Raviv about something that happened on the kibbutz shortly before I left—a minor event, in the scheme of things—but one that was still like poison to me.

One of the *lools* was due for a comprehensive cleaning. The egg-laying hens had reached the end of their cycle, and one night we herded them into crates for shipment to a slaughterhouse. The next morning, we began hosing down the walls and lifting out the raised slats, under which was three solid feet of chicken shit. I turned to the foreman of the house, a bitter man of thirty or so named Amir, who seemed to want to leave the kibbutz, but couldn't find the exit.

I asked him when we would begin shoveling out the house. "We're not cleaning the shit out," he said. "We get the Arabs to clean up the shit. That's why we have Arabs."

Raviv nodded. I don't think I was surprising him.

Standing by the fence of Block Four's kitchen late one afternoon, I asked Hamad what had landed him in the camp. Hamad was in his late twenties. He was from a refugee camp near Tulkarem, in the north of the West Bank, where he had made for himself, from scraps, a semblance of a life. He was fiercely bright and he earned a living as a tailor. He was a family man, and he owned a TV and a full spectrum of kitchen appliances. So what had sent him to the street, to fight the Israelis, I asked. Hamad would not tell me what he did to earn his sentence to Ketziot. He was a natural-born leader, and so I assumed he was a Fatah street commander in Tulkarem.

"You won't give me what I want, so there's nothing to say," he said. "We have nothing to talk about."

That's not true, I said. We're friends. (Hamad was always informing me of our friendship.) I told him I would happily visit him at home in Tulkarem after his release from jail.

He shook with laughter.

The issue between us, he was suggesting, was simple, and insurmountable. I have his land, and he wants it back. Such a return would right a wrong. A return would restore his sense of honor. He felt, he said, bested by the Jews.

I asked him about his land: I thought he was referring to Tulkarem, which Israel occupied in 1967. But he didn't mean Tulkarem. Instead, he named a village, now plowed under, that had sat southwest of the Israeli town of Hadera, on the Mediterranean. Near Hamad's wasted village—a stone's throw, in fact—sits a kibbutz called Ma'agan Michael, where I once lived for a short time. I studied Hebrew there, and worked in its banana fields, and, when it rained, in its plastics factory. This one manufactured, among other things, turkey nipple systems ("The Nipple System for Turkeys with Optimum Performance") and toilet tanks. The kibbutz, despite its soul-murdering devotion to plastics, was a good place. The earth was sweet, the beach pristine, and the people were not so pinched and sour as they were on my old kibbutz.

I want my land back, Hamad said, and I didn't tell him I once lived near his land. I also didn't tell him that he would never get his land back. What I could have said is, Enjoy Tulkarem, because that's where you're staying.

I pressed him, over time, to give me a more complicated answer to my question.

"What do you want from me?" he finally asked. "You want me to make you feel better?"

His time in Israel had evidently alerted him to the utility of Jewish guilt.

It is true, I said, that in a perfect world, he would be living on his family's land near Hadera, and Jews would live next door, and they would sit under the blossoming lemon trees and dance together a *debka,* and I would have no guilt and you would feel no shame. But it's not a perfect world, I said. For a Jew, in fact, it's a tragic world, because the world doesn't want us. So we came back to the place of our birth.

"You're from here?" he said, scornfully.

Yes, I am. This is my land, too.

"But look at you," he said. He was referring to my unaboriginal second-degree sunburn. I am, in complexion, a Ukrainian peasant. It was facially true that I lacked sufficient melanin for the desert: Ten minutes without sunblock and I was as red as May Day.

"Look at *you,*" I said. Hamad was equally unaboriginal. His roots were in the Sudan; his ancestors were brought to Palestine as slaves in the middle of the nineteenth century by Bedouins. His people were involuntary immigrants to the Holy Land.

"The Jews aren't from here," he said. "It's just not true."

"Who told you that?" I asked, astonished.

"Everyone knows it's true. You are the vanguard of European imperialism."

The vanguard of what?

Hamad said he read a book, in Arabic, about a tribe called the Khazars. The book argued that the Jews are not the Jews of the Bible, the Jews of ancient Israel, but a strange tribe of Caucasians that converted, en masse, to Judaism in the eighth century, moved to Poland, and became the Jews we know today. The book was undoubtedly a translation of Arthur Koestler's *The Thirteenth Tribe,* a loopy and widely discredited fantasy. But I saw how it could be used by Israel's enemies. If the Jews in Israel are not descended from the Israelites, but from a Caucasian tribe from the steppes of Central Asia, then we would truly be a foreign implant on Arab land.

I told him it was all nonsense.

Hamad smiled, and said, Go ask Abu Hamza.

Abu Hamza, a prisoner in Hamad's s sub-block, was, as best I could tell, a Hamas man. He was a figure of some mystery. He called himself Abu Hamza to me, but Abu Jibril to others. Abu Hamza was an expert lecturer. He taught Jewish history, in fact.

One of the oddities of Ketziot—one of its true absurdities, in fact—was that though the Palestinians were denied the right to possess flags and Palestine-shaped jewelry, they were allowed to hold lectures, in their tents, at all times of the day, on any subject. It was an early compromise negotiated between the prison commanders and the leaders of the Uprising: The Palestinians would refrain from murdering guards and in exchange they would be allowed to organize their own lives, even their political lives, more or less as they chose. Raviv Schwartz told me that on the first day of his service at the prison, his unit was visited by Ze'ev Shaltiel, the colonel in charge of the entire camp. Shaltiel justified the decision to allow the teaching of Palestinian nationalism by extolling the return benefit: peace. But the colonel joked that the Palestinians, if they ever received their independence, could name him their country's first minister of education.

The first time I saw a class in session I was taken aback. It was in the morning, after roll call and breakfast. In one of my sub-blocks three-quarters of the men suddenly disappeared inside a tent. The flaps remained open, so I walked down the chute—the path between the inner and outer fence of the sub-block—and came around the back, behind the open tents. I saw forty or so teenage boys gathered in a semicircle, listening to an older prisoner, thirty, perhaps, lecturing them. I stood in full view, but my presence did not bother them. I understood virtually nothing, but deduced, from what little I did get, that the students were being taught the aims of the Uprising, and the historic role that Abu Jihad, the onetime deputy to Yasser Arafat, who was assassinated by Israeli commandos in 1988, played in the historic struggle of the Palestinian people for a national home. I stayed long enough to take notice of the stillness of the students and the severity of the lecturer.

This scene was replicated every day in every block. Fatah lectured Fatah, Hamas lectured Hamas, Islamic Jihad lectured Islamic Jihad, and in times of calm among the factions, they would lecture each other. It was remarkable: Outside the prison, in Gaza and the West Bank, the army would shut down schools that taught the scarlet sins of Zionism.

At Ketziot, though, it was all perfectly acceptable, out in the open, and lunch was included.

Ketziot was, in some ways, a peerless gift to the PLO. Young Palestinians, ideologically illiterate, in the green years of life—high school kids, day laborers, and college students—were snatched off the streets of Gaza and the West Bank for the crime of throwing stones, or writing graffiti. They were tried, sentenced, and shipped to Ketziot, where they were housed and fed by the Israeli army and schooled by the PLO. Most of the prisoners arrived knowing nothing, just the exaltation of the street, the flash and bang of a Molotov cocktail and the sound of stone against jeep. They did not enter Ketziot as the elite of terror. They certainly weren't revolutionaries, and they weren't hard to the world.

When they matriculated at Ketziot, they were children, but at graduation they were heroes—the fighting generation, the first to resist the humiliation of the occupation. They knew the history of the Palestinian struggle now—their own idiosyncratic, narcissistic history, at least—and they came out of prison with memorized lists of names: of cell leaders, and ex-prisoners, who would make these new toughs useful to the Uprising, and not just as stone-throwers anymore.

Rafiq told me another Palestinian name for Ketziot: *Jama'a Thawria*. Revolutionary University.

One day I asked Rafiq why Fatah allowed Hamas to teach its principles at Ketziot. "Freedom of speech," he said.

The curricula were astonishingly different. The Hamas understanding of the world was purely theological: Its metaphysicians taught eschatology and numerology; the ideology of the Muslim Brotherhood, a fundamentalist group; and *shari'a,* Islamic law. Fatah, on the other hand, ran more of a trade school: There was some common ground with Hamas—both groups believed that the cultivation of correct group memory was supremely important—but Fatah instituted classes on such subjects as the smoking out of collaborators and the proper methods of resisting Shabak interrogators.

There were crucial differences in their approach to history. Fatah, unlike Hamas, differentiated between "Jews" and "Zionists." Hamas taught that the Jews were knights in Satan's service; Fatah took a slightly more sophisticated, though still wrongheaded, approach. One of the chief Fatah men in the block, a Gazan in his thirties named

Rashid Abu Shbak, explained, "There is no problem with Jews. It's with a European colonialist mentality that exploited the Jews for the purposes of imperialism."

Much Fatah talk was a stale echo of Third World liberation ideology. Its misunderstanding of Zionism was profound: Zionists were seen as the agents of Cecil Rhodes, sent off by London to put the wogs under heel. But it was a crime against history to call the Jews, Europe's longest-suffering victims, the new face of European imperialism.

This dissenting view was not mentioned, of course, in Revolutionary University. The atmosphere at Ketziot was not exactly one of raucous academic freedom, of course. The prisoners could not keep notebooks (though many did anyway), and we censored their reading material. Though I recognized that the First Amendment did not apply to a closed military zone in the Negev Desert, I nevertheless could not bring myself to be keenly vigilant in my enforcement of the censorship rules. The authorities had even banned *Hamlet* from the prison reading list. Shakespeare, after all, preemptively endorsed the Palestinian uprising, according to the army's reading of Hamlet's soliloquy.

"Whether 'tis nobler in the mind to suffer / The slings and arrows of outrageous fortune, / Or to take arms against a sea of troubles, / And by opposing end them?" Hamlet asks. I could not quite imagine that the ban by the prison administration on *Hamlet* was true, but I checked, and it was.

The prisoners *were* allowed to read the Quran and the *hadith,* a collection of the sayings of the Prophet Muhammad. I had not yet read the Quran, but I was told that it was not particularly friendly to the Jews, even more unfriendly than Shakespeare. But it would have been quite a mess to ban the Quran. Certain Israeli books—*The Revolt,* by Menachem Begin, for instance—were permitted. *The Revolt,* according to my unscientific poll, was the most popular book on the block. In it, Begin recounted the story of the Irgun's violent campaign against the Arabs and the British. The book was translated into Arabic, sometime before, by a high-ranking Fatah prisoner named Jibril Rajoub. It was read by the Palestinians as a playbook for revolutionaries, rather than for its justification of militant Zionism. Rafiq and I talked about it once. As ever, he forced me to defend a position I could not in good conscience defend, namely, the "iron wall" philosophy of Jabotinsky.

Rafiq said: "Begin proves that the Zionists would use any tactic to get the Jews an independent state."

Rafiq spent most of his time reading economic textbooks that found their way into the prison. He also read the memoirs of the Arafat aide Abu Iyad, whose nom de guerre was adopted by many Fatah men, who had been murdered by agents of the Saddam-sponsored terrorist Abu Nidal in Tunis just days before the start of the Gulf War. Abu Iyad, whose real name was Salah al-Khalaf, was a Gazan, a 1948 refugee, who founded the Black September terror cell for Arafat in 1971. But Abu Iyad softened his position on Israel after the 1973 war, and was writing in favor of a two-state solution when he was assassinated.

Most of the books in the small prison library were supplied by the International Committee of the Red Cross, an organization based in Geneva that is devoted to securing the rights of prisoners of war. The Red Cross was officially neutral in the conflict between the Jews and the Arabs. This was true on paper but untrue in practice. The Red Cross never much liked the Jews.

In order to maintain access to Ketziot—the ICRC's representatives visited regularly—the Red Cross did not provoke the army by bringing in copies of Muammar al-Qaddafi's *Green Book* or the anti-Semitic tracts of Henry Ford. But I noticed a pattern in the selection of reading material. The ICRC supplied many of Orwell's works, along with a biography of Karl Marx, Frantz Fanon's *The Wretched of the Earth,* and *The Flies,* by Sartre. These were mixed in with piles of innocuous detective stories, and dry sociology texts.

The prison commanders did not seem to understand the politics of the Red Cross library. If I had been in charge of Ketziot, and were censorious of mind, I would have disallowed Fanon from the entire military zone. Fanon was a psychiatrist from Martinique who became a leading theorist of the Algerian revolution in particular and Third World liberation in general ("Every brother on a rooftop can quote Fanon," Eldridge Cleaver once said). Fanon argued, in *The Wretched of the Earth,* for the cleansing power of violence: "It frees the native from his inferiority complex and from his despair and inaction; it makes him fearless and restores his self-respect."

The Flies, Sartre's updated treatment of the story of Orestes, was written in 1943, in Paris, under German occupation, and it was not overtly an anti-Nazi play, but its message was clearly understood by its French audience. "Justice is a matter between men, and I need no god to teach me it," Orestes tells Aegistheus, as he slays him. "It's right to stamp you out, like the foul brute you are, and to free the people of Argos from your evil influence. It is right to restore to them their sense of human dignity."

A Palestinian reader, of course, could draw his own conclusions about the political and psychological usefulness of Sartre's implicit endorsement of violent resistance.

Each week or two, a team from the ICRC came to the block to assess conditions and hear complaints. It was morally right for Israel to let these human rights workers in, but to me, they represented the world's pornographic interest in the failings of the Jews. The ICRC was a Swiss organization that was dedicated to securing the rights of prisoners around the world, except, as it happened, those of European Jewry during World War II. The ICRC, historians have shown, knew about the Shoah as it was happening, but its leaders made a deliberate decision to say nothing, in part because they feared the wrath of the Germans. The Swiss Red Cross's record in World War II will never be forgotten by Jews. So it was bile-making, watching the ICRC's representatives in Israel float through Ketziot on a cushion of moral vanity, passing instant and unbending judgment on our imperfections.

One morning, two officials came to the block. One was a woman of about forty, frizzy-haired and wan, who was not civil to the guards as she was let through the gates. The second was a man of about thirty-five who wore his blond hair short, and who came to visit in sandals and socks. We were not allowed to talk to them, but I could not contain myself in their presence. When I was bringing the Red Cross man—he wouldn't tell me his name—to one of the sub-blocks, I turned to him and said, "It's not as bad as Auschwitz, is it?" We were walking down Dizengoff, watching the prisoners play Ping-Pong.

He smiled.

"Of course," I went on, "you wouldn't know what Auschwitz looked like."

His grin remained fixed, but he said: "That was such a long time ago."

At the sub-block, I ordered the prisoners away from the gate and opened the lock. One of the guards said in Hebrew, "They're crazy to go in there." Actually, they weren't: They were friends to the prisoners. Of course it was safe.

I saw this official a few more times. Finally, I brought up the subject of the Red Cross lending library. I told him I thought it clever to bring in Fanon and *The Flies*. But what about Gandhi and Martin Luther King, Jr.? Why not propagate the idea of revolutionary nonviolence, rather than just revolutionary violence?

Maybe it was a rock to the skull that did it, but my affection for

Malcolm X, for his "by any means necessary" prescription for political liberation, was waning, replaced by an appreciation for King and the moral power of passive resistance.

The man from the Red Cross said the books were simply screened for their cultural value, that was all. He was either dumb, or playing dumb. I guessed the latter.

When I visited Abu Hamza, the scholar Hamad suggested I see, I asked him about the Khazars. He smiled beatifically. "You're a Khazar," he said. "You're from America, right?"

"No, Canada," I lied. This was during the Gulf War, and we, the American-born soldiers, were instructed to call ourselves Canadian. Jack and I practiced saying "aboot," rather than "about." Not that the prisoners knew the difference.

"But your parents came from Europe," he went on.

"Grandparents," I replied.

"You are European by origin," he said.

"And before that," I answered, "Middle Eastern."

"This is not correct," he said.

I pointed to a passing soldier, olive-skinned, obviously Sephardic, physiognomically indistinguishable from the Palestinians in the prison.

"The European Jews stole the Jews of Arab countries and brought them here," he said. "This was all part of the Zionist plan. The Jews and Arabs in the Middle East had very good relations until the start of Zionism." This was true, so far as I knew. But what do you say to someone who says nonsensically that the Zionists "stole" Jews from the lands of the Arabs.

Abu Hamza's theory of Zionism was simple: It was a Talmud-based ideology of world Jewish domination. This is what he taught his young charges. He based much of his theology on a book called *The Disappearance of Israel: An Imperative of the Koran,* which was written several years earlier by an Islamic Jihad cleric named Assad Bayoud al-Tamimi, who argued that the Quran demands of Muslims that they "cleanse" Palestine of the infidel Jews in order to bring about Judgment Day and the submission of the entire world to Allah.

"Our debasement is temporary," he said. I asked him to explain. "The *umma*"—the world community of Muslims—"will return to power, and the Jews will pay the price. This is an abnormal state, today." What he meant, I gathered, was that, in the natural order of things, the Muslims would rule the Jews (and everyone else) and not the reverse, as it was in Ketziot. "Do you know the achievements of the Muslims? Do you know what Muslims have done in science and art? We were a great people. We invented algebra. We invented astronomy. We discovered the weight of the sun. It is God's truth. We discovered the secrets of the stars."

Once, Muslims led the world in science. But that was a long time ago. The few jihadists among the prisoners lived in a fog of fantasy. One day, the *shaweesh* Abu Bassam, who was something of a prankster, introduced me to a monkish-looking prisoner, bearded and unsmiling. Abu Bassam, a smile spreading across his face, asked the prisoner to tell me a story. "Tell him about the Gharqad tree," Abu Bassam said, laughing. The prisoner seemed annoyed at Abu Bassam, but went to his tent and came out with a book of *hadith*. The prisoner, whose name I never learned, said in perfectly colloquial Hebrew, "I'll have to translate this from Arabic. It might not be exactly right."

The saying—it was number 6,985 in the collection of *hadith* compiled by the ninth-century scholar al-Bukhari—tells the story of the evil Gharqad tree, which is known as the "tree of the Jews." The Day of Judgment will not arrive until the *umma* rises up against the treachery of the Jews, the prisoner explained. The Muslims, the Prophet promises, will have great success in their campaign against the Jews, in part because the Jews will find themselves friendless. The remaining Jews will seek shelter behind the rocks and trees, but even the rocks and trees will turn against the Jews, and call out to the Muslims, "Come, oh Muslims! Look behind me, there is a Jew hiding! Come and kill him! But only one tree will disobey God in the end. It is called the Gharqad tree, the tree of the Jews."

The prisoner asked me: "Do you know who Lubaid bin al-Asaam was?" I shook my head. "He was the Jewish magician who put a curse on the Prophet. The Jews tried to kill the Prophet three times. They put a curse on him, they tried to poison goat meat he was to eat, and they tried to kill him with rocks. It is all true."

Abu Bassam said, mischievously, "What do you think of that?"

I said I didn't believe that Islam was so hostile to my people.

The prisoner said severely, "The world will end badly for the Jews."

These Hamas men were infatuated with violence. I asked the prisoner if he ever thought it possible to negotiate a peace with Israel. He said, "Impossible. The solution is only war." He walked away.

Abu Bassam looked at me and said, "Crazy."

"Crazy," I agreed. I asked him where his Hamas friend learned such good Hebrew.

"He worked in Tel Aviv," Abu Bassam said. "At the Burger Ranch."

I didn't care to spend too much time with the Hamas men. They had no regard for what was true. In any case, they were marginal to the story. They would not be deciding the fate of Israel.

It would be people like Rafiq, I thought, who would be deciding our fate. This idea gave me hope, for a while, until the day he admitted that he would kill me if the need arose. This confession froze over the ground between us. It was my fault, I suppose, for even asking him the definitive kitbag question. He said it wouldn't be personal—my murder, that is—but that was no consolation. It was a punishing truth he told me, and though I assured him that I would not hold his answer against him, I did. He was speaking against my life, after all. A flood of unexpressed feelings surged through me as I left him in his cage that day. I felt as if I had been betrayed.

Jack Ross, my doubting friend, did not mock me when I finally told him of Rafiq's answer. But Jack did ask me what I expected from him. He told me of a conversation he had had not long before with one of the *shaweeshim,* Jawdat Ahmed, the smooth-faced, debonair Bethlehemite who spoke a fluent Hebrew. Jawdat could mimic the full range of Israeli mannerisms—no prisoner could sneer the way Jawdat sneered—and he was not a sycophant, in the manner of some of the *shaweeshim*. Before the Intifada, he worked at a Sheraton in Tel Aviv, and he would tell American Jewish girls on two-week holidays he was Israeli, and they would believe him. "I've fucked more Jewish girls than you have," he told me once, trying to stir up my blood. "We're circumcised, too. They can't tell the difference."

Jack told me that Jawdat had lectured him on the immutable reality of the prison. "He said, 'We watch you leave the block to go home on leave and then come back again. We can't leave. That's the difference. You have everything and we have nothing.' "

You must remember, Jack told me, that they have good reasons to hate us. Even Rafiq, he said. Every day you rattle the locks on his cage in order to keep him inside. You're kidding yourself, Jack said, if you believed that Rafiq didn't think these thoughts.

Jack said one other thing that brought me up short. Our prisoners—Rafiq included, he said—believe that we are fully capable of killing *them*.

I hadn't thought of that.

I kept my distance from Rafiq for a while. But I was too determined to keep up a dialogue to stay away for long. We would weather this crisis, not only because my curiosity demanded feeding, but for reasons that were delusional, utopian, and, most of all, sincere. I believed that if Rafiq and I couldn't talk through our differences then there was no hope for any of us.

I stopped by after breakfast one day. We spoke about small things for a while. Then I asked, Do you want peace?

Yes, he said.

So how can you contemplate murder?

I must have seemed doleful, because he said, "Don't worry."

Then I asked him the essential question. Would you accept a state in the West Bank and Gaza and be done with your struggle, or would Israel's departure from the occupied territories simply whet your appetite for all of Palestine? Would the giving, to borrow from Eliot, famish the craving? If the Arabs would settle for nothing less than the whole of Palestine, then my presence in Ketziot was justified; these were men who, given the chance, would obliterate the national project of the Jewish people. But if these prisoners were working simply to remove Israel's soldiers and settlers from the lands seized in 1967, then the entire Israeli response to the Intifada—the rubber bullets, the broken limbs, the creation of Revolutionary University, was a cruel mistake.

Rafiq said patiently: "I told you what I think. I believe that we should have two states next to each other."

But you can't make peace by killing me, I said.

"You're the ones with the guns," my prisoner said.

I chose to believe him. I chose to believe that the PLO's decision in 1988 to accept Israel's existence was not merely a feint toward the West. The Israeli right believed that the PLO, once given charge of the West Bank and Gaza, would quickly revert to the spirit of its charter, which is unambiguous on the question of territory: "The Arab Palestinian people, expressing themselves by the armed Palestinian revolution, reject all solutions which are substitutes for the total liberation of Palestine."

In 1974, the PLO adopted a policy that became known as the

"stages plan." Any territory acquired by the Palestinians would be used as a launching pad for the conquest of more territory. In other words, Palestinians would accept a state on the West Bank and Gaza, but only as a means to an end, the end being the destruction of Israel.

But I thought that the world was changing. I did not share the Israeli right's bleak understanding of Palestinian motivation. Nor did I quite believe the left's assertion that an Israeli withdrawal from the occupied territories would usher in the eternal Sabbath of the Messiah. But I tended to believe an independent state in Gaza and the West Bank would have a moderating effect on the more zealous inclinations of the Palestinians, rather than an exacerbating one. Finally they would have something to lose.

"We just want a state," Rafiq said. "We know we can't destroy Israel. We're realistic."

I knew he believed I had no right to live here. Like Hamad, he would mock my broken Hebrew, and my paleness. I would point out to him that his last name carries the strong suggestion of foreignness—a Hijazi is someone from the Hijaz, a province of Arabia. He would respond by noting, "Everyone's from somewhere else." But, he once added, "I'm more from here than you."

Still, like most of the prisoners, he did not live in the false world of Hamas. Most of the prisoners did not lose themselves to the temptations of recondite fantasy. The lunatic eschatology of the fundamentalists seemed outlandish to them, and peripheral to the educational mission of Ketziot, a trade school in the service of national independence and, perhaps—just perhaps—eventual coexistence.

CHAPTER ELEVEN

LET MY PEOPLE GO

One evening, I was in the guardhouse at the far end of Dizengoff when a *shaweesh* came to the fence and called me over. He said a prisoner needed to go to the infirmary. "Diarrhea," he said.

I told the *shaweesh* to bring out the prisoner. He went back to a tent and emerged a few moments later with four prisoners carrying the sick man, prone on his bed of slats. My guards readied themselves, aiming their rifles at the Arabs, and I opened the gate. The four men carried the bed out and rested it on the ground. I locked the gate behind them. The sick man was buried under a pile of frayed blankets. I ordered the four prisoners to strip off the covers so I could inspect the bed, make sure this wasn't a scheme to— I don't know what, but procedures are procedures. Off came the blankets.

I blurted out, "Oh." I heard a sharp intake of breath from one of my guards. The prisoner was a seraphic boy, fifteen years old or so, with a slight, almost emaciated body and pensive black eyes. The bare mattress beneath him was flecked with blood.

How old is he? I asked the *shaweesh*. Sixteen. I told the *shaweesh* to come with us, to be with him.

The four stretcher-men carried the boy across the compound to the small infirmary tent near the command block. The tent was badly lit, and supplied only with the most basic of equipment and medicine. The medic on duty, a soft-spoken Sephardic man of about forty-five, was a pharmacist in civilian life. The medic turned to me and said, in Hebrew, quietly, just above a whisper, "It's not diarrhea."

He asked the guards to remove the stretcher-bearers from the tent. They were returned to their pen. The medic turned to the *shaweesh* and said something in Arabic I could not understand. The *shaweesh* flushed red with anger. He muttered something evil about the medic, and asked me—it came out very nearly as an order—to return him to the sub-block. He stormed out, the guards trailing.

"What do we do about this?" I asked the medic.

"What is there to do?" he asked tiredly. "There's nothing to do. It's their problem. We can't stop it."

The medic gently moved the boy to his side, and pulled down his pajama-like pants. I did not look.

"It's not so bad," he said. "I'll give him some cream and let him rest."

One of my guards returned and told me that the *shaweesh* who so desperately wanted to leave the infirmary now had a change of mind, and wanted to talk. I left the infirmary to see him.

"We get diarrhea from the bad water the army brings in," the *shaweesh* said petulantly. "Send him back to us. We'll take care of him."

I told him that would not be possible at the moment. He asked: "Did he say anything?" Nothing, I said. I stressed that the boy said nothing.

I rushed back to the infirmary. The medic had found a change of clothes for the boy, and they were talking about something other than the boy's condition. We decided to keep the boy overnight in the infirmary.

I went to Efrati to explain the situation.

"He gets treatment, then he goes back to his block," he said.

This was immoral, of course, but what else could I expect from Efrati?

Jack Ross learned about this kind of terror before I did. One night he came back to our tent flabbergasted at what he had just seen. A guard had shouted down to him from a watchtower, "They just brought a boy into one of the bathrooms!" Jack went to the sub-block, called out the *shaweesh,* and ordered him to clear the latrine. Two men and a teenage prisoner came out and returned to their tents. Jack warned the *shaweesh*. He told him to make sure this sort of thing didn't happen again. Jack didn't call the thing by its name, but it was still a murderous business to accuse an Arab of such perversions. The *shaweesh,* in a fury, accused Jack of slandering Islam. We are Muslims, he said. Shame on you. Jack was firm: No more than one man in the latrine at a time.

Jack, an unambiguously decent man, was shaken. I was shocked.

We were not entirely new to the world, but I could not believe that the Palestinians would ever let this happen. For one thing, they were awesomely disciplined. Every moment of every day was organized. The smallest infractions, the quickest flash of individual selfishness, would lead to punishment.

Until this incident, I had been in an expansive mood. Rafiq and I were getting along again, and Efrati was riding other MPs for a change. But this evidence of rape sent me back to a persistent question: If this is what they do to their own people . . . I was a bleeding heart, true, but now I was anemic.

A few days after that terrible night, I was walking down Dizengoff when I saw the boy in his sub-block. He saw me as well and, uncharacteristic for a prisoner—especially such a junior prisoner—he addressed me directly and impudently. "What are you looking at?" he demanded to know.

I noticed that he had a black eye. I didn't address him directly (it would be, by prison protocol, beneath me). I demanded to see his *shaweesh*. The boy behaved rudely, I said. The next time, I would take him to solitary. The *shaweesh* apologized and said he would scold the boy. I walked away. Then it struck me: Was the boy, by challenging me, trying to get himself removed from the block? And who gave him the black eye? Do they think he talked? Do they think he ratted them out? I had tried to make sure the *shaweesh* thought otherwise.

I left that boy to fend for himself in a lion's den. But what was I supposed to do, put him in solitary for the rest of his sentence? Exchange cruelty for cruelty? Should I have gone to Yehuda, rather than Efrati? I could only imagine what his answer would have been: Let them fuck each other to death.

I thought of going to Rafiq, then I reminded myself that he was a prisoner with a heart full of secrets, not merely my friend. His loyalty was to Fatah, not to my precious morals. Then an opportunity presented itself. The Red Cross was coming to visit. I decided to swallow my contempt for them, just this once, and tell them of this horrid situation.

When the man from the Red Cross came, I told him I had to speak to him. He was curious, of course. As we walked the length of Dizengoff, I told him, quietly, in English, the problem: Teenage prisoners were being raped. I didn't know how many, how often, but I knew it was happening.

He smiled. "This is a serious accusation," he said.

It's not an accusation, I said. It's the truth.

He didn't believe me. I suppose he thought it was Zionist propaganda.

I pressed him, and he said, without acknowledging the existence of the problem, "Maybe the prisoners should be separated by age."

Okay, I said, but what about the Palestinians themselves? You know all their leaders, they listen to you. Can't you ask the faction leaders to protect these teenagers in the meantime?

He was dismissive. "The Palestinians are not in charge of the camp," he said. "It's not their responsibility." In any case, he said, he wasn't about to accuse the Palestinians of such crimes.

"This is not an issue for the Red Cross," he said, as we stood by the gate.

My final chance came at a meeting with Ze'ev Shaltiel, the colonel who commanded the entire prison. The session was meant to air the gripes of military policemen. There were thirty or forty of us present.

Shaltiel, tall and lean, stood in the front of the room. His uniform was immaculate. I sweated in his presence. I looked on him as the Demiurge of Ketziot, the architect of this whole stinking universe. He spoke about security for a few minutes, and then went on about the implications of the American victory in the Gulf War. Finally, he opened the room to questions.

The first question concerned the irregular schedule of the PX truck. The second question concerned bus service in and out of the prison. Then I raised my hand.

The Israeli army has the flattest hierarchy of any army in the world. It has the esprit of a true democratic army. After basic training, officers are called by their first names, and no one salutes. Corporals believe they could do a sergeant's job; sergeants know in their hearts that they could, if called upon, out-lead their lieutenants; and everyone is smarter than the generals. Self-criticism is embedded in the system and complaints are not meant to be swallowed. Except at Ketziot.

"I just wanted to say," I said, "that I think we have a problem with the way we treat the young prisoners." Eyes turned my way. "I think it's a violation of the Fourth Geneva Convention to mix in prisoners younger than eighteen with older men. So I was thinking that maybe we should separate out the young prisoners from the adults, in order to protect them." I went on for a while longer, until Shaltiel's eyes seemed to roll up in derision.

Perhaps it was my invocation of the Fourth Geneva Convention—no doubt the colonel heard quite enough about the Fourth Geneva Convention from the human rights groups—that prompted his reaction to my request. Perhaps it was simply the wrong forum. Or maybe I presented my case maladroitly. It was certainly ungrammatical. My Hebrew sentences were filled with rococo constructions born of linguistic inadequacy. I forgot the word for rape, which forced me to describe the gruesome act in the manner of a prudish Victorian. Or perhaps it was my accent: It was quite possible that the colonel did not appreciate a lecture from a self-righteous, American-born corporal. Yes, that was certainly it. If I were Shaltiel, I would find me loathsome, a self-deputized moralist from the rich, smug, superficial, Indian-exterminating but holier-than-thou hyperpower that underwrites Israel's existence to the everlasting resentment of the Israelis themselves.

When I finally ran out of wind, he said: "It's not our problem. This is something for the prisoners to deal with."

Next question.

I slunk out of that meeting with my recherché morality and with the sudden expectation that I was going to be shunned. One soldier of my acquaintance said within my earshot: "Can you believe he's a military policeman?"

I walked to my tent. The air was stale and close. I sat on the edge of my bunk, and thought, They deserve each other: the Palestinians, who let violence into every corner of their lives, and the Israelis, these Jews devoid of pity. Let them suffer together in the desert. "The sun knows when to set," the psalmist wrote, and I needed to know when to shut my mouth.

Soon afterward, I was traveling to Jerusalem on a two-day leave. I waited at a fly-blown crossroads outside the base, squatting on my haunches like a Bedouin, waiting for a jeep to pass. An artillery officer gave me a ride to Be'er Sheva, where I caught the bus to Jerusalem. I sat next to a young woman, maybe twenty, flagrantly American, blond, un-Semitically leggy. I dropped my kitbag in the aisle, and squeezed myself next to her.

"Why are you pointing that gun at me?" she asked in English. She was agitated. I looked down. My rifle was sitting between my legs, the barrel aimed at the ceiling. It was, I suppose, a distressingly phallic sight, but the rifle wasn't loaded and it was on safety. Israeli buses are filled with guns and soldiers. She was new here, I guessed. "I'm not aiming my gun at you," I said. "Don't worry."

"Why do you need that gun?" she asked.

"I'm in the army," I said.

"Does it make you feel safe? Do you feel better with it?"

All I wanted to do was sleep.

"I'm in the army. It's my equipment."

"Do you think it solves any problems?"

Oh, right, a missionary. A missionary of peace and reconciliation. She probably took an undergraduate seminar on "Palestine" taught, no doubt, by an Episcopal in a keffiyeh. She was morally certain, despite lacking all knowledge, or *because* she lacked all knowledge.

"Yes, it solves problems," I said. "It protects people from violence."

She clucked her tongue, and shook her head.

By a coincidence of monotheism, Passover came during the Muslim holy month of Ramadan. During Ramadan, day becomes night. Breakfast was served after dusk, and dinner before dawn; Islam forbids its followers to eat or drink during daylight for the entire month. And, because it was Passover, the prisoners would be eating matzoh for part of Ramadan. The Israeli army is a kosher army, and a kosher army does not bake leavened bread during Passover. So there would be no pita, just matzoh at midnight. Ramadan opened up new avenues of complaint for the prisoners. One of the *shaweeshim,* the nudnik Abu Bassam, griped to me one day about the absence of a Ramadan cannon in the prison. A Ramadan cannon is fired each day in Muslim cities to let people know when it is time to end fasting. I couldn't find the words to answer him. The matzoh, of course, was the source of great unhappiness, though the prisoners made do: They crumbled it into their beans, drenched it in tubs and ate it wet.

Rafiq asked me one morning, "Do Jews like matzoh?"

"No, of course not," I said.

"Oh," he said, relieved. "I was wondering. Because it doesn't taste very good."

It is slave bread, I told him, baked by the Jews in flight from Egypt. It is not meant to taste good. It is to remind us of our escape from slavery to freedom—right past here, where we were standing, as a matter of fact. We were a few miles from Kadesh-Barnea, where the Children of Israel had camped.

I could not go to Jerusalem for Passover—holiday passes were reserved for married men—but I did not want to go. I was a Bible-reader now, and I read it as Ijo, my Bible guide from the kibbutz, would have me read it, as the atlas of my people. It was a blessing to mark Passover in the shade of Kadesh-Barnea.

The seder, organized by the military rabbinate, was held in shifts, in the mess tent. A tablecloth was set and the Moroccan cooks prepared all sorts of dishes unknown to me, which was a fine thing. Sephardim did not share the main culinary tradition of Ashkenazim, which is to boil the flavor out of food.

I took a seat at a long table. I was alone, but surrounded by people. The seder consisted of hurried readings, empty of feeling. Ignoring the chanting, I read a bit of the Book of Exodus to myself. The first of the Ten Commandments: "I am the Lord your God, who has led you out of the land of Egypt, the house of bondage."

The house of bondage? Here we were, celebrating Jewish freedom in a prison filled with our Arab captives! We had built a prison and planted it right along the pathway of Jewish freedom, and we had filled its cages with Palestinians who were demanding only what Jews themselves demanded, in the time of the Exodus and today: freedom.

No! I would not think this way. This was not the house of bondage. Israel was not Egypt. These Palestinians were not slaves.

A seder in prison? What was I thinking? It would have been better to boycott Passover.

Deliveries were slow during the holiday, and the kitchen complained. So did the *shaweeshim*. One afternoon, one of them called me over to the wire. He was furious. I asked him what was wrong.

"This!" he said, and held out an orange.

"Look at this orange! It's dented. We're not going to eat these oranges!"

I burst out laughing. I told him we all ate the same fruit, guards and prisoners alike. All of the food came off the same trucks, I said, but you know that, don't you?

He said his block would launch a hunger strike. *"Tfaddal,"* I said, in Arabic. "As you wish." He said he would inform the Red Cross. I stopped him then. I asked him to imagine a different scenario. Picture an Arab prison, I said, filled with Israelis. Do you really think, I asked, that the Arab prison wardens would be feeding Jews fresh fruit, or even dented fruit?

Later that day, a reserve lieutenant in camp only a few days approached me. He was actually an ensign in the Naval Reserve. He was far from the sea, and he was moody when we first met. Now he told me that Hassan, from the kitchen, had complained to him about the fruit. The oranges were brown and—

I know, I know, I interrupted. The oranges. The prisoners and their ridiculous complaints.

The lieutenant inquired if there was a way for us to find them better oranges. He asked me if I knew when the next shipment would arrive. He saw the condition of the fruit—Hassan put it all on display for him—and he had to agree, the oranges were damaged during shipping.

I rearranged the expression on my face and said, Yes, sure, let me find out.

The next morning, I met the delivery truck. The driver told me he had no fruit aboard, just matzoh and eggs. He said he thought there would be a separate delivery of apples and bananas, though.

I thanked him. Then I watched as the kitchen crew came out to unload the truck. Under guard, one of the prisoners climbed into the back of the truck and began handing down unwieldy cartons of matzoh. The remaining prisoners heaved the boxes onto their backs. They made a line and walked back to the kitchen, their backs bent under the weight of the bread of affliction.

The Israeli poet Natan Alterman, who was once a man of the Zionist center but who moved right, to the Greater Land of Israel movement, in the years of psychological upheaval following Israel's success in the Six-Day War, wrote a poem shortly before he died called "Then Satan Said," which explained to me my loss of grace. Alterman placed a question in the mouth of Satan: "How do I overcome this besieged one?" The besieged one—a metaphor for Israel—possesses talent, courage, and the implements of war. Satan is flummoxed. But then, being the embodiment of deviousness, Satan settles on a clever course of action: "I'll dull his mind," Satan concludes, "and cause him to forget the justice of his cause."

Doubt, T. E. Lawrence once said, is "our modern crown of thorns," one which the Arabs—a people "of primary colors" given to a "hardness of belief"—refused to wear. Alterman, like Lawrence's Arabs, despised doubt. The modern Jew's spiritual unease, his guilt, the infinite shadings of his thoughts, these were manifestations of Satan. It was this Satan who caused Israelis, in Alterman's mind, to doubt the righteousness of endless expansion, of the moral necessity to subjugate the Arabs, who would do the same thing to the Jews, if they had the chance.

I read Alterman not as Alterman would have his poem be read. The devil's work on me wasn't done by the devil, but by something in this world: Ketziot was the Satan that was making me forget the justice of my cause.

On our last day, Jack and I went from cage to cage, bidding farewell to the prisoners we favored. I promised a few of them—Capucci, Hamad, and especially Rafiq—that one day we would meet without a screen of barbed wire between us. It had become a compulsion for me. I wanted to see them as equals, and I wanted to prove to myself and to the world that my better angels were correct when they told me it was possible to bridge the chasm between us. Hamad thought this idea, a jaunt to Tulkarem, was the stupidest idea he'd ever heard, and told me so. But he gave his consent nevertheless. Capucci's reaction was inscrutably formal: "You are most welcome." When I asked Rafiq for his address, which he gave willingly, I could not help myself, and so I asked the question again: If I present myself to you in the Jebalya Refugee Camp, will that be the end of me?

He laughed. I wished that I could have looked into his heart and seen our future.

I wished him well. He was scheduled to be set free later in the year. I told him I hoped for his early release. "I'll see you soon," I said.

Jack was not moved to maintain relationships with the prisoners. He could not understand why I would wish for Rafiq's early release. He sensibly asked, "What if he gets out early and kills someone?" I became defensive. "It's just something to say," I said. But this was not true. I did wish for Rafiq's speedy release. I did not wish for him to suffer, for his sake and mine. Rafiq was a carrier of my hope. If he's treated well, I thought, he'll treat me well, and then he will work for peace.

Jack was more levelheaded than I was. Don't forget, he said: We're their jailers and they're our enemy.

We returned our rifles to the weapons room. Efrati was prowling about. I ducked him. I had last spoken with him a few days before.

Apparently, my inept speech on the inalienable human rights of underage prisoners had depreciated his stock among the senior officers. He was my immediate commander, and it was his job to keep his charges quiet.

"Any other complaints?" he asked, the last time we spoke.

Jack and I dragged our kitbags through the block. We opened the gate, walked through and shut it behind us. We were free men in Zion.

CHAPTER TWELVE

IN THE VALLEYS OF JERUSALEM

ARAB EDITOR ARRESTED FOR ISSUING INFLAMMATORY POEMS. So read a headline in the March 17, 1991, issue of the *The Jerusalem Post*. According to the story, one Attalah Mahmud Najar, the editor of a monthly magazine in East Jerusalem, had been arrested for distributing "nationalist" poems on the Golan Heights, arrested by a government—a Jewish government!—that banned Palestinian prisoners from reading *Hamlet*.

By late 1991, I was back at work at the *Post*. I was writing the humor column for the newspaper's weekend magazine. This was not a terrific formula for happiness, service as a left-wing humor writer at an unfunny, revanchist newspaper. I was surrounded by rightists. Settlers staffed the copy desk; the editorial page editor, David Bar-Illan, would eventually become Bibi Netanyahu's spokesman; the television reviewer, an Orthodox misanthrope named Moshe Saperstein, was a Kahane sympathizer.

On the other hand, how could I fail, with the absurd occupation as fodder?

"The three young Palestinians steal out of the Nablus casbah at dusk, crawling behind walls to avoid the army patrols sent to enforce the curfew," began my column on the plight of poor Attalah Mahmud Najar. "The oldest, a thin, fiery-eyed student named Hamad, carries two Molotov cocktails and a ragged copy of the *Norton Anthology of English Literature* in a small rucksack thrown over his shoulder."

I would not claim that my humor column was humorous. But I wrote with my spleen, which can tell a joke.

The editor of the paper at the time was a Colonel Blimp of a Zionist, with a mission to launder the sins of the occupation in the pages of his formerly great newspaper. He allowed some give in the column ("Take as much rope as you want," he said, "and hang yourself with it"), but in the feature pages of the newspaper I was proscribed in my writing, allowed only the use of euphemistic language to describe irrefutable reality. The word "occupation" was banned; we did not "occupy" the West Bank and Gaza, we "administered" them. Palestinians who collaborated with the Israelis in administering the territories were not collaborators, but "cooperators." Because, you see, the word "collaborator" is—and this is the quite unfortunate ruination of a perfectly adequate word, my editor said—tainted forever by its association with Vichy France. And so if the Palestinians who cooperate with Israel are in fact *collaborating* with Israel, that would make them the Middle Eastern equivalent of Vichy, and if these "cooperators" are the equivalent of Vichy, then the people they work for would be . . . well, need I say more, young Goldberg?

After work, on the way to meet friends or on the way home, I would see Arabs in the streets of West Jerusalem, despite the Intifada. One afternoon, outside my apartment building on Emek Refaim, the Valley of the Ghosts, my street in West Jerusalem, an Arab worker was laying stone for a new walkway. Sweat was pouring off him. I went up three flights of stairs to my apartment, filled a glass with orange juice, brought it down, and gave it to him. "You must be hot," I said. He looked at the glass skeptically. But I said, Go on, drink. He drank, and handed me the glass. He went back to laying stone.

I was not meant to be called for reserve duty for a year, but the military police were short on men. I was called to my reserve base outside of Be'er Sheva. The clerk, a woman of twenty or so, still on national service, took out my file. She wore her grass-stained uniform trousers low on her hips, and her face was a lava field of acne. It is the army diet that does it to them: potato chips, French fries, and cheap chocolate.

She was an artist of bureaucratic indifference. I said I'd prefer not to go to Ketziot. She said she didn't care. But I was sent to the prison in Gaza City. We crossed the border between Gaza and Israel and joined a convoy moving toward the sea. I spent my time there trying to keep my gaze fixed on the streaked blue sky. I complained about nothing, and talked to no one. I made myself, in other words, into a *rosh katan,* a "small head." I sketched out a column while there about steps we could take to make the "administration" of Gaza and the West Bank a bit kinder and gentler: I proposed the creation of a government-sponsored beauty pageant called "The Miss Occupied Territories" contest, for one thing.

Things were not working. A melancholy realization was coming over me: I was not at home here. It was an awful thing to recognize, but it seemed true: I felt alienated and untethered. Israel was a hard place, filled with hard people. I knew in my heart that I was failing to transform myself into an Israeli, and there were moments when I no longer believed I should have this as my goal. The coarseness of life in Intifada Israel was sometimes too much for me to bear. My love for Israel was so bottomless that my disappointment with it was bottomless, too. This wasn't fair, I knew: Israel is a flawed place, with flawed people, just like everywhere else. But it is not so easy to shake off dreams of Utopia.

I decided to spend some time in America. This wasn't an overly unpleasant idea, because as fate would have it, I had a girlfriend there. I had met Pamela a couple of years earlier, when I was on an extended sojourn in Washington. I found myself, over time, and at a great distance, falling irretrievably in love with her, which had been a problem, because though she had a great many virtues, Zionist ardor was not one of them. Pamela had spent a year as a graduate student at the Hebrew University in Jerusalem, and she felt all the right things about Israel, but what she felt was not enough to propel her on *aliyah*.

This mattered to me a great deal when I first met her. It didn't matter quite so much now.

It was not as if America had replaced Israel as the Promised Land of my affections. I still had my doubts. It still seemed to be an unhealthy place for Jews and Judaism. Pamela, however, labored under the delusion that America was a golden land. I did not trust her on this point, but I was willing to investigate the claim.

In my last months in Israel, I spent a great deal of time walking in Jerusalem. It is the only place where loneliness doesn't bother me. On Shabbat I would rise early, pack a tomato, an onion, and a piece of bread, and set off to unravel the mystery of God's city. In Islam there is a concept called *tawhid,* which means the oneness of God. Islam holds that everything on earth, no matter how seemingly contradictory or dissonant, is actually part of a coherent pattern that is the design of the one Creator. Islam calls this hidden pattern the "unity of the real."

I was searching for patterns in my random walks in the valleys of Jerusalem. I wanted to identify the things that might bind us all together. Judaism, of course, planted the idea of God's oneness in Islam; our profession of faith includes the words, "The Lord is God, the Lord is one." Christianity, too, seeks the unity of man in the End of Days. But Jerusalem throws up discord in the path of the person seeking unity, because in Jerusalem the three monotheistic religions have been in frantic ecclesiastical competition since Judaism gave birth to Christianity two thousand years ago. This is a conclusion that is topographically, architecturally, and politically unavoidable to an explorer in the city.

The Dome of the Rock, for example, was built as a challenge to the Church of the Holy Sepulcher, the traditional site of the crucifixion of Jesus. The church's dome was made of silver; when the armies of Islam swept into Jerusalem, the new caliph demanded a superior dome for his new shrine, one made of gold. And he built his Dome on Mount Moriah, the Temple Mount, because of its association with the Jews. The interior walls of the Dome are covered in fine, soothing calligraphy, but the words are angry words, Quranic refutations of the idea of the Trinity, and of the virgin birth of Jesus. Just beneath the Dome of the Rock, along the eastern retaining wall of the Mount, is the Golden Gate, which is sealed shut with stone. Tradition has it that the Muslims, knowing that both Judaism and Christianity say the Messiah will enter Jerusalem through this gate, planted a cemetery before it to keep out the Messiah, who, it is said, will be a member of the priesthood, and priests are forbidden to touch corpses.

So much discord! But there are other stories about Jerusalem that reflect large and forgiving spirits. There is the legend that concerns the Ottoman Sultan Salim, who conquered the city in 1517. When he arrived, the Western Wall had disappeared under a mound of garbage. One day the sultan saw a Christian woman deposit a pile of dung on a heap. The sultan grew angry and asked the woman why she did this. It was an order from the bishops, she said—they paid women to dump dung on the place where the Temple of Israel once stood, so that it would be covered and forgotten. The Sultan threw gold coins onto the dung pile. The poor of the city swarmed over it, digging out the gold and leveling the heap. The Western Wall had been made clean again. There were times, in other words, when Jews and Muslims approached each other with respect.

The police kept the Temple Mount closed to non-Muslims through much of the Intifada, so it was my rare good luck that I found it open one day—good luck except that by some lights I was placing my soul in mortal danger. Jews are not supposed to walk atop the Mount. The Holy of Holies—the chamber in which the High Priest uttered the ineffable name of God each Yom Kippur—was buried somewhere under the surface, and it was thought sacrilegious to tread atop it. But curiosity won out. I went straight for the Dome of the Rock. It was dark and damp inside. The carpets were thick and smelled of socks. I approached the Rock itself, and I felt a shiver of delight. It is massive, forty feet long, and ten feet thick. Pilgrims circled it, praying softly. Jews call the rock the *Even Ha-Shtiyyah,* the Foundation Stone. It is on this rock that Abraham is said to have readied himself to sacrifice his son, Isaac, until God in His mercy stayed Abraham's hand.

I did not think that God inhabited the rock, just as I did not think He inhabited the Western Wall below. But I felt as if this rock was the place of my birth.

One day, I walked the Via Dolorosa to the Damascus Gate, and then made a wide loop around the eastern walls of the Old City, past the great eastern buttressing walls of the Temple Mount, down through the Valley of Kidron, past the Garden of Gethsemane, and up the Mount of Olives. The Intifada saw to it that there were no tourists. I preferred this side of the city, which falls away into the desert. I was lost in thought, and I walked into the Arab village of Silwan, the biblical Siloam, the ancient source of water for the city. Silwan was empty; it might even have been under curfew. It was dusk, and there was a Border Police patrol on the Mount of Olives, but I didn't stop to make inquiries. Silwan is built against a hill, and its streets are crooked and narrow. From above me I heard noises. A group of young boys appeared on a flat stone roof. I waved. They laughed, and began to stone me. One rock caught me on the back. I ran. The boys gave chase, and rocks smacked the walls around me. I made a breathless sprint out of Silwan—another rock whistled by my ear—and I kept running, through the Hinnom Valley. I turned. The boys were gone. I finally stopped running. The Hinnom Valley is actually a narrow ravine that follows the curve of the Old City walls. The Bible reports that it is where worshippers of the pagan god Moloch sacrificed their children in fire. The word "Hinnom" gave Hebrew its word for hell: Gehenna.

Shortly before I left Israel, I had lunch with the family that took me in after I abandoned the kibbutz. They lived in Mevasseret Zion, a town outside Jerusalem, and they let me make their home mine. They were boisterous, argumentative, scandalously blunt, and selfless—that is to say, Israelis—and they had definite notions about everything, including the way I should lead my life.

With some trepidation, I announced at lunch that I was taking a sabbatical from Israel. I was going to move back to America for a while, to see what it was like, work a little, save some money. In support of this cowardly and ideologically dubious decision, I told a tired joke: How do you become a millionaire in Israel? Come with a billion.

One of the men at the table, a relative of my friends, spoke up. He was the son of American Jews who had moved to Israel long before, and I think he resented them for it. He said, through clenched teeth: "Who asked you to come here, anyway?"

An uncustomary and discomfiting silence fell across the table. "I mean, no one asked you to come," he said. "So what does it matter if you stay or leave?"

And so I became an American again. I returned to America with only an army-issue prayer book, a graduate-level understanding of chicken management, and a box filled with twice-confiscated Palestinian flags—confiscated by me from the prisoners and then confiscated from the prison by me.

Pamela told me that America would be a fine place even for a Jew with my particular neuroses. I loved her, but I didn't believe her. I was ill at ease in America. Only in Israel did I feel American. At Ketziot I felt like Thomas Jefferson. But I had raised myself to believe that Israel was the only proper and safe place for a Jew, and this was not a belief easily shed. Metaphorically I was born on Mount Moriah. It took some time for me to realize that births don't happen in metaphors.

It was undeniably true that most Jews in America were happy and at ease. But they tended to be Jews without a sense of responsibility to the past. It was only possible for them to embrace the geographical accident of their birth because they didn't think about themselves in history and they didn't think about history's lessons for the Jews. I was history-ridden and unhappy, but Pamela, though not without a sense of history herself, told me to relax.

She gave good advice. For this and other reasons, I asked her to marry me. Under the *chuppah* the rabbi mentioned my devotion to the State of Israel. He did so because I asked him to mention it. Twice I asked him to mention it.

We lived in New York, which is sort of like living in Israel but without Arabs or quite as much yelling. We ate at Barney Greengrass, and walked past quite a few synagogues on Saturday mornings. I went to work for the *Forward,* a Jewish newspaper, which was a substitute for religious devotion, because journalism is next to godliness. I wrote about American Jewish groups and their leaders in a disparaging way, because they were so small compared to Israelis, who were flawed, but grandly flawed.

What I liked best was writing about anti-Semites. I believed a red river of anti-Semitism ran under the surface of America and I wanted to discover its source. I insensibly sought the company of skinheads, Ku Kluxers, and Nation of Islam ministers, including one who called me a hook nosed motherfucker and blamed the Jews for global warming.

A friend asked me if I wanted to go back to Israel. Was all this exposure to Jew hatred pushing me back to the Jewish state? I was ambivalent. But I did say that there were people I wanted to see, in Jerusalem and Tel Aviv—and Gaza as well.

Gaza?

In truth, I was not ready for Gaza, and Pamela graciously provided me a way to avoid it. She was working as a missionary of sorts—an exporter of the American creed of optimism—building democracies on inhospitable terrain in Africa. The United Nations was sending her to Liberia, and so I commuted for a while between New York and Monrovia. Liberia's problems were catastrophic, but they weren't personal to me, and it was a relief to think about something other than Israel.

Pamela traveled a great deal, and I followed. She was in Tanzania for its elections in the fall of 1995 and I met her there. I went to Dar es Salaam from Sudan by way of Nairobi. I landed at night and took a taxi to a shabby portside hotel. Pamela was just then negotiating some fine point of Tanzanian election law, so I went to sleep.

"Rabin's been assassinated," she said the next morning as she shook me awake.

It seemed impossible. Rabin, dead? Yes, murdered by a Jew, not by the Arabs.

I went to the lobby. CNN was broadcasting live from Jerusalem. Rabin's body, the reporter said, would lie in state at the Knesset. I stayed planted in front of the television in this flea-filled hotel in a city of no Jews. A line of Israelis, stretching for miles, it seemed, waited to pass by Rabin's bier.

In 1987, at the outset of the Intifada, Rabin was serving as the minister of defense, and he famously ordered his soldiers to "break the arms and legs" of the Palestinians. His statement released the golems of occupation. But he was a changed man when he died. In 1993, he saw a way to break the code of the conflict, and he overcame, at least in part, the revulsion he felt toward Arafat. He was, when he was murdered, trying to lead his people to the Promised Land, and the Palestinians as well. He died giving birth to an independent Palestine. The people of Israel were with him in the end; not enough of them, but still a majority. Six years of Intifada had convinced Israelis of the futility of occupation.

There were three seats in the pantheon of Jewish national redemption. The first was claimed by Herzl, who had the dream, and the second was taken by Ben-Gurion, who made the dream concrete. The third seat was still empty, awaiting the leader who would bring lasting peace to the Jewish nation. Rabin should have been in that seat.

I watched again, a day later, as he was buried. The hotel had moved extra chairs around the television, and Tanzanian Muslims watched with me, silent and impassive as Rabin was buried. I felt then that I should go to Israel, but I had other business.

I flew to Entebbe a couple of days later. I was on my way to Rwanda, but I arranged a tour of the old airport, where the Jewish hostages were held in 1976. The terminal building, in which the Jews were corraled, was decomposing in the wet Ugandan heat. I climbed the stairs of the abandoned control tower. "Shlomo and Motti Were Here, 2/7/88," the wall read. I was not the only Jew to have had this idea. The windows of the control tower were smashed, the equipment long ago looted. I stepped out onto the balcony from which a Ugandan soldier is said to have fired down on the tarmac, killing Yoni Netanyahu. Then I went out to the spot where I thought he was struck down. I placed a small stone on the ground as a memorial. On the outside wall of the terminal there was another line of Hebrew graffiti: "We have returned."

For the first time in a long time, I was reminded that great things had once been done by men wearing the uniform of the Israeli army.

CHAPTER THIRTEEN

THE PAST IS THE PAST

On July 30, 1997, at one-fifteen in the afternoon, two men dressed in the black wool clothing of Hasidim walked into the main open-air market of Jewish West Jerusalem. They breached the checkpoint of the Border Police, walked another one hundred feet or so, and stopped. They looked at each other. Then the first man detonated his bomb—ten kilograms of TNT—which he carried in an attaché case. The case was filled with nails. Terrible screams could be heard. Bodies lay on the ground. People ran. Many ran in the direction of the second bomber. As they came close, he, too, blew himself up.

The sound made by the two blasts could be heard in downtown Jerusalem. I was close by. The police were entering the market as I arrived. They had not yet sealed it off.

I took an inventory. Scattered all about were bones stripped of flesh. A policeman covered body parts with a sheet. Broken ripe watermelons drew in clouds of flies. Blood and brain matter covered the stone walls. The ground was wet with spilled hummus and baba ghanoush.

Sirens screamed. The wounded lay still. An old woman, a Russian, sat on a curb, attended to by paramedics. Her heavy legs were cut. She rocked back and forth. A police officer held her hand.

The suicide bombers had murdered fifteen people. The next day's newspapers would carry stories, as they often did, about miracles of escape and survival, but that would be tomorrow.

The marketplace, which is called Mahane Yehuda, is run by Sephardic men of harsh and simple politics. They are all Likud voters, except for those who find the Likud too soft on the question of the Arabs. Labor Party politicians no longer ventured inside, to avoid the humiliation of thrown vegetables and shouted imprecations. The stall men cursed Yitzhak Rabin when he had visited.

A chant went up, *"Mavet l'Aravim, mavet l'Aravim!"*—"Death to the Arabs." These brown-skinned men could pass for Arab in any city in the world, just as Yigal Amir, the Yemeni assassin of Rabin, could have passed for Arab.

The furies were loosed. One of the men cried as he screamed. I went to him.

"I can't live anymore," he said.

Some of these same men demanding the murder of Arabs employ Palestinians to move boxes and chop vegetables. One young Arab jumped out from behind a cart and made a dash for a clutch of policemen. It is a rare event, a Palestinian seeking the protection of the Israeli police.

Soon the Orthodox men of the burial society arrived to make sure that every bit of dead flesh be given a Jewish burial, preferably with the body that surrendered it. These men started near the points of detonation, where the ground had been charred. First, they collected the larger body parts. Then they gathered up the viscera. The police had covered the bodies of the dead; white sheets for the victims, yellow for the presumed bombers. The lips of the burial society men were moving, saying prayers as they went about their work.

The marketplace was swarming now with soldiers, policemen, shopkeepers, and paramedics. Israelis are resolute in crisis, but they are not quiet, and the market rang with screaming and yelling. Reporters, foraging for quotations, pushed past the police line. I was a police reporter myself, once; I wasn't above invading an innocent person's privacy. But I was a bit stunned myself. An old Orthodox American man wandered by in search of his two grandsons, who had disappeared in the chaos. A television reporter for an American network stood in front of a cluster of sheeted bodies. He ran a comb through his beard. "Another tragic day in the Holy Land," he intoned, when his cameraman gave him the high sign.

The politicians massed. A right-wing Knesset member named Rehavam Ze'evi, the leader of the Moledet Party, the Homeland Party, gathered reporters around him. He was not soft on the Arabs. He desired their "transfer" from Israel, to points east. He was once a general, most famous for keeping two lions in a cage at his headquarters, and for banning the singing of the song "Shir LaShalom," the Song of Peace, in his encampments. It was a defeatist song, he said. Ze'evi was known by the nickname "Gandhi," but not for political reasons; he was said to have been an emaciated-looking infantryman.

"This," he said, acidly, pointing to the half- and quarter-corpses underneath the sheets, "is security cooperation."

The Oslo peace process was four years old, and it had provided the Middle East with a new political lexicon. Chief among the new terms was "security cooperation," which meant, in effect, that the Palestinian Authority of Yasser Arafat would cleanse itself of terrorists, with Israel's help.

Reporters asked Gandhi to repeat himself, in English this time, for the international news channels. "I won't speak English!" he said. "We are in the Jewish land! I will only speak the Jewish language!"

An Israeli reporter asked him, "What should be done?"

"We should take Arafat and send him express mail back to Tunis," he said.

A man from the prime minister's office came to the market: He wanted to see if it was safe—politically safe—for Bibi, Benjamin Netanyahu, to make an appearance. Bibi, the brother of Yoni, was prime minister now. I was standing near the police chief of Jerusalem when he told Bibi's man, "Not now. They want to kill someone." (A few days later, when Leah Rabin, the widow of Yitzhak, came to pay her respects, she was chased out of the market by men screaming "Daughter of a whore!")

The word spread through the media pack: The Izzedine al-Qassem Brigades of Hamas had just claimed responsibility for the bombing. The bombers would later be identified as Saad Sadeq al-Till and Majed al-Qaisiya, who were natives of the village of Dahariya, near the prison of the same name.

The goal of Hamas was to derail the peace process, but an English reporter asked me, when we heard of the Hamas claim: "What are they retaliating for?" His assumption, of course, was that the Israelis had struck first.

I had arrived in Israel a couple of weeks earlier, on assignment for *The New York Times Magazine*. My editors suggested I write about the Palestinian police. I knew that one day I would return to Gaza to look for Rafiq. But I wasn't quite ready, in 1997, to find him. I still believed there was a chance I could be killed in my search. Pamela had recently given birth to our first child, and it didn't seem wise to test Rafiq's commitment to the faltering promise of the Oslo peace accords. But I thought I could travel safely in the occupied territories—they weren't *that* small, after all. They held more than two million Palestinians. I didn't think it likely that I would run into an ex-prisoner, even though the veterans of Ketziot could surely be found in the ranks of the Palestinian security services.

Jack Ross, my friend from the prison, thought I should be more cautious. Jack and I lived near each other now in Washington, D.C. He was a student at the American University Law School, which was located a few blocks from my house. One day, before I left for Israel, Jack telephoned: "I saw one of our prisoners," he said, breathlessly. "I'm sure it was one of the prisoners." Jack tended to cultivate what the writer Norman Manea called the "Judaic taste for catastrophe." I told Jack he couldn't be right. When I mentioned that I would be spending time with the Palestinian secret police, Jack said I was losing my head. Our prisoners were free now and armed, he said. Only a fool would go near them.

But things were different, I argued. The Intifada had ended in 1993 with the signing of the Oslo accords. The Palestinians didn't believe they could expel Israel from the occupied territories by force. So they had adopted, for the first time in their national life, a realistic goal: the establishment of a state next to Israel rather than in place of Israel. They were no longer a tribe; they had a government with a flag, a foreign policy, and a publicly stated commitment to the idea of peace.

Jack spoke to me gently, the way one speaks to the delusional. "I'm not sure it's over yet," he said. This was undeniably true. The peace process was in trouble. It did, however, exist, and that to me was the important thing.

The most important thing of all, however, was that Ketziot was now closed. The army emptied it of prisoners after Oslo, and plowed it under, into the desert. How could this one fact alone not provoke feelings of hope? The only shame of Oslo was the shame of waiting. Six years of Intifada could have been avoided—Ketziot need never have been built—if Israel had conceded to the Palestinians in 1987 what it conceded to them in 1993.

I told Jack I wasn't stupid. It was not that I liked Yasser Arafat—any Jew who was charmed by Arafat was too much of a fool even for me—but he seemed ready to concede the necessary things in order to bring about a state for his people. But the crucial thing was that the momentum toward peace seemed unstoppable, which is why Yigal Amir murdered Yitzhak Rabin, and why Hamas was murdering Israelis—the extremists on both sides knew that history was breaking against them.

The media swarmed now, and I saw friends I hadn't seen in several years. We caught up with each other as the bodies were carried from the market. A *Jerusalem Post* reporter asked me where I was staying.

The American Colony, I said.

A look of disgust spread across her face. "The American Colony?" she asked. "But it's so *goyishe*."

"Goyishe?"

"It's for the Arabs," she said. "That's where the BBC stays. It's not even kosher. You should stay at a Jewish hotel."

Ah, no! I did not come back to Israel to hide among the Jews. I wanted to attach myself to a different tribe now, the tribe of reporters, and the American Colony was my tribe's home.

I couldn't bring myself to stay at one of the ugly stone-pile hotels of West Jerusalem. It was a new age, and what did it matter that the Colony was filled with Arabs, English reporters, and French television personalities wearing keffiyahs, and that each morning the hotel's demure waiters, Christian Arabs, most of them, set out at the breakfast buffet a huge pink ham with the bone in? The American Colony was such a beautiful hotel, a study in grace—its lovely old buildings, built as if for a pasha, its fragrant gardens, the discreet clerks who guarded the front desk in the lobby of cool, polished stone, the intimate, blue-tiled courtyard, the scene of secret assignations, political and libidinal, among foreign correspondents, freedom-fighters, and spies, shielded from the honking chaos of Jerusalem by high stone walls that were covered in flowers.

When I checked in, I hadn't had any experience with this new Middle East. I was a veteran of the old Middle East, the one segregated by barbed wire.

"Jeffrey *Goldberg*," I said, to the black-eyed woman at the front desk. She smiled and gave me a glass of fruit juice and the key to my room.

The aesthetic of the American Colony was perfectly calibrated to appeal to the fantasy life of the Western reporter in search of Eastern exoticism. There was a whiff of danger in the air, but just a whiff.

The night of the bombing, I met a friend at the bar of the American Colony, someone I knew from Africa. My colleagues were in a state of exhilaration, transported there by the day's story, by the knowledge that the night's newscasts, and the next day's papers, would lead with their stories. It was not only professional exhilaration. Proximity to violence is an unsurpassed stimulant.

The conversation did not dwell on the blood and gore. I was surprised at the speed with which the conversation turned to matters of geopolitics.

"Bibi's going to use this as another excuse," one reporter said, referring to Binjamin Netanyahu, the prime minister.

"The crackdown is going to be vicious," said another.

It seemed a feat of emotional detachment to work the conversation around so quickly to politics when the dead had not yet been buried. I didn't say anything, though. I had not paid sufficient attention to the peace process, and these reporters were streets ahead of me in knowledge and understanding. Besides, one wants to fit in with the tribe.

My colleagues seemed of one mind: Israel had brought this bombing on itself. Of course, Netanyahu was never popular with the international press. A few months earlier, he had announced the construction of a new Israeli neighborhood on a hill—Har Homa, it was called—just south of Jerusalem, on the West Bank. And a few months before that, Netanyahu ordered the opening of a tunnel in the Old City of Jerusalem that ran parallel to the Temple Mount, from the base of the Western Wall to the Christian Quarter. The Palestinians rioted, and during the course of a week, fifty-nine Palestinians and fourteen Israelis were killed. Palestinian leaders claimed that the tunnel's purpose was to undermine the foundation of the Dome of the Rock, and the al-Aksa mosque, both of which sit atop the Mount. So Netanyahu was seen as a provocateur, and a recalcitrant nationalist. His incessant demands for a crackdown were straining the Palestinian Authority to the point of collapse. The Palestinians could not shut down Hamas, one reporter explained, until Israel gave up more territory to the Palestinians. Otherwise Arafat stood the risk of looking like an Israeli puppet, and that, it was said, with sympathy, he would not do.

The next morning, I woke early and took a taxi to Jericho. I had an appointment with the chief of the Palestinian Preventative Security Service on the West Bank, Jibril Rajoub. His agency was said to be the largest of the twelve Palestinian security agencies and was staffed by "insiders"—Palestinians from the West Bank and Gaza, rather than from Tunis and the Diaspora. Rajoub had spent seventeen of his forty-four years in Israeli prisons. He did not serve in Ketziot during my time there, but his presence was felt: It was his translation of Menachem Begin's memoir, *The Revolt,* that was required reading among the prisoners. I was keen to talk to him about the Irgun, the 1948 war, and his time in prison. This is the way I would edge closer to my ultimate goal—to find Rafiq and make our own peace treaty.

It was an inauspicious time to meet Rajoub. The Israeli army had sealed off the West Bank and Gaza in the minutes after the Mahane Yehuda bombing, and the Palestinians were locked down inside their cities. But I found a taxi driver named Mustafa Nabulsi who knew the back roads. He said he would get me there and back. I trusted him. What else could I do?

Mustafa wound his way from the Colony to the Mount of Olives. Then he skirted the Arab town of Abu Dis, and took a dirt road to avoid an Israeli checkpoint. We made it past the enormous Jewish settlement of Ma'ale Adumim, and into the white desert. We dropped below sea level. The Dead Sea glimmered in the valley below. The mountains of Jordan were visible in the distance. Had we kept going straight we would have arrived at the Allenby Bridge, and Jordan, but we turned north, to, as it were, Palestine. Jericho was the first city to come under Arafat's control, in 1994. It was safe for Israel to hand over Jericho first because nothing ever happens there.

Despite the closure, it was still possible to enter the sealed cities of the West Bank, but on foot. Mustafa took me to the Israeli army barrier, and I walked the short distance to a makeshift Palestinian checkpoint. There, men with guns stood under a pole flying the Palestinian flag. The last time I was in Israel, it was illegal to fly this flag. And a Palestinian man holding a rifle would be shot and killed. Here, on the Jericho side, these men represented the law.

The Palestinian policemen arranged a taxi for me to Rajoub's headquarters, which was a five-minute drive away. His headquarters, a series of low, sand-colored buildings, shimmered in the heat as we approached.

A few years earlier, this run-down collection of buildings had served Israel as a police station; twenty-five years before that, it housed the Jordanian army; before that, it belonged to the British. Palestinian policemen walked singly, or in pairs, up the road. I ducked down low in the front seat. I was certain someone would recognize me.

Two policemen met me at the gate, and shooed my taxi away. They escorted me to Rajoub, who was seated heavily behind his desk. He didn't rise to greet me. He was mostly bald, thick-faced, and pallid with fatigue, and he was wearing a black mustache. He was dressed in the Israeli style, a white, buttoned shirt underneath a dark jacket, and no tie.

Rajoub was guarded by plainclothes officers, who appeared as spent as he did. He offered a limp handshake, and a seat. The office was decorated almost entirely in black, in what could be called the Levantine Guccione style. The desk was covered in black lacquer, the black display cases held mounted revolvers, and the walls were carpeted in black and gray. On his desk there was a nameplate from the Peres Institute for Peace.

Even on a good day, Rajoub was said to be a forbidding presence, a cold man whose primary method of persuasion was intimidation.

"I am under pressure, pressure, pressure," he said, speaking in a slow rasp. He rubbed his face with both hands. There was an air conditioner in the room, struggling to counter the deathly Jericho heat. "The Israelis are making a stupid mistake with this closure. This is collective punishment."

The Israelis believed that the bombers came from the zone under his control, and their assumption made him bitter. "They treat us like terrorists," he said, "but I am acting day and night to stop the planning of violence."

Rajoub had indeed stayed up all night, in Jerusalem, meeting his counterparts from the Shabak. They spent most of the time swapping accusations. The Israelis had presented Rajoub with a list of 150 Hamas men they wanted arrested. Rajoub belittled the Israeli demand. "We can't arrest hundreds of people without cause," he told his Israeli counterparts. "We aren't going to make arrests without specific information. We are not going to go to war against Hamas."

This, of course, was exactly what Israel demanded. "I am not working for the Israelis. I am not receiving instructions from the Israelis. I am working for my people. The Israelis are making a stupid mistake by telling me to arrest people blindly. We are not the police state the Israelis want us to be."

I asked him if he feared looking like a collaborator. His eyes narrowed to gun slits, and he leaned across his desk.

"Excuse me, excuse me," he said. "I am a godfather of the armed struggle. I am PLO! We were the armed struggle before there was Hamas or Islamic Jihad. Do not forget this!"

But Rajoub then switched course. He called the peace process irreversible. He said his people were shedding the culture of violence for the culture of peace. "I never believed we would win the armed struggle," he said. "We did not fight in order to destroy Israel. We did not use this slogan the Israelis say we use, that we are going to throw the Jews into the sea. We did fight for the sake of achieving international recognition for the existence of the Palestinian people. And as soon as we achieved this target, we terminated the armed struggle immediately."

Rajoub turned on the radio. It was eleven a.m., and the news from the Voice of Israel radio station was preoccupied with the aftermath of the bombing: the names of the victims, the schedule of funerals. When Rajoub lowered the volume, I suggested that Israelis might not care much right now about his national aspirations; they would be more interested to know that he was ready to cooperate in the dismantling of the terror networks.

"Please don't use this word with me," he said.

"Which word?"

" 'Cooperate.' This is a dirty word in Palestinian society."

Rajoub said he preferred the word "coordination."

"Cooperation is *mashtap*," he said, using the Hebrew acronym that means "collaborator." The Shabak uses the term to refer to its Palestinian informers.

I behaved as if these words were new to me. I had decided before the meeting that I would speak to Rajoub only in English, and that I would edit my past, should the subject arise.

"I will not give Palestinians to the Israelis," he said. "This will never happen."

Rajoub was in a more complicated spot than I knew. I only learned later that the Israelis were asking him to hand over his own brother, Nayef, the imam of a town called Dura, near Hebron. Nayef was a leader of Hamas in the southern West Bank, and he was the source of endless suffering for his brother. I met him once. He was a cold man, knife-thin, with brown, cracked hands. He seemed serene; he carried himself in the aloof manner I associated with that archetype of Islamic piety, the blind cleric. Nayef was a scholar of Islamic law, *shari'a* (he took his degree from the University of Jordan), and he found no theological fault in the suicide attacks at Mahane Yehuda or anywhere else. "The Israeli occupation has deprived the Palestinians of the right to act according to the principles of Islam," he said. "We are existing in circumstances outside the usual strictures of Islamic law."

Your brother Jibril doesn't think so, I told him. "He knows that the peace process is an abortion," Nayef said. "He uses words like 'stranded,' 'dead-ended,' which is his euphemistic language. I know what Jibril thinks. I know he will do what is right for the Palestinian people."

Jibril Rajoub was peevish when I mentioned Nayef's views to him. "I am not my brother's spokesman," he said. Nayef, he said, was wrong: "We cannot remove Israel from the world. We must make peace with it."

Here it was, then, the entire crisis reduced to an argument between two brothers. I let the mask of detachment slip free for a moment and said, "I hope you win."

"What?" he asked disagreeably.

I stuttered, "I mean, I hope the people are with you, not with your brother."

"Of course they are," he said.

Rajoub was tired of the subject, so I turned to Begin's memoir, *The Revolt*. Rajoub was said to be proud of his jailhouse translation. He worked on *The Revolt* together with his cellmate, Sameh Kenan, for over a year. "We wanted to be very accurate," he said. Kenan and Rajoub stayed together in freedom; Kenan was one of Rajoub's deputies in Preventative Security. "The friends you make in prison are your friends for life," Rajoub said.

I asked Rajoub what he learned from Begin's primer. "I learned that there is no compromise in true Zionism." Zionism, he said, is imperialism and imperialism means expansion. Begin and his mentor, Jabotinsky, did not hide their goals, in the manner of the labor Zionists. "They were very straight about what they wanted," Rajoub said.

Is this still true? I asked. "All Zionists have the same dreams, but some know they have to put off their dreams."

The Revolt taught Rajoub more than the nature of unsheathed Zionism, he said. It taught him that the Jews were the real terrorists of the Middle East. "Begin makes excuses for the acts of the Irgun, but you can tell he was not sorry."

The Revolt is an angrily self-exonerating book. Begin oversells the role played by the Irgun in the Jewish struggle, and at the same time, he understates the horrors of the terrorism committed in his name. Rajoub said he found Begin to be a hateful character—"I would not accept his apologies"—but he acknowledges the superior motivation and organization of the underground Irgun army. Reading *The Revolt*,

Rajoub said, was a revelation. For one thing, he said, Begin viewed the British in much the same way the Palestinians view the Jews today.

"Here," he said, reaching behind him for a copy of the book. He thumbed through the pages. "A British officer, who was Irish, and who was on the side of the Jews, once told Begin and his officers to remember that the English don't like to be killed. This is very true of the Jews today. They will do anything not to be killed. Maybe it was different just after the Shoah." He used, I noticed, the Hebrew word for the Holocaust. "But today, Begin would be very depressed to see how the Jews don't believe there is anything to sacrifice for. It is easy to kill people with sniper rifles or remote-control bombs, but it is our people who have the motivation."

He thumbed forward. "Begin was excellent at planning. Go and read the chapter he wrote on the bombing of the King David Hotel," he said, and paused. "And the Israelis call us terrorists! Their own people blew up a hotel! They even killed Jews."

My memory was incomplete, but I told Rajoub I thought the Irgun behaved in a more considerate manner than one would have expected of a terrorist group. Didn't they telephone the British and warn them of the bombs, in order to give them time to evacuate the hotel?

"Ha!" Rajoub said. "You are calling the murderer of Deir Yassin a humanitarian?"

Begin, Rajoub said, did not ever apologize for his actions. Not that Rajoub was rushing to repudiate his past, either. When I asked him if he regretted committing violence for the sake of independence, he demurred. The "armed struggle," he said, was a "practical means to achieve our national aspirations."

He did not excel in terrorism. Unlike his deputy, Sameh Kenan, who took part in a successful bombing campaign of Israeli supermarkets, Rajoub was arrested by the Israelis before he could do any sustained damage. He was a teenager in 1969 when soldiers caught him throwing a grenade at an Israeli bus. He said it was a military bus, though news accounts at the time said otherwise. As it happened, the grenade did not explode. He went in and out of jail. He became an organizer of Fatah, in the Hebron Hills, and it was bureaucratic work that got him into more permanent trouble.

Rajoub earned his red badge in jail, not on the streets. He became, over time, a commander of Palestinians inside the prison system, leading hunger strikes in 1980 and 1984. He was released from prison in 1985, but sent back in 1986, when he spent six months in administrative detention. When he came out, Fatah found him a job at the Center for Arabic Studies, under the supervision of Faisal Husseini, the leading PLO figure in Jerusalem. Husseini and Rajoub fell out and Rajoub returned to Hebron. He became a leader of the first Intifada, and was expelled by Israel to Lebanon in 1988. He quickly made his way to Arafat's headquarters in Tunis. Arafat took to calling him the "dynamo" of the Intifada, for his long-distance leadership of the Uprising. "The Shabak was very surprised by the work I did," he said.

I could not tell if this was a purely nostalgic pride.

It was time to go. We walked outside. A platoon of uniformed policemen stood on the parade ground. Each man was equipped with a sidearm and an AK-47, a heavy piece of equipment for a policeman. One of Rajoub's aides, a jumpy man named Jibreen al-Bakri, came over. He was Rajoub's man in Hebron. Al-Bakri and I watched the policemen on parade. These men, he said, were ready to do battle. "We will fight them in a very dangerous way. In 1967, we were Arabs," he said, nearly spitting on the word as it exited his mouth. "Today, we are Palestinians. All of our people will fight."

This was a reminder of a line of graffiti I once saw in Belfast: "Only a defeated army gives up its guns."

I asked Rajoub for a lift back to Israeli-controlled territory. He called for his aide, who called for his driver, and the three of us got in a Land Rover. As we drove down the main road, the barrier became visible. Parked just over the line were two jeeps filled with Israeli border policemen. The driver said something to Rajoub's aide, and the two men laughed. My battered Arabic was insufficient to the task. I asked the aide to repeat the joke. He said the driver told him he was going to make like Mahane Yehuda and turn the Land Rover into a suicide bomb. The driver picked up speed, and picked up more speed, aiming himself right at the Israeli jeeps. He braked just a few yards from the barrier. Then he collapsed into laughter.

There was an absence of war, but this was not peace. Even on the Israeli side—the Israel of Oslo—I found devastating contradictions. In Ramallah, the de facto capital of the Palestinian West Bank, I saw a city encircled by Jewish settlements. A local Fatah leader, an ex-schoolteacher named Marwan Barghouti, drove me around. Ramallah sits a few miles north of Jerusalem and it was experiencing a haphazard but lucrative building boom. Moneyed Palestinians from America were building second homes on the slopes of the wadis, and the city was becoming a tangle of banks, high-rise hotels, and expensive restaurants. But it was the frayed edges of the city that interested Barghouti the most. He was a hectic, diminutive man with curly black hair and a thick black mustache who was mercilessly self-critical in a very un-Palestinian way. He was born in 1959, in a village outside Ramallah, and was a Fatah mainstay from adolescence. He was one of the founders of the Shebiba, the Fatah youth movement. He was also a graduate of Birzeit University, and a natural politician. He was a reformer on the Palestine Legislative Council, who spoke feelingly about the thieving Palestinian Authority; this gave him great credibility among Palestinians who expected enfranchisement from their new leadership but received nothing instead. He was also a favorite of the Israeli left, a prized interlocutor of liberal Knesset members. Even among right-wing skeptics of Oslo, Barghouti was a favorite. He spoke Hebrew fluently—he learned it, of course, in jail.

We drove to the city's main cemetery. Looming in the distance was a Jewish settlement called Psagot. "Every day they build," he said bitterly. "We know exactly how many new apartments they put in. Do you know how? Because it is our people who build them! Men from Ramallah are the construction workers. They are building their own tombs." We drove a few minutes more, and came to a settlement called Beit-El, which marks the place where, the Bible says, Jacob wrestled with God. Barghouti was fluent in Judaism, as well as Hebrew, and he said: "We're wrestling against Beit-El and we're losing." At the outset of the Oslo process, the Israelis promised the Palestinians control over their cities, which they gave, but they were leaving little room for expansion.

"The Israelis want to put us in bottles like cockroaches," he said. "If the Israelis don't understand that the Palestinians require all of the West Bank and Gaza as the payment for quiet, they will once again face stones and Molotov cocktails and worse. I want my Israeli friends—I have a lot of Israeli friends—I want my Israeli friends to live in peace and quiet. But they won't have their peace and quiet unless I get my peace and quiet. These settlers will take us back to war. But believe me, I'm committed to peace."

I asked Barghouti if we could drive into Beit-El. "If I came with my hammer and my bucket and a tomato for lunch, they would let me in," he said.

I, of course, had no trouble penetrating Beit-El's defenses. I had a friend there, someone I met on the kibbutz. He had become religious. This didn't surprise me—he was a lost boy when I met him, and lost boys in Israel have a tendency to stumble into Jerusalem yeshivas and emerge three years later with black hats, wild beards, pregnant wives, and revanchist ideas.

My friend had discarded everything connected to his former life—his Argentine girlfriend, his badly played guitar, his sense of humor. When we met, he was dressed in the settler style: jeans, brown sandals, a flannel shirt—untucked, to hide his pistol—and a broad white-knit kippah. He wanted no reminders of his dissolute past. He only wanted to speak of the glorious messianic future. "God meant for me to live on this land," he said. He also said the Arabs were going to find another place to live or accept their status as *ger toshav,* resident aliens, and live under Jewish suzerainty. This was a person who at one time in his life spent most of his waking hours smoking marijuana and listening to Jethro Tull. Now he acted as if he had been born circumcised. "We're the bosses of the land," he said.

A short walk from the American Colony stands a building called Orient House, which served as the unofficial headquarters of the Palestinian Authority in Jerusalem. The man in charge of Orient House was Faisal Husseini, who had been the PLO's representative in the holy city even when the PLO was, by Israeli law, thoroughly illegal.

I went to see Husseini in the hope that he could make sense of my disorderly thoughts. I hoped Husseini would be able to transcend the moment. What I was looking for, in Orient House and everywhere else, were signs that the time was right for me to find my prisoners.

Husseini's uncle was the pro-Nazi mufti of Jerusalem during the period of the British Mandate. But the mufti's nephew was a man of moderation, and he was a rare find in Jerusalem. The main industry of Jerusalem is prayer—the poet Yehuda Amichai once wrote that the sky over Jerusalem is polluted with prayer—and these are not generally the prayers of conciliation. "We're ready for peace," Husseini said. "What you're hearing is emotion and noise. No one wants to be disappointed. We are arguing for our rights, but we have to argue, because everything here is an argument."

We were experiencing now the "birth pangs of the Messiah," he said, borrowing a Jewish religious image. "The Messiah in this case is a lasting peace," he said. Don't pay much mind to poisoned words, he cautioned. "We can't go back." Then he told me a story.

"My father was killed leading the Palestinian fighters here in 1948," he said. "My mother didn't cry when he was killed. You know, forty years later, my son was beaten up by Israeli troops in Ramallah. He went to a demonstration. We spent hours cleaning up his face. He wasn't a boy any longer when he came home. I recognize what this war does to families. I know there are many Israelis who see the same thing. We need to find arrangements now, so that these things don't happen anymore. These are hard things, but they aren't impossible. We will have peace."

Husseini was eloquent and charming, but my attention was diverted by one of his bodyguards. He had been looking at me curiously since the moment of my arrival. He was a thick-chested, dark-skinned man of about thirty. I knew that he recognized me, because I recognized him. I couldn't remember his name, but he had been a prisoner in Block Four.

I decided, as the interview came to an end, to introduce myself. As Husseini stood, I turned to the bodyguard and said—in Hebrew—"Don't I know you?"

The guard looked at me. "Yes. Ansar Three."

I told him my name. He said, "I'm Nasser."

"Nasser! Right, Nasser," I said. "Block Four, 1991, right?"

"You were a guard," he said.

"No, a *shoter,*" I said, a military policeman.

We shook hands.

Husseini seemed flummoxed—just who had he been speaking to all this time? I explained everything. In the back of my mind, of course, I was plotting my escape.

Husseini listened, and then said: Interesting.

Nasser was more effusive. He invited me to his house, to meet his family, but I begged off. I wasn't ready for this.

A short time later, I bumped into Marwan Barghouti. He was returning from a "peace meeting"—that's what he called it. It was a gathering of liberal Israelis and Palestinian intellectuals, making their own peace in advance of actual peace.

I decided to tell Barghouti about Ketziot. I was feeling badly about Nasser.

"Do you think we're all killers?" Barghouti asked, laughing. "We don't care what people did in the past. We're not going back to the past."

I was flown with joy. Here was Marwan Barghouti, a compelling new sort of Palestinian, telling me to ignore my doubts and listen to my desires.

CHAPTER FOURTEEN

PEACE WITHOUT GUNS

I wanted to go find Rafiq, but I still couldn't quite straighten out my spine. I was traveling around the West Bank regularly; I even visited Gaza, twice. Both times, a press pass was my camouflage and my shield. Luck was with me, and I went unrecognized. I even interviewed Sheikh Yassin, the founder of Hamas, in his home. It is one thing to be exposed as a Zionist spy in East Jerusalem—I could run, if necessary, to West Jerusalem—but there was no place I could hide in Gaza City.

Something else was stopping me from looking for Rafiq. It was fear, but not the physical kind. I feared that Rafiq would want nothing to do with me. He had become in my mind a barometer of sorts, and so I worried about the consequences of a failed reconciliation. But I could procrastinate only so long.

On the morning of the day I set out to find Rafiq, I rose to the sound of the muezzin—a taped, tinny sounding muezzin—that breached the thick walls of the American Colony. The drive from Jerusalem to Gaza is short and downhill, but I wanted to finish my business in Gaza in daylight. I would need some time there. It had been eight years since I last saw Rafiq. He could be dead, or in jail. I knew nothing of his whereabouts.

A week earlier, I asked an acquaintance of mine in the Shabak if he could help me locate Rafiq. I have great faith in the long arm of the Shabak. I assumed the existence of a computer buried underneath the Shabak's secret headquarters that could spit out on demand the exact location of every armed Arab on earth. Perhaps it was easy, I suggested to the Shabak man. Perhaps Rafiq was still in jail. The depth of his crimes, like everything else about him, remained a mystery. He was a blank slate onto which I wrote my fondest wishes, but how could I know he was not a murderer? The Shabaknik, in the Jewish manner, answered my question with a question: Why the interest in this random Fatah terrorist?

We were friends once, I said.

My sincerity was not paid back in scorn. This was during the period of Oslo, after all. "I have friends who are Palestinian," he said. I showed him my address book: Hijazi, Rafiq, Jebalya Refugee Camp, Gaza. There are a hundred thousand people in Jebalya, the Shabak man said.

He came back to me a few days later; there was no Rafiq Hijazi from the Jebalya Refugee Camp currently residing in the Israeli penal system. Your man is free. Beyond that, I can't say.

"Can't say, or won't say?" I asked.

"Can't say, won't say," he answered.

Then he recommended against this adventure. "Leave the dough to the baker," he said. In his view I was insufficiently paranoid to navigate Gaza. Some Palestinians, he said, had not yet absorbed the message of Oslo. Yes, yes, I said, I don't understand the mentality of the Arabs.

But he was wrong about my paranoia. The proof was under the front seat: a 9mm semiautomatic Beretta. A friend of mine had lent me the pistol. He thought it was foolish of me to look for Rafiq, foolish even to cross the border into the sardine can of Gaza, so he pressed the pistol on me, just in case.

I wanted to make peace with Rafiq, but I might just shoot him instead.

My plan was simple: I would cross the border and meet up with a local reporter, a man named Saud Abu Ramadan. Saud would guide me through the Gaza labyrinth. We spoke on the telephone, and arranged to meet. I said nothing about the task at hand.

My mind drifted as I drove. What, exactly, would I say to Rafiq? How would I greet him? Would I say, *Salaam*? That would be a touch obsequious, but it's his home, after all. No, no. I would say, *Shalom*, as a subtle assertion of my own unblemished conscience. I would hate to give Rafiq the idea that I'd come to Gaza as a supplicant.

Perhaps I could just say, Hello.

I arrived at the Israeli side of the Erez checkpoint and parked in an immense, empty lot. I felt the Beretta. I would hide it in my knapsack. The Israelis, I knew, didn't search anyone going into Gaza. No one, after all, brought bombs *into* Gaza. The Palestinians generally didn't bother to search anyone at all.

I stood in the parking lot, a one-man palaver. Finally, the rebuking *shmutznik* in me won the argument. I opened the trunk, and hid the gun under a mat. The point of this exercise, after all, was to make peace without guns.

I locked the car and walked. The sun was already high. Erez is a fortress of cement and gun turrets. It is the bridge between Gaza and Israel, but it is in design and appearance an inapt metaphor for reconciliation, and it is saturated with foreboding. To one side, behind a high wall of concrete painted gun-metal gray, sat a complex of factories. A platoon of armored personnel carriers was parked opposite the wall.

As I approached, I could hear the clanging of machines in the industrial zone, but no human sounds. The only person visible was a soldier in a booth. He was wearing body armor, and sweat had pooled on his forehead. I waved my passport at him, and he allowed me through, to the checkpoint itself.

There were two ways to travel through Erez. The first was reserved for Palestinians. It was a cattle chute. Early in the morning, Palestinians, by the thousands, gathered at the Gaza side of the checkpoint and entered the chute, which was a series of switchbacks and holding pens, under a tin roof. The Palestinians—day laborers, all—were searched and their magnetic ID cards were swiped by soldiers in flak jackets. *Jibili' weya*—Give me your identity card—is one Arabic phrase known to every Israeli who has put on a uniform since 1967. Then the workers are launched out of the chute and into the waiting vans of their Tel Aviv employers. They return twelve hours later, exhausted, but their pockets filled with shekels. The shekel was still the currency of Gaza, which meant that even the men of the Palestine Islamic Jihad carried in their wallets pictures of Golda Meir.

Then there was the second way to enter Gaza. This was the "VIP" line. That's what the sign said, in English: "VIP." This passage is reserved for aid workers, U.N. officials, journalists, and Palestinians of sufficient rank. These eminent personages were shuttled into an air-conditioned trailer, where their travel documents were inspected efficiently by Israeli soldiers in flak jackets.

"Goldberg?" the soldier reading my passport said. "Jewish?"

"Yes," I said.

"You're going to Gaza?" he asked.

There was nowhere else to go from Erez.

"Yes," I said.

He looked at me strangely.

"Okay," he said.

He gave me a blue slip. I walked out the door. A car pulled up outside just then, a Mercedes with diplomatic plates. Two blond-headed men stepped inside the trailer as I stepped out. I walked to the final Israeli checkpoint, an octagonal concrete pillbox. As I approached, a hand emerged from a slit. I gave the hand my blue transit slip. Then I was allowed into the funnel.

The funnel is about half a kilometer in length, and the width of a two-lane road. The ground was covered with broken glass. Brown weeds pushed through the tar. On both sides of the funnel stood high concrete walls. There was no escape from the funnel. I started walking. I stuck to one side, keeping to a narrow strip of shade. In the distance, hanging limp, was the red, green, and black Palestinian flag. I felt the Pavlovian urge to confiscate it. I heard a car behind me. It was the Mercedes. Diplomats, unlike journalists, are allowed to take their cars into Gaza. The car slowed. The driver looked at me. Then he sped away, leaving me to walk. Swiss, probably.

Finally I came to the Palestinian checkpoint, which consisted of a single un-air-conditioned shack. It had window frames but no windows. There was a black-and-white notebook open on a rickety desk, and a portrait of Arafat on the wall. A single police officer sat behind the desk. He inspected my passport, and said, "Welcome to Palestine." I signed the book, and went outside.

Saud saw me before I saw him. He was tall, and exceedingly friendly. He clapped me on my back as if we knew each other. This made me unhappy. Somehow, I had taken inside me the gloom and suspicion of the funnel. He steered me to a taxi, and we drove south, to Gaza City. The road was covered with sand. Donkey carts slowed traffic. The Israeli army had painted yellow stripes down the middle of certain roads through Gaza. The stripes told Jews that they were traveling in the direction of an army base or a fortified settlement. If you lost the stripe, you'd lose your life. It happened from time to time; an Israeli driver made a wrong turn into a refugee camp, and never came home.

A few minutes south of Erez, we left the stripe.

"So what do you want to do today?" Saud asked.

He knew me as an American reporter, and I guessed he expected the usual menu of requests: a Hamas spokesman before lunch; then some refugees—photogenic, oppressed by settlers, English-speaking, if you don't mind—and then perhaps an aide to Arafat, who would explain to me the continuing perfidies of Israel, then back to Erez, and on to the American Colony by dinner. For this, Saud could expect $100, perhaps $150; I always paid $150 when I went on my day tours of Gaza. Television reporters paid $250, but their profligate budgets made bargaining unnecessary.

"Actually," I said, taking the leap, "I'm looking for someone I knew in Ketziot." Then I told him the story.

When I finished, he smiled. "I was in Ketziot, too," he said.

He had served six months, in 1988, at the outset of the Intifada. He was a propagandist, a leaflet-writer. He was betrayed by a collaborator and he was placed under administrative detention. He never, he said, did violence to anyone. He was a man of peace. "Like you," he said hopefully.

Saud decided that our first stop should be the offices of the Society of Former Prisoners. The group is known by its Arabic acronym, Hussam. It is a group of wide influence. There are at least fifty thousand men in Gaza who are veterans of Israel's Intifada-era prisons. We drove in the direction of the sea. Hussam's offices were located in a two-story villa, within view of the water. The air smelled of salt and wet heat.

I followed Saud inside the villa. A group of men were sitting on benches. Saud explained our mission. They approved, and let me upstairs, to see the director. We walked into the director's office. I looked at the man behind the desk. Then I blurted out: "You're the guy who escaped."

Standing before us was Rafiq Hamdouna. He was a legend, one of the few men ever to escape from Ketziot. He had longish hair, impressive jowls, and a hawkish nose. In photographs, he was thinner, and dressed in simple clothing. Now he was wearing Italian loafers and a double-breasted sports coat. Heroism has its rewards.

He was pleased to be recognized. We sat, and drank coffee. Hamdouna said, "Would you like to speak Hebrew?"

His Hebrew was fluid, sophisticated, his vocabulary greater than mine. I asked him several times to slow down. He described for me, without prompting, the escape. It was not overly complex; unlocked gates certainly expedited the process.

Two of the escapees reached Egypt and freedom. Hamdouna did not. He spent the rest of the Intifada intensively guarded. "I always think this could be a movie. Don't you think so?" he asked. Certainly, I said.

Now what can I do for you? He asked.

I told him my story, framing my mission grandiosely, as one of peace, as well as curiosity.

"This is very beautiful," Hamdouna said. "We want peace like you." The Ketziot generation, he said, is the vanguard of peace. Only men who fought each other to a standstill, he said, could understand the importance of fighting no more. "Do you remember what Rabin said? He said, 'No more war!' This is how I feel."

I told him I had a list of ex-prisoners I hoped to see. The first one on the list was a fellow by the name of Rafiq Hijazi.

"This is no problem," Hamdouna said. "He is my cousin."

Saud Abu Ramadan said, "This is life in Gaza."

Hamdouna picked up the telephone. He called the Fatah headquarters in Jebalya. Find Rafiq Hijazi, he said.

You don't have his number? I asked.

"I have five thousand cousins," he answered.

Hamdouna wished us well. He cautioned me to be careful. There might not be people who understand your mission, he said, even in this time of peace. But he did not tell me how to discern friend from foe.

"B'hatzlacha," he said, in Hebrew. "Good luck."

Saud and I set out for Jebalya. It is not a refugee camp in the usual sense of the term. Perhaps fifty years ago, when it was founded, it looked like a proper refugee camp with leaky tents, mud paths, and dirty children. But the tents are gone. The Egyptians, who occupied Gaza until 1967, would not allow the Palestinians to leave Jebalya—ensuring that they would remain refugees—but they let them build as they saw fit. And so Jebalya today is a forest of squat, crude apartment blocks, their roofs a tangle of antennas and satellite dishes. It is indistinguishable from Gaza City, next door. The streets are mostly paved, but sand drifted across them; it is impossible to keep the sand in check in Gaza. Small shops occupied the first stories of these buildings; fruit stores, candy shops, a store called the Four Seasons Fashion Center, which sold wedding dresses. We drove down the main street, slowly. People moved grudgingly from our path. We turned onto a narrow side street, then turned again. A grooved alley led us to our destination, a sagging five-story building that had us in its shadow. I looked at my watch.

We climbed a slab staircase. A few years earlier, during the occupation, such an office could never exist openly. Now, the door before us read "Fatah-Jebalya."

There were ten men inside, a greeting party arranged by Hamdouna. They were rough in appearance. One of the men had a face scarred by knives. Another had a cauliflower ear. The hands I shook were callused. One of the men's hands, I noticed, was burned black on one side. Could this have been the result of what is known, delicately, as a "work accident"—a bomb that prematurely detonated?

We gathered around a long table. These men were the Fatah leaders of Jebalya and they were, until a short time earlier, among the hunted; a special Israeli unit, the Cherrypickers, roamed Gaza, killing PLO leaders like these men.

Saud introduced me, and I rushed out my story. I told them about Rafiq Hijazi. I employed the words "peace" and "friendship" so frequently that I sounded nearly Soviet. I made a promise to Rafiq, I said, that in the interest of peace and friendship, I would visit him in his home. And so here I was.

One of the men, who introduced himself as Iyad, said: "Do you mean Rafiq the professor?"

I said I didn't know. "The professor?" I whispered to Saud. He shrugged.

Iyad dispatched two of his comrades to find Rafiq. He was here, Iyad said. But Jebalya is big. This might take some time.

The room went quiet. The last hours had been crowded with talk. The shift to silence was jarring.

Finally, Iyad said, "I miss Ketziot."

I leaned forward.

"Those were good days," he said. "There was no money or status. Everybody was equal. We all knew who the enemy was." He paused, and then added, unnecessarily, "You."

I asked if everyone in the room had been jailed in Ketziot. They all said yes.

Today, things are different, Iyad continued. He described the current situation as purgatorial; the Palestinians were neither occupied nor free. The Israelis were no friends of his, he said, but they are partners in the peace process. The Palestinian flag flies over Gaza, but it is now the symbol of a corrupt and incompetent government.

It gets worse, Iyad said. The Palestinians from exile, the men who came with Arafat from Tunisia, Libya, and Iraq—they were pigs. The other men murmured their agreement.

"As soon as they came here, they wanted to take everything," Iyad said. "They came into the ministries, and they took all the foreign aid. It's disgusting what they've done. Jews would never do this to each other."

It seemed inconceivable to me that a sane Palestinian would yearn for the days of Ketziot, but the other men around the table echoed the words of Iyad. One of the men—his name was Hassan (it was he who had the burned hand), said, "You were *our* prisoners. We weren't prisoners. We were heroes. Because of us you had to come to Ketziot."

I went around the table, trying to figure out if any of these men were in Block Four during my time there. One of them, a retiring man of thirty named Kemal, said that, yes, he was in the *lool,* in 1991. He said, "I think I recognize you," but he was only saying that to be polite. Another man said he had been shuttled through Block Four in 1992. He told me the nickname the prisoners bestowed upon Yehuda, the block commander—Abu Dibhe, they called him, the fat man. They told me where they hid their radios and their knives; they told me how they bribed guards for extra cigarettes. One of them asked me if I remembered a military policeman named Abu Hatzeira. I said yes, I did. He was a corporal of no particular importance except that he was strikingly stupid. "He got very rich in Ketziot," the Fatah man said. "We would bribe him to buy us cameras and film, all sorts of things, good cigarettes. He made a lot of money in the army."

I told them how things worked on our side of the wire; which sort of prisoner I loathed (the flatterers and the whiners); which sort I liked (the secular nationalists, the ones who could tell a joke). We talked about flying faxes and the poison bean stews that issued from the kitchen. We were like old bunkmates from summer camp. Our common time at Ketziot had a cementing effect and our meeting became jolly. Someone brought out a box of cookies.

Then Rafiq walked into the room, looked at me, and said, "I knew it was you."

CHAPTER FIFTEEN

PRISONER NUMBER 26505

I got up and walked around the table.

"Salaam," I said. We shook hands. He put a hand on my shoulder. I put a hand on his. We kept shaking. This was new territory. I looked him over. He had put on weight. He looked prosperous. We were both wearing glasses. "You're reading too much," I said.

"You, too," he said.

Rafiq sat, and I sat with him. We asked after each other's family, which I thought odd, since we knew nothing of each other's family. These things weren't spoken of in prison.

He lived in the center of Jebalya, just a few blocks away. He asked me if I would like to come to visit. The sun was departing, and I decided against euphemism. I would prefer to leave Gaza before dark, I said. He laughed. We stayed seated.

This was the first time we ever spoke without barbed wire between us.

I asked him why they called him "the professor."

"Because I'm a professor," he said. He was teaching statistics at the Islamic University of Gaza, he said. The IUG is a Hamas school, I remembered. Are you in Hamas, I asked tentatively.

"Statistics is statistics," he said. "There's no Quranic view of statistics."

Suddenly I realized that Rafiq was speaking English. Accented, but fluent, English. I didn't recall him speaking English in prison.

He learned it in high school, he said. But it was greatly improved by his time at the American University. I thought he meant the American University in Cairo, but he meant the American University in Washington, D.C.

This was quite something. Pamela and I lived a few blocks from the main AU campus, in a neighborhood called American University Park. I asked him where he lived; he named a nearby street. He was there from 1995 until 1997, when he received his MA in applied statistics. For two years, we had lived a mile apart, oblivious to each other's presence. And, it turned out, we would be neighbors again. He was returning to AU shortly to begin studying for his Ph.D.

"Did you know," he asked, "that I was the top math student in Gaza before the Intifada?"

No, this wasn't mentioned to me by Efrati.

It was getting dark fast, but it didn't seem a wise time to go. The whole project seemed so fragile. I could stay and outrun the dark, I thought. But Rafiq made it easy. He told me to come back the next day. We would meet at his university and have lunch. I suggested that there were places I would sooner visit than the Islamic University of Gaza.

"Are you frightened?" he asked.

"How do I know you're not setting me up?"

"You're my guest," he said. There was a new coolness in his voice.

The time was right to dredge up the old threat.

"Remember what you once told me," I said, "that if the circumstances called for it, you'd kill me, because I'm your enemy?"

A smile broke out across his face.

"Yes," he said. "I remember that."

Here I was, naked before him. He was a Fatah man, as were the others in this room, in an anonymous building in the heart of the Jebalya Refugee Camp, the molten center of Palestinian terrorism. The eulogies would be uplifting, but I would be buried a fool.

He thought about the question for a moment. Then he said: "When I was growing up, my mother and father would always tell us to remember that even though we live in Gaza, it's not our home. Ashkelon is our home, and the Jews stole it. But today I'm almost ready to lie to my own children. I'm almost ready to lie to them and tell them that their family is from Gaza."

We made plans to meet the next morning, and Saud and I left for the border.

"Do you trust him?" I asked Saud, as if I could trust Saud.

"Were you nice to him in prison?" he asked.

I think so, I replied.

So you're safe, he said.

I wasn't sure it was quite as simple as that.

We arrived at the Palestinian checkpoint. I went into the guard shack, and signed out of Gaza. Saud walked me to the entrance of the funnel.

There was something on his mind.

"Why didn't you apologize?" he asked, as we said goodbye. I told him I didn't understand.

"Why didn't you apologize to Rafiq," Saud asked, "for keeping him in prison?"

On the drive back to Jerusalem, I called Jack Ross, to let him know that he was right. I told him he wasn't being paranoid. He had seen one of our prisoners. I just met him in Gaza, I told Jack. He was a graduate student. You probably bumped into him one day in Starbucks.

Jack asked for his name, and I told him. "I remember Rafiq," Jack said. "The guy I saw wasn't Rafiq. It was someone else." There existed in Jack's imagination an underground railroad that ran straight from Block Four to the campus of American University.

The next morning, I woke early again. I was happy with success. I had accomplished what I set out to do. Rafiq would be my friend in freedom.

I drove to Erez and passed through the checkpoint with a minimum of bother. The same soldier who questioned my last name the day before questioned my last name again. He shook his head, a single, almost imperceptible motion, and then let me go.

I walked down the funnel, found a taxi, and asked the driver to take me to the main entrance of the Islamic University. We were there in twenty minutes. The campus was giving off a racket. I couldn't make out the source of the noise. I walked through the main gate, and into the thrashing menace of a Hamas rally. There was a pullulating sea of black heads before me. In the distance, atop a broad platform draped in bunting, stood the Hamas leader Abdel Aziz Rantisi, once a prisoner in Block Four of Ketziot, exhorting the crowd to jihad. He was surrounded by the luminaries of the Hamas politburo. Oversized posters of young Palestinian men, martyred suicide killers, flapped in the wind. Several of the posters were photographs of the noble-faced Yayha Ayyash, the terrorist called "the Engineer" by Yitzhak Rabin, for his obvious technical gifts. Ayyash was the Saladin of bus bombings. He was a shy and introspective student who built the bombs that annihilated dozens of Jews a few years before. Ayyash was killed himself by the Shabak in January 1996, in a cunning operation. A *shtinker* gave him a cell phone the Shabak had packed with explosives. When Ayyash came on the line, the cell phone was detonated by a Shabak agent in a plane overhead. Ayyash died instantly, in a house half a mile from the Erez crossing. His death, to Jews, was like the death of Haman, or Eichmann. To the people of Gaza, his death was a cataclysm. One hundred thousand people came to his funeral. A Hamas man once gave me a copy of the death announcement: "The Izzedine al-Qassem Brigades, with great pride, announces the marriage of the Engineer, the martyr Yayha Ayyash, to the black-eyed," the leaflet stated. The "black-eyed" were the seventy-two black-eyed virgins promised to the martyr in heaven. A group of students carried a radio that played a devotional song: "Strike, oh Engineer. With an explosive belt you'll make glories."

Where the hell was Rafiq?

It is not easy for a large white person to make himself brown and small. A group of bearded men approached me with suspicion. Who are you? What are you doing here? they asked, in Arabic and English. I told them I was waiting for a friend. Who? I didn't think it was wise, for Rafiq's sake, to say. A friend, I said, a friend. More people came over. A man with a gun put his hand on my chest and said, "What's your name?" He had a face like an axe.

And then Rafiq arrived. He said I was a guest of his, and of the university's. He said my presence at the rally was an innocent mistake. We walked outside the gates, and I made note of the obvious: You could have had me killed back there.

"Why," he asked, "would I do that?"

He laughed, and put his hand on my shoulder. "Don't worry," he said. "I'm not with them."

I was flooded, just then, with a kind of joy. It was not so much that Rafiq liked me. It was that Rafiq was *like* me. If he was not with *them,* he was with *me*. I was giddy with good feeling. We walked for an hour in the sun, and he bought me falafel. It would be an insult for me to offer to pay; we were, after all, on his land. "Israelis say falafel is Jewish food," he said. "But everyone knows it's Arab. You can't stop stealing from the Arabs, can you?"

"We didn't steal it," I said. "We made it better."

We sat in the sun and talked as if our relationship had not suffered an eight-year pause. We turned to politics almost right away. We both were confused; we both oscillated between hope and doubt, our opinions about the future shaped disproportionately by the previous day's news. But Rafiq saw an inevitability to the peace process, as did I. We negotiated together as if our negotiations mattered.

The settlements would have to go, at least most of them, he said. Check. Hamas would have to be suppressed, I said. Check. The refugees of 1948 would have to be brought back to their homes inside Israel.

Huh? Or, Rafiq rushed to add, they could be paid for the property they lost. Check. Jews should be allowed to pray in Hebron and other holy sites located inside the future state of Palestine. Check again.

What about Jerusalem? I asked.

Jerusalem is hard, he said.

No doubt. But what's your red line?

The Temple Mount—*Haram al-Sharif*, the noble enclosure, as he called it—was Muslim property and would have to revert to Muslim ownership.

Well, that's a sticky one, I said.

"I've been saying for years that Jerusalem is the hardest thing," he said.

We changed the subject.

That was an off-putting rally, I said, referring to the Hamas demonstration at the Islamic University.

"I knew the Engineer, you know," Rafiq said.

"You did?" I asked, surprised.

"I didn't really know him. But we were both students at Birzeit," the West Bank university from which Rafiq received his BS.

"What was he like?" I asked.

"He was nice."

He was *nice*?

I told Rafiq that I knew the man responsible for killing the Engineer. His name was Carmi Gillon and he was the director of the Shabak at the time Ayyash was assassinated.

"He's nice," I said.

We wandered some more and soon found ourselves near the beach. Rafiq said he wanted to show me something. We had arrived at a Palestinian security base. I recognized it immediately—in the time of the occupation, it was known as the beach prison, the main prison in Gaza, Ansar Two. It was an intake-and-interrogation prison. Here is where young Palestinians were assimiliated into the apparatus of occupation, where the Shabak extracted from the Arabs what they could and then trucked them to the desert.

A guard stood lazily at the gate. Rafiq spoke to him and then turned to me. "Don't say anything, okay?" In particular, he said, don't mention to anyone that you're Jewish. I told him I generally preferred not to lie. This was true for technical reasons—a lie such as this would be a hard sell for a Goldberg—and for larger reasons, too. I did not believe that I should hide my Jewishness. It would feel so Diasporaish.

"Just don't say you're Jewish," he repeated.

The guards let us pass and we walked through the base, toward the sea. Rafiq stopped at a weedy basketball court. "Here is where I was tortured," he said. He didn't look at me. He was arrested three times during the Intifada; twice he was first brought here. The policy of Ansar Two was consistent: Prisoners being prepped for interrogation were made to stand on the basketball court under the sun for four, or five, or six hours. They were forced to raise their arms, and they were not allowed to sit, or drink. When Rafiq's arms dropped from exhaustion, he was struck. He was in high school at the time of his first arrest.

He was not meant to be a soldier of the Intifada. He was bookish, and introspective, and became the valedictorian of his high school. But nearly everyone in Jebalya was drafted into the army of the street. Jebalya was the Fort Sumter of the Intifada. The first riot erupted there, and the first death came there, too, on December 8, 1987.

The next morning, the riots spread to the flanking camps. The men of Jebalya led the way. The Israelis sent in two armored personnel carriers to smash through a roadblock. The people of Jebalya were ready with Molotov cocktails. The APCs were forced to retreat. A riot broke out in another corner of the camp. The Israelis were outnumbered; their commander ordered his men to fire at the legs of the protesters. Two people were wounded. This sent up a howl across the camp. Another man was shot. The Israelis again were forced to withdraw. One of the injured Palestinians, Hatem Sisi, was already dead. He was seventeen years old. Most days of the week, he would walk to school, the Falouja High School, with Rafiq. They had done so the day before.

"It could have been anyone," Rafiq said, "but it was him."

Rafiq was not present at that first riot, or the riots to come. His father, he said, was a man committed to the betterment of his family, and issued his ruling: No Intifada until Rafiq finished high school. His father told him that he had special gifts. The revolution would have to proceed without him. The students of Falouja High School left Rafiq alone as well. "They would not say, Come out and throw stones. I was known as a studious guy."

You never once threw a stone? I asked.

"I don't like running around like that," he said.

So what happened? How did you wind up in jail?

We were still standing on the basketball court. There was no shade. "You're getting a sunburn," Rafiq said. "Your skin isn't right for Gaza." He smiled as he said this; an old joke, resurrected.

Rafiq was avoiding my question. He was, I remembered, given to deliberation and circumspection; he didn't answer any question, however banal, in a rush. I pressed him, though, and he said, "I helped Fatah, that's all."

Rafiq was first arrested in a roundup in May 1989, just before he graduated. He remained unconnected to the Intifada, but he prayed in a mosque near his house, the al-Khulafa'a al-Rashideen mosque, which was popular with Jebalya's strong contingent of Hamas men. In later years, several of the group's suicide bombers would pray their last communal prayer at this mosque.

Rafiq was arrested in a retaliatory sweep. Hamas had just kidnapped and killed an Israeli soldier, and the Shabak and the army swept through Gaza. Rafiq's mosque, like Gaza itself, was riddled with collaborators, and one of them gave the Shabak Rafiq's name.

The soldiers came at night, to Rafiq's front door. "There were a lot of soldiers outside. I saw forty or fifty soldiers on the street. I was sleeping when they came. My father opened the door. 'Where is Rafiq?' they asked him. They got me and said, 'We will take him.' My father asked how long? My father didn't cry when his beloved sister died. He didn't show emotion. The only time I ever saw him cry was when they said I would have to go to prison."

Rafiq, the apple of his father's eye, was taken away by soldiers of the Golani Brigade, who had made a reputation in the territories for their freehanded abuse of Palestinians. "I looked out on the street and there were soldiers everywhere," Rafiq said. "They were arresting people all over Jebalya. They handcuffed me, and put a blindfold on me. They gave me little punches. One of the soldiers lit a cigarette and put it out on the leg of one of the prisoners in the jeep.

"They took us to the civil administration office in Jebalya. There were a lot of people. They would smack you if you spoke. They were playing the drums on our heads. They would do stupid things to you. They wouldn't let us go to the bathroom. But none of us went in our pants." They were kept awake all night. The soldiers forced the Palestinians to sing the anthem of their brigade, "Golani Sheli," or "My Golani." Roughly translated, it goes, "My Golani is the War of Independence, my Golani is the story of all Israel, that returned and comes back to me."

Rafiq was soon transferred to the beach prison, Ansar Two. He was made to stand on a shadeless concrete apron and then he was taken inside for questioning.

"I was good in the interrogation," Rafiq told me. "I didn't say anything." The man who interrogated him, he said, was called Abu Hani. Shabak agents, by custom, take on Arab names. Abu Hani was the agent in charge of Jebalya. He was a potbellied man, Rafiq said, who spoke Arabic "with a Jewish accent." Rafiq was smacked around a bit, but he had nothing much to tell his interrogator. He was a math student who was caught praying in the wrong mosque.

After a few days in Ansar Two, Rafiq was bused to Ansar Three, Ketziot. It was a three-hour ride. Rafiq and the other *shebab* were deposited in the intake wing of Ketziot. Rafiq had not been charged with a crime. But he was held, all the same, on the recommendation of Shabak.

"My first number was 9706," he said. "The second time I was put in prison, my number was 26505."

The intake compound of Ketziot was organized along the lines of the intake base of the Israeli army. The Israelis gave each prisoner a brief medical checkup, and then the prisoners were released into a yard that was, in essence, a recruiting facility. At the Israeli army intake base, different units competed for the attention of new draftees. Each unit made elaborate promises about the joy and challenges of their mission and of the grand fighting history of their units. And the girls, the recruiters said, love the color of our berets.

At Ketziot, the Palestinian factions competed for new recruits in much the same manner. The promise of delayed sexual conquest was not held out as an enticement, except, elliptically, by the Communists, who had pretty much nothing else to offer. Fatah had the sweetest pitch: Align yourself with us, and you'll be the aristocrats of the place. Kitchen work could be yours, and hot showers, smuggled chocolate, all the perks of power. "It was like a fraternity at American University," Rafiq said. "Everyone was telling us why they were the best."

Rafiq was raw to this world and he made a mistake. His friends from the mosque were Hamas, so he signed on with Hamas. "They came to me and said, 'Are you a Muslim?' Of course I was a Muslim. But it was a big mistake. I didn't like their way of thinking. They started reading the Quran all the time, nothing else. I changed my allegiance to Fatah."

By the time he came out of Ketziot, two months later, he was a Fatah man of considerable promise.

In the summer of 1989, he took charge of a Jebalya cell. "We distributed leaflets. We did that sort of thing," he said. By the fall, he once again found himself in the hands of the Shabak's Abu Hani. This time, Rafiq went to trial. The charge was affiliation with a banned group. He faced a military tribunal consisting of three uniformed Israeli army judges. Rafiq had no lawyer; all the Gaza lawyers were at that moment on strike. The judges heard the evidence, but postponed their decision until a lawyer could be present. "Our lawyers came back the next time," Rafiq said, "but they didn't say anything. The evidence was already heard by the judges." Nearly everyone was found guilty in the Gaza military court, not least because the defense lawyers were not allowed to see the evidence collected against their clients. They were present mainly to plead for leniency.

There were others from his Jebalya cell with him. They were also found guilty, in fifteen minutes. Before he was led away, the judges asked if he wanted to make a statement. "I asked them for mercy. I started to make a political speech. But I mainly said I didn't do it. I didn't do the things they said I did."

Did you do them? I asked.

Rafiq smiled.

One of his five sisters came to the courtroom to wish him goodbye. He was sent back to Ketziot; first to Jail Seven, an outpost of the prison outside the main wire, then to the *lool* of Block Four.

The *lool*? I asked. Wasn't that for dangerous men?

"I was dangerous. I had a lot of knowledge," he said.

"You weren't put in there for violence?" I asked.

"I told you," he said, "I don't like to run."

Within three weeks at Ketziot, he was teaching courses on Fatah, its principles, and its history. "I started out as a TA," he said, a teaching assistant. But the commanders of the prisoners were impressed by Rafiq's intellectual gifts, and he was quickly marked for bigger things.

Do you remember hearing about the List? He asked me.

Of course I did—the List. The notorious collaborator list. It was the Rosetta Stone of prison intelligence. The List contained the names of prisoners who Fatah suspected might be cooperating with Israel. We were forever hunting for the List. We needed to know, of course, which of our collaborators had been uncovered by the Palestinians, to prevent them from being murdered by the Fatah security committees.

"I had the List," Rafiq said. "It was with me."

"You?"

I didn't know quite how to respond.

Why did you have the List? I asked.

"Because I was in charge of the security committee," he said.

This made Rafiq the man in charge of ferreting out collaborators, in charge, then, of torturing confessions out of his brother Palestinians, burning them with cigarettes, supervising their beatings, ordering their executions.

"You killed your own people, then?" I asked, deflated and bewildered.

No, not at all, he said. "First of all, we weren't allowed to kill collaborators in prison. The sentences could only be carried out outside the prison."

Then how did he explain the corpses tucked neatly in their beds at first light?

Well, sometimes, he said, the interrogators tended to overestimate the defensive capabilities of kidneys and livers. They lost control of the situation, but when he took charge he put in some reforms, he said. "I began to use the psychological methods of interrogation. I didn't kill anyone."

But did anyone get hurt?

"During my work we tried to create something new: no hitting, no burns, just psychological pressure. At least in three cases it worked. It was something great for us." The other factions were responsible for rooting out their own traitors, and they looked down at Rafiq's reforms. "There was one time the Popular Front guys in the block next to mine thought they found a collaborator," he told me. "They covered his mouth and they beat him and beat him, for two days." Rafiq told them Fatah could handle the interrogation, "but these guys wanted to do it their own way." They wound up beating the prisoner to death.

Rafiq's methods seemed to have been informed by television police procedurals. One technique he used to break the will of suspected collaborators was to have them write their life stories, four or five times. "After they wrote it, I would go to them and say that there was a search going on and they found the archives, or a *shoter* was coming so I had to burn it." Rafiq would ask the suspected collaborator to write it again. Lies were unsustainable over time, he said.

Rafiq's role as the chief of the internal security committee made him one of the most powerful prisoners in the block.

"Why do you think I was allowed to talk to you?" Rafiq asked. "I was in charge of the committee that decided which of the prisoners could talk to the Israelis."

We left the beach prison, and started walking toward town. "Let's go see the grass," Rafiq said, smiling. There is one street in Gaza City that could be called a boulevard, and separating the lanes of the traffic is a strip of grass, slightly yellowed, but still technically green grass. "The settlers use up most of the Gaza water," he said.

We stopped for coffee.

"It was not only the collaborators who had to write reports. Every newcomer had to write a report, everything about him, everything they did outside," he said. "We would get information from the outside. A prisoner who was leaving would carry information to the Tanzim"—the Fatah cadres—"and ask about So-and-So. So-and-So is from Jebalya, what do you know about him? We had a good system."

Rafiq was a prodigy of counterintelligence. His elders hoped he would take his proper place among the elite of Fatah. But after his release from prison, late in 1991, he wished instead to continue his studies. He was a mathematician. He preferred the precision of numbers to the messiness of politics.

He enrolled in Birzeit. He extracted permission from the Israelis to transit across southern Israel to the West Bank. The Fatah men at Birzeit knew of Rafiq's reputation; they press-ganged him into service. They put him on the ballot for the Fatah executive committee at the university. Rafiq didn't campaign, but he won anyway. He was detailed to the Fatah finance committee. "I didn't really want to run for office, but they made me feel I should."

On his first winter break, he went home, and to his surprise, he was arrested again. Abu Hani showed up at his house. It was just before January 1, the anniversary of Fatah's founding. The Shabak was doing a little preemptive arresting, to make sure that Jebalya stayed quiet.

"Abu Hani said, 'This time you're going to go to jail for ten years.' I said to Abu Hani, 'Why? What do you think I'm going to do? Kill Shamir?,' he said, referring to Yitzhak Shamir, who was then the prime minister.

"Abu Hani laughed," Rafiq said. "The soldiers who were with him asked what I said—we were speaking in Arabic. He told them what I said, and they started to laugh, too."

Rafiq's mother came outside as Rafiq was led away. She was devastated, he remembered. "My mother heard him say I would go to prison for ten years, and she started crying. I told her, 'I'll be out of jail in fourteen days.' "

He was released in twelve.

"That was a turning point for me," Rafiq said. "I tried to stay out of politics after that. I wanted to pursue my studies. My GPA jumped up to an eighty-nine after I stopped the politics. Anything above eighty-five is considered excellent in the system they use at Birzeit."

Fatah kept up the pressure. "Right now I could be high up in the security services, like the other guys we were with," he said. "But I didn't want to stay involved."

Rafiq soon found himself recruited for graduate studies at American University. An Arab foundation in London paid his way. Rafiq passed two years of quiet in Washington and then returned home to teach. But things weren't going well, he said. He was glad to be getting out. The problem was the politicization of everything: appointments, raises, class assignments—decisions about these vital matters, he said, were made without respect for merit. The Islamic University was under the direct control of Hamas, and Rafiq wasn't. The disappointments of Palestine—the venal Palestinian Authority, the inadequacies of the education system, the cruelty of the security services—all these things, he said, made him ready to return to Washington.

"You know, when you see something from the inside, you see all the corruption," he said.

CHAPTER SIXTEEN

REFUGEES

Rafiq wanted me to meet his father. A crumbling taxi—the floor was ventilated—took us to the center of Jebalya. The smell of dung and frying oil hung over the street. This was it, Rafiq said, the Hijazi homestead. He motioned to a low, mean, concrete shell. I liked to imagine that Rafiq and I had lived our lives on parallel tracks, but who was I kidding? Compared to his immiserated existence, I grew up in splendor. We had a *den*, after all.

A pile of dirt sat outside the front door like a bulwark against intruders. A stooped old man came out to greet us. He was dark brown and weathered. He wore a kepi-like hat on his head. His pants and shirt were stained with grease and his knuckles were swollen.

Hamed Hijazi said he was pleased to meet me. I asked after his health and he asked after mine. He asked after my children and I asked after his. "I have five daughters!" he said, like a Muslim Tevye. We sat on mats in the front room. The rooms made a crooked line that traveled back to the kitchen. Hamed went to bring us juice. I heard women's voices in the back of the house. Rafiq made no attempt to introduce me to his mother, or his sisters; he did not even explain their presence.

On the stained walls of the room were two diplomas: Rafiq's, from American University, and another from the University of Massachusetts. This belonged to his brother, Kemal. Kemal, Rafiq said, was a Ph.D. already. His field was gerontology. I asked if I could meet him. Yes, of course, Rafiq said, as soon as you return to Washington: Kemal works for the U.S. Department of Health and Human Services. His office is located three blocks from the Capitol.

His father returned with a tray of tea and orange soda. He gave me a pillow, so I could lean comfortably against the wall. He sat on the ground next to me. He smiled. He had only eight teeth.

He asked me what I thought of his son. I told him I liked his son very much. "He's very smart," Hamed said.

I turned to Rafiq and asked him in English: Does your father know how we met?

"Of course," he said.

"And it doesn't bother him?" I asked.

"He doesn't like Jews but he likes Jews who visit him," Rafiq said.

Hamed looked at his son in awe: a son who spoke English.

With the barest of preambles, Hamed told me his story, as Rafiq translated. The Hijazis lived in Majdal, the town the Jews today call Ashkelon. It is just up the coast from Gaza. His father's father, he said, was a graduate of al-Azhar University in Cairo, the great center of Sunni Muslim learning. He himself was born in Cairo. His father came home to Palestine and preached in a mosque in Majdal. It was like heaven, Majdal. Then came the war. The Jews attacked one night in 1948. The people ran in terror, because they knew what the Jews did in Deir Yassin.

"We took everything we could carry," Hamed said. "We went out at night, on the beach. We walked for hours. Then we heard the Jews coming. In the distance, we could hear that the army was coming. I dug a hole in the sand, and I buried the gold, the family's gold. And jewelry. I tried to mark the spot, and remember where it was. We ran away. Later, we saw that it wasn't the Jews." It was, he said, a column of Egyptian troops, coming to save them from the Jews. He returned to the spot where he buried the gold, he said, but the sands had shifted. The family fortune was lost.

The family wandered as far as the small village of Jebalya. Thousands of other refugees flowed into Gaza as well. They lived in a tent, and then a shack. Life goes on, and the family soon arranged a match between Hamed and his cousin Sarah. She was a refugee, too, from Majdal. He found work as a handyman and mechanic and Sarah had babies. Their first child was a daughter they called Amal, or hope. The family lived a shrunken life under Egyptian military rule. Then, 1967 came. "The Jews followed us all the way to Gaza," he said, laughing at his joke.

The 1967 war was a famously catastrophic insult to Arab honor but it had a practical benefit for Rafiq's family. The new occupiers provided more in the way of material goods than the old. The Israelis built schools and brought steady electricity to Jebalya. Before, when the family wanted to watch Egyptian soap operas on Friday afternoon, a black-and-white television was set up in the street and run off a car battery.

Hamed found regular work on a kibbutz near Ashdod. He repaired machinery and made himself available for all sorts of jobs. It was a religious kibbutz, and on Shabbat, when the farmers were in *shul,* he would come especially to feed the chickens. Rafiq told me that, as a teenager, he picked fruit on the kibbutz during summer vacations. Kemal, too. Rafiq's dislike of the kibbutz was acute; he certainly stayed away from the chicken houses. "It made me want to stay in school," he said. As Hamed grew older his desire to work in Israel diminished. In recent years he remade himself as a scrap dealer.

I was curious to know how these two academics, Rafiq and Kemal, sprung from this dirt-floor house. Rafiq laughed. "My father thought education was more important than the Intifada. He always believed in education more than anything else."

His father told me with pride that even his daughter Intissar was a math teacher in a U.N. school nearby. "Women can be educated, too," he said.

Hamed's politics were simple: He didn't like Israel at all but he didn't think his sons should die fighting it. "There are people for this, and people for that."

Rafiq told me, "He was really angry at me when I got arrested."

It was getting late. Rafiq asked me if I wanted to stay the night. I begged off. I had to return to Jerusalem. But I came back several times to Gaza on this trip. There was some business that needed tending, including an interview with Abdel Aziz Rantisi, the Hamas leader and graduate of Block Four. "Why do you want to see him?" Rafiq asked me dubiously. I told him I had interviewed Rantisi once already, about politics, but this time I also wanted to broach the subject of Ketziot with him, though we barely overlapped in Block Four. Rafiq didn't think this was smart but I explained that I was compelled for some reason to meet men who would theoretically kill me merely because I was Jewish. "Like you, for instance," I said.

"Do you still think I'm waiting for the right time?" he asked, smiling, and I said no, obviously not, but of course I was secretly worried that his mask would slip.

On the last day of our reunion, Rafiq finally asked me what, exactly, I was doing. He had been too polite to ask until then. I told him I wanted to reestablish our friendship for its own sake, and I wanted to see the conflict through his eyes, in order to answer a crucial question: Could the Arabs finally accept—accept, not merely tolerate—the presence of Jews in their midst, and not just Jews, but a Jewish state? Or would we forever be viewed as invaders?

Rafiq turned the question on me. Could the Jews live with the Palestinians without fear, without guns?

Yes, I said. I believed so. Not ten years ago, during the Uprising, but now, yes. Israel was educated by your stones, I said.

I went by Rafiq's house to say goodbye to his father. I asked Hamed if he thought he would ever come to America to be with his two sons. "I had to leave my house once," he said. "I don't want to leave my house again."

Rafiq disappeared for a minute and came back carrying a plastic bag. It contained two gifts, he said—one for his faculty adviser at American University, the other for his brother, Kemal. He asked me if I could carry these gifts to Washington.

I, of course, said yes. He removed from the sack a clock, six inches by eight inches. It was meant to look like a Swiss chalet. It was kitsch, made in China of cheap plastic. I noticed then that it ticked. The clock was meant for his adviser; her name was Mary Gray. Her office was in the Mathematics Department, just off Nebraska Avenue, he said. The second gift looked, on first glance, like a bag of dirt. "Seeds," Rafiq said. Kemal misses the vegetables of Gaza. But now he had a backyard and he wanted to plant vegetables.

The seeds were brown, black, and red. He handed the bag to me.

"Thank you," he said.

How could I be such a patsy? It was a setup. I had been played. I didn't even put up a fight. Once a *freier,* always a *freier.*

It was two a.m. I was alone in my room at the American Colony. My bags were packed. I should have been sleeping. Mustafa, my driver, would be coming for me in three hours. My plane would take off in six hours. And in seven hours it would explode over Cyprus.

I stared at the ceiling, writing headlines: Clock Held Bomb That Killed 300; Reporter Duped by Terror Cell; "Seeds" Contained Botulinum Toxin, Cyprus under Quarantine. And: Hijazi Surfaces in Damascus, Called Hero by Assad.

The story of a woman named Anne-Marie Murphy lay heavily on

my mind. Murphy was a noticeably unworldly thirty-two-year-old Irishwoman who one day in 1986 presented herself at the El Al counter in London's Heathrow Airport. She passed without interference through airport security and then she was interviewed, as all passengers are, by an El Al security agent. She told the agent she was traveling to Israel to marry her fiancé, who was Jordanian, the father of her unborn child. Two aspects of Murphy's story seemed irregular to the agent. Murphy said she would be staying in Israel for a week, but she had no checked luggage with her, just a carry-on bag. And she was booked into the Tel Aviv Hilton, though the credit card she carried, the agent discovered, was good for use only in the United Kingdom. This would not be significant, except that her fiancé, she reported, was not yet in Israel; he would be traveling there in a few days' time. This was considered unusual, because pregnant women seldom travel alone, according to the behavioral protocols of El Al security.

Murphy did not pass this first, cursory inspection. The screeners took her bag and emptied it. Its weight was suspicious so they cut open the lining and discovered three pounds of plastic explosive.

Murphy's fiancé, a man named Nezar Hindawi, was a Palestinian terrorist. He wooed her, impregnated her, and proposed marriage to her all in order to murder her, along with the passengers on the El Al flight he hoped to destroy. Three hundred seventy-five people were scheduled to fly that day to Israel. The story of Anne-Marie Murphy is taught as a cautionary tale to security officials at airports around the world.

And now I was Anne-Marie Murphy.

Did you pack your own bags?

Yes.

Have your bags been with you at all times?

Yes.

Has anyone given you anything to carry with you?

Yes.

Yes?

What are you carrying?

A clock. And some seeds.

And who gave you this clock and these seeds?

A friend.

What is your friend's name?

Rafiq Hijazi.

Say again?

Rafiq Hijazi.

How do you know Mr. Hijazi?

We met in Ketziot.

Ketziot?

He was my prisoner.

Which bag contains the material from Mr. Hijazi?

This one, I would say. It's a Tumi, it's made of ballistic material, you know. You could hold it up to your face if you were being shot, and you'd be perfectly fine.

In a steel-lined room the bags would be examined. I would deliver a panegyric in Rafiq's defense. You see, he's a peace-seeking Palestinian. He supports the Oslo peace process.

The device in my luggage was brilliant, the agents would tell me. The plastic explosives were molded into the shape of a Swiss chalet. The security men would be palmy in triumph, and I would have a new career warning Jews to beware of Arabs bearing gifts.

I got off the bed. I opened my bag and removed the clock. I shook it. I put it down. I picked it up. I turned it upside down and right side up. I shook it harder.

There was an all-night grocery across the street from my hotel window. The young men of East Jerusalem wandered in and out. They talked on the street, in low gutturals. It sounded like Ketziot. I was in a waking nightmare. Acid filled my throat.

I took the seed bag in my hand. I opened it. I stuck a pen in it. I poked and prodded. I smelled it. It smelled like the ground.

The clock, though, that was the thing. Who could really know what evil lurked inside that clock?

It all made sense to me, at three in the morning. The stage had been set. All that was needed was an actor, and then I appeared. I skipped right into Rafiq Hamdouna's office. Everyone I met in Gaza wanted peace. Peace, peace, peace. I should have known.

I picked up the clock. I pulled at it. One of the sides came off. I just wanted to work it loose, but it came off. Shit. The glue between the walls was yellow. I tugged at the opposite wall. Then I peeled off the roof, and ripped out the workings, and smashed the base on the stone floor. The clock stopped ticking. I picked up the scattered pieces. Then I threw them all in the trash.

It was just a clock.

I examined the seeds once more. They seemed harmless. I zipped my bag and I watched *MacGyver* on Lebanese TV until Mustafa came and drove me to the airport.

In the terminal the El Al agent asked me: Did anyone give you anything to carry?

No, I said.

A few days after I arrived home, I went to see Kemal Hijazi. He lived in a split-level house in Rockville, Maryland, which is about twenty minutes north of Washington, in a slightly tattered neighborhood of striving immigrants.

I saw a man in the side yard on a stepladder, pruning a bush. He wore black-frame eyeglasses, and he had thinning hair. He also had Rafiq's padded face.

I introduced myself. Kemal wiped his hands and stepped off the ladder.

We shook hands. Kemal's smile was wide. Rafiq, he said, called a few days before. "He told me you'd be coming."

"It's nice to meet you," I said.

He looked at the bag in my hand.

"Did you bring the anthrax?" he asked.

CHAPTER SEVENTEEN

YOU WERE THE DEVIL TO ME

These were the days of accelerating hope in Israel and the territories it didn't quite occupy, and the situation no longer made me feel like a drowning man slapping at the water. The promise of reconciliation was so tangible that it even imbued the misanthrope Yasser Arafat with a superficial largeness of spirit. "We are brothers," he told me in Gaza one spring day. "Brothers!" His handshake was like herring in cream sauce, the spit danced on his lips, and I could not put from my mind his many contributions to the Jewish martyrology, but even he seemed to believe, against the grimness of Ecclesiastes, that soon we would have something new under the sun.

Bibi Netanyahu was gone, replaced as prime minister by the gallant general Ehud Barak, who put peace at the forefront of his capacious mind. There was still violence here and there but Barak's impatience to break the code was matched by a broad desire for tranquillity among Jew and Arab alike. Bill Clinton was in the last year of his second term as president, and he, too, sought to make Middle East peace his immortal legacy. Arafat didn't seem rushed, but he wasn't wrong-footing the chances, either.

"I am ready to sacrifice everything for the sake of peace," he said. I asked him if he thought his people were equally ready. His eyes widened in a vaudevillean manner. "Do you know who I am?" he asked, poking his finger at my chest. "I am the president of Palestine! You are speaking to the president of Palestine!" The people and Arafat are one, that is to say.

I asked him one other question, provoked by Rafiq, who argued with impressive constancy that the peace process could break apart on the hard stone of Jerusalem. I believed, on the other hand, that the issue of the refugees would be the most difficult to surmount. I think it was Rafiq's devotion to statistics that took him to his conclusion. Virtually everything in this fight was quantifiable: There were a certain number of settlements that needed dismantling, a set number of refugees whose needs had to be met, borders that needed redrawing. All this was math. Jerusalem, however, was not. "They shouldn't talk about Jerusalem," Rafiq said. He was convinced that a preoccupation with Jerusalem would bring only misery in its train.

All this prompted me to put the question of Jerusalem to Arafat, who said vehemently, "Do you know what Jerusalem is? Jerusalem is the capital of Palestine. This is my promise. Jerusalem is the capital of Palestine."

Well, sure. This is what he was meant to say. But this didn't mean that Jerusalem couldn't remain the capital of Israel as well. Encounters with Arafat always left me confused. He was a reminder that the Middle East is a complication of half-feints, jaw-dropping lies, chest-thumpery, burst hopes, devilish violence, and improbable progress, and you can break your head trying to figure it all out.

But the tide was no longer dimmed by blood. It was possible to hear in the days of Barak the unembarrassed expression of the most reckless hopes. The director of the Palestinian Authority's tourism ministry, a man named Nabil Sarraj, announced that his new slogan would be "Tourism Is the Oil of Palestine." Two nightclubs had opened in Gaza and Sarraj had taken it upon himself to lead the cleanup of Gaza's beaches. It was like Hercules' Fifth Labor, but he was rashly confident. "We still have a problem with people going to the bathroom on the beach, or dumping their trash," he said, but he advised me to take note of the new multicolored umbrellas decorating the coast, as well as the creation of a lifeguard-training program. The tourists were mostly Israeli Arabs, so far. "The Jews will come to Gaza, too, I think." Gaza, Sarraj noted, is where Samson pulled down the Temple of Dagon onto the heads of the Philistines, and Jews would certainly like to celebrate this noble prophet's achievements. The story of Samson is an advertisement against Jewish tourism in Gaza, but the very Chamber of Commerce–like Sarraj was unversed in the moral ambiguities of Samson's death.

Rafiq, for his part, couldn't quite believe that Jews would come in numbers to Gaza, but he had his hopes as well. He was placid and big-hearted. He even threw himself into my project, and we went in search of other prisoners.

We checked a few off my list right away. Imad al-Alami was the chief representative of Hamas in Iran, for instance, and not easily accessible. And then there were the dead, including Hassan, the chief of the kitchen, who was shot by Israeli soldiers a few years earlier on the frontier with Egypt. Hassan was a Bedouin who viewed borders as nuisances, but the exact circumstances of his death were clouded by rumor. One of his friends from the prison, a Jebalya resident named Rashid Abu Shbak, told me that Hassan did nothing to provoke the soldiers. Abu Shbak suggested that Hassan might have been dabbling in smuggling when he walked into an army patrol. "You know, 'Shoot first' is still sometimes the policy," he said.

Abu Shbak was a senior Fatah man in Block Four. When we met in Gaza he was the deputy chief of Preventative Security and the chief aide to Muhammad Dahlan, the leading secret policeman in Gaza and Jibril Rajoub's peer and rival. Abu Shbak was a stylish man. He kept his mustache in the Saddam style and he had longish hair, which was atypical for a Palestinian secret policeman. He wore Armani, but he still had a Gaza mouth—uneven and deeply yellow teeth planted in rotting brown gums.

Like everyone else, he oscillated between hope and weariness, and he was cynical about the intentions of the Israelis, but when I saw him at his headquarters he spoke without sarcasm about his "dream," which was to bring about the permanent end to war between Jews and Arabs. "The question is, Do the Israelis learn from their mistakes?" he asked. The peace process was a way for Israel to undo the damage it inflicted on itself in the Intifada, the greatest *fashla*—cock-up—in Israeli history.

"It was a big mistake to arrest all those people," he told me, referring to the tens of thousands of Palestinians who passed through Ketziot. "Seventy to 80 percent of the people they arrested had nothing to do with the resistance. Maybe the Israelis took 1 or 2 percent of them and made them collaborators, but we got 30 percent of them to become resistance fighters. The Israelis helped us to straighten up Palestinian society. They arrested drug-takers and sent them to jail, and this allowed us to engage people in the proper way." He gave me a superior smile. "How can the Israelis be so clever and be so naïve at the same time?"

Abu Shbak, who was in his early forties, had made the grand tour of the Israeli prison system. In the Be'er Sheva jail he shared a cell for a while with Capucci. "He was very clean," Abu Shabak recalled. Ketziot was inferior to Be'er Sheva, he said. "I remember the stars and the sky and that there were dirty covers on the bed." But he said the conditions were superior to those of the prisons in Libya. He fell into trouble in Tripoli, once, while in Israeli-imposed exile; the Libyans believed he was operating against their interests, he said, without further elaboration. "I can definitely say that the Israelis have better jails than the Libyans."

I asked Abu Shbak about the men from Block Four. I mentioned Hamad, the Yiddish-speaking Sudanese baklava baker. "Hamad dropped out, I think," Abu Shbak said. "He's just a civilian now."

Not long after, I went to the refugee camp at Tulkarem, in the northernmost West Bank, to find Hamad. It was no trouble at all.

"The black?" one of the camp administrators asked, except that he didn't use a neutral Arabic term to describe Hamad's skin, but instead a word that meant something akin to *shvartse*. The camp was muddy, its alleys rutted. The flat-roofed cement houses were piled atop each other. Children rolled bicycle tires through pools of brackish water.

Hamad's wife met us at the door. She had a sweet smile and many children. My escort from the camp administration explained who I was. The house was dark, lit only by the television. Hamad was returning from work, she said. One of the children was sent outside, and returned with Hamad's brother. It would not do for his wife to be seen welcoming strange men into the house without a suitable male chaperone. I played with Hamad's baby daughter. His wife introduced the children; one was born while Hamad was in prison.

Then I heard, in Arabic, "Who are you?"

Hamad filled the door frame. I had his baby in my arms.

"It's Jeff, from Ketziot," I said, in Hebrew. He squinted. Then he rushed over and kissed me three times on each cheek. I was kissed by more Arab men in those months than I've ever been kissed by Jewish women.

Hamad still had a quicksilver wit, and was acerbic as ever. "Did you learn Yiddish yet?" he asked. No, I said. "What a Jew," he muttered. Hamad had quit the Fatah life, he said—there were too many children now to entertain an interest in politics. He didn't give much thought to the situation, he said. He was certainly happy with the upturn in the economy. Every day in his taxi he took carloads of Palestinian workers to the border with Israel.

In Ketziot, Hamad had told me that he wanted to go "home"—to a home he's never seen in a disappeared village on the Mediterranean, where his family had lived for generations before the birth of Israel in 1948. I reminded him of his dream. He said, *"Nu?"*

"Do you still want to go to this place?" I asked.

"I want quiet and peace," he said. "I don't want anyone bothering me."

There was a surprising consistency of emotion and thought among my former prisoners. They said all the things about peace and compromise that I hoped to hear.

But there were still a few prisoners on my list who I thought would introduce darker themes into the conversation. And then there was Capucci. I wasn't keen to seek out Capucci alone. There was something about him, I remembered, that suggested coiled violence. So I brought Rafiq with me.

The air was cottony on the day we set out to find Capucci, and by nine in the morning I was sweating in a most undignified way. Rafiq said he heard that Capucci had become one of Arafat's bodyguards, so we went first to the headquarters of Force 17. Rafiq said that hundreds of Ketziot veterans had found their way into the security services. He wasn't pleased by this. It was no way to cure unemployment, he said. There were so few taxpayers in Gaza and so many bureaucrats to pay, he said, playing with the numbers in his head.

Besides, I said, these were armed bureaucrats. That can't be a good thing. For *my* tribe, at least.

We went inside. There were eight or ten men hanging about, untasked, oblivious to the clock, but very polite. Rafiq spoke to them in Arabic; I understood only passingly what he was saying. He seemed to be sharing only parts of the truth. Even now, in this time of promise, he seemed to think that certain things should remain concealed.

The men had heard of Capucci, but only vaguely. We left the office filled with coffee but not substantially illuminated. Capucci's family, Rafiq remembered, once lived in Khan Younis, at the other end of Gaza. We found a taxi and went south, tracking the sea for a few minutes and then turning inland. Suddenly the traffic stopped. Before us was Netzarim junction. Netzarim was one of the two most isolated

Jewish settlements in Gaza. Three hundred Jews lived there, along with two battalions of soldiers to protect them. Netzarim was a Jewish Alamo, enveloped entirely by the Nusseirat Refugee Camp.

There was no logical or theological reason for Netzarim's existence. In the Bible this was the land of the Philistines, and yet these Jews, abetted by one Israeli government after another, decreed that Gaza's holiness was not negotiable. It was Ariel Sharon who placed Netzarim here, like a choke collar on Gaza's neck. Once, in 1980, the army commander of Gaza complained to Sharon about the impossibility of defending Netzarim. Anyway, he asked, what's the point? According to one account, Sharon answered, "I want the Arabs to see Jewish lights every night five hundred meters from them."

The injustice here was not slight. Most of the Gaza settlements were clustered in a single block called Gush Katif, which was located on the sea, opposite Khan Younis, a particularly impoverished Palestinian city. Gush Katif occupied 20 percent of the Strip. It was home to seven thousand settlers. Khan Younis, which covered a smaller piece of land than Gush Katif and which was cut off from the sea, was home to one hundred thousand Palestinians.

Traffic was frozen. I stepped out to look. In the distance, I could see an Israeli armored personnel carrier blocking the road. A soldier sat behind a machine gun mounted on its roof. A group of settlers was exiting Netzarim, driving to Israel proper. Each time a settler left the settlement to go to work or to buy vegetables or to take his dog to the veterinarian the army cleaved the Strip into two, paralyzing traffic on the main road until the settlers were safely on their way. There was another pressure point, as well, farther south. On days of punitive closures, the army could divide Gaza into three, like Gaul.

Along the rutted sides of the road, Arab men stood and smoked and watched. Some squatted by their cars. No one complained. The women stayed like prisoners inside the taxis. I was not patient like an Arab. I suggested we devise another plan. Rafiq searched his mind; a relative of Capucci's lived nearby. We were off.

Even now, I can't say for sure how Rafiq conjured up Capucci, but it was without a doubt Capucci who presented himself to us at yet another Force 17 base later that afternoon. His beard was trim, but his eyes still shone as I remembered them. He carried an AK-47, but he was not in uniform. He seemed smaller in freedom than he did in prison.

The three of us and Capucci's second, another ex-prisoner of Block

Four named Mahmoud Kalkili, sat down for tea. Kalkili was also armed and he watched me carefully. Capucci remained grave, speaking in soft, even tones, but he was perfectly polite. I told him I was happy to see him. He smiled.

"We are not enemies anymore," Capucci said. My heart nearly burst with liberal feeling. You were once the devil to me, he said, but not now. Now, he said, he held no grudges against Jews. He felt sad, he said, when Rabin was killed.

His thoughts on making peace, alas, were not quite mine. He believed in the "right of return" of Palestinian refugees, along with their children and grandchildren. Such a right, granted symbolically, might help counter the humiliation Palestinians feel in exile. Such a right implemented in fact—the end of the actual exile of Palestinians—would mean the end of Israel.

Then he said something even more bothersome. "It's good to have one state, not Arab or Jewish. Just a state," he said.

I'd like to believe that he said this without knowledge of its implications. In the mouths of the clever, this utopian-sounding ideal, a single, shared state for Arabs and Jews, is an argument against the survival of the Jewish people. In the 1960s, the PLO called for a single, *Judenrein* state between the river and the sea. By the late 1990s, only Hamas and the Islamic Jihad were arguing for the sea as a solution to the Jewish problem. But there were rejectionists in the PLO who still argued for Israel's destruction by demographic, rather than literal, drowning. Farouk Kaddoumi, the second-ranking member of the PLO, who rejected the Oslo peace process and stayed in Tunis when Arafat came to Gaza, told me he still believed in the "stages" plan for Palestinian victory, the notion that each piece of "liberated" territory should be used to liberate the next. But when this strategy succeeds, he said, or when the Jews accede to the inevitable, there would still be a place for them in Palestine. "Zionism will undermine itself, and we will be victorious, but this does not mean that the Jews cannot participate in our democracy," he said, adding magnanimously that the Jews would be an honored and protected minority in a Palestinian state. Capucci argued the Kaddoumi line, but I think he did so without fully understanding its consequences.

Capucci's role in Force 17 was obscure to me; he was adept at sidestepping questions. But he was a full colonel, he said. He was responsible, like everyone else, for keeping the chairman safe from those who would do him harm.

Finally, I realized that it was my responsibility to adjourn the meeting. I was their guest. It would have been impolite for them to go without my blessing. I stood up. Capucci and Kalkili jumped up, too. We shook hands and exchanged telephone numbers. You will come to Khan Younis, to visit the *hamoula,* the clan, soon. *"Inshallah,"* I said, if God wills it.

Capucci held on to my hand. "There was a fence between us," he said, not letting go. "Now there's nothing between us."

Rafiq and I drove back to his house in Jebalya. Kemal, his brother, was visiting from Washington and I wanted to say hello.

We wiped the dust of the road off our clothes and sat in the bare front room. Kemal was in good spirits, though tired from the inundation of relatives. His children were playing outside, running between reefs of sand. "They think they're at the beach," Kemal said. His oldest son, he said, was out chasing rats with a stick.

Kemal was helping Rafiq plan for his return to America, though Rafiq seemed quite organized, quite handy at list-making. Students of applied statistics, I gathered, were methodical. His plan, he told me, was to work part-time as a teaching assistant and to fill the rest of his time with study. He had already found an apartment on Tunlaw Street near Georgetown, just ten minutes from my house. The apartment, he said, was in a dormitory for married students. "My wife will be coming a few months after I get there," he said.

Your wife?

Tahani was her name. When we finally met in America, not in Gaza—I learned that she wore the hijab, the head-covering worn by traditional Muslim women. I found her to be amiable, sweet, intelligent, and deferential.

In retrospect I should not have been surprised to discover that Rafiq was married, but I was innocent of his profound commitment to the most orthodox expressions of Islam, in particular his devotion to the idea of *purdah*—the complete seclusion of women from the world of men—and so therefore I was unaware that the existence of his wife was none of my business.

Rafiq and Tahani were married in 1996, he told me as he packed for Washington. It was an arranged marriage, made by the fathers. Tahani is eight years younger than Rafiq. She came from a refugee camp close to Jebalya. Tahani has eight brothers. Her family's allegiance, Rafiq said, was to Hamas, but it was a passive kind of loyalty. None of the brothers, he noted, had ever been arrested. Still, the family was more religious than his, he said.

The disclosure of Tahani's existence interrupted a set of daydreams I was then enjoying, brought on by Rafiq's imminent return to Washington. Maybe, I thought, I would take him to an Orioles game. Perhaps we would go out for sushi. Does he like sushi? He would come over to visit and play with the kids. We probably wouldn't go to the movies. He had never mentioned a movie. And we would certainly not be splitting a six-pack since he had the sincere Muslim contempt for alcohol. But he could go to Starbucks—he is a Palestinian, and drinking coffee is the national sport of Palestine. We would sit and chat and be reasonable about the Middle East. We would run into friends, and they would say, How do you two know each other? and we'd laugh and say, Well, that's a story.

What *did* we talk about, anyway? It had been months since we first met in the Fatah office in his refugee camp. We never talked about sports. We didn't talk about cars. Nothing quotidian ever injected itself into our conversations, which was unfortunate because it is the ordinary details of a person's life that often illuminate the important things. I needed him to be knowable. But it was not clear, sitting in Gaza, that I would even be allowed to meet his wife.

I ventured an invitation: I said I hoped that he and Tahani would be able to visit us in our home.

"Why not?" he asked.

By the time Tahani arrived in America Rafiq had settled into the semimonastic routine of a graduate student in applied statistics. I saw him a few times in those first months of his Ph.D. program, but he was frenetically driven; his anxiety about achievement reminded me of stories about first-generation Jewish immigrants. He spent most of his days squinting in front of a computer, and the remainder of his time either in the makeshift mosque on campus or teaching ill-mannered undergraduates. The lives of his students did not seem to interest him. As we sat one day drinking coffee in the student union, he unburdened himself: His students, many of them, anyway, were spoiled and unserious. This was a position any self-respecting teaching assistant would take. But Rafiq said his students also complained, on occasion, about his accent, and he didn't like that very much. The student union was crowded, and I noticed that the girls on line for coffee were outfitted in flip-flops, short-shorts, and midriff-baring tank tops. I also noticed that all this exposed flesh never provoked even a flicker of attention from Rafiq.

We walked back to his undecorated office in the cinder block building that housed the math department. His office was just down the hall from that of Mary Gray, his thesis adviser. She was said to be a talented teacher, a pioneer in her mostly male field. She was also a woman with grudges; one of her special grudges was against Israel, which helped explain why she recruited Palestinians to be her graduate students.

I went to say hello. Gray was once the chairwoman of the American board of Amnesty International and she could be smug in the way that human rights activists can be when they don't hear how they sound. I felt guilty about breaking her clock, however, so I heard out her opinions. She would often complain about Israel's cavalier treatment of Palestinian universities on the West Bank, for instance, without noting that there were no universities on the West Bank at all before the arrival of the Israelis. I still couldn't abide Christians who sit in judgment of Israel. Worry about the plank in your eye before removing the mote from mine, that revolutionary Jew from Nazareth told his followers on the Mount of Beatitudes.

Gray and I shared one common interest, though—Rafiq's welfare. She issued only the best reports about Rafiq's adjustment to the life of a Ph.D. student, and sympathized with him about his students. "Rafiq's just not used to spoiled American brats," she said. She also saw nothing worrisome about Rafiq's desire to keep Tahani at home. Rafiq would not send Tahani to work. They could certainly use the money, he said, but it wouldn't be "appropriate" for her to take a job. I imagined that this bit of information was hard for a person like Mary Gray to accept, though she managed. In any case, she said, her Muslim graduate students didn't discriminate against her: She told me that women with Ph.D.'s were treated like men by her Palestinian students.

Despite his commitment to the rules of *purdah* and his desire to quick-march his way to a Ph.D., Rafiq did take a moment out of one weekend to bring Tahani to our house. She wore a hijab and an abaya, the neck-to-foot cloak that hid her shape and her youth and was meant to deflect male lust. It was not a trifling garment in the swampy Washington heat. Rafiq and Tahani came in the company of Kemal and his wife, Manal. Manal, too, wore the hijab and an abaya of Saudi black.

In anticipation of the visit, I suggested to Pamela that, in order to place our guests at ease, she should consider wearing the lovely, draping, indigo-colored burka that I bought for her a short while earlier on a visit to Afghanistan. It was made of Georgette polyester, and it had surprisingly good hand, as the Long Island garmentos would say, and it came with a three-layer niqab, a veil that allowed its wearer only limited peripheral vision. The impenetrable niqab came standard on these Afghan burkas, which is why women in Kabul were killed while crossing the street in far greater numbers than men.

Pamela was not amused. But my obvious desire to please Rafiq and his family led her to offer, without any extravagant pleading on my part, to serve everyone tea from a tray. She also offered to cover her arms and to resist the temptation to make comments, true though they might be, about the misery of women's lives under the yoke of Islam.

The awkwardness dissipated almost immediately. The wives spoke of wifely things while Rafiq, Kemal, and I talked about developments in the Middle East peace process at our usual granular level. Kemal was harder-edged than Rafiq. Unlike Rafiq, he was never a soldier in the Uprising. He is older than Rafiq by five years. At the start of the Intifada, in 1987, he had already graduated college—a Baptist college in Jerusalem—and was working as a nurse in a Gaza hospital. He was enmeshed in the Intifada, however. His emergency room received many casualties, and he had feared seeing Rafiq bleeding on a stretcher. But he was, like his younger brother, famed in Jebalya for his studiousness, and his father and his friends encouraged him to separate himself from the Uprising so that he could pursue his academic interests unmolested. One day, soon after the eruption of the Intifada, one of his best friends, a medical student named Mustafa Liddawi, approached Kemal with a request. They were old friends and they worshipped at the same mosque.

"This wasn't the main mosque where the sermons were written by the Waqf," the official Muslim Trust, Kemal explained. "Mustafa told me one day that I shouldn't pray there. You'll be watched and arrested. It was true. It was the sermons of Hamas in that mosque. So I didn't go there anymore."

Liddawi was a member of Hamas, and though he wanted to recruit new members, he also wanted to protect Kemal from the hard life of the underground. "I don't know why," Kemal said. "Maybe he saw a weakness in my character."

I said that Mustafa Liddawi was the one with the dubious character. He had dropped out of medical school, and by the time we spoke, he was the commander of Hamas forces in Lebanon. He was a killer, not a hero.

"Well, I guess it depends on how you look at things," Kemal said. "He was a big hero to everyone in Gaza."

Isn't that the problem with Gaza?

Kemal just smiled.

I said I thought that Kemal made a bigger contribution to the Palestinian cause than did Liddawi. "How? By making money in America?" he asked in a self-lacerating way. No, I said, by building, not destroying. Then it struck me to ask: You're not with the suicide bombers, are you?

No, he said, but without much conviction.

Rafiq was more vehement on the subject of suicide killing. "The Quran is very clear about suicide," he said. "It is against it and it is against the killing of innocent people." He felt anger, he said, toward the men who dispatched suicide bombers to their deaths. A couple of years earlier, he reminded me, he took part in a demonstration in Gaza City against suicide bombing.

Rafiq felt no guilt about his level of contribution to the cause. Kemal, I think, did. In 1988 he moved to Boston and though he returned to Gaza for visits, he never went back to live.

By the time I got to know him, Kemal was an American citizen of long standing. He arrived in America with nothing, but immigrant desire carried him to graduate school. He married Manal in Gaza, brought her to America, and now they had three sons who were by no means deracinated but nevertheless conspicuously American in demeanor and posture, though when I visited, the older boys uncomplainingly waited on Kemal and me. The boys attended public school in Maryland, though they also went to an after-school program at their mosque. Kemal would have preferred to send his boys to an Islamic school, he said, but they were inferior academically to the public schools of Montgomery County.

That afternoon I tried to engage Tahani and Manal in conversation, mostly to no avail (Pamela had much greater luck). At one point, though, I asked Tahani about her trip to Washington. Unlike Rafiq, who was still banned from entering Israel (he flew out of Cairo), she was allowed to use Ben-Gurion. Suddenly I saw an imp under the hijab.

"The next time I go home I'll travel with you," she told me. "Rafiq can't fly from Israel because he's a terrorist."

Of course, she would no sooner be seen alone with me than expose her navel at a fraternity party. But still, there was some irreverence there, which I found a relief. In fact, the whole afternoon was delightful. Rafiq even held one of my babies on his lap. It was a heart-catching thing to see.

I would talk to Tahani from time to time, when I visited Rafiq in their apartment. I was curious about her adjustment to solitude. In Shata, her refugee camp, she lived in a house with her parents, her brothers, their wives, and their many children. (Her father would add a floor to his house each time a son married.) Now she was more or less alone much of the day in an antiseptic one-bedroom apartment in a building filled with Chinese graduate students. But over time she made friends with the wives of other Palestinian students, and though she didn't drive—Rafiq didn't want her to—she made small forays into Washington. She seemed to spend a good part of her day cleaning. She vacuumed with great geometric precision and the whole apartment gleamed with cleanliness. It was an attractive, simple apartment. There was little luxury, just Ikea bookshelves for Rafiq's math texts. The walls were hung with framed Arabic calligraphy, sayings from the Quran, and a small prayer rug was rolled up under the couch.

"I have a new thing that I do," Rafiq told me one day. "I put the alarm clock at the opposite end of the bedroom from our bed, so when it rings I have to get up and turn it off."

How unpleasant, I thought. "The first prayer of the day is so important," he said. "I don't want to risk staying in bed."

It seemed to me he was praying more than usual, and I said so. This irked him. "I always pray five times a day," he said. "You know that."

For some reason, I said: "You know that I'm still a Zionist, don't you?"

"Really?"

"Absolutely."

Rafiq asked me why.

"It's still the answer."

The answer for what?

"The answer for the Jews."

He looked at me skeptically. "It's not the answer for the Palestinians," he said.

"You could have accepted us," I said.

"No. That could not happen. There were too many crimes."

I asked him if he believed that the Quran contained only literal truth.

"Of course," he said. "Why do you ask?"

I told him why. I had recently been in Ramallah, where I saw a friend named Akram Haniya, who was the publisher of a daily newspaper called *Al-Ayyam*. Akram was a former aide to the late master terrorist Abu Jihad. Though he was a moderate, Akram believed that nothing Israel did in the cause of peace was good enough. He told me that even Ehud Barak didn't understand that the choice he faced was between Arafat and the abyss. "We're the only ones they can negotiate with," he said, meaning the PLO. "We're the only secular nationalists left in the whole Middle East. They can't talk to Hamas because they can't negotiate with Islam. Islam will give them a set of nonnegotiable demands."

This argument was blackmail, but it was true. If the Palestinians one day subsumed their national interests to their theological interests, then there would never be peace. Even a cursory reading of the Quran would suggest this.

Rafiq didn't like this line of argument. "The Quran says nothing about peace talks," he said. I pointed out that the Jews are the villains of the Quran.

"The Jews in the Quran are not the Jews of today," he said. "The Jews in the Quran are specific Jews in the time of the Prophet, peace be unto him."

He went on, "There are good Jews and bad Jews in the Quran, just like there are good Muslims and bad Muslims."

I first read the Quran at Ketziot. I wasn't much moved, which was surprising, because even the Christian Bible moves me: Who could not be stirred by the eloquent vision of radical justice outlined in the Book of Matthew? But I didn't quite understand the appeal of the Quran.

"It's beautiful in Arabic," Rafiq said. "It really can't be translated."

I had an impudent thought: If Shakespeare can be rendered into Arabic, the Quran can be translated into English. The Bible contains passages of unmistakable beauty and I could find nothing to match the transcendence of its language in the Quran. Nor could I find the sort of parables and poems that make the Jewish Bible peerless in its exploration of good and evil and redemption and desire.

But of course Rafiq didn't grow up in a culture that subjected holy texts to withering criticism. I dropped the subject. I also acknowledged that reading unfamiliar scripture without the guidance of learned commentary is like stargazing in sunglasses.

I did not mind confessing to Rafiq the limitations of my knowledge, but he would not do the same. He believed the Quran was given to man by God to correct the errors of the Bible, and this belief was, I came to learn, immune to scholarship, skepticism, and reason. "When the Bible and the Quran contradict each other, it's always the Quran that is right," he said, while admitting that he had not read the Bible.

Though I couldn't find majesty in the Quran itself, I could certainly locate it in the infinite faith of its readers. I was traveling frequently in Muslim lands and on Friday afternoons I would watch thousands of mosque-bound Muslims spill into the streets of Cairo and Beirut and Karachi—rich and poor, young and old, of every color known to man—and join together with an egalitarianism and a unity that created in me feelings of awe and envy, because my own people were so fractious, not to mention so modest in number.

As I went deeper into the Quran, something else nagged at me, something more serious than the literary shortcomings of Islamic scripture. The God of Judaism is a jealous God, but not like Allah, who seemed to want every soul. Judaism doesn't present itself as the only alternative to hell. Its rebellious offspring, on the other hand, have taught that there is no path but the one true path. Many Christian churches today have softened to the idea that multiple truths might exist about the one God. But no such reformation has visited Islam. For Rafiq, there was one truth that imposed itself on every other truth.

I decided to reread the Quran through the prism of our friendship. It was not the most pleasant experience. I was reminded of the malevolent things Allah thought about my people. The Quran calls the Jews "men who will listen to any lie." It teaches, "Strongest among men in enmity to the believers wilt thou find the Jews and Pagans." In the chapter called "The Children of Israel" I came across this idea, presented in the voice of Allah: "And we decreed for the Children of Israel in the Book, that twice would they do mischief on the earth and be elated with mighty arrogance (And twice would they be punished)!"

I asked Rafiq if this curse was meant to be taken literally. No, he said. "It's a warning about arrogance. It is warning people against the arrogance of not following God's way."

So the Jews are not meant to be punished twice by God?

He smiled. "You don't have to read it literally," he said.

But I was to discover in my travels through the Muslim world at the turn of the millennium that millions did.

CHAPTER EIGHTEEN

YOU ARE MOST WELCOME HERE

In the center of Kandahar, the crushed and shattered city in southwestern Afghanistan that gave birth to the Taliban, stands an elegant building called the Shrine of the Respectable Cloak of Muhammad. The cloak in question allegedly belonged to the Prophet himself and the faithful believe it radiates a holiness that cures the sick and heals the lame.

I wanted to see the cloak, which is locked away in a vault deep inside the shrine, but the man assigned by the Taliban to be my minder, a slight fellow called Mullah Muhammad, opposed my wish, because I was an infidel and therefore unclean, and, in any case, even if he agreed, the men of the Taliban's Committee for the Propagation of Virtue and the Suppression of Vice, who wear black turbans and diabolical black eyeliner, would object, and they carried whips. But I broke free of Muhammad and made my way up to the crease of the shrine. There was no sensible reason for me to go inside except the desire to experience something that was so eloquently, palpably foreign.

I was wrapped in a cloak myself and I had a beard, which I had grown in order to endear myself to the fundamentalists of Pakistan and Afghanistan, but it was reddish and patchy and the cloak did not quite hide my Levi's and so my attempt to push through the narrow mouth of the crowded shrine quickly came undone. The Taliban guards waved their batons and picked up rocks to throw and screamed *"Kafir,"* infidel, at me. I moved aerobically to a waiting taxi, whose driver turned out to be, *Allahu Akbar,* a superior wheel man. As he drove he yelled at me in Pashto (I assumed he was critiquing my gimcrack ideas) and we drove past Osama bin Laden's house, right to the gate of the city's small United Nations compound, which was raided by the Taliban, but not until the day after I departed Kandahar for Pakistan, where I could talk in a more superficially tranquil setting to the terrorists who would soon transform the world.

What do you want? I asked one of them, the Pakistani terrorist leader Fazlur Rahman Khalil, when I met him in Rawalpindi. "I want the West to die," he said. He was seated under a poster that spelled out the word "Allah" in bullets. We were in a shabby building by a bus station. Khalil had signed bin Laden's 1998 fatwa that called for the murder of Americans and Jews. The fatwa was issued by a group called the World Islamic Front for Jihad Against the Crusaders and Jews.

"Why Jews?" I asked.

"Because you are from Satan," he said.

I asked him if he would use nuclear weapons against his enemies, and he said, smiling, "We don't have nuclear weapons. We wish we had nuclear weapons. If we had them, we would use them as necessary. But they're very expensive."

Three years later, a group of Khalil's associates beheaded *Wall Street Journal* reporter Daniel Pearl in Karachi for being, among other things, Jewish.

I told Rafiq about my visits with Muslim fundamentalists in Pakistan and Afghanistan. Rafiq didn't think much of their brute Islam. The Afghans were the hillbillies of the *umma,* and Pakistan was not even an Arab country. There was always a snobbish cast to Rafiq's comments about non-Arab Muslims. In any case, he thought I was overestimating the importance of this strain of Islam. I told him I was trying to learn wherever I could. I was dropping a hint: Rafiq had resisted my thoughtfully and understatedly expressed desire to accompany him to Friday prayers. I didn't see how he could blame me for seeking other teachers.

I found such teachers at a madrasa, a seminary, called Haqqania, which sits about two hours east of the Khyber Pass in Pakistan's North-West Frontier Province. *"Madrasa"* is an Arabic word that shares its root with the Hebrew word for study, *"midrash."* This linguistic consanguinity proved, once again, despite appearances, the indissoluble cousinship between Jews and Muslims. At least to me it did.

Haqqania is one of the largest madrasas in Pakistan: Its mosques, classrooms, and dormitories are spread across eight ungroomed acres. Its three thousand students were recruited from the dire poor, mostly from Pakistan and Afghanistan, but also from Central Asia, and from among the Arabs as well. The students at Haqqania ranged in age from eight and nine to thirty or so. These were men without women. Most of the students had not even hugged their shrouded mothers and sisters since reaching puberty.

The youngest boys at the madrasa spent their days seated cross-legged in dusty, airless classrooms, memorizing the Quran. The older boys were studying the properly sanctioned interpretations of the Quran and of the *hadith*. These students also studied Islamic jurisprudence and Islamic history. The oldest of those attending Haqqania—the postgraduates—attended the "mufti course." A mufti is a cleric who is authorized to issue fatwas on matters ranging from family law to the conduct of jihad. Haqqania was notable not only because of its size and its militancy but because it was the Kennedy School of the Taliban; it graduated more members of the Afghan junta than any other madrasa.

One day I presented myself at the office of the chancellor of the madrasa, a mullah named Samiul Haq. Maulana Haq—*"maulana"* means "our master"—was a well-known Islamist with passionate anti-American views. His sympathizers included Osama bin Laden, and a few years earlier he had granted bin Laden's protector, the Taliban leader Mullah Omar, an honorary degree. The maulana came into his office in a rush and sat down beside me. He was a man of sixty-five. He was barefoot, and his toenails were the color of rust. He had a long beard dyed a bright brown and he wore a turban wrapped loosely around his head. He has two wives and eight children, and he seemed to be a happy man. He was pleased by my appearance at his school and he wanted to let me know that I should feel at home. We talked for a while about the course of study, our mutual love for comity, and our shared loathing for lying and small-mindedness.

Then he sighed. "The problem," he said, "is not between us Muslims and Christians. The only enemy Islam and Christianity have is the Jews."

He went on, "It was the Jews who crucified Christ, you know. The Jews are using America to fight Islam. Clinton is a good man, but he's surrounded by Jews. Madeleine Albright's father was the founder of Zionism."

"I'm Jewish," I said.

There was a pause. "Well, you are most welcome here," he said.

And so I was.

The day began at dawn, in dormitories that were cramped and threadbare, and collected the dust of the Grand Trunk Road nearby. The boys stumbled into the mosque for prayers and then to the kitchen, where they were fed curries and nan. I remember most the smells of the morning; unwashed clothing, burned bread, and diesel fumes drifting over the walls from the road.

The youngest students had not yet been armored in the hard casing of jihadist ideology and yet they seemed to incorporate the politics of the madrasa into their play. Two eleven-year-old boys, both Afghan refugees, would often jump out from behind trees and scream "Osama!" when they saw me.

The students were inquisitive, though most of their questions to me concerned bin Laden. In several classes, I was asked why America hated bin Laden. Well, bin Laden kills innocent people, I would explain, and it was the Prophet Muhammad who said it was *haram,* forbidden, to kill civilians. The students in one class did not like it when I drafted Muhammad for the defense, and they began chanting, "Osama, Osama, Osama."

One day, I attended a small mufti class that concerned the rules of jihad. The word *"jihad"* means "striving." There are, in the common understanding of the word, two types of jihad: "greater jihad" and "lesser jihad." Greater Jihad is an interior jihad, the struggle to conquer one's own evil inclinations. "Lesser jihad" refers to war to protect or expand the Islamic realm.

The teacher in the mufti-level course was a middle-aged cleric named Abdallah who had tobacco-stained hands and a lined, unhappy face. He taught the lessons of jihad through the *hadith*. There are thousands of *hadith,* which collectively answer a universe of Muslim concerns, including those on prayer, the slaughter of animals, the burying of the dead, even the proper washing of genitalia.

My Judaism was no secret at the madrasa, and Mullah Abdallah turned, for my benefit, to a set of sayings having to do with my people's evil impudence. Abdallah read a *hadith* that was originally narrated by Aisha, one of Muhammad's wives: "Once the Jews came to the Prophet, peace be unto him, and said, 'Death be upon you.' So I cursed them. . . . I said, 'Have you not heard what they said?' The Prophet said, 'Have you not heard what I said to them? The same is upon you!' "

The students laughed into their beards. This recitation was supposed to put me in my place.

I answered his *hadith* with a *hadith* of my own. I had already mined the collections for positive references to Jews. I did not find much, but there was this, which I read aloud: "A funeral procession passed in front of us and the Prophet, peace be unto him, stood up and we too stood up. We said 'O Allah's messenger, this is the funeral procession of a Jew.' He said, 'Whenever you see a funeral procession, you should stand up.' "

The teacher addressed me: "What does this mean to you?"

I answered: "The Prophet, peace be upon him, had respect for all people, because man is created in the image of God." I went on to attribute to the Prophet great respect for the Jews, in particular. In the earliest days of Islam, Muhammad instructed his followers to pray in the direction of Jerusalem, rather than Mecca, as a means of honoring the Jews.

One of the students, a thickly bearded fellow from Peshawar, rose: "I would like to challenge the Jew," he said.

"Please," Mullah Abdullah replied.

"It is true, the Prophet, peace be unto him, had respect for the Jews as humans and as receivers of the word of God," he said. "But the Jews strayed from the path of Allah, and they answered the criticism of the Prophet, peace be unto him, with insolence and insults. So it is a fact that while the Muslim had respect for the Jew, the Jew had no respect for the Muslim."

The students applauded.

Abdallah, the teacher, said, "The brother is correct."

The most popular compilation of *hadith* contains 199 sayings of the Prophet on jihad, and every one of them refers to the jihad of war rather than to the "greater jihad" of spiritual betterment. Classical Islam was not overly concerned with "greater jihad," the therapeutic jihad. The men at the madrasa were not abashed about this: Islam was a warrior religion, they said. Christians might foolishly celebrate their Savior's passive surrender to evil, but Muhammad would never have allowed himself to be humiliated in such a way. The maulana boasted that the Prophet Muhammad fought in more than seventy battles, virtually every one meant to expand the borders of the House of Islam.

The *hadith* on jihad address all sorts of questions, including when to fight, how to fight, and who should fight. One *hadith* suggests that it is, in fact, permissible to kill civilians when waging jihad: "The Prophet, peace be unto him, passed by a place and was asked whether it was permissible to attack the polytheists and pagans at night, with the probability of exposing their women and children to danger. The Prophet, peace be unto him, replied, 'They [the women and children] are from them, the polytheists and idolaters.' "

I asked how this might apply to Israel. The Jews are not polytheists, but people of the Book. So surely the killing of Jewish children is *haram*.

One of the students answered, "In the case of Israel, the Jews are too strong militarily, so the only means to hurt them are through their civilians—"

"There are no Israeli civilians," Mullah Abdallah interrupted, looking at me.

"—Yes, right," the student said. "This is why they are so strong. So it is permissible to strike at their civilians."

Abdallah cited another saying that forecast the destruction of the Jews. It is a *hadith* the theologians of Hamas quote regularly: "The Muslims will fight against the Jews till some of them will hide behind stones. The stones will betray them, saying, 'O, Abdallah [Abdallah means "slave of God"], there is a Jew hiding behind me, so kill him. The Hour will not come until you fight against the Jew,' " the saying concludes.

Maulana Haq seemed to find it perversely enjoyable to talk about Islam with me. He certainly had a sense of humor about it. "The Holy Quran teaches us that the Jews do not listen to the word of God," he said, giving me a green leather Saudi Quran as a gift. Then he smiled. "We will see."

I noticed one particular footnote in this Quran, one obviously influenced by Shakespeare: "The Jews in their arrogance claimed that all wisdom and all knowledge of Allah were enclosed in their hearts. But there were more things in heaven and earth than were dreamt of in their philosophy. Their claim was not only arrogance but blasphemy." This Saudi Quran, I was seeing, was a catalogue of Jewish sin.

Haq asked me a question. "I have never understood this," he said.

"The Jews should have been the very first people in the world to accept the word of Muhammad, peace be unto him. They were acquainted with God. So why do you reject the message of Muhammad? I would like you to become a Muslim."

Well, that's very good, I said, but I'll be staying Jewish.

"It is so arrogant of the Jews to ignore Muhammad," he said. "He is the final Prophet."

"It is so arrogant of you to ignore the Bible," I said.

"But we don't! The Jewish prophets are our prophets as well." This is true, but in name only; the Jewish prophets are also found in the Quran, but their stories are distorted—the Quran, for example, has Abraham giving his blessing to Ishmael, not Isaac.

"Would you say the *shahada* with me?" he asked. The *shahada* is the Muslim testimony of faith. An infidel who states the *shahada* with a clean heart before two Muslim witnesses is then considered a Muslim. "I bear witness that there is no God but Allah," the *shahada* goes, "and I bear witness Muhammad is His slave and messenger."

"I'm not interested in conversion," I said.

"It's not conversion," he said. "We are all born Muslim. Islam is the original word of God."

No thank you.

"I am offering you Paradise, and you say no."

"How do you know Paradise even exists?" I asked.

His face took on a hard cast.

"This is blasphemy," he said. "The word of God tells us of Paradise."

I said, "I choose to stay Jewish."

"You would be a fine Muslim," he said. He suggested a new name for me: "Imad Udeen," which means "pillar of faith."

Imad Udeen Goldberg.

"There is no compulsion in religion," I said, quoting the Quran.

"I am not compelling you. I am just telling you honestly that you can have life in heaven with God, or eternal hellfire."

I asked the maulana if the Jews were in fact twice cursed by God.

Yes, he said. The first curse has already befallen your impious people, he said. It happened in ancient times, when the Babylonians destroyed your cities and enslaved your ancestors. The second curse, he said, is coming: "Allah in His magnificence will wipe the stain of Israel from the clean face of the earth. This is the promise of Islam."

I stayed at the madrasa for a few weeks, leaving only for occasional appointments in Islamabad, such as the birthday party for Pakistan's nuclear bomb, which was thrown by the dictator Pervez Musharraf. A man on a motorcycle delivered the invitation to me one day. The invitation read, "To celebrate the Second Anniversary of 'Yaum-e-Takbeer,' the Minister for Science & Technology, Prof. Dr. Atta-ur-Rahman, requests the pleasure of your company."

"Yaum-e-Takbeer" means "the day of God's greatness," a reference to the day Pakistan's nuclear scientists detonated an atomic bomb under the Chagai Hills in western Pakistan. It was a great day for Pakistan, and for Muslims in general: The events of the Day of God's Greatness officially qualified them for membership in the nuclear club. Pakistanis had gone pie-eyed over the bomb. Full-scale models of the country's long-range ballistic missile took aim at the sky from traffic circles across the country. In the metropolises stood thirty-foot-high models of the Chagai Hills, which were lighted up at night in fiery oranges and reds.

The party was held at the National Library Auditorium in Islamabad in the presence of General Musharraf, and the beau monde of Pakistan's defense establishment. There were speeches and songs and a vast vanilla sheet cake, the words "Yaum-e-Takbeer" written in lemon frosting.

"We bow our heads to Allah almighty for restoring greatness to Pakistan on May 28, 1998," proclaimed Rahman, the science minister. The room was humid and the speeches stultifying but General Musharraf told me afterward that things went very well, in his view. I was standing in a circle of men, all of us eating cake. One of the men, in a bespoke suit, noted the absence of foreign dignitaries at the ceremony, to which another man said, "The world can't accustom itself to our strength."

"Why do you think that is?" I asked.

The second man answered: "Because the world is frightened of Muslim power. They don't call the American bomb a Christian bomb. They don't call India's bomb a Hindu bomb. The Jews have a bomb and the Muslims didn't. What's fair about this? Israel is an aggressor state and needs to be confronted."

There was something odd about this statement. The Pakistani bomb was meant to counter the Indian bomb, or so the experts said. But this fellow, a physicist whose name I later learned was A. Q. Khan, had the Jews on his mind. "Why is there such a double standard?" he asked. "All the West is an enemy of Islam. The West has been leading a crusade against the Muslims for a thousand years. Israel is the leader of the crusade. The West will have Israel use its bomb on the Muslims. The crusades have not ended. The war against our religion has not stopped."

The Pakistanis nodded in agreement.

"Why do the Americans want to destroy Islam?" one of them asked me.

A. Q. Khan left in the company of General Musharraf. I was ignorant at the time of his importance, but this was the man the Pakistanis called the father of their bomb. Several years later, he would be accused of selling Pakistani nuclear technology to, among others, the Islamic Republic of Iran.

CHAPTER NINETEEN

ABRAHAM WAS A MUSLIM

"Allahu Akbar! Allahu Akbar!"

I was on the ground, the victim of an expertly administered horse collar tackle. A stampede of students poured past me into the streets around Cairo University. "Open the door to jihad!" they screamed. The man who sacked me had bad intentions and a hard gleam in his eyes but the others who trampled me were merely riding a cresting wave. I scrambled to the sidewalk and watched a gang of men demolish a Kentucky Fried Chicken. Then the swarm set off for the Israeli embassy, but the riot police arrived swinging truncheons. Tear gas canisters hissed through the air. Palestinians would know what to do in such moments, but these bourgeois Egyptians were too sensitive to be tear-gassed and they retreated, wet faced. A canister came down near me and I covered my face with my sleeve and made a blind dash for anywhere inside.

All of Cairo was boiling. Demonstrators thronged the mosques. The police rolled water cannons up to the entrance of the al-Azhar Mosque to threaten the worshippers. The crowds burned Israeli flags and chanted, "There is no God but Allah and the Jews are the enemy of Allah." All the while the radio broadcast morbidly hysterical songs: "Jerusalem, death is on the loose among us," one singer cried.

By October 2000 the seven-year hope of Oslo was turning to ash. The new Intifada—the second Intifada, the al-Aksa Intifada, named after the mosque that looms over the Western Wall—was rampant, bloody, and unstoppable. The Likud leader Ariel Sharon had lit the match three weeks earlier when he made a well-policed pilgrimage to the Temple Mount. The players knew their roles: The Arabs rioted and the Israeli police broke out their stores of live ammunition, and soon the peace process was collapsing under the weight of the accumulating dead.

Arab leaders would soon be gathering in Cairo to condemn the Israeli barbarians and make sumptuous promises to the Palestinians, who knew better than to believe their brethren. The students of Cairo University required militancy from their leaders, who would not satisfy the demand. Some of the leaders struck radical poses, though. Muammar Qaddafi left early to protest what he saw as the impotence of the moderate Arab states. The Iraqis, the Syrians, and the Yemenis would leave dispirited as well, calling the final declaration of the summit an impotent response to Israeli genocide. They wanted instead a declaration of jihad against Israel that would expire with the last Jew. "The Jews will be taught a lesson," the Iraqi vice president, Izzat Ibrahim al-Duri, said as he left his hotel one morning. I pressed near to ask him another question and for this impertinence the secret police expelled me from the summit, but my banishment had the useful consequence of sending me out into the city to gather its fury.

The Jews were cursed in the mosques and on television. The most stunning lies were called brave truths. I visited a film producer named Munir Radhi, who was planning to turn a book called *The Matzoh of Zion* into a movie. The book was written by the Syrian defense minister, Mustafa Tlass, who treated as fact the Damascus blood libel of 1840, in which the city's Jews were accused of murdering a priest and his servant and baking their blood into their Passover matzoh. The predictable pogrom had ensued.

"The Muslim world needs to know about these Jewish rituals," Radhi said, though he promised an understated approach to the violence of the Jews: While he would dramatize the slaughter of the priest, he would only imply the actual draining of his blood. I noted that *The Matzoh of Zion* was an anti-Semitic tract, to which he said: "How can the truth be anti-Semitic?"

Cairo is the cultural center of the Arab world. Its books and newspapers are read in Europe and America, its television stations transmit to six continents. And yet many of its most intelligent citizens were on a flight from reason. "You have to admit that Ariel Sharon shows the classic Jewish characteristics of aggression and duplicity," an editor of Cairo's leading magazine said. "No one in the world is as violent as the Jews," an editor of Cairo's biggest newspaper told me.

I took an afternoon off, seeking a bit of quiet in the halls of the Egyptian Museum, the repository of the country's expired greatness.

Its director, Mamdouh Eldamaty, was an acquaintance, and he offered to walk through the exhibit halls with me. He showed me the new humidity-controlled mummy room—twelve pharaohs in all, supine in immortal humiliation. The dry, emaciated body of Rameses II was covered by a length of cloth, but his collapsed, eyeless face was visible inside his glass sarcophagus. Some archaeologists believe that Rameses II may have been the pharaoh of Exodus.

We soon came upon a huge slab of stone, a stele on which was carved in hieroglyphics the exploits of one of Rameses' sons, the pharaoh Merneptah. The stele contains the first reference to the existence of Jews outside the Bible. It is not a pleasant reference, or an accurate one. "Israel is laid waste, her seed is no more," the stele asserts.

Well, fuck you, I thought.

Mamdouh said, "The stele doesn't refer to Israel as a nation. It refers to a group of people, like a clan. Not a nation."

But it was a nation, I said, and it *is* a nation, whether you like it or not.

I was becoming estranged from usual feeling. For a moment I wasn't interested in celebrating the ties that bind Arab and Jew together. I was interested instead in standing with my people. My blood was on the rise.

And so, I learned, was Rafiq's.

I went to see him on my return from Cairo, to measure his mood. We met at a Starbucks on Massachusetts Avenue, near campus. He was furious at Israel, but I reassured him that our friendship would survive. He wasn't the one who needed reassuring. I had recovered from my dark tribal mood, and I wanted to make sure I could still have it all: my parochialism, my universalism, a clean conscience, and a friendship with my enemy. I was glad Rafiq didn't seem angry at me. On the other hand, his face was closed and shadowed when he spoke.

I scraped around for signs of promise. I noted that our two peoples were still negotiating. But this was thin borscht, and I knew it.

"It's all Israel's fault," he said bitterly. "Barak allowed Sharon to go to the Haram al-Sharif. You know why, right? Because Barak is the same as all of them." Rafiq never called it the Temple Mount. "Of course they all knew this would happen. There's no Muslim who would allow Sharon to walk on the Haram."

I assumed a pained expression and kept my more complicated feelings to myself. I was becoming convinced, for one thing, that the Intifada was not exclusively Sharon's fault. But I moved the conversation away from the Middle East and to the safety of American politics, to the upcoming election. But it turned out that Rafiq had strong feelings about this as well. He told me he feared Al Gore and much preferred George W. Bush. Bush's father was no friend of Israel, he said, while Gore was a notorious Zionist, and his running mate was an Orthodox Jew, an idea that frightened Rafiq.

I drove Rafiq home. Our route took us past the rear entrance of the U.S. Naval Observatory, which sits at the top of a hill along Embassy Row. A house on the observatory grounds is the official residence of the vice president. The front of the complex, along Massachusetts Avenue, was always stringently guarded, but its flanks appeared exposed. I noted that a shrewd terrorist could find his way into the vice president's house.

"We'll wait until Joe Lieberman moves in," Rafiq said, and laughed for the first time that day.

As we parted I told Rafiq I was going to Israel soon, in order to see Sharon. He could not quite absorb the information—it was as if I told him I was going off to play pinochle with Satan.

"You know, the Quran doesn't mention Jerusalem once," Ariel Sharon was saying. "In the Bible it is mentioned 676 times. Muhammad was never in Jerusalem. When the Muslims occupied Jerusalem, it was seven years after Muhammad's death. They say he came here and went to heaven. Yeah—seven years after he died."

We were sitting in his farmhouse at the edge of the Negev, within rocket range of Gaza. He was eating from a tube of Pringles. "You know, when the Jews pray, all over the world, they face the Temple Mount," he said. "When an Arab prays, he prays to Mecca. Even when an Arab is on the Mount, his back is to it. Also some of his lower parts."

Sharon did not believe he was the cause of this new Uprising. I asked him to name the spark.

"The Arabs don't want the Jews to be here," he said. "That is the secret of this whole story. This land we are on is considered by the Muslims to be holy land. They will never let anyone else possess it. Read the Quran—you'll see what they think about the Jews."

Sharon was avuncular and unpretentious. He had a capacity for charm when it suited his needs. I first met him in New York in 1992. He asked me at the time why I had left Israel. I manfully transferred most of the blame to Pamela. So he decided to write her a letter. "Dear Pamela," it read, "Come to Israel. We need you in our beautiful country." She was touched, but not moved. "You liked him, didn't you?" she asked, surprised.

No, I didn't. I was still partial to fighting Jews, but I preferred fighting Jews who knew when to stop fighting, and Sharon never stopped. He didn't stop, most consequentially, in Beirut in 1982, when he was serving as Menachem Begin's defense minister. The result was the massacre of Palestinians in the Sabra and Shatila refugee camps by Sharon's Christian Phalange allies.

Sharon's visit to the Temple Mount came when the peace process was at its most frail. The Camp David peace talks had ended two months earlier. The prime minister, Ehud Barak, had offered Yasser Arafat a state that would have occupied roughly 90 percent of the West Bank and 100 percent of Gaza, and which would have had its capital in East Jerusalem. In the Barak vision of peace, the Temple Mount would have been shared by Muslim and Jew. For the first time in Israeli history—for the first time in Jewish history, in fact—a Jewish leader offered to cede control of a part of Jerusalem to his enemy. Neither Titus nor Nebuchadnezzar stood at the gates; Jerusalem was safely in Jewish hands. And yet Barak was willing to sacrifice a piece of our holiest city in order to gain peace.

The Palestinians were unimpressed. To the stunned surprise of Barak and President Clinton, the Palestinians announced that they did not believe the Jews had a historic claim on Jerusalem. The chief Palestinian negotiator, the ostensibly secular Saeb Erekat, told me shortly after Camp David, "I have never seen any proof that there was a Jewish temple on the Haram al-Sharif. The Haram must be Muslim in its entirety."

Rafiq had been right: It would have been best to leave Jerusalem off the agenda.

Arafat left Camp David without even making Barak a counteroffer. Instead, he gave him an Intifada.

By late autumn Barak was an outcast. But he found solace where he could. "I tried to do something brave," he told me one day in his office. "I feel I know what I'm doing is right."

There was nobility in his failure. Barak charged into the unknown because he knew his nation could not withstand the moral damage of an occupation without end. The first Intifada, he said, was a kind of payment for Israeli hubris. "It was a misjudgment of reality to believe that a Jewish state could rule over another people for twenty years." At Camp David he was searching for a future free of Ketziots. "I had decided that in order to avoid a tragedy, a deterioration into full-scale violence, that we have to—without breaking from our vital interests—just put everything on the table and try to solve it."

And yet Barak could not claim all my sympathy. The world was massed against Sharon, but what was his crime? To assert the right of a Jew to visit the holiest site in Judaism?

This question first nagged at me in Cairo. Egypt's most important cleric, the sheikh of al-Azhar, Muhammad Sayyed Tantawi, told me, as Erekat would, that the Temple Mount was never the site of a Jewish temple. This was an absurd idea, though mainstream in the Muslim world. But Tantawi, a spry man with a false smile, went even further. The Western Wall, he said, wasn't Jewish either. The Western Wall was called al-Buraq, after Muhammad's miraculous flying steed, which Muslims believe carried the Prophet to Jerusalem and then on to heaven. Although Jerusalem is not mentioned in the Quran—Sharon was right about this—Muslims have surmised that it was Muhammad's final stop on earth. The Western Wall was where he tethered al-Buraq before his ascent.

"So it is Muslim property just like the Haram," the sheikh said. He also told me that Islam is older than Judaism. "Abraham was a Muslim," he said. "Moses was a Muslim, Solomon was a Muslim. All of the figures of the Bible were Muslims."

This was too much.

When Alice meets the Queen of Hearts, she says: "One can't believe impossible things." The Queen responds: "I daresay you haven't had much practice. . . . When I was your age, I always did it for half-an-hour a day. Why sometimes, I've believed as many as six impossible things before breakfast."

Tantawi wasn't delusional, but something worse: He was a thief of history. Jerusalem is where I found my deepest self, and he wanted to take it from me. We argued; I said that the Foundation Stone, the massive rock that is now sheltered by the golden Muslim dome, was the physical core of Jewish national existence, but he said it had nothing to do with Jews. I was not denying a Muslim connection to the Mount; I was simply noting a Jewish one. And I certainly didn't want to refuse Muslims the satisfaction of prayer at one of their holy places. But there was something he needed to understand: Before there was a Dome of the Rock and a Prophet Muhammad, there was a Jewish Temple and a King Solomon.

Tantawi sat serenely as I spoke. But his deputy, who sat with us, was fibrillating with anger. Stupidly, I gave him his moment. I happened to cross my legs as the sheikh was answering a question, and in so doing I gave him a glimpse of the sole of my shoe. It is a terrible insult to show an Arab the sole of your shoe. The deputy whacked my foot down with the back of his hand. "Don't show him your shoe!" he yelled.

"Very sorry," I said reflexively—and regretfully. If they didn't like the sole of my shoe, well, there was a lot I didn't like about them—their cloying certainty, their smugness, and their callow misinterpretations of a sister faith, my faith.

Ariel Sharon said that day on his farm: "The Arabs want you to believe that history began in 1967. . . . They know I would never give them what Barak wanted to give them, but they turned on Barak. Do you know why? Because they don't want the West Bank. They want everything."

God help me but I began to believe him. The first Uprising—the Uprising that built Ketziot—was meant to reverse the occupation of 1967. But this second Uprising was different—it was an attempt to undo the outcome of the 1948 war, the war that returned my people home.

It was a different Uprising in other ways as well. It was bloodier than the first Uprising and it was also less popular. In the first Intifada the war cry of Fatah—"Where are the millions?"—would go up in the streets and the millions would rush out to confront the army and fill its jails. But this time the villages of the West Bank were quiet, and the people of East Jerusalem, after discharging their rage in the days immediately after Sharon's visit, vanished from the streets. Even at the confrontation lines outside the cities of the West Bank the army faced hundreds of Palestinians at a time, not the thousands of the late 1980s.

I asked Marwan Barghouti one day where the millions went. He was still the favorite of Israel's fast-shrinking left, though he was now commanding Fatah's street forces on the West Bank and had no time to participate in encounter groups. "The people's anger is the same," he explained, "but it's harder now to find the Israelis to confront. They stay outside the cities." This was true—the Israelis had ceded the cities to the Palestinian Authority at the outset of the peace process.

We went together to the Ayyosh junction, at the northern end of Ramallah, to see what little action there was. The junction, just south of the Jewish settlement of Beit-El, was by unspoken agreement the main friction point between the army and the Palestinians. A man selling baklava had set up shop a few dozen yards from the front line. We bought Cokes. Barghouti went to speak to his lieutenants, who were hiding in a shot-up apartment building nearby. The high schools had let out for the day, and a group of girls in uniforms arrived to break rocks for the boys, who were up ahead, forty or fifty of them, hiding behind a burned-out bus.

Four Israeli jeeps were parked in a tight line about forty yards from the bus, across a stony field. The soldiers inside wore helmets and flak jackets and stepped out to fire tear gas. The Palestinians threw rocks at the jeeps, but they were new to this, and their aim was poor.

After dark, the Tanzim, the Fatah militia under Barghouti's command, would bring out the guns, but during daylight this was the province of children. I drank my Coke and watched. It seemed tame, even languid, not serious at all, until the boy next to me was shot. A geyser of blood erupted sideways out of his neck. He was sixteen, at most. He collapsed fast. Medics rushed to grab him. They threw him on a stretcher and ran.

I was stunned. There was no need to shoot the boy. The Israelis were safe in their jeeps.

"You see what they do?" Barghouti screamed at me. I was running up the street, looking for a taxi to take me to the Israeli line. I found one, which took me in a wide loop around the junction, to the Israeli side, and within five minutes we were behind the Israelis. What a strange and terrible war! I walked with upturned palms to the jeeps. I found a sergeant smoking behind a low wall. I let out a booming *"Shalom."* He nodded in return.

I asked him in Hebrew why his men were shooting down Palestinians.

"They have guns," he said.

No they don't, I said. They have stones.

"No, they have guns."

Bullshit. I was just there, they don't have guns.

"They will," he said, as his comrades continued shooting into the mass of unarmed Arabs.

And they say that the Jews have a gift for learning.

The army would kill more men in Ramallah. Osama Khalil and Majed Hussein Radwan were two of them. They were shot down outside a settlement a few days later. The army said they were firing rifles at Jews. The Palestinians said they were unarmed. I couldn't figure out who was lying.

Thousands of Palestinians, their faces like thunder, marched in the funeral procession for the two men. This grim parade cascaded down narrow streets to the cemetery. Many of the marchers were armed. The bodies were carried on trucks. A Fatah man in the bed of a pickup screamed into a megaphone: "Give us weapons, O Abu Ammar, and we will set the West Bank on fire!" "Abu Ammar" is Arafat's nom de guerre. The crowd chanted, "O, Saddam, send your missiles to Tel Aviv!" I picked up other scraps of slogans, and then I heard, from behind me, another sort of slogan entirely: *"Khaybar, Khaybar, ya Yahud, jaysh Muhammad sawf ya'ud!"*

It meant, "O Jews of Khaybar, the army of Muhammad is returning!" I had not heard this slogan since Ketziot. It was the fundamentalists of Hamas who had chanted it then. This, however, was a Fatah funeral. These people were beardless. They were nationalists. They were violent, yes, but they weren't apocalyptic. And yet, the "Khaybar" in the slogan refers to a tribe of Jews defeated 1,400 years ago by the Prophet Muhammad. The intent was plain: These men of Ramallah made up the new army of Muhammad. The Palestinians were not only refighting the war of 1948, they were fighting an even older battle as well.

Barghouti stood over the open graves. His eulogy was not a remembrance of the dead, but a war cry. "Heaven is opening its doors to receive these martyrs of al-Aksa!" he screamed, tearing away at his vocal cords. "The Israelis are sending our people to heaven every day. They are killing us every day with helicopters, but they will never be able to destroy us. Look at that settlement!" He pointed to Psagot, on the hill. "Those settlers will learn, I promise!"

"Allahu Akbar!" the mourners shouted.

I left with Barghouti. We drove past his office. He was working in a third-floor apartment of a five-story residential building that housed families with small children. He put his office there because he feared assassination, and the children served as a shield. He was unconstrained by Western notions of chivalric behavior, notions he assumed, correctly, that Israel would respect.

In the car, Barghouti was jumpy and fidgeting, and he seemed hollowed out by fatigue. A bodyguard sat in the front seat, affecting a gangster lean, his elbow out the window. We sped by the skeleton of the Ramallah police station, which was destroyed in an Israeli rocket attack, in retaliation for the lynching of two Israeli reservists inside its walls. Barghouti couldn't bring himself to condemn the murders. "Let's talk about Israeli crimes," he said. "Let's talk about shooting kids at the junction."

"Why Khaybar?" I asked.

"It's a Jewish story," he said.

"Are you fighting against settlements or are you fighting against Jews?"

"We're fighting to free Palestine," he said.

Didn't you tell me once that peace was irrevocable? I asked.

"It always depended on the Israelis," he said. "Look, I know what you're going to say. Barak offered 90 percent of this, 70 percent of that. I don't care. I don't care what he offered. We want 100 percent. We can't take less than 100 percent."

And if you get it, you'll put an end to the conflict.

He laughed. "Then we could talk about bigger things."

Barghouti admitted that the Intifada would have erupted without Sharon.

"It was necessary in order to protect Palestinian rights," he said. "But Sharon provided a good excuse." By 1999, he said, he realized that the "unilateral disarmament" of the Palestinians was a mistake. "It became a negotiation between a slave and a master. We had an Intifada for six years without negotiations and then we had seven years of negotiating without Intifada. Now we should try both together. Unfortunately, the Israelis understand only violence."

No, I said, you're wrong.

He let out a dry, mean laugh. "No, we're right. We couldn't accept any more humiliation."

After dark, leaving Ramallah for Jerusalem, my taxi was pulled over by agents of Preventative Security. It was a moonless night. We were on a back road. There was no one to help me. Get out of the car, an agent said in English. I gave him my passport. His partner searched my bag, and searched me. They wheeled me around and put my hands on the hood of the taxi. One of the agents kicked my feet apart. He ran his hands up my thighs. "What are you doing here?" he asked.

I explained my business, then asked if I could turn around to face them.

"No!" the English-speaking agent yelled. I was still up against the taxi. The two men spoke in Arabic, and laughed. They were laughing at me.

"Why are you on this road?" they asked.

"To get around the checkpoint."

They lost interest in me quickly. They turned to the driver and yelled at him for a minute or two. One of the men threw my passport at me. "Don't take this road again," he said. Then they drove off.

My lungs were constricted, my palms were sweaty, and every bad feeling I ever had about this conflict came back to me in a flood.

CHAPTER TWENTY

A KITBAG QUESTION

"We know you were in Ketziot."

The smile of the secret policeman in that Gaza interrogation room was broad and gleeful. That was it, then, the end of my double life in Palestine. I could no longer travel the territories wearing the cloak of neutrality.

I was seated in a room that smelled of aftershave and cigarettes, in a building that belonged to a Palestinian security agency, one I didn't know. The lights burned whitely. The furniture was warped. There was a Judas window high up on the wall.

I thought at first I had been arrested by the Preventative Security Service of Muhammad Dahlan. It would have been my preference. Dahlan was a reasonable man, sort of, and I knew his deputy, Rashid Abu Shbak, who was once a prisoner of Block Four. He could attest in full candor that I did not have the capacities of a Shabak agent, which is what my interrogator, Abu Hamad, evidently believed me to be.

If this wasn't a Preventative Security facility, then Abu Hamad might represent the interests of Force 17, the personal bodyguard unit of Yasser Arafat. I had just been on a Force 17 base, which the previous evening had been bombed by the Israeli Air Force, a bombing that set the teeth of Force 17 on edge, as could be expected. It was at the Force 17 base that I had a fleeting, unsettling encounter with Capucci. I saw him across a courtyard, but he left without saying hello. This could have been an act of self-preservation on his part: We first met again in the time of Oslo, when such encounters could be more readily excused.

Abu Hamad said, no, he did not represent Force 17. He could have been lying, of course. Perhaps he was from the Mukhabarat, the secret police, of Amin al-Hindi. This would be disconcerting: Amin al-Hindi was not a Jew's idea of a good time—he was the chief plotter of the 1972 massacre of Israel's athletes at the Munich Olympics.

"I'll be back in a moment," Abu Hamad said.

He was clever. He had tricked me with kindness into speaking Hebrew and now he was grinding me down with his absences. Each time he left, he would lock the door from the outside, leaving me alone with my thoughts, which was not a good thing.

"When are you going to let me go?" I asked when he returned.

"Savlanut, habibi," he said. "Patience, my friend."

He brought someone with him this time, a fellow officer. The second man looked at me unemotionally. I thought I recognized him. The two muttered to each other in Arabic. Then the man left.

It was now more than a couple of hours since I had been arrested by these men at that café on Izzedine al-Qassem Street. My hope for a speedy denouement was fading.

"Tell me what you did in prison."

"Was that man a prisoner in Ketziot?" I asked.

"Everyone was a prisoner."

I know, I said. "Who was he?"

"No one. So, tell me about the prison."

"What can I say? I was a *shoter*. A *rosh katan*." A small head. "Block Four, 1991."

"Yehuda."

Yehuda, yes.

He asked why I made no mention of Ketziot previously.

"Would you?" I asked.

"Yes, I understand. I would be ashamed, I think," he said.

Touché.

"That's not what I meant."

"Who are you spying for?"

"I'm not a spy."

"Why were you at the Force 17 base? Why are you in Gaza?"

This was the third time he asked. Each time I provided elaborate answers. This time I told him, in so many words, that I was compelled by some inexplicable, self-destructive force to get close to bad things.

I asked him, again, for my telephone. I was pressing him to call the Palestinians listed in my address book.

Abu Hamad stepped out again. Then I realized that my telephone book also contained the numbers of senior officials of the Jewish settlement movement, along with the number for Ariel Sharon's farm.

Abu Hamad came back a half-hour later with the telephone. My imagination kicked in again and I decided that he had put a bomb inside. I could practically smell his scheming. He's another engineer, a son of Ayyash.

I thought back suddenly to one of the stranger days at Ketziot. My comrade, Jack Ross, had just received a gift from his family in America, a package of chemical foot warmers. I was in the funnel of the *lool,* talking to Capucci, when Jack brought one over. Capucci was curious, so we demonstrated its use. Shake it, and it gets hot. Really something, huh?

Capucci asked for one.

Ummm, sure. Why not? We handed it over and left the *lool* and then the cold hand of terror seized us. There are *chemicals* in that thing, for God's sake. We were such chumps. Never send an American to do an Israeli's job.

We decided to retrieve the foot warmer. We concocted a story for Capucci. Efrati, we said, had seen us give you the foot warmer. We will be in desperate trouble if we didn't get it back. Capucci studied us carefully. Okay, he said. He spoke to his deputy, who spoke to another prisoner, who called out to another pen in the *lool,* from which a shout went up, clear across Dizengoff, to someone in the West Bank sub-blocks, one hundred meters away.

Capucci said, "Go over there," meaning, across Dizengoff. "The *shaweesh* will have it."

It was astonishing. In ten minutes, the foot warmer had been delivered to a cage clear across the block. We went to the *shaweesh* and collected it. From then on, Jack and I referred to that particular sub-block as the laboratory.

Abu Hamad was scrolling down my address list. "I see Israelis," he said. I countered by reciting other names, Palestinian names, in my phone book: Abu Mazen, Abu Alaa, Abu Shanab—

He interrupted me to ask why I had joined the Israeli army.

I told him that I wanted to kill Hitler, but I was too late.

He didn't understand. "We know how it works," he said. "The Israelis recruit Jewish children for this purpose from a very early age. They tell them that their enemies are the Arabs. Everyone hates them, everyone is surrounding them, and they must come to Israel and learn to protect Israel from the Arabs. It's indoctrination. They take Americans and Russians and make them into Zionists. It's brainwashing. It's a very big operation."

I thought back to the dilapidated dining hall of Camp Shomria.

"You're describing the Hamas recruitment program," I said. He laughed.

"Do you do *milium*?" he asked, using the Hebrew word for army reserve duty.

I used to, I said. But now I'm very much an American.

I made this statement to Abu Hamad with unmixed pride. It was not merely a tactical assertion. I was proud to be an American, and I was no longer embarrassed to be an American Jew. There were many Israeli traits I still admired—the physicality, the bluntness, the contempt for powerlessness. But there were American Jewish traits I now had come to appreciate: irony, tolerance, and ambivalence about the possession of physical power and the use of force. These were not, after all, shameful traits.

These thoughts first appeared in my mind in, of all places, the Nusseirat Refugee Camp, in Gaza, where I had been visiting a couple of ex-prisoners. One of them was named Abed. He was a short, slight fellow, but he had a gun in his waistband and he was in a state of agitation the day I stopped by. "I've just got to kill an Israeli," he said, his face taut with fury. "I just have to kill one."

I waited for him to shoot me, but he just paced the room. Another of the ex-prisoners, Yihya, a student of political science, asked me, "Do you remember there was an attack at Erez a little while ago?"

I didn't. Erez was a preferred target of Palestinian attackers and their attacks were jumbled in my mind. "A martyr-bomber went to the Israeli side and wanted to blow up," Yihya said, "but he was shot by the soldiers. Remember? It was supposed to be Abed. Abed was supposed to be martyred that day. But he couldn't get the right permits to cross to the Israeli side. So they sent someone else."

I was shocked. I asked Abed: Why do you want to kill yourself? You have children.

Abed said, "I have to have revenge. My children have no life anyway. No one has a life."

I asked someone standing nearby, a Fatah man named Mustafa, if I should be worried in Abed's presence. He said, "Don't worry."

Abed heard this and came over.

Mustafa said, "He's worried you want to kill him."

Abed said, "No, I want to kill a real Israeli."

"I'm a real Israeli," I said, unconvincingly.

"No you're not."

"Yes I am. I was in the army, you know that."

Abed just laughed. "You're an American."

A few years before I would have been insulted. But at that moment I felt a kind of tranquillity, and not just because he wasn't going to kill me.

My Americanness did not accrue me any benefits, however, in the interrogation room.

Abu Hamad asked, "Why does America give so much support to Israel?"

I'd be happier discussing this in a restaurant, I said.

"Israel is only strong because it has the great power of America behind it," he said. "The only reason America supports Israel is because of the Jewish political power.

"You're going to have to stay with us for a while." He looked closely at me, monitoring my face for signs of distress. "Are you scared?" he asked.

No, I'm not, I said.

"But you don't have any Apaches or tanks," he said. "I think the Jews are scared except when they sit in their F-16s and bomb Arabs."

You know, you can't do this, I said. But he left the room.

In fact, of course, he could do this. He could do exactly as he pleased. Israel had given him its prisons.

Two hours went by. I finally knocked on the door. One of the guards eventually found the will to answer. I told him I needed a bathroom. He left, in order to seek the appropriate permissions. I stood there for ten minutes. This is what it is like to be someone's prisoner. Even your bladder belongs to someone else.

Finally, he came back. He searched me. Then we walked to the bathroom. We passed Abu Hamad in the hall.

"Did you call Rajoub? What about Dahlan?" I asked, but he would only say, *"Shweya, shweya,"* which is Arabic for "Slowly, slowly."

One of my prisoners, the dearly departed Bedouin cook Hassan, once taught me a song that went, *"Ra'anili, shweya, shweya, Ra'anili, aychuta aynaya."* It was a song of unrequited love about a girl named

Ra'ana. Translated, it meant, "My Ra'ana, slowly, slowly, I poke my eyes out."

I whistled this song on the way to the bathroom. I was faking insouciance, because now Jewish honor was at stake.

"Yalla," the guard said. "Move it." I fiddled around at the sink. There was no toilet paper, I noticed. I washed my face with silty Gaza water.

I finally decided that Capucci had betrayed me. He was my own personal *shtinker.* I arrived at this conclusion without facts, only intuition. Capucci held resentments, and deep suspicions, and his secrets were more carefully tended to than those of the Sphinx.

But perhaps it was that doubtful-looking clerk at the Deira Hotel. Perhaps it was my driver, who melted away in my moment of need.

No, it was Capucci.

On the other hand, Rashid Abu Shbak could be behind this. He had no personal reason to punish me, but I had long before learned that the personal in Palestine was not the political. Abu Shbak was the only Palestinian security official of high station who knew of my army service in Ketziot, or so I believed. When we first met, before the Intifada, I asked him to keep my history to himself, and he agreed.

But that was then.

A month or so before my arrest, I was asking questions in Gaza about a bus bombing. The bombing had taken place the previous November, outside Kfar Darom, one of the Jewish outposts in Gaza. This is the attack in which two adults died, and three small children of the same family lost limbs. The Israelis insisted that the bombing was conducted on the orders of Rashid Abu Shbak, and one of his aides, Suleiman Abu Matlaq. So I went to Abu Shbak and asked him directly. He denied it. "If they think I'm a terrorist, why do they keep calling me?" he asked. He was referring to his regular, semi-clandestine contacts with the Israeli security services. "Of course we had nothing to do with it. We're trying to control the Tanzim," the Fatah foot soldiers. "We're trying to stop violence." But the Israelis said they had Abu Shbak on tape, discussing the planting of the bomb. I made a choice for agnosticism on the issue. But did Rashid know that? Perhaps he thought I was spying on him.

I sat in the interrogation room in silence.

Another hour went by, then another. No one knew where I was. Pamela and I had a friend in Jerusalem named Esther Abramowitz who made it her job to worry about me when I went to Gaza, and she had ordered me to telephone the minute I stepped through Erez. Esther would raise the alert, though not for a while.

Abu Hamad came back into the room.

"You can go," he said.

"Why?" I asked.

Never in the history of Israel had someone asked such a sublimely stupid kitbag question.

It was after dark when they drove me back to my hotel. It was too late to leave Gaza. I ate dinner alone on the veranda. Then I went to sleep without even checking the locks.

"How was Palestine?" Rafiq asked.

"Interesting," I said.

"How's school?" I asked.

"Okay," he said, but he didn't seem to mean it.

He told me a group of Jewish students had recently held an "Israel Day" event on campus. He was walking across the green when one of his students, a Jewish boy—"I always grade him fairly," Rafiq said, preemptively—called him over. The students were distributing literature about Israel and selling food. "They had falafel," Rafiq said. "I said, 'First you steal our land, then you steal our food.' They thought I was just joking."

We caught up on events. He recited for me a litany of recent Israeli crimes. It was obvious he was spending a lot of time on the Web.

"I pay taxes," Rafiq said. "Did you know that? My tax money goes to send weapons to Israel that kill Palestinians. It's terrible."

Many of the misfortunes afflicting the Palestinians are caused not by American aid or Israeli criminality, but by the self-destructiveness of the Palestinians themselves, I said. He accused me of blaming the victim. I told him that the underdog isn't axiomatically right.

Something was bothering me. I asked him: "Rafiq, do you believe that there was a temple on the Temple Mount?"

He said, "I've never seen proof."

Get out of this, I told myself. Don't argue about religion. Friendships die in these sorts of cul-de-sacs. But I couldn't stop.

"Have you seen proof that Muhammad flew to heaven from Jerusalem on a winged steed?"

"It's written in the Quran."

No, actually it's not. The word "Jerusalem" isn't in the Quran, I said.

"Yes it is."

"No, it isn't."

"Hey, *shoter,*" he said, "it is."

"I'm not a *shoter.*"

"I'm just kidding," he said.

I told him I was going back to Gaza. Prudence demanded that I keep away, but I was going. Rafiq asked if I could take a package of clothing for his sister Intissar. Of course, I said. He said he would drop it by my house before I left.

He came by a few days later with Tahani. I invited them in, but they declined. We talked on the steps for a few minutes. Then Pamela came home. She was wearing shorts and a tank top. Tahani was wearing a gray cloak and a hijab. I hoped Rafiq wouldn't fall over from shock. He said hello while staring at the ground. I watched Tahani's eyes, but they said nothing. We all chatted in a warm and friendly way for a few minutes. They thanked me graciously and then left to go shopping.

"Another package," Pamela said dubiously when we went inside.

"You probably started another Intifada with that tank top," I said.

"You're really going to bring another package?" she asked. What she meant was, "I can't believe I married such a *freier.*"

"Have faith," I said, but a part of me knew she was right. I was mocking fate. Pamela had been—and not for nothing—unhappy about my recent arrest.

Our three-year-old daughter wandered by and pawed the package. Pamela gave me a look.

My flight back to Israel was nearly empty. Hardly anyone traveled there anymore. The news tended to dissuade sensible tourists, the latest news, especially: A suicide bomber from Hamas had just murdered twenty-one people, mostly teenagers, outside a disco in Tel Aviv called the Dolphinarium. The bomber, a twenty-two-year-old Hamas acolyte, was infected with hepatitis B and his flying body parts may have infected some of the survivors.

In other words, the American Colony was the only busy hotel in Jerusalem. I chose to stay at one of the Jewish hotels, though. I had a floor to myself.

The crossing into Gaza was painless. A friend met me on the Arab side of Erez. I made a round of prudential visits to the security services, though I decided to put off my search for Capucci. My questions for him could wait, especially because I dreaded the answers.

I went to Intissar's house. She was older than Rafiq by several years, and matronly; she had a handful of children—Rafiq couldn't remember the exact number, and she wouldn't tell me, out of superstition. We stood in the anteroom. She sent one of her sons to fetch her brother-in-law. Her husband was in Egypt, and she couldn't be seen having unsupervised visits from strange men. Intissar was a math teacher in a U.N.-run school—she and her husband had a fair income, but she was grateful for the clothing from Rafiq. The Intifada, she explained, was destroying the economy, the schools, life itself. I felt sympathetic just then. I thought she was suggesting that the Uprising was pointless. But she wasn't. In fact, she was quite hard-boiled. The students in her school wanted to become suicide bombers, and while she encouraged them to finish their studies, she could not think of a reason to tamp down their dreams.

Fayez, her husband's brother, struck a lordly pose upon his entrance. He questioned Intissar closely on my intentions and origins. Intissar knew the story, and she was opaque in her explanation of Rafiq's friendship with me, and I was glad for this, because Fayez was giving off vibrations of unreliability.

Intissar dutifully ceded the floor to Fayez, who lectured me unoriginally. "Israel is ruining our lives," he said. "Of course we will have suicide bombers. Tell the Americans to give us Apaches and we will fight them with Apaches."

Intissar nodded. When Fayez had spent his anger, she said, "I could send my own son to be a bomber. That's the way I feel."

I hoped I hadn't heard her right.

What was going on here?

This was too painful to contemplate. Intissar was a smart woman, the product of a smart family. But this was depraved. She was a sane woman who saw her womb as a bomb factory.

I told Intissar that Rafiq opposed suicide bombings. "Rafiq doesn't live here anymore," she said flatly.

If he did, I thought, he would have seen his society ravaged by a cult of death. Schools were named for suicide bombers; photographs of suicide bombers were pasted to the walls; kindergartens hung signs that read "Martyrs of tomorrow"; and children played "Martyrs and Jews" in the alleys.

One day in the Shejaiya neighborhood, an Islamic Jihad garrison in Gaza City, I watched a group of young boys play such a game. The youngest boy, named Ahmed, was the *shaheed*. He charged an imaginary bunker. The other boys made the sounds of firing rifles. Ahmed pretended to die. Two other boys—a five-year-old and a six-year-old—carried Ahmed's limp body down the sand-filled alleyway and held his funeral. They laid him out on the ground. The game ended when Ahmed rose from his imaginary grave, shouted *Allahu Akbar,* and giggled.

I later asked Ahmed's father, Abdullah Shami, the chief of the Islamic Jihad in Gaza, whether he wanted his eldest son, Hussam, to become a suicide bomber. "Of course I do," he said. "But it's his own choice. I won't push him in either direction."

The advocates of suicide killing seldom offered their own children for sacrifice, but they certainly encouraged others. "It is the youngest martyrs who I respect the most," the mufti of Jerusalem, Ikrima Sabri, told me. "They are like lions."

Everywhere the young were exhorted to sacrifice their lives. At a Hamas initiation ceremony I attended in Deir al-Balah, a refugee camp south of Gaza City, the message was simple: The moral consequences of continued existence on earth were unbearably burdensome for true Muslims. Only the grave provided absolution. "God will never forgive us if we don't kill the Jews," one of the initiates said. "The best way to kill them is to make the sacred explosion near them."

Who taught you this? I asked.

"The imams of my mosque."

The ceremony was held in a dank room in a shattered gray building at the end of an alley. An acquaintance from the prison named Muhammad brought me. We went up a dark staircase into a windowless room. There were twenty-five men there, covered from head to ankle in satin sheets. These were not like the billowing robes of the Ku Klux Klan—the Hamas robes fit the athletic forms of the men hidden underneath. The robes were tied with a sash at the waist, and the headpiece was held tightly. The eye slits were narrow, and there was no opening for the mouth. Each man wore a yellow band around his head that declared the wearer's fealty to the desires of Allah. There was a painting of the Dome of the Rock on one wall. The Dome was surrounded by green birds flying skyward. The birds stood for the suicide bomber on his flight to heaven.

There was little light. Two lanterns burned in front. Standing before us was a man wearing black; his face, too, was covered. He held an M-16 and a Quran.

Muhammad told me: "These men are about to become living martyrs."

The man in black read from the eighth and ninth chapters of the Quran—from the chapter called al-Anfal, "The Spoils of War," and from at-Tawba, "Repentance."

"Fight those who believe not in Allah nor the last Day," he read, "nor hold that forbidden which has been forbidden by Allah and his messenger, nor acknowledge the religion of truth, from among the people of the Book, until they pay the *Jizyah* with willing submission, and feel themselves subdued." The *Jizyah* is a special tax Jews and Christians—the people of the Book—were required to pay when they lived under Muslim rule. At-Tawba is the only chapter of the Quran that does not open with the words, *"Bismillah ir-rahman ir-raheem"*—"in the name of Allah, the compassionate and merciful"—because it is a hard, unforgiving chapter.

One by one, the men were called forward: The man dressed in black, the suicide instructor, placed the Quran against each man's forehead.

"May God protect the human bombs," he said, his voice muffled and harsh.

"What is your highest goal?" he asked the group.

"To walk in the path of martyrdom," the men responded.

Again: What is your highest goal? Again they made their delirious death pledge.

After the ceremony Muhammad introduced me to two members of this collegium of martyrs-in-waiting.

The first one said: "I want to make the sacred explosion today. I want the Jews to die from my anger." His assignment could come, he said, with as little as forty-eight hours' notice. Because of this, the martyrs-in-waiting passed their days in study and fasting. They fortified each other with descriptions of Paradise, of the seventy-two virgins.

The bombers also believed that their final act in life would bring such happiness to Allah that He would grant these martyrs permission to bring seventy of their relatives directly to Paradise upon their deaths. "My family and I will be together forever," one of the men said. "Because of what I will do, they will not have to pass through the fires and trials of God's judgment."

And so in their spare time these men made lists of the seventy blessed souls who would gain admission to Paradise.

The second man told me the bombers practiced their Hebrew with each other whenever possible. Success would depend on their ability to mix with their victims. The first man described for me his fantasy of death. He would follow the orders of his cell leader, of course, and blow himself up in a bus, if that is what he was told to do, but he would prefer to detonate his bomb in Tel Aviv, in a specific café, as a matter of fact. He would not name the café, which was smart of him, because I would have been compelled to tell the Shabak.

"I will walk in and order an alcohol drink," he said. "This way the Jews won't notice me. I will wait until the café becomes very crowded, after the working day is over. I will have to make the explosion standing up, because my bomb will have a thousand nails, and I don't want them going into the floor. I will look at the people who come into the café, and know their secret, that they are about to die. I will count the people around me. If it is more than fifty, I will yell *Allahu Akbar!* Then I will push the button. I know I have to yell very loudly because the cafes have music and people talking. But they need to hear the words *'Allahu Akbar,'* before they die. I think I can kill at least twenty Jews this way. I've asked God to allow me to kill thirty."

Why the nails? I asked.

"To go into the eyes of the Jews," he said.

He said he would like to destroy this particular café because its owner once humiliated his cousin. "The owner was a Jew from Morocco. My cousin washed dishes in the kitchen. The owner called him a dirty Arab. He fired him, and he didn't give my cousin ten days' salary."

His cousin, he said, would like to blow himself up as well, but the café was off-limits for him for fear that he would be recognized.

These men were young, and not yet married. I asked if they thought they would miss the satisfactions of marriage and fatherhood.

"Satisfaction is found in Paradise, not on earth," one of the men said. "I can't wait to be in the presence of Allah, in his garden. I am ready for it. Paradise will be so much better than this."

At the time I visited these future bombers, the death cult in Islam was mainly the concern of Jews, who were its target. But a great change was coming. Once I thought that the Palestinians were immune to the death theology of the jihadists in Afghanistan and Pakistan. But they weren't. In fact, they were innovators. The last will of Muhammad Atta, the epoch-making terrorist of American Airlines Flight 11, was no different linguistically or morally to those of the Hamas men I knew. Jihad Abu Swerah, the Gaza killer of my acquaintance, once told me that he hated this world. "Paradise is the goal," he said.

In his will, which was later found in his suitcase, Atta encouraged jihadists to remember that a better time was coming: "Strike like champions who do not want to go back to this world. Shout, '*Allahu Akbar*,' because this strikes fear in the hearts of the nonbelievers. . . . Know that the gardens of Paradise are waiting for you in all their beauty and the women of Paradise are waiting, calling out, 'Come hither, friend of God.' "

CHAPTER TWENTY-ONE

A LESSON FOR AMERICA

Muhammad Atta also wrote, "You should dedicate the slaughter to your fathers . . . because you have obligations toward them."

Atta's own father was seized by hallucinations in the weeks following September 11. His son, he told me, had nothing to do with the attacks—he had spoken to Muhammad several days after September 11—but in his dream state he was not alone, because much of the Arab world had become gripped by fantastical ideas concerning September 11, including the conspiratorial notion that the Mossad played a crucial role in the attacks. Atta's father, who is also named Muhammad, told me in Cairo later that September that his son was a naïve boy who was outmatched by nefarious Westerners—Jews, Americans, both, perhaps—who framed him for their crime, which had as a coming chapter the targeting of Muslims in America.

What was notable in America in the days after September 11 was the fairly comprehensive absence of revenge attacks on Muslims, but I was a great distance away and so images suggested by Atta's father and by the mythopoetical Cairo press—which was rather nakedly hoping for violence against Muslims in America—visited me, images of Rafiq's wife, Tahani, running a gauntlet of rednecks in the produce aisle of the Safeway. So I called Rafiq right upon my return. I couldn't reach him, so I called Kemal, who told me that Rafiq was preoccupied because he was accelerating his studies. But all was well, he said. Kemal's neighbors in suburban Maryland were solicitous in the days after the attacks, a couple of them offering to take Manal shopping, worried that she might feel self-conscious wearing the hijab in public.

Kemal told me of one strange incident, though, at his office, at the headquarters of the Health and Human Services Department. The police came one day and arrested another employee, a Pakistani-American. "He received some kind of chain e-mail that was suspicious," Kemal said. "They took him away in handcuffs." Was he a jihadist? Kemal laughed. "He worked in the health care finance division," he said. Kemal said there were no al-Qaeda operatives at Health and Human Services. He was philosophical about the incident, though. "These things happen. Everyone in the first days was angry, but there weren't any real problems," he said.

It turned out that Rafiq was more worried than Kemal suggested. When we finally spoke, he told me that he kept Tahani in the apartment for two weeks after September 11.

"There are so many things that a Muslim shouldn't see when you walk down the street in America," Rafiq said one day. "Do you know what *munkar* is?"

I did not. "*Munkar* is anything that is an abomination, things that are disliked by God," he said. He gave examples: "If you walk down the street you see bars and liquor stores everywhere and video stores that are selling pornographic videos. Something that is *munkar* is trying to draw you away from the right path."

Rafiq himself was not tempted by the *munkar* attractions of America. In Catholic terms, he avoided occasions for sin. His few non-Muslim friends edited their behavior in ways that pleased him. He stopped attending math department parties, he said, because pork and alcohol were served, and only ended his boycott when Mary Gray realized the faux pas. She decided to ban *haram* food and drink from these gatherings, and Rafiq once again attended.

No one, of course, was forcing beer down his throat. "This is true, but I don't want to be near such behavior."

"But you're in America," I said. "It's a free society."

"Have you ever watched *The Montel Williams Show*?" he asked. "There was a woman on with two men. She had just had a baby. And she said to these two men, 'You're both not the father.' It was so crazy. Nothing is normal here."

Kemal, he said, was even having trouble with his sons. They were growing up to become insolent Americans, and this was unacceptable. "You know, you can't hit your children here without someone calling 911," Rafiq said.

I asked him what he thought of the World Trade Center attack. We had avoided the subject for quite a while.

"It was too much," he said, his eyes cast downward. "It was too exaggerated. But America needed to be taught a lesson."

"What lesson?" I asked. "What lesson did America deserve?"

"Look at the way America behaves around the world. Look at how it behaves here."

America, I said, is the greatest country in the history of the earth.

Rafiq clucked his tongue. "How can you think that America is so great? Do you think your democracy is so great? You only have two political parties. If someone else wants to run you crush him. America has so many choices—look at all these stores, people always buying and buying—but there's no freedom in the important things."

"A lesson?" I asked. "You want a lesson taught? What kind of lesson kills children? That's your kind of lesson?"

"The Israelis kill children all the time. The Americans kill children!"

"For God's sake, we don't *try* to kill children. We don't go out of our way to kill children!"

My chest was in a clench.

America was giving him an education, and in return he wished for our deaths. Not all of our deaths—he made that clear. September 11 was, he said, "too much."

So, I asked, would the deaths of one thousand Americans have been sufficient?

"I said, it was too much," he answered.

How can you curse the country that gives itself to you?

Now *he* was upset. "Do you think they educate me out of goodness?" he asked. "They have a goal. They aren't doing this for nothing. They want to change the world according to the way they want." By this, he meant a world made receptive to consumerism and secularism.

We were all infidels in Rafiq's angry creed. I made one last reach across the divide.

"You went to a rally against suicide bombing in Gaza," I said. "You're against terrorism."

Then Rafiq said, "I wouldn't go to that rally today."

Rafiq stayed in America. He would take what he needed to take. Kemal, however, was making his exit.

"I don't want to raise my children here," he said one day. We were having lunch near the Capitol. A hospital in Saudi Arabia had hired him to make sense of its management, but it wasn't the professional challenge that drew him; it was the chance to raise his sons in a place that would make them proper Muslims. Kemal and I had differing notions about child discipline. "Islam teaches us that corporal punishment is permissible but should be used as a last resort," he said once. "It's a corrective, not a punishment. And you shouldn't hit your child in the face or in any sensitive places. It shouldn't be used much at all. But what is the alternative in America? In America the children are in charge and the parents are the children."

Do you think your family will be safer in Saudi Arabia? I asked.

"Yes," he said. "They won't be exposed to the *jahili* environment." *Jahili* refers to a state of pre-Islamic ignorance.

Kemal said he would miss many things about America—its material plenty, its culture of hard work—but it was time to be among Muslims. "It's better to stay with your own kind," he said.

And then he was gone.

I imagined that Rafiq would miss Kemal terribly. His brother's departure must have magnified Rafiq's feelings of isolation. I didn't know for certain, because I didn't call him for a very long time. I had decided not to abandon hope, but I needed a rest from his hostility. I called him, though, shortly before I left on another trip to the Middle East. He updated me on his studies. He told me Kemal was not entirely happy in Saudi Arabia, but he recognized that all beginnings are difficult.

I told him I was planning on visiting Gaza. It was time, I thought, to find Capucci.

There was a pause.

"Capucci's dead," he said.

I couldn't believe it. "How did he die?" I asked.

"It was a clan feud," Rafiq said.

A clan feud? You mean Palestinians killed him?

"Yes," he said. In Khan Younis.

I felt a perverse sort of relief. At least it wasn't my army that killed him.

Later, I thought to myself: How were we supposed to make peace with people who murder so many of their heroes?

"Capucci's clan has been fighting this other clan for a long time," Rafiq's cousin, Rafiq Hamdouna, explained a few days later. We were in his office at the seaside villa in Gaza City that housed the Society of Former Prisoners. "The men of the other clan came to his neighborhood and they shot eight or nine of the men in Capucci's clan. Everyone was sad about Capucci. Even the other clan liked Capucci. No one wanted him to die."

It was a hot day, but the windows and doors were closed, and the shades were drawn—Hamdouna had locked us in so we could speak Hebrew together. The darkness matched his mood. He was usually even-keeled but now he was grim, for good reason. It was a bleak time in Gaza. The borders were sealed, the work had disappeared. Violence was everywhere.

Capucci's death must have hit you hard, I said.

"I want to leave," he said. "I want to be a refugee. I've had enough. I have to leave. I can't take it anymore."

"You can't," I said abruptly. "These people need you."

Hamdouna ignored me. He told me his dream. "I want to go to Sweden. I want to open a falafel restaurant. I think I would be successful. I don't want to be here. I don't want my children to have the same miserable life."

A restaurant in Sweden. Takeout only, at first, but then a dining room, he said. Middle Eastern food, he said, was very popular in Northern Europe.

He was entertaining an even more outlandish dream as well.

"Do you think I could get to America?" he asked.

I'm not sure that would be so easy, I said.

"September 11?"

His past might interfere with his present, I said. Viewed in a certain light, Hamdouna was a terrorist and such information would make its way to the American embassy in Tel Aviv as it considered his request. He noted that his cousin Rafiq Hijazi was the recipient of a student visa. Hamdouna, though, was a terrorist of higher standing; he was once part of a cell that killed settlers. Rafiq Hijazi was a dilettante by comparison.

In any case, I said, Gaza needs you.

Hamdouna was an authentic moderate who stood at the barricades fighting the death cult. I told him, and myself, that things could change. We were enemies, but knowledge has made us friends. He stirred for a moment. "We have an expression like this in Arabic," he said. "To know your enemy brings you halfway to victory."

Well, no, that's not what I meant. But never mind. These connections, I said, can't be severed, and in their strength is hope that the world around us will change, and to this he agreed unconditionally. Then he asked me to write on his behalf to the consular section of the American embassy, but this I could not do, for any number of tragic reasons, including my inability to search his heart for secret malice, and my fear that exposure to America would turn him against America, as it had done to his cousin.

I wished him luck with the Swedes, and went in search of Capucci's martyr poster. I found several in downtown Gaza City. His photograph was superimposed over the Dome of the Rock. The text gave the dates of his various imprisonments, some general details of his service to Fatah (he worked, it said, in the "security and military" fields), and it labeled him, in large black letters, a "martyr." Nowhere on the poster were his murderers identified. Force 17, which published the poster, wanted the people of Gaza to assume that Israel was to blame.

I stared at his stony features against the backdrop of a gray wall smeared with graffiti. I would never know if he was the *shtinker*. But this was a petty concern. He left a family behind and that was the true tragedy. I went to Khan Younis to pay my respects to his wife, but it turned out that she was in hiding in Gaza City. I couldn't find anyone from his family. Finally, I stumbled upon one of his nephews, who spoke to me for a brief moment. The Jews killed my uncle, he said. No they didn't, I said. He knew, of course, that he was perpetrating a lie. But it was a lie that gave meaning to Capucci's death. Eventually, I found someone who filled in some blanks. He was a Block Four veteran named Atallah, a neighbor of Capucci's, and he told me that feuding was savaging Gaza. The impetus for the feud that took Capucci's life, Atallah said, could be located generally in a broader feud between two competing security organizations. There are protections built into Palestinian society against the escalation of feuds, but in this case none of the usual solutions worked. Mediators—the chiefs of other clans, generally—were brought in, and they proposed the outlines for a *sulha,* the stylized reconciliation ceremony that restores the honor of the aggrieved, but the power of spilled blood overwhelmed the good intentions of those who wanted to end the violence. The discussion had not even advanced to the matter of the blood-price. In Gaza, it generally cost \$25,000 or \$30,000, paid by the murderer to the victim's family, to neutralize a feud.

I told Atallah I was surprised by the size of the blood-price. This gave him an opening to introduce a new subject. He was hoping he could borrow money from me. He wouldn't ordinarily ask, he said, but the need was great. A doctor had botched his wife's episiotomy. He was out of work, he had no money, and his in-laws were feeding the children, which shamed him. He didn't want to become a bomber, he said, but one of the factions would pay his family \$8,000 or more if he became a martyr.

He was blackmailing me, of course. He was offering me the chance to prevent a suicide bombing. I asked how much the corrective surgery would cost.

The money wasn't for surgery, he said. It was to hire a gunman to kill the doctor.

CHAPTER TWENTY-TWO

A HAPPY MAN IN PALESTINE

It was an overcast, windy day at the Kalandia checkpoint. There were four or five hundred Palestinians bunched together, hoping to pass swiftly and without incident through the Israeli army lines. Kalandia separates Jerusalem from the besieged city of Ramallah. Green-plated Palestinian taxis waited on the Ramallah side for passengers, who were slow in coming. The checkpoint was manned by soldiers of the Nachal Brigade—Nachal is an acronym that means "Fighting Pioneer Youth"—and, by their looks there were new immigrants among them. Nachal frequently assembles *garinim,* seed groups, of recent immigrants, and teaches them to be Israeli. Today's lesson was in humiliation.

It wasn't necessary for me to wait with the Arabs. My press pass could have expedited my passage. But there was no rush—I was hoping to see Yasser Arafat at his headquarters, but it was still daylight and I had hours to kill before the midnight call from his aides. So I chose to make the trip to Ramallah in the Palestinian fashion: disagreeably. A shroud of ill feeling overhung Kalandia, which had the correct aesthetics for a military checkpoint: Jersey barriers funneled us into lines that wound past piles of quarried stone and spools of barbed wire. Our feet kicked up gray dust. It took a half-hour for me to reach the bottleneck, which was manned by three soldiers in flak jackets. I became angry as I got close. The soldiers were yelling at the Palestinians the way our drill sergeants once yelled at us. *"Yalla, yalla!"* one of them screamed at a man with a cane.

My turn came. I held up my passport for inspection.

"Shame on you," the soldier said in English. His accent was New York. He was tall and smooth-skinned. I watched his Adam's apple ratchet up and down. He was trying to contain himself, but couldn't.

"Excuse me?" I said. I had passed through many such checkpoints without commentary. His glandular hostility threw me.

"Shame on you for going to them," he said.

I told him to mind his own business.

"You're on *their* side?" the soldier asked.

"What do you know about me?" I said.

We went on like this for a minute and I left the funnel, bringing to an end the colloquy.

I walked to the waiting taxis. I had become a hero to the Palestinians who saw the confrontation. And I was with them in spirit—I was an enemy of checkpoints and a champion of honor. This feeling lasted three entire days. On the fourth day a suicide bomber penetrated the screen of checkpoints around Jerusalem and committed murder. I had made an unthinking assumption at Kalandia: I had assumed the innocence of the Palestinians around me, when one of them could quite easily have been strapped with a bomb meant to kill Jews. This was undeniably what contributed to the unbalanced state of my Nachal friend. The checkpoints were the curse of Palestinian existence, but whenever the army let some slack into the system, the suicide bombers breached the lines and committed murder.

Soon enough, Hamas would make sure there would be no slack.

The end of all pretense came on March 27, 2002, when a Hamas bomber walked through the front door of the Park Hotel in Netanya, on the coast north of Tel Aviv, and detonated himself in the middle of a Passover seder. He killed thirty Jews and injured another 140. Ariel Sharon quickly ended the fiction of Palestinian autonomy and ordered an invasion of the West Bank. In the refugee camp at Jenin, in the northern West Bank, soldiers went house-to-booby-trapped-house in the hunt for bombers. They killed dozens, and lost twenty-three of their own in the fight.

After the incursion into Jenin, the Palestinians, abetted by some of the more credulous members of the American Colony press corps, accused the army of committing a massacre. This was the opposite of truth: The army in Jenin killed the makers of massacres. Of course, the Palestinians knew this to be the case. They boasted to themselves of Jenin's faithful production of murderers. In a document captured by the army after the attack, Fatah officials referred to Jenin as the "capital of suicide."

The document in question was addressed to Marwan Barghouti, who, in that haywire month, was given the chance to martyr himself but declined. When the army came to arrest him at his safe house in Ramallah he came out with his hands up. An Israeli officer gave him a bottle of water and drove him to jail.

More than seven thousand Palestinians had been swept up in the Israeli incursion. There was no place, of course, to warehouse them all. So on April 17, the army decided to resurrect Ketziot.

The only happy men in Palestine then were the killers. It was proximity to the abyss that induced this happinesss. Sheikh Yassin was elated. He told me his martyr bombers would soon force the disintegration of Israel. The Jews will run away from our warriors, he said, even as his people were fleeing the guns of Jewish tanks.

The dour Abdel Aziz Rantisi seemed happy as well. He was ordinarily a petulant man, disliked even within Hamas for his mean temper. I had particular prejudices against him, both because he was a pediatrician who murdered Jewish children and because he gave Rafiq a hard time in Block Four. In Ketziot, Rantisi made absurd demands on Fatah. "He thought he owned the prison," Rafiq told me once. "But Fatah was in charge."

Actually, *we* were in charge, I said, which caused Rafiq to break out laughing.

In the summer of 2002, the revolt was proceeding apace, and Hamas was strong in the streets of Gaza. Rantisi was pleased. We passed one afternoon talking in a most relaxed way, even reminiscing about Ketziot. "Do you remember Shaltiel?" he asked, referring to the colonel who commanded the prison.

"Sure I do," I said.

"Shaltiel called the Palestinians for a meeting, the prisoner leaders, and I was one of them," he said. "They brought us from our tents by bus, to his office. We took our chairs inside, and then an officer came in and asked us to stand for Shaltiel. Really, all the prisoners just stood, but I refused. Shaltiel came in, and said 'You have to stand.' I said, 'You are not Allah, I stand just for Allah.' After a few minutes of talking, he said to me, What will be the solution? I said, I will continue sitting or I'll return to my tent. He said, 'Okay, you can return.' Then he sentenced me to solitary confinement for three months."

He was taken immediately to *zinzana*. "One of the policemen in charge of the cells was really astonished by this. 'Three months,' he said. 'Usually it's one day.' Really, he sympathized with me. He gave me sympathy."

So this *shoter* was a good Israeli?

"This is a strange question," Rantisi said. He preferred to dwell on the sins of Shaltiel. "He will suffer as I suffered," Rantisi said. His meaning was unclear to me. Was he planning a Levantine version of the Count of Monte Cristo? Or was he merely saying that Shaltiel would suffer the judgment of Allah? "All the Jews will suffer," he said.

Rantisi was one of the seven founders of Hamas. He was born in the town of Yibna, in October 1947. His family fled six months later to Khan Younis. Yibna is known today by its original name, Yavneh, and it is wholly Jewish. In the time of the destruction of the Second Temple, Yavneh was a center of Jewish learning.

Rantisi attended medical school at the University of Alexandria in Egypt, and it was there that he was introduced to the ideology of the Muslim Brotherhood, and to the thinking of its most essential theologians, including Hassan al-Banna, who founded the movement in 1928, and Sayyid Qutb, whose book, *Signposts on the Road,* is the Islamist *Guide for the Perplexed*. Qutb's masterwork, a thirty-volume compendium called *In the Shade of the Quran,* revivified and radicalized the fundamentalist strain of Islam. Qutb's Islam is a harsh desert religion, spiteful to Christians and Jews, unforgiving of those believers who do not live up to its implacable demands. It spoke to Rantisi. He came back to Gaza as a fully fledged Muslim Brother.

"Qutb is the most important thinker," he said. "He said that Islam is the answer to all parts of our lives, that it can be integrated with science, with your family life, with everything. It's the answer. The world is in chaos, but Islam stands with clarity and beauty. Everything else fails except Islam."

Rantisi maintained a medical practice in Gaza but became a Muslim activist. He also became a discordant figure at the Islamic University of Gaza, where he taught genetics. He devoted himself to purging the school of PLO influence. The goal of the Muslim Brotherhood acolytes in Gaza was to turn the Palestinian people to God; the confrontation with Israel could begin once the people were united under the banner of Islam.

But the first Intifada erupted before the Brotherhood could shepherd the masses into the Quran's shade. Expediency won the day, and the Muslim Brothers joined the liberation struggle, announcing the birth of Hamas and issuing a charter, a prolix, hateful document that mentions nothing of "occupation," as the word is generally understood—that is to say, the temporal occupation by Israel of the West Bank and Gaza. According to the charter, Jewish control of Palestine is an insult to God. "Our struggle against the Jews is very great and very serious," it reads. "It strives to raise the banner of Allah over every inch of Palestine. The Prophet, Allah bless him and grant him salvation, has said, 'The Day of Judgment will not come about until Muslims fight the Jews.' "

Hamas, more than any other force, transformed the dispute between Arabs and Israelis into one between Muslims and Jews. There was no category called "Israeli" in Rantisi's bifurcated understanding of the world. There is the *umma,* which represents the light, and then there are the Jews, who are darkness. "The Quran says that they will be behind violence and wars everywhere," he said. "This is true throughout history. They stole money from everyone. People always talk about what the Germans did to the Jews, but the true question is, What did the Jews do to the Germans?"

There was a small chance that Rantisi's ancestors were Jewish—Yavneh was home to many Jews in the time of the Muslim conquest of Palestine, and there is a scholarly notion that some of these Jews were converted to Islam. I mentioned this to Rantisi in order to annoy him.

"Impossible," he said. "Do I look Jewish?"

"Well, actually, yes."

"Are you crazy?"

"You know, Isaac and Ishmael came from the same father. Maybe you have a little Isaac in you," I said.

"Go to hell."

It was, of course, ridiculous to think that Rantisi would ever admit kinship with Jews. After all, he had no compassion even for Muslims. When I asked him if he supported a cease-fire that would ease the misery of his people, he said, "We must all suffer for justice." It would take time, he said, but Palestine would be won. "God is on our side. Everything is going our way."

If God was on his side, I asked, then why did he live in impoverished exile?

He thought for a moment. It is the Jews who are cursed by God, he said. "You say you are chosen, but look how God has punished you. For thousands of years He has punished you."

But the Jews own Jerusalem. Jewish soldiers even control the Haram al-Sharif. So how can you say that it is the Jews who are cursed?

"The Jews are put before us as a test," he said. "Allah has sent you today to me as a test. We have failed a test, which is why we are being punished today. We are not true enough to Allah. But Allah has promised that He will bless us."

I left his apartment and walked into the bright sunshine. I was on the street outside his building when my cell phone rang. It was my friend Esther, in Jerusalem. She worked at the Hebrew University, and she said, "There was just an explosion." I asked where. "Here. Outside," she said.

When?

"Now! Just now."

I told her to stay inside, but she didn't.

It was a Hamas bomb, hidden in the cafeteria just across a plaza from Esther's office. She ran outside, she told me later, into the ionized air. Students, dripping blood, crawled out from the skull of the ruined cafeteria. Then the klaxons sounded. Esther helped the wounded, and searched for her friends. Nine people were killed in the bombing, including a woman named Marla Bennett, one of Esther's friends. Bennett was a twenty-four-year-old student from San Diego who reminded me of my earlier self, because she loved Israel the way I loved Israel. A few weeks before she was murdered, she wrote: "Here in Jerusalem, I've found a community of seekers: people who, like me, want to try living in another country, who want to know more about Judaism; people who are trying to figure out exactly what they want their lives to look like."

Four hours after the bombing, Rantisi issued a statement on behalf of Hamas. "The Zionists," he said, "are paying the price of their terror." He called on the Arab world to give Hamas "five years to fight the Zionists, the way they gave the Palestinian Authority five years to try to make peace. Give us five years and you'll see for yourselves."

That night I read the notes of our conversation. Rantisi told me: "The Jews will lose because they crave life, but a true Muslim loves death."

The humiliation of the checkpoints did not cause Marla Bennett's death. She was killed by the followers of Moloch, the pagan god who, the Bible tells us, demanded the lives of Jerusalem's children.

CHAPTER TWENTY-THREE

GOOD GUYS

The Dar al-Hijrah Mosque in Falls Church, a Virginia suburb near Washington, is exceptionally popular with newer immigrants to America. It is located in a neighborhood of small single-family houses, off a commercial strip of car dealerships and mattress stores. On Fridays, the parking lot of Dar al-Hijrah is filled with the taxis of the Somali, Egyptian, and Pakistani faithful.

The mosque of establishment Muslims in Washington is the International Islamic Center, which is located on Embassy Row and counts among its board members the ambassadors of fifty-four Muslim countries. Dar al-Hijrah was founded in 1983 by a group of Arab students who had grown contemptuous of the safe pieties dispensed by the Islamic Center, where one could not hear a bad word about the dictators and monarchs who ruled the Middle East, in part because their financial largesse funded the Islamic Center's landscaping and tile work.

The members of Dar al-Hijrah first met in a house in Falls Church, and only years later found the money to build today's mosque, which is squat and functional, not at all soaring like the Islamic Center. To the satisfaction of its founders, however, it pulses with activity. Unlike the Islamic Center, Dar al-Hijrah is an openly political mosque, and, before September 11 especially, its Friday sermons were bracingly militant. In December 1998, one of the mosque's leaders, a man named Ibrahim Hanooti, delivered a sermon in which he cried out: "Allah will give us the victory over our tyrannical enemies in our country. Allah, the infidel Americans and British are fighting against you. Allah, the curse of Allah will become true on the infidel Jews and on the tyrannical Americans."

In 2001, a young imam known for his scorching sermons came to Dar al-Hijrah to teach. He was a Yemeni named Anwar al-Aulaqi, and though he enjoyed the company of prostitutes, a vice that was no secret at Dar al-Hijrah, he won many followers, including Nawaf al-Hazmi and Hani Hanjour, two of the September 11 hijackers, who turned to al-Aulaqi for spiritual advice when they moved to nearby Alexandria in the beginning of 2001.

After the attacks, German police found the telephone number for Dar al-Hijrah in the apartment of a central September 11 conspirator. The FBI began conducting surveillance of the mosque, which continued even after al-Aulaqi left for Yemen. This means that in an FBI file somewhere there is probably a photograph of Rafiq Hijazi, who, after a time, started praying at Dar al-Hijrah, rather than at the Islamic Center and rather than at the small makeshift mosque on the campus of American University.

Dar al-Hijrah is an inspiring mosque for study and prayer, Rafiq told me one afternoon in his apartment. I was admiring the vacuum-and-mop work of Tahani, and admiring as well the volumes and volumes of Sayyid Qutb's writings on Rafiq's shelves, which either I hadn't noticed before, or represented a recent purchase.

I hadn't given up on Rafiq. A single remark, however awful, would not destroy my dream of coexistence. On certain sunlit mornings I still found it possible to believe that the two of us could love our own tribes and yet maintain a bond of authentic affection. I believed this because the maintenance of faith in the absence of almost any hope is the American way. Nonetheless, my curiosity about him was now cooler and more clinical.

Rafiq said he joined Dar al-Hijrah not for the politics, but for the purity of its worship. He was boycotting the prayer service at American University, he said, because the imam delivered a sermon calling on Muslims to celebrate Thanksgiving in the American manner. "He said that we could make Thanksgiving part of our Muslim worship."

When I asked him why this was such a heinous idea, he said, "Thanksgiving is okay for Americans, but it doesn't have anything to do with Islam."

You don't give thanks in Islam?

"Of course we do," he said. "But it's already in our prayers."

When I was growing up in Malverne, a columnist in the local newspaper wrote of learning, to his delight, that his Jewish neighbors also celebrated Thanksgiving. I remember my mother believing this columnist to be a very stupid man and boycotting—always with the boycotts—the dry cleaning store he owned. Of course Jews celebrate Thanksgiving—we're American!

I had no strong feelings about Thanksgiving early in life, but I realized, in my post-Israel incarnation, that Thanksgiving was my favorite holiday, not because it complements Judaism, which it does, but because it is a way to embrace America the way America has embraced me.

"You shouldn't be so offended by Thanksgiving," I told Rafiq, who had himself been embraced by America.

"No, it's not Thanksgiving that bothers me," Rafiq said. "It's that these Muslims in America think they have to behave like Americans. They're trying to bend too far toward America." Then he told me a story.

"You know, Kemal prayed at the Capitol—every Friday there are Muslim prayers at the Capitol—and the girls who come there are dressed just like American girls. They go around and talk to guys. They make believe they are Muslim but they are not." A friend of Rafiq's named Adil Radwan, who was also a graduate student at American University, once gave the *khutba*—the sermon—at Friday prayers at the Capitol, and was criticized for his efforts. "His *khutba* was about sincerity in your worship," Rafiq said. "He said that Islamic women praying and not wearing hijab was proof of hypocrisy and insincerity. After he spoke the organizer of the prayer service got up and said, 'What was just mentioned in this *khutba* does not reflect what is in Islam.' But of course it did."

Rafiq struck this theme incessantly. America—leering, libidinous America—was too great a temptation for Muslims. He had contempt for American culture, and he built walls around himself, but his scorn was mainly directed at Muslims who fell from the path. "Before I came to Washington, there was a professor in Gaza who taught here once, and he said to me, 'When you go to Washington, you have to go to the good place.' I didn't know what he meant, 'the good place.' Then I figured out that he meant 'Good Guys.' "

Good Guys was a topless bar on Wisconsin Avenue, not far from Rafiq's apartment. "He thought I should go to the strip club."

I asked Rafiq if he was ever tempted to drink alcohol, visit a strip club, read a pornographic magazine. The answer was always no.

A more basic question struck me: When you were single, did you ever go out on a date?

"No, of course not."

He told me he had single friends at school, Muslim men, who had yielded to temptation and were dating American women. This was *haram,* he said, forbidden. "I tell them, you don't have to stay with girls to become American. You can stick to your culture. In Islam I am required to try to stop them. I can't use my hand, so I have to use my tongue. I'm always saying, 'Hassan, you shouldn't have a girlfriend,' 'Saeed, you shouldn't have a girlfriend.' "

Does it work?

"The only thing I can do is try," he said. "Islam gives me no choice."

The suggestion heard in Washington after September 11 was that the government should make a more strenuous effort to bring Muslim students to America. How could they not like us, once they got to know us?

The Israeli novelist Amos Oz once described in a corrosive way this sort of American sunniness. We were speaking shortly after the disintegration of the peace talks at Camp David, and he said, "There is something very American, very Christian, if you don't mind, about this process. They speak of liking one another, of the need to understand one another. But we do understand each other. Perhaps that is the problem."

Millions of Muslims, I am sure, love America, but its charms are not universally felt. Muhammad Atta did not succumb. Neither did the al-Qaeda terrorist Khalid Sheikh Muhammad, the architect of the World Trade Center attacks and a 1986 graduate of North Carolina Agricultural and Technical State University.

The life of Sayyid Qutb is instructive here. Qutb came to America for a visit in 1949. He was horrified by what he saw—wanton women, emasculated men, churches empty of spirit. He reported later, in tones of horror and disgust, that a drunk woman once propositioned him on a boat. When he returned to Egypt, he announced, in uncompromising terms, that America was no place for a Muslim.

After Rafiq prayed, we left his apartment and went out for coffee. I carried with me a copy of the Quran, the Saudi version given me by Samiul Haq, the chancellor of the Taliban madrasa. I wanted to read it with Rafiq. Against his better judgment, he agreed.

We went to the student union. I asked him to go to Starbucks, but he said he was boycotting Starbucks because it was notorious for its support of Zionism.

I took the Quran out of my bag. "You have to wash your hands!" he said. But his panic was fleeting. "It's okay, it's okay," he said. He held infidels to necessarily low standards.

I showed Rafiq Samiul Haq's inscription to me: "Presented to Mr. Jeffrey Goldberg with a hope that it will remain with you and will be a beacon of light for you." Rafiq said, with real adamance, "It *is* a beacon of light. It's a complete guide for life."

He turned to the second chapter of the Quran, and read: "Those who believe in the Quran, and those who follow the Jewish scriptures, and the Christians and the Sabians, and who believe in Allah and the Last Day, shall have their reward." This passage, he said, "shows that you still have good Jews. I don't know if this will include you," he said, smiling.

"The Jews," he went on, "say that the Quran is against them, but the Quran does not say that all Jews are bad. It judges people on their behavior. There are Jews who follow Allah's will, and there are some Jews that don't. Every person has good and bad points. God criticized Muhammad in one of the chapters. All humans make mistakes."

I pointed Rafiq to another passage that accused the Jews of repeatedly covering themselves in "humiliation and misery." They drew the wrath of Allah, the passage read, because they went on rejecting the signs of Allah and slaying his Messengers without just cause.

Rafiq said, "It's true that the Jews killed the Prophets without cause."

Like who?

"Jesus," he said.

The footnote to this passage is grossly anti-Jewish. The Jews, it reports, "got the Promised Land. But they continued to rebel against Allah. And their humiliation and misery became a national disaster. They were carried in captivity to Assyria. They were restored under the Persians, but still remained under the Persian yoke, and they were under the yoke of the Greeks, the Romans, and Arabs. They were scattered all over the earth, and have been a wandering people ever since."

This particular Quran was printed in 1995. Israel was founded in 1948. It seems, I said, to be missing a bit of history. There is no more wandering.

The chapter called Bani Israil catalogues the flaws of Jews, particularly their faithlessness. But the Jews are given a chance by God to return to His fold: "To the believers who work deeds of righteousness . . . they shall have a magnificent reward." The footnote to this passage states, "The instability and crookedness of the Jewish soul having been mentioned, the healing balm which should have cured it is now pointed out."

Rafiq then said he doubted that the Jews, having strayed so often from the path of God, were capable of finding Him again.

He read: "And We decreed for the children of Israel in the Book that twice would they do mischief on the earth and be elated with mighty arrogance (And twice would they be punished)!"

Once, a more enlightened Rafiq told me that this was a general admonition against arrogance. Now, though, he offered a more specific interpretation of the passage. "History shows that the Jews betrayed God and so God sent the Babylonians to conquer them," he said. "The passage says that the Jews would twice do mischief. There's a debate about this. Some people think this refers to events that have already happened, such as when the Jews rejected the prophecy of Jesus. But I also think this can mean something that hasn't happened yet."

In other words, the eventual disappearance of Israel is the second curse, the curse that has not yet materialized?

"I'm not saying it will happen soon," he said.

But it will happen. "When the first of the warnings [from God] came to pass," the passage continued, "we sent against you Our servants given to terrible warfare; they entered the very inmost parts of your homes; and it was a warning completely fulfilled."

The servants of Allah, he said, are today's Muslims, and they will one day, Rafiq said, "completely eliminate the Jews."

Genocide, then?

I was losing my temper. Rafiq saw this.

"This is a prophecy about the future," he said.

I asked him finally if Islam is a supremacist religion.

"It is the final word of God." He showed me something in the second chapter of the Quran: "Never will the Jews or the Christians be satisfied with thee unless thou follow their form of religion. Say [to them], 'The guidance of Allah—that is the only Guidance.'

"This is the part I like," Rafiq said. "The Jews won't accept the guidance of Allah. We're in the second phase of Jewish arrogance today."

I realized that it was theologically insufferable for Rafiq to feel subjugated by Jews. For him, such a feeling went against history, God, and nature. Sayyid Qutb once made an observation that has lodged in my mind. He wrote that the Quran exposed the "contemptible characteristics of Jews, their craven desire to live, no matter at what price and regardless of quality, honor, and dignity."

It was terribly hard for Muslims to accept that their inferiors—the Jews who scorned Muhammad, the Jews who cling to life, the Jews who lived for a thousand years in fetid little ghettos at the sufferance of condescending and heavily taxing caliphs and kings—now ruled Palestine, now ruled, if you believe what al-Qaeda and Hamas believe, the entire world.

Islam's fundamentalists—and Rafiq was now one—see both Judaism and Christianity as competition. But Islam's relationship to Christianity is different; these two giants fought for hundreds of years for control of the Middle East and Europe. They were enemies, but they respected each other's strength.

The Jews were something else. After the defeat at Khaybar, the Jews put up no resistance to the expansion of Islam. They accepted their second-class status. They were protected in some measure by their passivity. In the Palestine of the Ottomans, the Arabs called the Jews who lived in Jerusalem, Safed, and Hebron *"ibn maut,"* the children of death, because they were spectral and stayed deep in the shadows. "Our Jews knew how to behave very nicely," the PLO leader Ziad Abu Ziad told me once.

But then came Zionism, a movement that demanded for Jews equal rights as a nation. This made no sense in the worldview of many Arab Muslims, who, if secretly insecure about their primacy in the world, were at least sure that they were better than the Jews.

The cognitive dissonance was too great. Here was Rafiq, one of God's chosen people, possessor of His final truth, the foe of His betrayers, those contemptible Jews, and yet reality presented him undeniable truths: a vital, powerful Israel, a hyper-power America, Palestine in a state of abjection, and a broken-down Muslim world, afflicted by a spectrum of troubles that a statistics professor would have no trouble quantifying.

There were still two sides to his soul, I thought: One side was rational, and could coexist with me. But for the other side of his soul, concessions to a Jew, much less a Jewish state, were an abomination.

If you really believe in jihad, why don't you just go do it? I asked.

"There are all different kinds of jihad," he said. "You can make a jihad in statistics."

I said: "There's a little bit of Sayyid Qutb in you."

And then he said: "There's a little Kahane in you."

CHAPTER TWENTY-FOUR

STOP BEING JEWISH

The road that runs down the mountain spine of the West Bank is called by Jews "The Way of the Fathers," because it links Shechem, or Nablus, the place where Abraham first entered the Promised Land, to Hebron in the south, where he is said to be buried. During the Intifada it was a deadly road, but settlers go with God, and so did I, in soft-skinned rental cars. I was driving one day with a man named Moshe Dann, a former American whose former first name was Marty and who found God and Israel after undergoing a spiritual crisis brought on when the History Department of the City College of New York denied him tenure. We were leaving the most radical block of settlements, those gathered around Shechem, where his daughter and her husband lived in a trailer with guns and a dog.

It is customary to pick up Jewish hitchhikers on this road, and so outside the settlement of Kfar Tappuach we took on three young boys wearing kippot and sidelocks. The youngest was no more than eight. They were going home to Jerusalem after a visit with their sister. I was astonished to see such young children traveling alone, and I asked them about their parents, and it was only a few minutes before I realized that they were the grandchildren of Meir Kahane, the racist Brooklyn rabbi.

"I knew your grandfather," I said.

The oldest boy said, "The Arabs killed him."

Kahane was shot to death in November 1990 in a hotel in New York by an Islamist. The funeral in Jerusalem a few days later was a disgrace. Thousands of his followers screamed, "Death to the Arabs!" The procession fractured between those who wanted to bury Kahane and those who wanted to kill Arabs. I was standing outside the Mifgash

Ha'esh restaurant, across the street from *The Jerusalem Post,* when the procession surged past. A gang of Kahanists broke off from the main body and tried to ram through the doors of the restaurant, screaming together, "Let the Arabs out!" I followed the crowd down the road to the Center One shopping center. "We'll find the Arabs!" someone cried. Then the mob attacked a bus. "There's Arabs on it!" "We're going to kill you!" someone screamed. A passenger yelled from the window, "There aren't any Arabs here!" The Kahanists saw an Arab running from another bus. The gang caught the Arab and smashed his head with a rock. He lay on the ground as Israeli soldiers rushed to protect him from the madness of their Jewish brothers.

Kahane would have been proud of his mourners, and he would have called the Jewish soldiers who beat them back kapos and quislings. There was no space in my heart for such a man but when his grandsons asked me what I remembered of him, I answered, "He had very profound thoughts," which was true.

By the time I first met Kahane, at the University of Pennsylvania, I had long before grown disenchanted with his ideas. But in a speech he gave to hundreds of students—most of whom were properly liberal and predisposed to loathe him—he laid out what he saw as the hypocrisy of Jewish life in America in an unapologetic, ribald, and revolutionary way, and we surrendered momentarily to his charisma. "It's just idiocy to have a bar mitzvah when you can't understand a word that's being said and when you know that the whole thing is just a chance for your parents to spend $20,000 on shrimp and show off for their friends," he said, to laughter. And he excoriated us: "You're all cowards, you know. Unless you come and join in the fight for Israel's survival, you're all cowards. If you make the pursuit of money the only purpose of your lives, then you're nothing." And he yelled at us, too, for knowing nothing about Judaism and for knowing no Hebrew. "You know more about Christianity than you do about your own religion!" he said, and we knew this was true.

But Kahane was incapable of lifting Jews up without tearing everyone else down. He was the mirror image of an Islamic supremacist. In that speech at Penn, he ended up calling Arabs dogs. Later on, when I asked him about his reflexive anti-Arabism, he called me a *shaygetz,* a dirty Christian.

Not everyone at the *Jerusalem Post* was upset by the funeral riot. Moshe Saperstein, for one, was not. Saperstein, the one-armed, one-eyed, cigar-chewing misanthrope from the Lower East Side who was the *Post*'s right-wing television reviewer, loved Kahane, in fact.

I noted once to him that Kahane wanted to expel all the Arabs.

Moshe arched an eyebrow. "And the problem is?"

I couldn't totally blame Moshe for having unkind feelings about Arabs—it was an Arab rocket that tore off his arm in the Yom Kippur War, but his hostility was unbearable.

I lost track of Moshe over the years, but I had heard a rumor that he had left Jerusalem and moved to Gaza, to the Gush Katif block of settlements opposite the Palestinian city of Khan Younis. I looked him up, and we arranged to meet one day not long ago.

Moshe picked me up at the junction that marks the border between southern Gaza and Israel. The junction, called Kissufim, was an armored camp. Three dozen tanks and bulldozers stood ready to pass through the gates into Gaza. The only civilians present were the settlers of Gush Katif, waiting for the all-clear to go home.

The road from the border to the settlement was under Israeli control—concrete pillboxes were planted intermittently along the way—but Palestinians often fired on the settlers' cars. In 2001, Moshe told me, he was ambushed near Kissufim; Palestinian gunfire tore off two fingers of his remaining hand. He had the presence of mind to push down on the accelerator, and he struck a Palestinian gunman. Moshe pointed to the spot that marked the attack. "Here's where I tried to run over the peace-loving Muslim," he said. Sometimes, he said, he was overcome by a feeling that "Ahmed is trying to kill me." Moshe referred to Arabs generically as "Ahmed."

Just before we reached the fortified entrance to the Gush Katif block, we passed the ramshackle Bedouin village of Muwassi. "They like to live like pigs in shit," Moshe said. I was loud in my objections, and he said, "I'm sorry, that's politically incorrect. 'They have a different cultural aesthetic.' Is that what I'm supposed to say?"

Moshe and his wife, Rachel, came to the settlement of Neveh Dekalim, the largest village in the block, to retire. Their children were grown and lived elsewhere in Israel. The couple's ranch house, which overlooked the sea, would not have seemed out of place in Boca Raton. The settlement was made up of dozens of whitewashed houses and sand-dune playgrounds, and it was the frequent target of Palestinian attacks. A fifty-foot-high wall of concrete slabs sits about five hundred yards from the Sapersteins' house, separating the Jews from the Arabs. Rachel taught English in the girls' school on the settlement. I asked the Sapersteins why they had chosen this outlying village in Gaza rather than one of the urban settlements near Jerusalem. "We like the weather," Moshe said. "We never lived near the sea."

Then he became serious for a moment. "I'm here because of a religious commandment, believe it or not, as irrational as that may seem to you."

Ariel Sharon had just publicly suggested that his government would soon empty Gaza of Jews. Sharon had, late in life, a change of heart about Gaza. He had come to see the settlement project as politically, militarily, and demographically disastrous. So he had announced a plan to "disengage" from Gaza.

Moshe and Rachel saw a unilateral withdrawal from Gaza as theological heresy and political suicide. They moved here from Jerusalem in 1997 as a protest against the Oslo peace process. "Oslo meant the abandonment of land that was meant for the Jews," Moshe said. "Call me an extremist. I don't care."

What seemed to offend Moshe the most about the disengagement proposal was that Arabs might one day live in his house. "I had this Ahmed in here once, doing repairs, and he said, 'Do you know why I'm doing such good work? Because one day I'm going to live here.' And I told him, 'If I'm kicked out of here, I'm going to blow this place up before I let someone like you have it.' "

Moshe did say, however, that he would leave if he thought his departure could bring peace. This drew a look from Rachel.

"I wouldn't," she said.

Moshe was skeptical about this scenario, however. He considered the idea that peace will come to Israel only when it cedes territory to the Arabs to be a Diaspora psychosis. "We've lived for so many years in exile, we've forgotten what it is to be a powerful and ruling people," he said. "We have always depended on the kindness of strangers, wherever we were; the czar, or some Polish landowner. We had to kiss ass because we couldn't defend ourselves. Now that we have the strength to defend ourselves, we don't know how. Most of this country has an exile mentality. Most of the population here takes the attitude that the Jews are at fault. But what have we done to provoke those poor Palestinians?"

"Do we have to kill ourselves? Is that Jewish?" Rachel asked. "You have to teach them: No more. You want to do evil, you're going to take the consequences. This is what America did to Germany. You finish them. Bomb the hell out of them. Just bomb the hell out of them."

I asked Rachel about her youth, in Brooklyn.

"The blacks hit me, of course," she said. "We were raised in a very Jewish area. Then the blacks came in and the Jews ran. The first blacks came in and the Jews flew out of there so fast. Everybody went to Crown Heights. I don't want to run away. I always see Jews running and running."

Many of the American-born settlers I know had early encounters with anti-Semitic roughnecks and many of them see an explicit link between the Palestinians and the *"shvartses"* of their youth. Jews were chased from Brooklyn, in other words, and they won't be chased again. Maybe it was because I was beaten up by Irish boys who couldn't be mistaken for Palestinians, but I did not sympathize with Moshe's ghetto bluster.

"Goyim used their hands. Jews used their brains," he said, describing his version of a Diaspora mentality. "That's nothing more than a justification for weakness."

Weren't they overdoing it, I asked. I, too, had been punished for the death of Christ, but it wasn't Arabs who dealt me the suffering. Moshe gave me an indulgent smile.

"Do you really think we're going to give the Arabs Gaza and then they'll leave us alone? Don't be such a *shtadlan,"* he said, using a Yiddish word for "middleman," a reference to the intermediary appointed by Jewish communities to negotiate with the gentiles. "Answer me. Do you?"

No, I said, I didn't think so, not anymore. But I also didn't think that a pullout would cause the death of Israel. It would be better for the Jews to be out of Gaza than in Gaza. These settlements weren't doing much for our morality, and our morality was something we used to prize.

"Oh, please," Moshe said. "You think there's a connection between the Arabs living in shit and my being here? Let me tell you, there isn't."

This was probably true. The Gaza Arabs did not thrive under Egyptian rule either, and their per capita income, even in the middle of the Intifada, was no worse than the per capita income in many places around the Arab world. But there was something else: death. The presence of Jews here, on this sand spit, caused death—the deaths of Jews, settlers and soldiers, and the deaths of Palestinians, some of whom didn't even deserve it, I said. I suggested to Moshe that he try to imagine himself in the place of a Palestinian.

"You're a Palestinian, you're here, you have your farm, your grandparents are from here, and—"

But Moshe interrupted me. *"Stop being Jewish!"* he yelled. "Stop being Jewish! Only a Jew would say, 'Imagine yourself as a Palestinian.' Could you imagine a Palestinian imagining himself as a Jew?"

One afternoon I left Gush Katif through Kissufim, traveled north to the Erez checkpoint, and crossed over into Palestinian Gaza. Rafiq had come home, and I was going to congratulate him on his Ph.D. His departure from America was quick, unceremonious, and, for him, a relief. Before he left I had asked him if he had plans for the July 4 holiday. I thought I would invite him over for a barbecue.

"I'll go to mosque," he said tetchily.

His departure from America was a relief for me as well.

He was home in Gaza only on vacation. He had won a tenure-track position at a university in the United Arab Emirates. He was, like Kemal, too much the professional to tolerate the corruption and disruptions of academic life in Gaza.

We went one evening, with Tahani and a collection of his cousins, to the Deira, where we sat outside under a dark sky and drank tea. "The truth is, I won't miss America," he said. "The people are ignorant and arrogant."

Was it really so bad? I asked.

You can't understand, he said.

Everything about America seemed to bother him, but especially President George W. Bush. The Iraq war offended his sensibilities and reinforced an idea he had shared with me before, that America was threatened by the power of Sunni Muslims. "America wants to exist every place on earth. It's arrogant. They want everybody to be obedient to them. That's what's most important to them. That everyone listen to them. Most Americans live in a Clint Eastwood movie, but this isn't a movie."

The next day, we met up in Jebalya, in the early evening. The heat had broken, and we took a walk through the camp. Donkey dung, melon rinds, and sand filled the gutters.

"The Palestinian Authority doesn't exist anymore," he said. "Even when it did no one picked up the garbage."

We walked past his old mosque. "My first arrest was because of this mosque," he said, reminding me that the Shabak learned his name from a *shtinker* among the faithful. The mosque was a three-story building of concrete and faded yellow stucco. Graffiti covered the walls. "Reject the Life of Dishonor," it said on one wall.

We walked to a memorial dedicated to the victims of the first Intifada. It was built by the National Union for Martyr Families of Palestine. There, Rafiq pointed, there's Hatem al-Sisi's name. He was the schoolmate of Rafiq's who fell on the first day of the first Intifada.

"If the Israelis hadn't overreacted, who knows what could have happened," Rafiq said.

It would have happened sooner or later, I said.

The first Intifada was better than this one, he said.

I agreed. There was a clarity to it. And it had rational goals. The next one, I said, will be even worse this one.

"Do you think there will be a next one?" Rafiq asked.

Yes, I said.

Why?

Because there's something wrong in Palestine, I said. You've lost yourselves. All you think about is death. The Bible tells us that love is as strong as death. But in Islam today, death is stronger.

It's the opposite, he said. It is Israel that can't stop killing.

Moshe Saperstein came to mind. Once I thought Rafiq could imagine himself as a Jew. I asked him now if he could imagine how a Jew might feel today, hunted by murderers for the crime of living in his homeland.

"I don't have to think of that since I have the answer in the Quran," he said. And then he quoted: "And we gave clear warning to the Children of Israel in the Book, that twice would they do mischief on the earth and be elated and arrogant, and twice would they be punished!"

"I told you," he said, "read the Quran and you'll find out why Muslims love the Jews."

We went by the school where his sister Intissar was a teacher. Martyr posters hung on its walls, images of black-haired boys and young men with mustaches and winning smiles. Rafiq told me that one of his former students at the Islamic University, a boy named Hamad Helis, had not long before "martyred" himself in a bombing.

"I could never be that brave," Rafiq said.

We came upon a torn poster dedicated to the memory of Rachel Corrie, a young American from Washington who died at a protest in

Gaza. She had joined a group of foreigners, advocates of the Palestinian cause, who stood one day against a line of Israeli bulldozers. She came too close to one and she was plowed under. "Rachel was a girl from Olympia who came to stop the tanks" read the poster, which was printed by the Fatah Youth Organization. "She came to be a witness to American policy."

Corrie's face had been razored out of the poster. It was a sin to display pictures of uncovered women, even those who martyred themselves for the cause.

Hamed, Rafiq's father, was waiting for us when we came back. It was dark, and everyone in Jebalya was outside, escaping the built-up heat of their concrete boxes. We sat and drank tea. The streets were crowded. An infinite number of cousins came by. I could see that Rafiq was tiring of his family obligations.

A young nephew of Rafiq's named Baha'a turned up. He was the son of Rafiq's sister Amal. He was fifteen or so. "Baha'a means brightness," Rafiq said. "His name is a contradiction. He's not very smart. He beats dogs for a living."

Rafiq decided to have some fun at Baha'a's expense.

"Baha'a," he called out. "You see this guy? This guy is Jewish." Baha'a stared at me.

"No," he said, gape-mouthed. The other cousins laughed.

"Yes," Rafiq said. Baha'a looked at me.

"Yes, Jewish. One hundred percent," I said in Arabic.

Baha'a thrust out his chest at me. "I will be a martyr one day and kill Jews," he said. Everyone broke up at this.

Why don't you like Jews? Rafiq asked.

Baha'a said, "They will die a donkey's death."

I asked, "Why would you want to become a martyr?"

He had no answer. He had never prepared one. This wasn't necessary in Gaza.

"It will probably be better if he does become a martyr bomber," Rafiq said. "He's not very good in school."

We sat. Hamed said, "I like the kind of Jew who sits and talks."

Never one to let anything alone, I asked, Doesn't the Quran warn Muslims against friendship with non-Muslims? The exact passage reads as follows: "O ye who believe! Take not the Jews and Christians for your friends and protectors; they are but friends and protectors to each other. And he amongst you that turns to them is of them."

Rafiq looked surprised. "It warns against friendship with bad Jews and Christians, not all of them," he said. After all, he said, "We're friends."

It was time for me to go. I said I would visit him in Abu Dhabi, and we shook hands.

"See you soon," he said, and I took a taxi to the hotel.

I was surprised to learn that he considered me a friend. How could he be a friend, when he couldn't imagine himself in my place. In an alien idiom—the idiom of Ketziot—he didn't understand my mentality. What I worried about more, though, was that I understood his.

CHAPTER TWENTY-FIVE

I WANT YOU TO LIVE

Psalm 137, the rhapsody of Zionism, gives beautiful, aching expression to a transcendent desire, the desire to go home: "By the rivers of Babylon, / there we sat down, / and yea, we wept, / when we remembered Zion."

The first two verses are written in this lamenting tone. In the second verse, the psalmist promises his beloved city, "If I forget thee, O Jerusalem, let my right hand lose its cunning."

It is my favorite psalm, though it reminds me of my failures as a Jew. Israel represents the biggest portion of the Jewish future, and I am not a part of it, so I read the first two verses of Psalm 137 as a rebuke. If America was Babylon—if we were refuseniks in America—then I could assign the blame for my condition elsewhere. But America is not Babylon. At worst, America is an outstandingly comfortable exile. At best, it is another Promised Land. It has certainly become my Promised Land.

Though I've come to realize that my Americanness is unconquerable, Zionism is no worm-eaten ideology to me. It answered a need, and answers even today. I am still susceptible to the demands of blood and tribe.

There is a third verse to psalm 137, one that people don't often remember or recite. If the first two verses of the psalm remind us not to forget Jerusalem, the third verse is an inadvertent reminder of the cost of loving it too much. In the third verse, the psalm's tone shifts from mournfulness to vengeance:

O daughter of Babylon, that are to be destroyed
Happy shall he be that repayeth thee

As thou has served us
Happy shall he be, that taketh
And dasheth thy little ones
Against the rock.

The Jews in captivity dreamed of revenge against the Babylonians. This is natural. The horror of this verse is the wish to see the deaths of Babylon's children as well. But the horror instructs: The holiness of the land can poison the man who sanctifies only stone and forgets the supreme value of life.

The settlement of Tekoa sits on the edge of the Judean desert, northeast of the holy city of Hebron. It was built near the site of the ancient Jewish village of the same name, as well as near a modern Arab village, which is called Tequa. The bones of ancient Tekoa sit underneath the Arab village. It is in this ancient Tekoa that a shepherd and fig gatherer named Amos was born.

Two hundred and fifty Jewish families, half of them Orthodox, most of modest means, live in the settlement of Tekoa. It is average in size and appearance for a West Bank colony. Among its residents is an acquaintance of mine named Seth Mandell. Seth is an Orthodox rabbi, and he and his wife, Sherri, brought their children to Israel from Maryland in 1997.

I met Seth at his house one morning. It was a clear, cold day, and we went for a walk into a steep ravine outside the gates of the settlement, following a narrow path to a cave. At the beginning of the Intifada, Seth's son Koby and a friend skipped school for the day and came to the wadi. They were fourteen years old. Their bodies were found the next day in this cave; they had been beaten to death with rocks.

I had visited the cave before with Seth. This time we didn't speak much. The cave is low-ceilinged, dank, and dark. The remnants of memorial candles, hundreds of them, covered the wet stone.

On the way back to Seth's house, we talked about Amos, as we walked where he once walked.

In the time of Amos, Tekoa was part of the Kingdom of Judah, the rival to the northern Kingdom of Israel. Amos first heard the voice of God in Tekoa. He left his sycamore trees and his sheep and carried his prophecies to the northern kingdom, a place, the Bible says, of avarice, decadence, and empty ritual. When Amos arrived, he condemned the sins of foreigners but told the Israelites that the greatest share of God's anger was reserved for them, His people. He said God believed that they had "sold the righteous for silver, and the poor for a pair of shoes."

Amos did not believe that the Jews were worse than their neighbors, but he believed that being chosen by God brought with it a burden: the burden of moral stringency. Ritual worship would not please God, Amos said, when the poor went hungry. "I hate, I despise your feast days, and I will not be appeased by your solemn assemblies," he told the Israelites. Amos wrote in fire, "Let judgment run down as waters, and righteousness as a mighty stream."

Amos is a favored prophet of liberal-minded Jews. How could he not be? His call for universal justice seemed to include even the Palestinians. Amos, I said to Seth, carries a different message from the one carried by the men who conceived of the settlement project, who saw the Six-Day War as a sign from heaven that the Jews were blessed and the Arabs cursed. Amos's concerns were not those of conquering land but those of spreading justice.

Seth corrected me. He recognized the universality of Amos's message, but he also remembered his audience. "We can reinterpret Amos into universal meaning, but Amos, like Jesus, was talking to Jews," he said.

But wasn't Amos demanding universal moral behavior?

"Of course," Seth replied. "But he was also telling Jews that the reward for righteousness was the land we're on. The universalists don't see the Zionism in Amos, and the hard-right Zionists don't see the universalism."

I then asked Seth an indecent question. I asked him if he thought he still would have come to this settlement had he known the price his family would pay. No, he said, he wouldn't. If there had been no other place for a Jew to go, then so be it, he would have come. But there were safer places. He could have lived behind the 1967 lines, in Israel proper. It wasn't safe, but it was safer. And it was no sin. God gave the land of Israel to the Jews as their birthright. But the conquest of every last stone and every last dry riverbed was not worth the life of a fourteen-year-old boy.

I asked Seth how he kept his faith. He said, "The world is full of pain. But without God it is only pain. I can't imagine a world without God."

He is a skeptic about the possibility of peace with his Muslim neighbors. This does not mean, he said, that peace is impossible; it is just not available at the moment. "Of course I have my hopes. To believe in God is to have hope," he said. Should the day come when the Muslims seem ready for peace, he said, he would be willing to hand over Tekoa to his neighbors.

This was no small thing for Seth Mandell to say. The evacuation of Tekoa would mean moving Koby's grave and abandoning the site of his murder.

An inscription on the memorial stone erected by the government in memory of the two boys reads: MAY GOD AVENGE THEIR BLOOD. This is not quite so ruthless as it sounds; it is a traditional Jewish formulation that warns against the taking of earthly vengeance. Vengeance is the responsibility of God, not a right of man. Still, Seth said, "I wish they didn't put that there."

Seth Mandell has somehow maintained his hope, his faith, and a love that extended beyond the boundaries of his tribe.

I had spent years searching for people like Seth Mandell in the House of Islam, right-hearted people who could see the tears of Jews as well as the tears of Muslims. I wasn't having much success, but despair is a sin in my religion, so I called Rafiq and said that I'd like to drop by.

I arrived in Abu Dhabi at night. Rafiq lived two hours from the city, in a university town called al-Ain, but Kemal, his brother, lived in the capital itself, and we had dinner. He picked me up at my hotel in the same minivan he drove in Washington.

Kemal and his family had left Saudi Arabia a while earlier. It turned out not to be quite the paradise he had expected. "The education system is not very good," Kemal said. "I was worried about how my sons were learning." Now he was working for the health ministry in Abu Dhabi; he was, among other things, its point man on bird flu.

Kemal had a beard, which gave him the appearance of a Muslim Brother. "My father hates the beard," he said. "He says it reminds him of Hamas."

I asked him if the beard meant that he was, in fact, a Muslim Brother. "Muslims wear beards, that's all," he said. He was, however, trying to adhere scrupulously to Islamic tenets. He no longer listened to any music at all, and his wife, Manal, now covered her face with a veil, in addition to wearing the hijab. I wondered how a woman could stand the pitiless Arabian heat under so much drapery, but Kemal said, "She's very comfortable."

The family in Gaza thought that he and Rafiq were becoming terribly righteous. "My sister Amal said, 'Come to my boy's wedding.' And I asked her if they were going to have music and dancing. She said yes, and I said I couldn't go. She said, 'Why not? Everyone's doing it.' But you know, keeping Islam is like holding fire in your hand. It's not easy." Kemal would not return to America. It was no place to raise a Muslim family, he said, and besides, he was infuriated by the war in Iraq. He didn't see the war as one against Islam, as it has been interpreted in some quarters, but one waged in favor of Shiites. As a devout Sunni, he said, this was incomprehensible. "The Shiites are apostates and murderers. Why does America take their side?"

I asked about Rafiq. Kemal said his brother was happy. The university was a well-managed place. It was run by an American, "so of course the standards are very high," he said.

I went the next morning to al-Ain on an empty highway that ran in a straight line through the desert. Al-Ain is an untroubled city that sits on the border with Oman. Its streets were laid out cleanly, and its water was apparently used judiciously, because the median strips were green. I checked into my subdued and elegant hotel. It was impossible to avoid the conclusion that al-Ain was the opposite of Gaza.

Rafiq came by an hour later. He hugged me, and I hugged him back. There was no cheek kissing, but we never did go in for that. He looked well, and relaxed. His face no longer seemed creased and dark. He was wearing clothing he bought at Costco. He seemed content and satisfied now.

He took the afternoon off in order to show me the modestly interesting sites of al-Ain. He told me about his life: His students were earnest, his salary sufficient, and his house was so big he would be ashamed to show it to his father, which wasn't a possibility, because everyone knew that Hamed Hijazi would never leave Gaza. Tahani was doing well, he said—she was finishing her high school studies, which had been interrupted by their marriage, and she was also attending a seminary for the memorization of the Quran. She had memorized quite a bit already, he said. I said I hoped to see her, and Rafiq smiled. I told him I had brought her a box of chocolates. I'll give them to her, he said.

He had been in Gaza a few months earlier as well. Unlike Kemal, he had shaved his beard before he saw his father. "He would have said, 'What is that, shit on your face? Or just dirt?'

"He doesn't want us looking like Hamas," Rafiq went on. "I don't want to look like them either, to tell you the truth."

He explained: "They're crazy. They started launching rockets at Israel from our neighborhood. One morning there was a lot of noise outside and we saw the Hamas guys with the rockets running up and down the streets and on the roofs."

His father mocked the Hamas men. "He said to everyone, 'Okay, let's pack our bags, we're going back to Ashkelon. Hamas is about to defeat Israel.' "

We caught up on common acquaintances. Prisoners I did not remember were dead. He mentioned one man who had just recently blown himself up. We spoke briefly about Capucci, and Hassan, from the kitchen. Both had been shot dead.

We spoke of Sheikh Yassin, who was in his grave, as was Abdel Aziz Rantisi. Both men were executed in Israeli rocket attacks. Rafiq never cared for Rantisi, but now he said he thought of him as a martyr. "Anyone who is killed by the Israelis is a martyr, I think."

I told Rafiq about my last visit with Rantisi. This came after a first, unsuccessful attempt on his life, and Rantisi had cloistered himself inside his apartment. He was also using his grandchildren as a shield. They were crawling all about the apartment. Rantisi even used them to answer the telephone. Once, the telephone rang when the grandchildren weren't in the room and Rantisi asked me to pick it up. I declined.

"That was smart of you," Rafiq said. Rantisi was assassinated shortly after my visit. Rafiq named others who had died. One of his math teachers, he said, was newly dead, killed a few weeks earlier in a rocket attack. Rafiq knew lists and lists of dead people.

There was a pause.

On the other hand, I said, Jack Ross was now the president of the Jewish Community Center of Tampa, Florida.

Rafiq told me to pass on his regards.

It was mid-afternoon and the streets were empty. We were still touring the city.

"Have you ever seen a camel market?" he asked.

We came up to al-Ain's permanent livestock fair, up against the border fence with Oman. Bedouin boys were herding camels into the beds of dented pickup trucks. The camels—dun-colored camels, gray-haired camels, camels the color of skinned figs—bleated and bellowed and spit profusely.

"Are these for riding?" I asked.

"For eating," Rafiq said.

We walked down a wobbly dirt lane that separated two lines of wooden pens. The camels pushed needily against the fences, churning up clouds of dust.

"Does this place remind you of something?" Rafiq asked.

"We fed you better in prison," I said.

"No, that's not true. The camels eat better."

We got back in the car. "I'm going to stop at a mosque to pray," he said.

I waited for him outside. The desert brimmed over into the half-empty parking lot. He came out and we drove to his house. I realized when we arrived that I would not be seeing Tahani, but I did get a momentary glimpse of a pair of eyes peering out from behind an almost-closed door.

Is Tahani wearing a veil now? I asked.

"Yes," Rafiq said. "She wants to."

I spent a week in al-Ain, and we passed many hours together. Once he offered to take me to a Starbucks in al-Ain's leading mall.

"I thought you were boycotting Starbucks," I said.

He shrugged. "It's okay, I think," he said. "I thought you would like to go there."

Some sort of change had come over him. He was no longer so strident and unforgiving. I mentioned this to him rather directly. "It seems," I said, "like you don't hate America anymore."

"I never hated America," he said.

"Oh, please," I said.

He smiled. "You know, maybe I was trying to hate it because I knew I was leaving," he said.

So now you like it?

"I didn't say that!" he said. "I don't want to live there, if that's what you mean."

This was not at all what I was expecting when I got off the plane in Abu Dhabi. But I shouldn't have been surprised. The only constant in the Middle East, the saying goes, is sudden and dramatic change.

This was not to suggest that he had abandoned his faith or his cause. He hadn't changed his views about the inerrancy of the Quran, for one thing, though he did acknowledge that nothing in Islam prohibited its followers from making compromises in politics. I said I hoped the Palestinians would follow the example of Ariel Sharon, who had just the previous summer discarded a violently held belief for the sake of peace, evacuating all eight thousand Jewish settlers from Gaza (Moshe and Rachel Saperstein among them) because it made no sense to keep them there.

Rafiq was unconvinced. He didn't believe Israel's attachment to Gaza was the equivalent of his feelings for Palestine. He did allow, however, that the Gaza pullout was a "good start."

I pressed a point. "I think he's changed," I said of Sharon. "He knows that sacrifices have to be made. He might even pull out of part of the West Bank. It's not that he doesn't think it's Jewish land, he just knows that compromises have to be made."

"Jewish land?" Rafiq asked dubiously. "How long do you have to go back in history to find Jews there? It's a long time ago. Don't you think there should be a time limit on this claim?"

His question reminded me of a conversation I once had with a man named Muhammad Hussein Fadlallah, who is the "spiritual leader" of Hezbollah, the Shiite terror group. I met him in Beirut, and he gave me a harangue about the perfidious crimes of Zionism. At one point, he put a question to me: "How would you feel if the Indians came to your house and said, 'We were here first, get out.' "

I didn't understand him at first. It had always been my impression that the world thought of the Jews as the cowboys. It seemed too good to be true: Sheikh Fadlallah was casting the Jews in the role of the American Indians and the Arabs as the white settlers who came from Europe to steal Indian land.

"What would you say to that?" he asked, and I answered in the only way a liberal American Jew could: "I'd let them share my house," I said, mournfully and self-righteously.

Rafiq was suggesting, inadvertently, perhaps, that the Jewish claim on the land, though ancient, was not manufactured, but rooted in history. I was going to bang home this point—Take that, Rafiq!—but something kept me from doing so. Perhaps it was the recognition that I had a propensity to torment him with my ceaseless questions in the futile and arrogant hope that I could turn him into the perfect Muslim—a Muslim, in other words, who agrees with me.

He was game for arguing, though—al-Ain, in its sunstruck orderliness, was a bit too serene for him—and we went back and forth in the usual manner. Eventually we arrived at the question of Jerusalem.

He asked me if I could imagine agreeing to Islamic control of the Temple Mount. Of course, I said, just so long as you recognize that it's mine.

This is the way he feels about the Western Wall, he said. "If you just say it's Muslim then it can stay Jewish."

We were silent for a moment.

Well, then: Two men, wholly without power, working at the subatomic level in a Starbucks in distant Arabia, had just solved the Middle East crisis.

"I didn't know it would be so easy," I said.

"Well, all you have to do is try," he said, laughing.

Then I asked him a question I had never asked him before.

"Do you think that our friendship means anything?" I asked, using the word "friendship" quite on purpose, because that is what, at the moment, I thought we had.

"Yes, I think so," he said.

"What does it mean?"

"If this could be done between a million different people, then situation would be a lot different," he said. "People would at least know what the other person thinks."

I said, "This doesn't mean we agree on anything, though."

No, he answered, but it lets us talk, at least.

I was flush with hope for a moment, but I didn't forget that billions of words had been spoken in the years of the peace process, and to what effect? An irreducible truth remained: The maximum Israel could give did not match the minimum the Palestinians would accept.

And soon after this conversation would come the dismantling of even the remnant of hope. Ariel Sharon, who might have been the only Israeli leader strong enough to close down the West Bank settlements, suffered an incapacitating stroke. His replacement, Ehud Olmert, was more inclined to compromise than Sharon but less equipped to do so—he is a mere politician, not a founding father of Israel. But even Olmert's best offer would still not have been enough to satiate the Palestinians; his aim was to rope several large settlement blocks to Israel by means of a separation fence. To me, the removal of every last settlement in exchange for peace seems like a bargain, but I recognize that even this would not satisfy the men of Hamas, and their rise was unstoppable. The win by Hamas in the Palestinian elections early in 2006 was convincing, but the group's hold seemed tenuous—Rafiq thought a full-on civil war between Hamas and Fatah was possible. The wretched fact of Hamas rule meant, however, that history was once again siding with the pessimists. And then there was the true existential threat from nuclear-obsessed Iran. Its president seemed to be possessed by the spirit of Berlin, circa 1938, and it did not seem wise to take his threats to annihilate Israel as mere rhetoric. Once, in Teheran, Ramadan Shallah, the leader of the Islamic Jihad, told me that his allies among the mullahs wished more than anything to bring about the physical eradication of Israel. "We will show the Jews a black day. We won't stop until we're finished," he said, reminding me that the world is a heartless place for small peoples.

I have not stopped wanting what I have always wanted: security and justice for Israel, and security and justice for the Palestinians. By the middle of 2006, though, the Middle East was a landscape of wasting sadness and obliterating furies, Hezbollah was at war with Israel, and despair was coming easily to me. Except when I recalled my last conversation with Rafiq in al-Ain.

We were having coffee. I had been thinking, in the most rational way, that if Rafiq and I could allow friendship to triumph over anger, then it wasn't impossible to believe that the rest of Isaac's children, and the rest of Ishmael's children, could stop their long and dismal war. Jews believe, of course, that Isaac is Abraham's chosen son; Islam came along and settled on Ishmael as Abraham's favorite. Without a direct statement from God, this is not a winnable argument. But what can be won is the recognition that both men came together as brothers to bury their father. The rest is commentary.

In that last conversation I told Rafiq that I believed in the power of reconciliation because his life was more valuable to me than any rock or stone.

"You know," I said, "when I hear about something terrible happening in Jebalya, my first thoughts are of you and your father."

Rafiq smiled. "It's the same thing for me. When I hear that there is a bombing in Jerusalem and I know you're there, I get worried."

I must have looked surprised just then, because Rafiq said: "I mean, I don't want you to die. I want you to live."

And this, I thought, might be the start of something.

ACKNOWLEDGMENTS

I am indebted to a great many people. My debt to Rafiq Hijazi is obvious. He has been a gracious host to me in Jebalya and in al-Ain, he has patiently answered my endless questions, and he has done all this while knowing, to a statistical certainty, that he would disagree with many of my observations and conclusions. It is my most sincere hope that he takes this book in the spirit in which it was written, as a wish for a future unconsumed by hate. I also owe Kemal Hijazi, Hamed Hijazi, and the rest of Rafiq's family my sincere thanks.

Jibril Rajoub told me once that the friends you make in prison are your friends for life. Jack Ross, my comrade-in-arms, is such a friend. He is a true son of his people. Esther Abramowitz has been a friend through thick and thin. Her parents, Molly and Stanley Abramowitz, took me into their home and made me a part of their family. Assa and Nechama Lifshitz did the same. My debt to them is profound. On Mishmar Ha'Emek, Bini and Simi Talmi were devoted surrogate parents as well.

I am grateful to the Woodrow Wilson International Center for Scholars in Washington, D.C., which gave me time and room to work on a first draft of this book. Lee Hamilton, Michael Van Dusen, Robert Litwak, and Haleh Esfandiari at the Wilson Center were particularly supportive. Rameez Abbas was a brilliant researcher. My friend Walter Reich introduced me to Lee Hamilton, for which I am grateful, and I am grateful to Walter as well for his wisdom.

I am also grateful to the Jerusalem Foundation for appointing me its Marie Syrkin Fellow in Letters. The Jerusalem Foundation's guest house, Mishkenot Sha'ananim, has been a refuge and a delight. Michael Shiloh and Liat Cohen have been generous and understanding hosts.

Sloan Harris has been my friend and agent for a dozen years. This book would not have been written without him. He is a true member of the tribe.

Sonny Mehta understood the idea for this book in an instant, and in his bones. I am grateful for his devotion and attention. Jon Segal, a wizard of an editor, has given himself to this book in ways that have caused me to stand back in wonder. Alfred A. Knopf is filled with other people of extraordinary talent, including Paul Bogaards, Sarah Robinson, Leyla Aker, and Maria Massey.

My friends and colleagues at *The New Yorker* have helped me in ways too many to count. My thanks go to David Remnick, and to Dorothy Wickenden, John Bennet, Perri Dorset, Boris Fishman, Jonathan Shainin, Tara Gallagher, Nana Asfour, Pamela McCarthy, Peter Canby, Marina Harss, Amy Davidson, George Packer, Seymour Hersh, Jane Mayer, Steve Coll, and Alexander Dryer. Jeffrey Frank has been my wise and forgiving editor for several years. He, Dorothy Wickenden, and David Remnick read early drafts of this book, and they saved me from myself on nearly every page.

My friends James Bennet, Jonathan Rosen, and Amy Hawthorne also read early versions of the book, and their advice and encouragement were invaluable. So too, was the learned counsel of Leon Wieseltier.

Many others have helped me along the way, including my teacher, Seth Lipsky, Adam Moss and Gerald Marzorati, Ari Shavit, Michael Oren, Warren Adelman, David Brooks, Mustafa Nabulsi, Samer Shalabi, Daniel Greenberg, Hussam Madhoum, Akram Haniya, Adila Laidi, Herb Keinon, Faye Bittker, Saud Abu Ramadan, Ghassan Khattib, Robert Satloff, Daniel Schwartz, and Katharine Cluverius.

My mother has encouraged me in everything I have ever done, for which I am eternally grateful.

My children, Talia, Elisheva, and William Ze'ev, are my joy. They were never out of mind as I wrote this book. One day, when they read *Prisoners,* I hope they will see it as an antique document, one written in the time before peace.

My wife, Pamela, is my partner in all things. She has sacrificed so much for this book, and for me. She is the greatest blessing of my life. This book is hers.

A NOTE ABOUT THE AUTHOR

Jeffrey Goldberg is the Washington correspondent of *The New Yorker*. He previously served as a Middle East correspondent for the magazine. Before joining *The New Yorker*, Goldberg wrote about the Middle East and Africa for *The New York Times Magazine*. He has also written for *New York* magazine, for which he covered organized crime, *The Jerusalem Post*, and the *Forward*. He began his career as a police reporter for *The Washington Post*. He is the recipient of the National Magazine Award for Reporting, for his coverage of Hezbollah. His other prizes include the Overseas Press Club Award for Human Rights Reporting; the Abraham Cahan Prize in Journalism; and the Daniel Pearl Prize in Journalism. He was named International Investigative Reporter of the year by the International Consortium of Investigative Journalists. In 2001, he was made the Marie Syrkin Fellow in Letters of the Jerusalem Foundation, and in 2003 he was appointed a Public Policy Scholar at the Woodrow Wilson International Center for Scholars in Washington, D.C. He lives in Washington with his wife and their three children.

A NOTE ON THE TYPE

The text of this book was composed in Apollo, the first typeface ever originated specifically for film composition. Designed by Adrian Frutiger and issued by the Monotype Corporation of London in 1964, Apollo is not only a versatile typeface suitable for many uses but also pleasant to read in all of its sizes.

Composed by Creative Graphics, Inc., Allentown, Pennsylvania

Printed and bound by Berryville Graphics, Berryville, Virginia

Designed by Robert C. Olsson